The
Alaska Almanac®

Facts About Alaska

31st Edition

Alaska Northwest Books®
Anchorage • Portland

First edition published 1976
Thirty-first edition 2007
Previously published as FACTS ABOUT ALASKA: The ALASKA ALMANAC®

ISBN 978-0-88240-698-5
ISSN 0270-5370
Key title: The Alaska Almanac

Cover and interior design: Elizabeth Watson
Composition: Jean Andrews
Editor: Nancy Gates
Maps: Gray Mouse Graphics

Alaska Northwest Books®
An imprint of Graphic Arts Center Publishing Company
P.O. Box 10306, Portland, OR 97296-0306
(503) 226-2402
www.gacpc.com

Printed in the United States of America

To Our Readers

Alaska Northwest Books® once again welcomes the wisdom, wit
and wackiness of Mr. Whitekeys to this, our 31st edition of
The Alaska Almanac®. For more than 25 years, thousands
of visitors and Alaskans alike enjoyed his Alaska-based
comedy, songs and dance showcased at Anchorage's
dearly departed Fly By Night Club. Originator of the
infamous "Whale Fat Follies," Mr. Whitekeys brings
his distinctive insights on Northland life—from
moose nuggets to politics—to the pages of
The Alaska Almanac®.

Contents

Fast Facts About Alaska

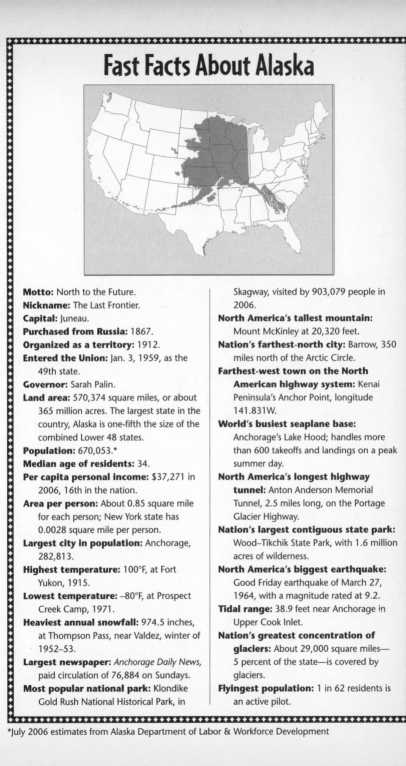

Motto: North to the Future.

Nickname: The Last Frontier.

Capital: Juneau.

Purchased from Russia: 1867.

Organized as a territory: 1912.

Entered the Union: Jan. 3, 1959, as the 49th state.

Governor: Sarah Palin.

Land area: 570,374 square miles, or about 365 million acres. The largest state in the country, Alaska is one-fifth the size of the combined Lower 48 states.

Population: 670,053.*

Median age of residents: 34.

Per capita personal income: $37,271 in 2006, 16th in the nation.

Area per person: About 0.85 square mile for each person; New York state has 0.0028 square mile per person.

Largest city in population: Anchorage, 282,813.

Highest temperature: 100°F, at Fort Yukon, 1915.

Lowest temperature: –80°F, at Prospect Creek Camp, 1971.

Heaviest annual snowfall: 974.5 inches, at Thompson Pass, near Valdez, winter of 1952–53.

Largest newspaper: *Anchorage Daily News,* paid circulation of 76,884 on Sundays.

Most popular national park: Klondike Gold Rush National Historical Park, in Skagway, visited by 903,079 people in 2006.

North America's tallest mountain: Mount McKinley at 20,320 feet.

Nation's farthest-north city: Barrow, 350 miles north of the Arctic Circle.

Farthest-west town on the North American highway system: Kenai Peninsula's Anchor Point, longitude 141.831W.

World's busiest seaplane base: Anchorage's Lake Hood; handles more than 600 takeoffs and landings on a peak summer day.

North America's longest highway tunnel: Anton Anderson Memorial Tunnel, 2.5 miles long, on the Portage Glacier Highway.

Nation's largest contiguous state park: Wood–Tikchik State Park, with 1.6 million acres of wilderness.

North America's biggest earthquake: Good Friday earthquake of March 27, 1964, with a magnitude rated at 9.2.

Tidal range: 38.9 feet near Anchorage in Upper Cook Inlet.

Nation's greatest concentration of glaciers: About 29,000 square miles— 5 percent of the state—is covered by glaciers.

Flyingest population: 1 in 62 residents is an active pilot.

*July 2006 estimates from Alaska Department of Labor & Workforce Development

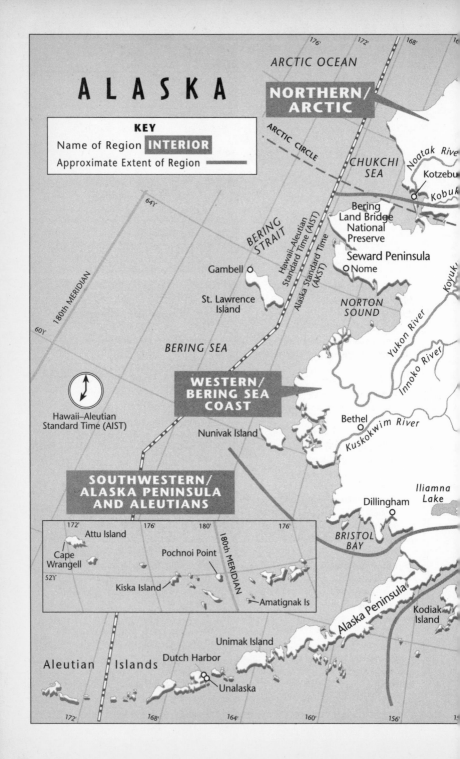

ALASKA

KEY
Name of Region INTERIOR
Approximate Extent of Region ——

ARCTIC OCEAN

NORTHERN/ARCTIC

ARCTIC CIRCLE

CHUKCHI SEA

Noatak River

Kotzebue

Kobuk

Bering Land Bridge National Preserve

Seward Peninsula
Nome

NORTON SOUND

Koyukuk

Yukon River

Innoko River

BERING STRAIT

Gambell

St. Lawrence Island

Hawaii–Aleutian Standard Time (AIST)

Alaska Standard Time (AKST)

64°

60°

180th MERIDIAN

BERING SEA

WESTERN/BERING SEA COAST

Nunivak Island

Bethel

Kuskokwim River

Hawaii–Aleutian Standard Time (AIST)

Iliamna Lake

Dillingham

SOUTHWESTERN/ALASKA PENINSULA AND ALEUTIANS

BRISTOL BAY

172'   176'   180'   176'
Attu Island
Cape Wrangell
Pochnoi Point
52°
Kiska Island
180th MERIDIAN
Amatignak Is

Alaska Peninsula

Kodiak Island

Unimak Island

Aleutian   Islands   Dutch Harbor

Unalaska

172'   168'   164'   160'   156'

176'   172'   168'   16

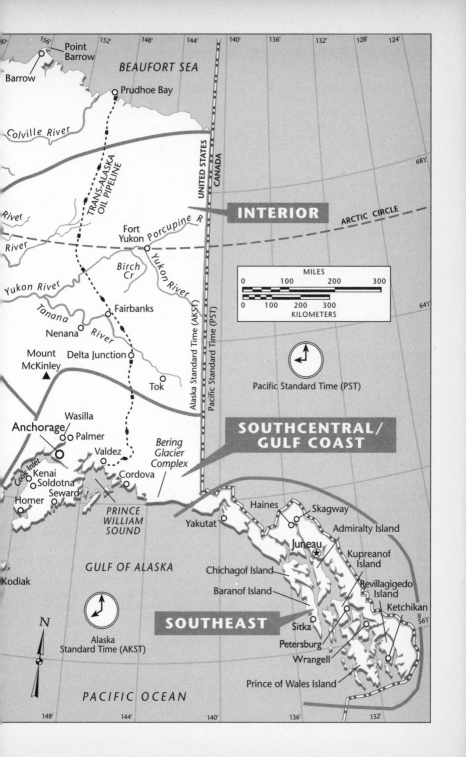

BEAUFORT SEA

Point Barrow

Barrow

Prudhoe Bay

Colville River

TRANS-ALASKA OIL PIPELINE

UNITED STATES

CANADA

INTERIOR

ARCTIC CIRCLE

River

Fort Yukon

Porcupine R

Yukon River

Birch Cr

River

Yukon River

Fairbanks

Tanana

River

Nenana

Mount McKinley

Delta Junction

Tok

Alaska Standard Time (AKST)

Pacific Standard Time (PST)

MILES
0   100   200   300

0   100   200   300
KILOMETERS

Pacific Standard Time (PST)

Wasilla

Anchorage

Palmer

Valdez

Bering Glacier Complex

SOUTHCENTRAL/ GULF COAST

Cook Inlet

Kenai

Soldotna

Seward

Homer

Cordova

PRINCE WILLIAM SOUND

Haines

Skagway

Yakutat

Admiralty Island

Juneau

Kupreanof Island

Kodiak

GULF OF ALASKA

Chichagof Island

Baranof Island

Revillagigedo Island

Ketchikan

N

Alaska Standard Time (AKST)

SOUTHEAST

Sitka

Petersburg

Wrangell

Prince of Wales Island

PACIFIC OCEAN

68Y

64Y

56Y

Acknowledgments

This 31st edition of The Alaska Almanac®
*has been compiled and updated from information
supplied by many helpful state and federal
offices, publications, consultants, organizations,
experts and individuals. The editors gratefully
acknowledge:*

Alaska magazine
Laura Achee, Alaska Permanent Fund
    Corporation
Anchorage Daily News
Jeanne Anglin, Alaska Department of Health and
    Social Services
Jo Antonson, Alaska Department of Natural
    Resources
Chuck Becker, Alaska Export Assistance Center
Sue Benz, Alaska Agricultural Statistics Service
Kalei Brooks, Department of Military & Veterans
    Affairs, Alaska National Guard
Bill Brophy, Usibelli Coal Mine, Inc.
Tammy Bruce, Mat-Su Convention and Visitors
    Bureau
Linda Bustamante, Alaska Department of
    Transportation
Norm and Linda Carson, Pelican Visitors
    Association
Leslie Chapel, Ketchikan Convention and
    Visitors Bureau
Susan Christensen, Alaska Department of
    Natural Resources
Linda Close, Alaska Department of
    Transportation
Vera Crews, Hostelling International, Alaska
    Council
Fairbanks Daily News-Miner
Tom Findtner, U.S. Army Corps of Engineers
Earl Finkler, KBRW AM & FM, Barrow
Neal Fried, Alaska Department of Labor
Kasey Gillam, Fairbanks Convention and Visitors
    Bureau
Donna Gindle, Alaska Command
Doug Hanson, Alaska Department of Natural
    Resources
Gretchen Hazen, National Audubon Society,
    Alaska State Office
Sean Jordan, Alaska Department of
    Transportation
Juneau Empire
Barry Lane, U.S. Coast Guard Public Affairs
Brian Lepley, U.S. Army Alaska Public Affairs
Gilbert Lucero, Alaska Agricultural Statistics
    Service
Chris Maisch, Alaska Department of Natural
    Resources

Julia March Crocetto, Talkeetna Ranger
    Station
Marlene McCluskey, Skagway Convention and
    Visitors Bureau
Caryl McConkie, Alaska Department of
    Commerce, Community & Economic
    Development
Bryon McGarry, 1st Lt., U.S. Air Force Public
    Affairs
Steve McMains, Alaska Department of
    Administration
Terry Miller, Juneau Convention and Visitors
    Bureau
Simone Montayne, Alaska Department of
    Natural Resources
Christina Neal, Alaska Volcano Observatory
Will Nebesky, Alaska Department of Natural
    Resources
Linda Nelson, Alaska Heritage Tours
Catherine Opinski, AT&T Alascom
Steve Packel, Anchorage Bucs
Michael Plotnick, Alaska Department of Fish
    and Game
Cathryn Posey, Anchorage Convention and
    Visitors Bureau
Jack Reneau, Boone and Crockett Club
Linda Resseguie, Bureau of Land Management
Susan Shirley, Alaska Department of Fish
    and Game
Julie Shook, Haines Convention and Visitors
    Bureau
Erin Slaughter, 2nd Lt., U.S. Air Force Public
    Affairs
Debbie Smith, Alaska Department of
    Administration
Missy Smothers, Talkeetna Ranger Station
Liz Stone, Alaska Forest Association
David Szumigala, Alaska Division of Geological
    & Geophysical Surveys
Tim Thompson, Alaska Railroad
Rene Tuttle, Sitka Convention and Visitors
    Bureau
Krystlyn Westre, Petersburg Visitors Center
Tim Workman, Alaska Department of Education
    and Early Development

Mr. Whitekeys wishes to gratefully acknowledge
the slightly twisted contributions of the
Anchorage Daily News, Jenny Haggar, The Azul J.,
Ron Eagley, Paul & Cecily Fritz, James Huettl,
Donald A. Haggar, Mike Wiedmer, and Nancy &
Bruce Wade. They all realize that everything
they have told me is true, whether it really
happened or not.

AGRICULTURE

Agriculture in Alaska ranges from backyard gardens to 3,000-acre farms. Extremes of weather and a short growing season challenge cultivation in the state, but certain crops—notably potatoes, cabbage and carrots—thrive in the cool soil temperatures. Overall, climate is not the greatest impediment to Alaska farming. More significant hurdles are high production costs, lack of available, accessible farm ground and competition from the Lower 48.

Alaska's traditional farming is concentrated in two regions: the Matanuska Valley (northeast of Anchorage), which in 2005 contributed 61 percent of the state's farm production value, and the Tanana Valley (running from Fairbanks to Delta Junction), which was responsible for 33 percent.

An estimated 15 million to 18 million acres in Alaska are believed to be arable, but only 900,000 acres—less than one-half of 1 percent of the state—are currently considered land in farms. In 2005, crops covered 30,000 acres; the balance was in pasture and uncleared land.

Total market value of Alaska's agricultural products in 2005 was $49 million. Feed crops accounted for $4.9 million of total market receipts, and vegetables (including potatoes) were $4.7 million of the total.

Aquaculture now accounts for the largest portion of the Alaska market basket, at $17.0 million. Shellfish farming and private nonprofit hatcheries make up these market receipts.

Greenhouse and nursery industries—a substantial portion of the state's agricultural picture—amounted to $14.6 million, or 30 percent of total cash receipts for 2005.

Almost 98 percent of the barley grown in 2006 was harvested in the Tanana Valley. Total production netted 157,000 bushels, yielding 37.4 bushels an acre. Production value for the 2006 barley crop was $557,000, down from the 2005 crop of $759,000. Harvest of oats yielded 35.0 bushels an acre for a total of 28,000 bushels at an estimated value of $69,000. This reflects a decrease from 58,000 bushels valued at $148,000 in 2005.

Another Alaska agriculture enterprise is the raising of reindeer. Officials estimate there are a total of 15,000 head in herds throughout Alaska. Most of the reindeer are located on the Seward Peninsula, where they contribute significantly to the local economies. Among the by-products of reindeer is the powder made from clipped antler, most of which is exported to the Far East, where it is believed to be an aphrodisiac. Sales related to reindeer were valued at $585,000 in 2005, up from $575,000 in 2004.

Alaska has fewer than one dozen Grade A dairies supporting 800 milk cows that produced 1.1 million gallons of milk in 2006. This is a decrease of over 500,000 gallons from 2005. These figures contrast with those of the 1960s when there were more than 50 Grade A dairies with approximately 2,800 milk cows producing 2.7 million gallons of milk. Economic stresses continue to hold down the number of farmers involved in this capital-intensive industry.

The small vegetable gardens of the Russian fur traders are believed to constitute the first Alaska agriculture. Gold-rush days saw growing interest in local farming possibilities, but it wasn't until 1935 that there was a concerted effort to introduce commercial growing. President Franklin Roosevelt's New Deal resettlement plan transplanted 200 farm families from the Midwest to the Matanuska Valley, where they were to create a food source for the territory.

Although most produce comes from Outside, local farmers still supply the state with fresh produce and dairy products. During the growing season, grocery stores and farmers' markets feature "Alaska Grown . . . Fresher by Far" produce. In Anchorage, the growing season averages 117 days; there are some days with more than 19 hours of sunlight in the summer (which help produce giant-size vegetables).

The Tanana Valley growing season is shorter than that of the Matanuska Valley, with about 106 frost-free days. Because growing-season temperatures are warmer in the Tanana Valley, many experts consider the area to have greater agricultural potential. Barley and oats are raised for grain and hay. Most Alaska-grown grain is

Crops	Volume	Acres Harvested	2006 Value
Hay	22,000 tons	20,000	$5.50 million
Potatoes	186,000 cwt	840	$3.74 million
Barley, for grain	157,000 bushels	4,200	$557,000
Oats, for grain	28,000 bushels	800	$69,000

used for domestic livestock feed. All are spring varieties since few winter types survive the cold.

Beef, pork, hay, eggs and fresh produce are produced throughout the Railbelt region and are easily transported to major markets. (The Railbelt is the region linked by the Alaska Railroad, from Seward north to Fairbanks.) There are nearly 1,000 sheep in Alaska, down from 27,000 in 1970.

Across Alaska, the pressure of urban development is reducing the number of accessible acres available for farming. At the same time, the state is attempting to increase the number of farms through sales of agriculture tracts. Many Alaskans rely on farming to supplement other income. In 2006, there were 640 farms with annual sales of $1,000 or more.

Since 1978, state land sales have placed more than 165,000 acres of potential agricultural land into private ownership. Most of this acreage is in the Delta Junction area, south of Fairbanks, where tracts of up to 3,200 acres were sold by lottery for farming.

The Nenana area, southwest of Fairbanks, and the Fish Creek area of the Mat-Su Valley are among those under consideration for future agricultural development.

Additional information is available from the Alaska Agricultural Statistics Service, P.O. Box 799, Palmer 98547; (907) 745-4272; www.nass.usda.gov/ak.

Total Acreage of Alaska Cropland by Region, 2005

Region	Percent	Acres
Tanana Valley	54.6	16,337
Matanuska Valley	36.7	10,948
Rest of Alaska*	8.7	2,610

*Includes the Kenai Peninsula, Southeast and Southwestern portions of the state.

AIR TRAVEL Alaska is the flyingest state in the Union; the only practical way to reach many areas of rural Alaska is by airplane. According to the Federal Aviation Administration, Alaska Region, in February 2006 there were 10,805 active pilots and 9,902 registered aircraft.

Since 1982, the federal Airport Improvement Program provided $2.1 billion for airport construction, development and planning throughout the state. These federal funds were provided for more than 1,000 projects within the state. In 2006, the FAA, Alaska Region distributed $229 million in grants to state and local airport sponsors.

According to the FAA, Alaska has approximately 731 recorded landing areas (including 136 seaplane bases and 41 heliports). Additionally, pilots land on many of the thousands of lakes and gravel bars across the state where no constructed facility exists. Of the seaplane bases, Lake Hood in Anchorage is the largest and busiest in the world. It accommodates an average of 110 takeoffs and

NUGGETS

Carl F. Brady Sr. died in his Anchorage home in August 2005. Credited as the man who brought the helicopter to Alaska, Brady was a significant figure in aviation, business and political circles during his 60 years in the state. His company, Economy Helicopters, was later renamed Era Aviation. Brady served in the Alaska House of Representatives and the state Senate.

—1996 *The Alaska Almanac*®

As a flying game warden before, during and after statehood, Ray Tremblay battled the elements as well as the bad guys. Photo courtesy C. D. Evans. From *On Patrol* by Ray Tremblay.

landings daily, and more than 600 on a peak summer day.

Merrill Field in Anchorage recorded 190,287 flight operations as of May 2007. Ted Stevens Anchorage International Airport saw 5,043,147 passengers pass through in 2006.

Ted Stevens Anchorage International is the No. 1 airport in the United States for cargo traffic, based on all-cargo aircraft landed weight. In fiscal 2006, international cargo aircraft landed weight was 20.7 billion pounds. Operating revenue for fiscal 2006 was more than $96 million. The airport counted 47,091 revenue landings of cargo aircraft during the fiscal year, up from 45,950 in 2005.

Pilots who wish to fly their own planes to Alaska should have the latest federal government flight information publication, *Alaska Supplement*. Travel and safety information is available from the Federal Aviation Administration, 222 W. Seventh Ave., No. 14, Anchorage 99513-7587; www.alaska.faa.gov; and akweathercams.faa.gov.

Air-taxi operators are found in most Alaska communities, and aircraft can be chartered to fly you to a wilderness spot and pick you up later at a prearranged time and location. Most charter operators charge an hourly rate, either per planeload or per passenger (sometimes with a minimum passenger

requirement); others may charge on a per-mile basis.

Flightseeing trips to area attractions are often available at a fixed price per passenger, ranging from $95 to $295 ($550 to $695 for bear viewing).

Charter fares begin at $375 per hour for a four-passenger flight, to $1,150 per hour for a ten-passenger flight. A wide range of aircraft is used for charter and scheduled passenger service in Alaska. The larger interstate airlines—Alaska, American, Continental, Delta, Northwest and United—use jets (Boeing 737, 757, 767 and Airbus comparable aircraft). Prop jets and single- or twin-engine prop planes on wheels, skis and floats are used for most intrastate travel. A few of these types of aircraft flown in Alaska are 19-passenger de Havilland Twin Otter, Cessna Caravan,

The *Nome Nugget* reported that "you are a real Alaskan if you have ever gone to the bathroom on a plane that doesn't have a bathroom."

Fish Collides with Jet

Just before April Fools' Day, a flying fish collided with an Alaska Airlines Boeing 737 jet. It was no joke. The plane was taking off from the Juneau airport and about 400 feet past the runway's end, the jet crossed the flight path of a bald eagle, fish in talons. The eagle dropped the fish as the jet approached. The flight was delayed for about an hour as a mechanic, dispatched to the plane's next stop in Yakutat, inspected the plane. He reported finding a greasy spot with some scales, but no damage. The eagle escaped injury.

—1989 *The Alaska Almanac®*

SAAB, Metroliner, 10-passenger Britten-Norman Islander, 7-passenger Grumman Goose (amphibious), DC-3, 4-passenger Cessna 185, 9-passenger twin-engine Piper Navajo Chieftain, 5- to 8-passenger de Havilland Beaver, 3- to 4-passenger Cessna 180, 5- to 6-passenger Cessna 206 and single-passenger Piper Super Cub.

International Service. Several international carriers provide cargo or passenger service in Alaska through the Anchorage gateway. The list includes Air China, Air HongKong, Air Canada, Alaska Airlines (to Canada and Mexico), American-Trans-Air, Asiana Airlines, Atlas Air, Cathay Pacific Airways, China Airlines, China Cargo Airlines, Condor, Evergreen International, Fed Ex, Gemini Air Cargo, Japan Air Charter, Japan Airlines, Korean Air, Nippon Cargo Airlines, Northwest Airlines, Polar Air Cargo, Singapore Airlines, United Airlines and United Parcel Service.

Interstate Service. U.S. carriers providing interstate cargo or passenger service: Alaska Airlines, American Airlines, American-Trans-Air, America West Airlines, Continental Airlines, Delta Air Lines, Frontier Airlines, F. S. Air Service, Hawaiian Vacations, North American Airlines, Northern Air Cargo, Northwest Airlines, Omni Air International, Sun Country Airlines, United Airlines and US Airways.

Intrastate Service. Cargo or passenger carriers include Era Aviation, Frontier Flying Service, Grant Aviation, Hageland Aviation, PenAir and Shared Services Aviation. Cargo carriers include ACE Air Cargo, Alaska Airlines, Everts Air Cargo, Lynden Air Cargo and Northern Air Cargo.

ALASKA–CANADA BOUNDARY

In 1825, Russia, in possession of Alaska, and Great Britain, in possession of Canada, established the original boundary between Alaska and Canada. The demarcation was to begin at 54°40' north latitude, just north of the mouth of Portland Canal, follow the canal to 56° north latitude, then traverse the mountain summits parallel to the coast as far as 141° west longitude. From there it would conform with that meridian north to the Arctic Ocean. The boundary line along the mountain summits in southeastern Alaska was never to be farther inland than 10 leagues—about 30 miles.

After purchasing Alaska in 1867, the United States found that the wording about

In spite of ice, snow berms and unshovelled sidewalks, *Prevention Magazine* and the American Podiatric Medical Association named Anchorage the 18th Most Walkable City in the nation. We were ranked better than Phoenix, Tucson or Reno. Sometimes the only exercise you need is just rolling your eyes!

the boundary line was interpreted differently by the Canadians, who held that the measurements should be made inland from the mouths of bays. The Americans argued the measurements should be made from the heads of the bays. In 1903, an international tribunal upheld the American interpretation of the treaty, providing Alaska the 1,538-mile-long border it has with Canada today. The southeastern Alaska border is 891 miles long, and 181 miles of that border are over water. If the Canadians had won their argument, they would have had access to the sea, and Haines, Dyea and Skagway now would be in Canada.

A 20-foot-wide vista—a swath of land 10 feet on each side of the boundary between southeastern Alaska, British Columbia and Yukon Territory—was surveyed and cleared between 1904 and 1914. Portions of the 710-mile-long land portion of the boundary were again cleared in 1925, 1948, 1978 and 1982 by the International Boundary Commission. Monument and vista maintenance in 1978 and 1982 was conducted by the Canadian section of the commission and by the U.S. section in 1983, 1984 and 1985.

The Alaska–Canada border along the 141st meridian was surveyed and cleared between 1904 and 1920. Astronomical observations were made to find the meridian's intersection with the Yukon River; then, under the direction of the International Boundary Commission, engineers and surveyors of the U.S. Coast and Geodetic Survey and the Canadian Department of the Interior worked together north and south from the Yukon. The straight-line vista extends from Demarcation Point on the Arctic Ocean south to Mount St. Elias in the Wrangell Mountains (from there the border cuts east to encompass southeastern Alaska). This part of the border stretches for 647 miles in one of the world's longest straight lines, as well as the world's longest unguarded border.

Monuments are the actual markers of the boundary and are located so they tie in with survey networks of both the United States and Canada. Along the Alaska boundary most monuments are 2½-foot-high cones of aluminum-bronze set in concrete bases or occasionally cemented into rock. A large pair of concrete monuments with a pebbled finish marks major boundary road crossings. Because the boundary is not just a line but in fact a vertical plane dividing land and sky between the two nations, bronze plates mark tunnel and bridge crossings. Along the meridian, 191 monuments are placed, beginning 200 feet from the Arctic Ocean and ending at the south side of Logan Glacier.

ALASKA HIGHWAY (See also Highways)

The Alaska Highway runs 1,422 miles through Canada and Alaska from Milepost 0 at Dawson Creek, British Columbia, through Yukon Territory to its official finish in Delta Junction, Alaska, then onward to its unofficial finish in Fairbanks at Milepost 1,523. (Each town claims an "end of the road" status and has a much-photographed milepost marker outside its visitor center.) Until this overland link between Alaska and the Lower 48 was built in 1942, travel to and from Alaska was primarily by water.

History. The highway was built to relieve Alaska from the hazards of shipping by water and to supply a land route for equipment during World War II.

By agreement between the governments of Canada and the United States, the highway was built in eight months by the U.S. Army Corps of Engineers and was dedicated in November 1942. Crews worked south from Delta Junction, Alaska, north and south from Whitehorse, Yukon, and north from Dawson Creek, British Columbia.

RV travel on the Alaska Highway and its spur roads continues to increase with road improvements. Photo by Tricia Brown.

The building of the highway was recognized as one of the greatest engineering feats of the 20th century. Two major sections of the highway were connected on Sept. 23, 1942, at Contact Creek, Milepost 588.1, where the 35th Engineer Combat Regiment working west from Fort Nelson met the 340th Engineer General Service Regiment working east from Whitehorse. The last link in the highway was completed Nov. 20, 1942, when the 97th Engineer General Service Regiment, heading east from Tanacross, met the 18th Engineer Combat Regiment, coming northwest from Kluane Lake, at Milepost 1200.9. A ceremony commemorating the event was held at Soldiers Summit on Kluane Lake, and the first truck to negotiate the entire highway left that day from Soldiers Summit and arrived in Fairbanks the next day.

After World War II, the Alaska Highway was turned over to civilian contractors for widening and graveling, replacing log bridges with steel and rerouting at many points. Road improvements on the Alaska Highway continue today.

Preparation for Driving the Alaska Highway. Make sure your vehicle and tires are in good condition before starting out. A widely available item to include is clear plastic headlight covers to protect your headlights from flying rocks and gravel.

You might also consider a wire-mesh screen across the front of your vehicle to protect paint, radiator and headlights from flying gravel. For those hauling trailers, a piece of quarter-inch plywood fitted over the front of your trailer offers protection from rocks and gravel.

> Every Alaskan knows it gets so cold in the winter that your tires freeze flat, and it takes a couple of miles of driving for them to get round again.

NUGGETS

Motorcyclist Garrett Edgmon, 40, was traveling south at about 45 or 50 mph and rounding a bend of the Old Glenn Highway when he caught a glimpse of reddish-brown fur barreling down the hill toward him. The bear slammed into his front wheel and sent the bike skidding across the road. Edgmon was thrown onto the bear's head and neck as they slid together for a short distance. A witness stated that the bear did a flip, then scrambled off under the guardrail. Edgmon only remembers painfully staggering to his feet in shock, and trying to drag his new 750-pound 1200cc Kawasaki Voyager off the roadway. He credited his full-face helmet with saving his life.

—2006 *The Alaska Almanac*®

You'll find well-stocked auto shops in the North, but may wish to carry your own emergency items: flares; first-aid kit; mosquito repellent; trailer bearings; good bumper jack with lug wrench; a simple set of tools, such as hammer, screwdrivers, pliers, wire, crescent wrenches, socket and/or open-end wrenches, pry bar; electrician's tape; small assortment of nuts and bolts; fan belt; one or two spare tires (two spares for traveling any remote road); and any parts for your vehicle that might not be available along the way.

Include a few extra gallons of gas and water, especially for remote roads. You may wish to carry a can each of brake, power steering and automatic transmission fluids.

While the main route is nearly all paved, long stretches of the Alaska Highway undergo widening or other improvements, and delays are possible. Dust is worst during dry spells, following heavy rain (which disturbs the road surface) and in construction areas. If you encounter much dust, check your air filter frequently. To help keep dust out of your vehicle, try to keep air pressure in the car by closing all windows and turning on the fan. Filtered heating and air-conditioning ducts in a vehicle bring in much less dust than open windows or vents.

ALCOHOLIC BEVERAGES

The legal age for possession, purchase and consumption of alcoholic beverages is 21 in Alaska. Underage drinkers may lose their driver's licenses for 90 days.

Any business that serves or distributes alcoholic beverages must be licensed by the state. The population in a geographic area limits the number of different types of licenses issued. Generally one license of each type may be issued for each 3,000 persons or fraction thereof. Licensed premises include bars, some restaurants and clubs. Packaged liquor, beer and wine are sold by licensed package stores. Licenses are renewed biennially.

Recreational site licenses, caterer's permits and special events permits allow the holder of a permit or license to sell at special events, and allow nonprofit fraternal, civic or patriotic organizations to serve beer and wine at certain activities.

State law allows liquor outlets to operate from 8 A.M. to 5 A.M., but provides that local governments may impose tighter restrictions.

Dozens of communities have banned possession and/or sale and importation of alcoholic beverages (knowingly bringing, sending or transporting alcoholic beverages into the community). Others have banned the sale of all alcoholic beverages. Contact the Alcoholic Beverage Control Board at (907) 269-0350 for a current list or check www.dps.state.ak.us/abc.

ALYESKA (See also Skiing) Pronounced

Al-YES-ka, this Aleut word means "the great land" and was one of the original names for Alaska. Mount Alyeska, a 3,939-foot peak in the Chugach Mountains south of Anchorage, is the site of the state's largest ski resort.

AMPHIBIANS Three species of

salamander, two species of frog and one species of toad are found in Alaska. In the salamander order are the rough-skinned newt, long-toed salamander and northwestern salamander. In the frog and toad order are the boreal toad, wood frog and spotted frog. The northern limit of each species may be the latitude at which the larvae fail to complete their development in one summer. While some species of salamander can overwinter as larvae in temperate southeastern Alaska, the shallow ponds of central Alaska freeze solid during the winter. All these amphibians are found primarily in southeastern Alaska, except for the wood frog, *Rana sylvatica,* which with its shortened larval period is found widespread throughout the state and north of the Brooks Range.

ANCHORAGE (See also Regions of

Alaska) Anchorage is located on a broad peninsula in Cook Inlet, defined by Knik Arm and Turnagain Arm, and bordered to the east by the Chugach Mountains. Anchorage and the Kenai Peninsula make up the region Alaskans call Southcentral, a region milder in climate than the Interior, with average temperatures of 15°F in January and 58°F in July and an average snowfall of about 70 inches a year.

Anchorage's daylight has a daily maximum of 19 hours, 21 minutes

NUGGETS

As the deep snow north of Anchorage began to melt in early spring 1990, the grim tally of just how hard the winter had been on Alaska's moose became clear. Official estimates showed 4,600 moose died of starvation or from being hit by highway and railroad vehicles in the Susitna Drainage Area. Snow depth was the primary factor behind the deaths. It forces them to walk on trails, roads and railroad tracks where contact with humans is more likely.

—1990 *The Alaska Almanac®*

15

Neither Snow nor Rain nor . . .

It all began on a Thursday afternoon in October 2005, when an unarmed robber made off with a man's wallet in downtown Anchorage. Next he dashed into the KeyBank down the street, demanded money from a teller and fled. A person in line at the bank took off in hot pursuit, yelling, "Stop! Thief!" Then U.S. mail carrier Jonathan Higgins, who was just leaving the Alaska Center for the Performing Arts with his mail cart, heard the commotion. Quickly assessing the situation, he chased down the robber and a struggle ensued. Meanwhile, two nearby police officer candidates, who had been busy writing parking tickets, saw the two men and quickly joined in the fray. Ultimately the robber was handcuffed, the money was recovered and Higgins received the Carrier of the Week award.

—2006 *The Alaska Almanac*®

in summer and reaches a minimum of 5 hours, 28 minutes in winter.

The population of Anchorage was 1,856 in 1920, and remained at a few thousand until well after World War II. In 1994, Alaska's most populous city broke the quarter-million mark for the first time; in 2006 it was home to 282,813 people (about 42 percent of the state's population).

Anchorage suffered millions of dollars in damage in a devastating earthquake on March 27, 1964, originally measured at 8.6 on the Richter scale but later upgraded to a magnitude of 9.2—the strongest ever recorded in North America. (SEE ALSO Earthquakes)

In early 2007, Anchorage adopted a new "brand" to increase its appeal to tourists. "The Big Wild Life" was immediately attacked by wags throughout the city. The critics were unimpressed by the economic gains of neighboring towns when they adopted mottos such as "Cordova—Like Taking a Cold Shower with Your Clothes On," and "Point McKenzie—Come Smell Our Dairy Air!"

Sometimes called the "Air Crossroads of the World," Anchorage is a gateway for international travelers. Surrounded by dense spruce, birch and aspen forests, it is just a step away from wilderness and multiple recreational opportunities. Anchorage also serves as a jump-off point for tourists—heading 200 miles north to visit Denali National Park and Mount McKinley, North America's highest mountain; or south 52 miles to view Portage Glacier, one of the state's most-visited sights; or even to one of Alaska's Bush locations for hunting, fishing, skiing, hiking, nature photography or sightseeing.

Although bear and moose may occasionally wander the city's highways and byways, Anchorage offers many of the attractions of any large metropolis, such as art galleries, museums, libraries, cultural diversity, music—including a symphony orchestra, opera and dance—and theaters big enough to stage productions by national touring companies.

Anchorage has more than 200 churches and more than 130 public and private schools, including the University of Alaska Anchorage and Alaska Pacific University. Restaurants offer everything from fine dining and ethnic cuisine to fast food. Anchorage has more than 8,000 hotel/motel rooms and 800 bed-and-breakfast or hostel beds.

Contact the Anchorage Convention and Visitors Bureau for a free visitor's guide, maps and additional information: 524 W. Fourth Ave., Anchorage 99501; (800) 478-1255; www.anchorage.net.

ANTIQUITIES LAWS (See also National Historic Places)

State and federal laws prohibit excavation or removal of historic and prehistoric cultural materials without a permit. Nearly all 50 states have historic preservation laws; Alaska's extends even to tidal lands, making it illegal to pick up artifacts on the beach while beachcombing.

It sometimes is difficult to distinguish between historic sites and abandoned property. Old gold-mining towns and cabins, as well as areas such as the Chilkoot and Iditarod Trails, should always be considered historic sites or private property. Also, cabins that appear to be abandoned may be seasonally used trapping cabins; the structure and possessions are vital to the owner.

Alaska law prohibits the disturbance of fossils, including those of prehistoric animals such as mammoths.

ARCHAEOLOGY (See also Bering Land Bridge)

Alaska has a long and rich archaeological history. Many experts believe the first human migrants to North and South America some 40,000 to 15,000 years ago came first to Alaska, crossing over the now-submerged Bering Land Bridge that connected Siberia to Alaska during the Ice Age.

Archaeological investigations over the last decade have produced some of the earliest evidence of human occupation in Alaska. These sites, in the Tanana drainage of central Alaska, include the Broken Mammoth, Meade and Swan Point sites. They have produced deposits ranging back to more than 13,000 years old. Small hunting tools have been found throughout Alaska, probably belonging to nomadic hunting and gathering peoples. The archaeological record becomes more complex about 4,000 years ago, when it reveals cultural patterns that can be traced lineally to Alaska Native groups still extant at the time of contact with Europeans.

There is still much to discover about Alaska's prehistory. Many archaeological sites are small, representing the camps of wandering hunters and gatherers; some

sites, especially along the coast where rich natural resources allowed people to become more sedentary and established, are large and deep. Where permafrost occurs, preservation of even the most perishable organic materials offers a wealth of information on life in the past. There are several thousand known archaeological sites in the state. One of the most famous is the 500-year-old Utkeaviq Site at Barrow, where a "frozen family" was unearthed from Mound 44 in the Birnirk archaeological site during 1982–83.

In 1993, another of the oldest documented sites of human habitation in North America was discovered. Called the Mesa Site, it is located about 150 miles north of the Arctic Circle in the foothills of the Brooks Range. The 11,500-year-old hunting site, perched atop a 200-foot mesa overlooking the surrounding plain, has produced stone tools reminiscent of "Paleo Indian" sites of the continental U.S. and Canada. It probably was used for 2,000 years as a hunters' lookout for prey such as caribou.

Archaeological excavations, or digs, are generally confined to the summer months. The University of Alaska frequently sponsors digs, as do several state and federal agencies. Recent excavations have taken place near Unalaska, Tok, Kodiak,

NUGGETS

A University of Alaska Fairbanks student, taking part in a field study course in Denali National Park and Preserve, discovered a track left by a three-toed dinosaur perhaps some 70 million years ago. Susi Tomsich discovered the three-toed Cretaceous-period dinosaur's paw print, which looks like an oversized bird footprint, on the underside of a ledge. From the size of the track, the meat eater is estimated to have been 9 to 13 feet long.

—2006 *The Alaska Almanac*®

Fairbanks, Prince William Sound, Point Franklin, Sitka and on the Kenai Peninsula.

Participants are invited, for a fee, to take part in a dig on Afognak Island. Inquire with the Native Village of Afognak, 204 E. Rezanof Dr., Suite 100; (907) 486-6357; www.afognak.org/dig.php.

Additional information about projects is available from the Alaska Office of History and Archaeology, www.dnr.state.ak.us/parks/oha/index.htm.

ARCTIC CIRCLE (See also Daylight Hours)

The Arctic Circle (See map, pages 6–7) is the latitude at which the sun does not set for one day at summer solstice and does not rise for one day at winter solstice. The latitude, which varies slightly from year to year, is approximately 66°34' north from the equator and circumscribes the northern frigid zone.

A solstice occurs when the sun is at its greatest distance from the celestial equator. On the day of summer solstice, June 20 or 21, the sun does not set at the Arctic Circle, and because of refraction of sunlight, it appears not to set for four days. Farther north, at Barrow (the northernmost community in the United States), the sun does not set from May 10 to Aug. 2.

At winter solstice, Dec. 21 or 22, the sun does not rise for one day at the Arctic Circle. At Barrow, it does not rise for 67 days.

ARCTIC WINTER GAMES

The Arctic Winter Games are held every two years in mid-March for northern athletes from Alaska, northern Alberta, Greenland, Northwest Territories, Nunavut, Nunavik–Northern Quebec, Yukon Territory and Russia. The first games were held in 1970 in Yellowknife, Northwest Territories, and have since been held in Fairbanks and on Alaska's Kenai Peninsula, Whitehorse, Yukon and Wood Buffalo, Alberta. Yellowknife will again host the games in March 2008.

In 2006, some 375 athletes and coaches from Alaska participated in the games held in the Kenai Peninsula Borough. Competition includes alpine skiing, arctic sports (traditional Inuit and Dene games), badminton, basketball, curling, cross-country skiing, dog mushing, figure skating, gymnastics, hockey, short track speed skating, ski biathlon, snowboarding, snowshoeing, indoor soccer, volleyball and wrestling. Cultural events and performances encourage participation by people of all ages. Information: www.awg.ca.

AREA CODE

The area code for nearly all of Alaska is 907. The one exception is the tiny community of Hyder in Southeast Alaska, which shares an area code with nearby Stewart, British Columbia—250. Although virtually all Alaska Bush communities now have full telephone service, the situation today differs greatly from 1979, when RCA Alaska Communications reported that 140 of the 291 communities it served had only a single phone monitored by an operator.

AURORA BOREALIS

The aurora borealis—the northern lights—is produced by charged electrons and protons striking gas particles in Earth's upper atmosphere. The electrons and protons are released through sunspot activity on the Sun and emanate into space. A few drift the one- to two-day course to Earth, where they are pulled to the most northern and southern latitudes by the planet's magnetic forces.

The color of the aurora borealis varies, depending on how hard the gas particles are being struck. Auroras can range from simple arcs to drapery-like forms in green, red, blue and purple. The lights occur in a pattern rather than as a solid glow because electric

A visitor trying to get to Kotzebue asked an Anchorage Convention & Visitors Bureau Information Center volunteer, "How do you get to Keo-pec-tate?" While visiting Portage, another tourist asked, "Are these glaciers here year-round?"

Alaskan Athletes at the Winter Games

The 2006 Arctic Winter Games were held in Alaska's Kenai Peninsula Borough on March 5 to 11. Among the Alaskan winners were these:

Inuit Games:

One-Foot High Kick: Open Male, Gold: David Thomas. Open Female, Silver: Elizabeth Rexford. Junior Female, Silver: Dannielle Malchoff.

Two-Foot High Kick: Open Male, Silver: David Thomas. Bronze: Philip Blanchett. Open Female, Bronze: Elizabeth Rexford. Junior Female, Gold: Jasmin Simeon. Bronze: Dannielle Malchoff.

Alaskan High Kick: Open Male, Gold: Billy Bodfish. Silver: David Thomas. Open Female, Gold: Elizabeth Rexford. Silver: Alissa Joseph. Bronze: Katherine Commack. Junior Female, Gold: Tanya Slim. Silver: Virginia Angaiak. Bronze: Dannielle Malchoff.

Kneel Jump: Open Female, Gold: Elizabeth Rexford. Silver: Alissa Joseph.

One Hand Reach: Open Male, Gold: David Thomas. Bronze: Billy Bodfish and Manuel Tumulak.

Knuckle Hop: Open Male, Gold: David Thomas.

Arm Pull: Open Female, Bronze: Elizabeth Rexford.

Sledge Jump: Open Female, Bronze: Elizabeth Rexford.

Dene Games:

Finger Pull: Open Male, Gold: Faustino Morrow. Junior Male, Gold: Kohren Green. Junior Female, Silver: Lindsay Merculief.

Hand Games: Junior Male, Bronze: Team Alaska. Juvenile Female, Bronze: Team Alaska.

Snow Snake: Junior Male, Silver: Christian Warrior. Bronze: Kohren Green. Junior Female, Silver: Linnette Stettinger.

Stick Pull: Open Male, Gold: Garry Hull. Junior Female, Silver: Marjorie Tahbone. Juvenile Female, Bronze: Meda Warrior.

Pole Push: Open Male, Silver: Team Alaska. Junior Male, Silver: Team Alaska. Junior Female, Gold: Team Alaska. Juvenile Female, Bronze: Team Alaska.

All Around: Open Male, Bronze: Garry Hull. Junior Male, Silver: Kohren Green. Junior Female, Gold: Linnette Stettinger.

—Source: Arctic Winter Games, www.awg.ca

current sheets flowing through gases create V-shaped potential double layers. Electrons near the center of the current sheet move faster, hit the atmosphere harder and cause the different intensities of light observed in the aurora.

Displays take place as low as 40 miles above Earth's surface, but usually begin about 68 miles above and extend hundreds of miles into space. They concentrate in two bands roughly centered above the Arctic Circle and Antarctic Circle (the latter known as the aurora australis) that are about 2,500 miles in diameter. In northern latitudes the greatest occurrence of auroral displays is in the spring and fall months, because of the tilt of the planet in relationship to the sun's plane. Displays may occur on dark nights throughout the winter.

If sunspot activity is particularly intense and the denser-than-usual solar wind heads to Earth, the resulting auroras can be so great that they cover all but the tropical latitudes.

Some observers claim that the northern lights make a sound similar to the rustle of taffeta, but scientists say the displays cannot be heard in the audible frequency range.

Residents of Fairbanks, located on the 65th parallel, see the aurora borealis an average of 240 nights a year. The University of Alaska Fairbanks issues weekly aurora forecasts in winter. Additional information and forecasts can be found at www.pfrr.alaska.edu/aurora.

Photographing the Aurora Borealis. To capture the northern lights on film, you will need a digital SLR camera or a 35mm camera that has adjustable f-stop and shutter speed, a sturdy tripod, a locking-type cable release (if needed for a long exposure) and an f3.5 lens (or faster). It is best to photograph the lights on a night when they are not moving too rapidly. And as a general rule, photos improve if you manage to include recognizable subjects in the foreground—trees and lighted cabins are favorites of many photographers. Set up your camera at least 75 feet back from the foreground objects to make sure that both the foreground and aurora are in sharp focus.

Normal and wide-angle lenses are best. Try to keep your exposures under a minute—a 10- to 30-second exposure is generally best. The lens openings and exposure times are only starting points, since the amount of light generated by the aurora is inconsistent. (For best results, bracket widely.)

f-stop	ISO 400	ISO 800
f1.2	3 sec.	1.5 sec.
f1.4	4	2
f1.8	5	3
f2	10	5
f2.8	20	10
f3.5	30	15

Fujichrome Provia 100F color film can be push-processed to 200, 400 and 800 ISO in any professional lab. Provia 400F can be push-processed to 800 and 1600 ISO. (Consult your local camera store for details.)

A few notes of caution: Protect the camera from low temperatures until you are ready to make your exposures. Cameras with electronically controlled shutters may not function properly at low temperatures. Having several sets of extra batteries (kept warm in a pocket close to your body and changed frequently) is a good idea. Prefocus the camera at infinity in the daylight—before shooting the aurora. When using film, wind it slowly to reduce the possibility of static electricity, which can lead to streaks on the film. Grounding the camera when rewinding can help prevent the static-electricity problem. (To ground the camera, hold it against a water pipe, drain pipe, metal fence post or other grounded object.) Follow the basic rules and experiment with exposures.

The first photographs to show the aurora borealis in its entirety were published in early 1982. These historic photographs were taken from satellite-mounted cameras specially adapted to filter unwanted light from the sunlit portion of the Earth, which is a million times brighter than the aurora. From space, the aurora has the appearance of a nearly perfect circle.

BAIDARKA The *baidarka* (also spelled bidarka or bidarkee), or Aleut kayak, is a portable decked boat made of skins (usually seal) stretched over wood frames. The *baidarka* (a Russian term for the skin boats) was widely used by Aleuts and Alaska coastal Natives for transportation and hunting in areas associated with Russian influence. Baidarkas were the only form of kayak commonly built with three hatchways—two for the Aleut paddlers and one for the Russian passenger.

Three-hatch *baidarka*, about 1909.
Photo by J. E. Thwaites, courtesy Anchorage Museum of History and Art. From *Baidarka* by George Dyson.

BALEEN (See also Baskets; Whales) Baleen (often mistakenly called "whalebone") hangs from the upper jaw of baleen whales in long, fringed, bonelike strips. Baleen whales, such as humpback, bowhead, minke and gray, feed by taking in seawater and filtering through the baleen small fish, plankton and the tiny, shrimplike creatures called krill. Baleen is made of keratin, a substance found in human fingernails. The outer edge of baleen is hard; the inside edges of the baleen plates form a fringe of coarse bristles that resembles matted goat hair.

The number of plates along the jaw of an adult humpback, the largest of the baleen whales, varies from 600 to 800 (300 to 400 a side); the roof of the mouth is empty of plates. The bowhead whale has 600 plates, some of which reach 14 feet or more in length. Baleen varies in thickness and texture. Baleen from humpback whales is coarse; sei whales have finely textured baleen.

Baleen was once used for corset stays, Venetian blinds, hairbrushes and buggy whips. It is no longer of significant commercial use, although Alaska Natives use brownish-black bowhead baleen to craft fine baskets and model ships, or apply scrimshaw to raw pieces before selling them as gift items.

BARABARA Pronounced buh-RAH-buh-ruh, this traditional Aleut or Eskimo dwelling is semi-subterranean and built of sod supported by driftwood or whale ribs.

BARANOV, ALEXANDER

(See also Sitka) Alexander Andreyevich Baranov (1747–1819), sometimes called "Lord of Alaska," was manager of the fur-trading Russian–American Co. and the first governor of Russian Alaska.

A failed Siberian fur businessman, Baranov seemed an unlikely choice for overseeing the expansion of the Russian–American empire when he arrived at Kodiak in 1790. But his aggressiveness and tough political skills proved indispensable. Within seven years, he had eliminated all competitors and secured the entire south Alaska coast, from the Aleutian Islands to Yakutat, for the Russian–American Co.

NUGGETS

It was 12 below zero in December 1993, when Anchorage watercolor artist Nancy Stonington and her intended, Chuck Beatie, exchanged vows on the Chukchi Sea ice pack just off Barrow. The eight-minute ceremony was kept short for two reasons: "It was real cold out there, and because of all the reports of polar bears in the area," explained the maid of honor.

—1998 *The Alaska Almanac®*

Learning to handle a *baidarka* and navigate a seagoing sloop, he established Fort St. Michael at remote Sitka Bay in 1799, and in 1804 reestablished the post following its destruction by Tlingit warriors.

Baranov was a pragmatic ruler. He encouraged marriage between European men and Native women. The settlement's need for clerks and artisans led him to require basic schooling for all children. Lacking military support to exclude British and American ships from Alaska waters, he cultivated cordial relations with foreign captains. By the time he retired in 1818, Russian influence in the North Pacific stretched from Siberia to Fort Ross in northern California.

Baranov died of fever aboard ship en route to St. Petersburg in 1819.

A Coast Guard survey of Alaskan boating safety concluded that approximately 50 percent of all man-overboard accidents resulted from the victim trying to relieve himself over the side of the vessel.

BARROW (See also Museums; Native Peoples; Regions of Alaska)

Situated 350 miles north of the Arctic Circle, Barrow is the northernmost city in the United States and the largest Iñupiat Eskimo community in the world.

Barrow was called Utqiagvik by its Iñupiat founders. Because of its key location at the junction of the Chukchi and Beaufort Seas, Barrow became an important whaling site. The town remains a center of subsistence whaling and harvesting of other land and water species.

Nearly 4,100 people live in this polar environment, unconnected to any other community by road. Within the 21-square-mile city limits, however, are 127 miles of maintained roadway covering three distinct areas of settlement: the traditional Iñupiat community of Barrow, the former Naval Arctic Research Laboratory and portions of the former Distant Early Warning (DEW) Line station.

Barrow is the seat of government of the North Slope Borough, and serves as a regional center for the 89,000-square-mile borough. It is also the corporate headquarters for the Arctic Slope Regional Corp. and the Ukpeagvik Iñupiat Corp., which were established under the Native Claims Settlement Act.

Barrow has a strong and growing tourist industry. Visitors are attracted by everything from traditional whaling celebrations to polar bear watching, northern lights and the midnight sun. A monument across from the airport is dedicated to American humorist Will Rogers and famed pilot Wiley Post, who were killed in a 1935 airplane crash 15 miles south of Barrow.

Men's Health magazine found out that Alaska has the lowest rate of skin cancer in the nation. They called Alaska to find out why, and their source simply answered, "You don't get skin cancer where the sun doesn't shine."

BASEBALL

Six teams make up the Alaska Baseball League: Alaska Goldpanners of Fairbanks, Anchorage Bucs, Athletes in Action Fire of Fairbanks, Anchorage Glacier Pilots, Kenai Peninsula Oilers and Mat–Su Miners.

Baseball season opens in June and runs through the end of July. Each team plays a round-robin schedule with the other Alaska teams in addition to scheduling games with visiting Lower 48 teams. The caliber of play in Alaska is some of the best nationwide at the amateur level. Major league scouts rate Alaska baseball at A to AA, visiting each season to check out talent for possible recruitment.

The Anchorage Bucs began playing during the 1981 season. They defeated Team USA in 1991, defeated the Moscow Red Devils in 1992 and won the Alaska League championship several times. In 1993, the Bucs were recognized as America's No. 1 summer collegiate team.

The Anchorage Glacier Pilots are entering their 38th year. This semipro team drafts collegiate athletes from all over the United States. The Pilots consistently finish in the top seven when they compete in the annual National Baseball Congress Championships in Wichita, Kansas, most recently taking first place in 2001. More than 80 former players have gone on to play in the major leagues. Twelve former Glacier Pilots were playing in the majors in 2007, including Jeff Francis, Eric Hinske, Josh Wilson, Greg Dobbs, Mark Teahen, Mike Zagurski, Matt Wise, Ryan Ludwick, Russ Springer, Scott Hatteburg, Aaron Boone and Randy Johnson.

The list of other major league players who were once on Alaska teams is equally impressive, and includes stars Tom Seaver, Mark McGwire, Chris Chambliss and Dave Winfield. Ten former Bucs currently playing in the majors are Geoff Jenkins, Mark Redman, Jeff Kent, Jeff Francis, Jered Weaver, Heath Bell, David Bush, Geoff Geary, Kirk Saarloos and CJ Wilson. Find more information on the Alaska Baseball League at www.alaskabaseballleague.org.

BASKETS (See also Baleen; Native Arts and Crafts)

Native basketry varies greatly according to materials locally available. Athabascan Indians of the Interior, for example, weave baskets from willow root gathered in late spring. The roots are steamed and heated over a fire to loosen the outer bark. Weavers then separate the material into fine strips by pulling the roots through their teeth.

Yup'ik Eskimo grass baskets are made in river delta areas of Southwestern Alaska from Bristol Bay north to Norton Sound and from Nunivak Island east to interior Eskimo river villages. Weavers use very fine grass harvested in fall. A coil basketry technique is followed, using coils from ⅛- to ¾-inch wide. Seal gut, traditionally dyed with berries (today with commercial dyes), is often interwoven into the baskets.

Baleen, a glossy, hard material that extends in slats from the upper jaw of some types of whales, is also used for baskets. Baleen basketry in the Iñupiat region originated about 1905 when Charles D. Brower, trader for a whaling company at Point Barrow, suggested, after the decline of the whalebone (baleen) industry for women's corsets, that local Native men make the baskets as a source of income. The baskets were not produced in any number until 1916. The weave and shape of the baskets were copied from the split-willow Athabascan baskets acquired in trade. A decorative "knob" of ivory is often added. Later, baleen baskets were also made in Point Hope and Wainwright.

Most birch-bark baskets are made by Athabascan Indians, although a few Eskimos also produce them. Baskets are shaped as simple cylinders, or canoe shapes, held together with spruce root lashings. Sometimes the birch bark is cut into thin strips and woven into diamond or checkerboard patterns. Birch bark is usually collected in spring and early summer; large pieces free of knots are preferred. Birch-bark baskets traditionally were used as cooking vessels. Food was placed in them and hot stones added. Birch-bark baby carriers also are still made, chiefly for collectors.

Among the finest of Alaska baskets are the tiny, intricately woven Aleut baskets made of rye grass, which in the Aleutians is abundant, pliable and very tough. The three

Tlingit spruce-root basket. From *Indian Baskets of the Pacific Northwest and Alaska* by Allen Lobb, Art Wolfe and Barbara Paxson.

main styles of Aleut baskets—Attu, Atka and Unalaska—are named after the islands where the styles originated. Although the small baskets are the best known, Aleuts also traditionally made large, coarsely woven baskets for utilitarian purposes.

Tlingit, Haida and Tsimshian Indians make baskets of spruce roots and cedar bark. South of Frederick Sound, basket material usually consists of strands split from the inner bark of red cedar. To the north of the sound, spruce roots are used. Maidenhair ferns are sometimes interwoven into spruce root baskets to form patterns resembling embroidery. A large spruce root basket may take months to complete.

Examples of Alaska Native basketry may be viewed in many museums, including the University of Alaska Museum of the North, Fairbanks; the Anchorage Museum at Rasmuson Center, Anchorage; the Sheldon Jackson Museum, Sitka; and the Alaska State Museum, Juneau.

Prices for Native baskets vary greatly. A finely woven coiled beach-grass basket may cost from $100 to $700; birch-bark baskets may range from $35 to $200; willow-root trays may cost $800; finely woven Aleut baskets may cost $200 to $800; cedar-bark baskets may range from $30 to $80; and baleen baskets range in price from $800 to more than $2,400 for medium-size baskets. These prices are approximate and are based on the weave, material used, size and decoration added, such as beads, embroidery or ivory.

BEADWORK (See also Native Arts and Crafts; Parka)

Eskimo and Indian women create a variety of handsomely beaded items. Before contact with Europeans, Indian women sometimes carved beads of willow wood or made them from seeds of certain shrubs and trees. Glass seed beads became available to Alaska's Athabascan Indians in the mid-19th century, although some types of larger trade beads were in use earlier. Beads quickly became a coveted trade item. The Cornaline d'aleppo, an opaque red bead with a white center, and the faceted Russian blue beads were among the most popular types.

The introduction of small glass beads sparked changes in beadwork style and design. More colors were available and the smaller, more easily maneuvered beads made it possible to work out delicate floral patterns impossible with larger trade beads.

Historically, beads were sewn directly onto leather garments or other items with the overlay stitch. Contemporary beadwork is often done on a separate piece of felt that is not visible once the beads are stitched in place.

Alaska's Athabascan beadworkers sometimes use paper patterns, often combining several motifs and tracing their outline on the surface to be worked. The most common designs include flowers, leaves and berries, some in very stylized form. Many patterns are drawn simply from the sewer's environment. Since the gold rush, magazines, graphic art, advertising and patriotic motifs have inspired Athabascan beadworkers, although stylized floral designs are still the most popular.

Designs vary regionally, as do the ways in which they are applied to garments or footgear. Skilled practitioners execute beadwork so distinctive it can be recognized at a glance.

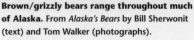

Brown/grizzly bears range throughout much of Alaska. From *Alaska's Bears* by Bill Sherwonit (text) and Tom Walker (photographs).

BEARS (See also Mammals; McNeil River State Game Sanctuary)

Three species of bear inhabit Alaska: the black, the brown/grizzly and the polar bear. Most of Alaska can be considered bear country, and for those wishing to spend time in Alaska's great outdoors, bear country becomes "beware" country. Sows are extremely aggressive if their young are around, and bears will guard a moose kill against all passersby. Bear behavior should always be considered unpredictable. Bear scat or a large concentration of flies in one area are signs for hikers to watch for and retreat from. The Alaska Department of Fish and Game publishes *Bear Facts,* recommended reading for hikers and campers. Excellent

> According to the latest figures, law enforcement and wildlife officials receive more annual calls in Anchorage concerning problem moose and bears than they do for holdup alarms, bomb scares, liquor violations, escaped criminals, subjects resisting arrest, prostitution and illegal aliens COMBINED!

bear information is also available from the Alaska Department of Natural Resources, www.dnr.state.ak.us/parks/safety/bears.htm.

Black Bears. Black bears are usually jet black or brown with a brown-yellow muzzle, and weigh from 100 to 200 pounds as adults. The brown color phase can sometimes be confused with grizzlies, but black bears are generally smaller and lack the grizzly's distinct shoulder hump. Black bear habitat covers three-fourths of Alaska, with high concentrations found in the Southeast, Prince William Sound and the coastal mountains and lowlands of Southcentral Alaska. Low to moderate densities are found in Interior and Western Alaska. Their range is semi-open forests, and though omnivorous, their diet consists mainly of vegetation due to the difficulty of getting meat or fish. Black bears often spend their lives within five miles of their birthplace and will frequently return to their home range if transplanted. They easily climb trees; both cubs and adults use trees as a place of escape. Cubs are generally born in late January or February weighing 8 to 10 ounces. Average litter size is two cubs, but three or four cubs in a litter is not unusual. Black bears den in winter for up to six months but are not true hibernators. Their body temperature remains high and they awaken easily—even in midwinter.

Brown/Grizzly Bears. Fur colors of brown/grizzly bears vary from blond to black with shades of brown and gray in between. As adults, they can weigh over 1,000 pounds, but are usually smaller; size depends on sex, age, time of year and geographic location. Coastal bears, referred to as "browns" or "brownies," are the largest living omnivorous land mammals in the world and grow larger than Interior "grizzlies." Browns or grizzlies are found in most of Alaska except for islands in the extreme southeastern part of the state.

The lowest populations are found in the northern Interior and the Arctic. Their range is wherever food is abundant, but the bears prefer open tundra and grasslands. Diet consists of a wide variety of plants and animals, including their own kind, and humans under some circumstances. In their realm, grizzlies are king and fear no other animal except humans with a firearm. While

---

Bear Cub Entertains Tourists

Tourists in Ketchikan were able to go home with a story about Alaska that will be hard to top, thanks to a feisty bear cub who wandered into the airport. The 25-pound cub tripped an electronic eye on the airport's automatic doors and found his way over to a crowded baggage carousel. Finding himself surrounded by tourists, he bolted for a stairway, but was grabbed by an airport employee, who put him in a portable dog kennel. The little guy was held overnight by the state wildlife protection agency for observation and released the next morning in the area where his mother had last been seen.

—1990 *The Alaska Almanac*®

---

attacks on people are the exception, the results can be tragic. These bears are also tremendously strong and have been seen carrying—off the ground—an 800-pound moose. One to two hairless cubs are usually born in late January or February weighing 8 to 10 ounces, and sows have been known to adopt orphaned cubs. Time of year and duration of denning varies with the location and physical condition of the bear, and can be up to six months of the year. Dens are frequently on hillsides or on mountain slopes.

Polar Bears. The only areas on a polar bear not covered with heavy, white fur are its eyes and large, black nose. The bear, seemingly aware that his nose gives him away to prey, will hold a paw up to hide it when hunting. An adult polar bear weighs 1,500 pounds or more and has a long neck with a proportionately small head. Polar bear habitat is the Canadian–eastern Alaska Arctic and the western Alaska Arctic–eastern Russia, the latter being home to the world's largest polar bears. Polar bear range is the arctic ice cap, with the species being more

Spanish Exploration

When residents think of explorers who came to Alaska, they usually think of Captain Cook. But Britain was not the only country to explore northern waters. For 30 years after Vitus Bering's 1741 voyage, Russians dominated the area. Then European countries began to make inroads. In 1773 and on several other occasions, Spain sent explorers to Alaska to document Russian activities, make land claims and search for a Northwest Passage. Spain withdrew from the region in 1795 when it surrendered a plot of land at Nootka Sound to the British. However the Spanish legacy is still evident in such place-names as Valdez, Cordova, Revillagigedo and Malaspina.

numerous toward the southern edge of the ice pack. Occasionally polar bears will come ashore, but they generally stay near the coast. While ashore they eat some vegetation, but their diet consists primarily of ringed seals, walrus, stranded whales, birds and fish.

Cannibalism of cubs and young bears by older males is not unusual. Polar bears are strong swimmers; reports exist of swimming bears found 50 miles from the nearest land or ice. When swimming, they use their front paws for propulsion and trail their rear paws.

Mother bears have been seen with cubs hanging onto their tails, towing them through the water. Cubs are born in December with two being the common litter size. They weigh about a pound at birth and remain with their mother for about 28 months. Usually only pregnant sows den up, for an average of six months in the winter. Polar bears need stable, cold areas for denning, and dens in Alaska have been found 30 miles inland, along the coast, on offshore islands, on shore-fast ice and on drifting sea ice.

BERING, VITUS Vitus Jonassen

Bering (1681–1741) is credited as the first European to discover Alaska. A Danish captain serving Russia under the crown of Peter the Great, Bering was in command of an expedition to find out if the continents of Asia and America were connected and to claim new lands for Russia.

He piloted his first expedition in 1728 through the strait that now bears his name,

concluding that Asia and America were not joined. On that voyage, however, he never saw the fog-shrouded Alaska mainland. The expedition was considered a failure.

In June 1741, Bering set sail again as captain of the ill-fated *St. Peter.* Also on board was German naturalist Georg Wilhelm Steller; the Steller sea lion and Steller's jay owe their names to his fieldwork on the journey. A second ship, the *St. Paul,* piloted by Aleksei Chirikov, accompanied the *St. Peter.*

During the voyage, Bering and Chirikov lost contact in foul weather, never to meet again. In July both ships sighted southern Alaska. On July 16, Steller led a landing party on what is now Kayak Island at Cape St. Elias, just east of Prince William Sound.

Short of food and weakened with scurvy, Bering was anxious to set sail for Kamchatka before winter. Against the advice of Steller, the explorer sailed for home. In heavy seas the *St. Peter* ran aground on a rocky island off the Siberian coast, since known as Bering Island. Twenty sailors, including Bering, died of scurvy.

The remaining sailors survived by eating fish and seals, eventually built a boat from the wreckage of the *St. Peter,* and returned to Russia.

Bering's voyage not only laid the basis for Russian claims to Alaska but also opened the fur trade. His crews brought back many pelts, among them 800 sea otter skins. By the late 1700s, the Russian fur trade had become the richest fur enterprise in the world, setting the stage for the extinction of the Steller's sea cow by 1768 and the near-extinction of the sea otter in the 1820s.

BERING LAND BRIDGE

The Bering Land Bridge was formed when the glaciers of the Wisconsinan period flowed across the northern cap of Earth. Millions of cubic miles of water from Earth's oceans were bound in these glaciers, causing the ocean levels to lower by more than 300 feet. Between 40,000 and 15,000 years ago, the lowered sea levels exposed a 1,000-mile-wide corridor of dry land connecting North America with Asia. Now known as the Bering Land Bridge, it enabled the migration of plants and animals, including humans, between the Old World and the New World.

When the glaciers retreated, the water returned to the sea, covering the bridge and creating the Bering Strait between Alaska and Siberia. Recognizing the need to preserve the area's unique paleontological and archaeological resources, in 1980 the U.S. Congress created the Bering Land Bridge National Preserve, managed by the National Park Service. The preserve occupies 2.7 million acres of the Seward Peninsula in northwest Alaska.

Visitors will find extensive lava flows and maar lakes (formed by ash and steam explosions), sandy beaches, tundra and Serpentine Hot Springs, which is considered one of the preserve's highlights. Located in a valley of granite spires called tors, the hot springs attract those who come to bathe, hike, relax and observe wildlife.

More than 400 species of plants have been found in the preserve. The Bering Land Bridge Preserve also has a rich and diversified bird life. Animals found here include musk oxen, bears, moose, wolves, wolverines, reindeer, caribou, foxes and other smaller species.

Depending on the season, access is possible only by aircraft (special permit required for helicopter), boat, dogsled, foot, skis or snowmobile. Recreational options include camping, backpacking, hiking, photography, wildlife viewing and coastal boating.

Federal highway access ends 400 miles from Bering Land Bridge National Preserve, but the information superhighway leads right to it. The preserve's Web site, www.nps.gov/bela, offers a detailed look at the region.

BERRIES

Wild berries abound in Alaska, with the circumboreal lingonberry/lowbush cranberry (Vaccinium vitisidaea) being the most widespread. Blueberries of one species or another grow in most of the state. Some 50 other species of wild fruit are found in Alaska including strawberries, raspberries, cloudberries, salmonberries, crowberries, nagoonberries and crab apples. High-bush cranberries (which are not really cranberries) can be found on bushes even in the dead of winter; the frozen berries provide a refreshing treat to the hiker.

The fruit of the wild rose, or rose hip, is not strictly a berry but is an ideal source of vitamin C for Bush dweller and city resident alike. A few hips will provide as much of the vitamin as a medium-size orange. The farther north the hips are found, the richer they are in vitamin C.

Alaska does have one poisonous berry, the baneberry. Sometimes called doll's eyes or chinaberries, baneberries may be white or scarlet in color. As few as six berries can induce violent symptoms of poisoning in an adult.

BILLIKEN

This smiling ivory figure with a pointed head, though long a popular Northland souvenir, is not an Eskimo invention. Florence Pretz of Kansas City patented the billiken in 1908.

A small, seated, Buddha-like figure, the original billiken was manufactured by the Billiken Co. of Chicago and sold as a good luck charm. Thousands of these figurines were sold during the 1909 Alaska–Yukon–Pacific Exposition in Seattle.

The owner of a Wasilla butcher shop told the *Anchorage Daily News* that customers frequently call to ask the price of turning their MOOSE into sausage. When he asked one *moose*-hunting customer, "What kind of sausage would you like?" the man replied, "*REINDEER* sausage!"

Crondahl's Fresh Berry Pie

Raspberries, blueberries and strawberries all work beautifully in this classic recipe from Jay and Judy Crondahl's bed-and-breakfast in Juneau. When Jay, an enthusiastic canoeist, goes camping in berry country, he takes along a prepared pie shell, premeasured sugar and cornstarch, and canned whipping cream, and creates this pie with whatever berries he finds.

1 prebaked 9-inch pie shell	1 cup water
¼ cup sugar	4 cups fresh berries
2½ tablespoons cornstarch	Whipped cream, for serving

Combine the sugar and cornstarch in a heavy-bottomed saucepan. Add the water and cook over moderate heat, stirring, until thickened. Remove from the heat. Puree or crush 1 cup of the berries and stir them into the cornstarch mixture. Arrange the remaining berries in the pie shell and pour the crushed berry mixture on top. Chill the pie thoroughly to set, and serve with whipped cream. Makes 8 servings.

—Sarah Eppenbach, *Baked Alaska: Recipes for Sweet Comforts from the North Country*

Billikens vanished soon afterward from most Lower 48 shops; however, someone had brought them to Nome, and the Eskimos of King Island, Little Diomede and Wales began carving replicas of the billikens from walrus ivory and walrus teeth.

A popular notion contends that rubbing a billiken's tummy brings good fortune.

BIRDS The Alaska State Office of the National Audubon Society acknowledges 478 naturally occurring bird species in Alaska. If unsubstantiated sightings are included, the species total increases.

Millions of ducks, geese and swans wing north to breeding grounds each spring. Millions of seabirds congregate in nesting colonies on exposed cliffs along Alaska's coastline, particularly on the Aleutian Islands and on islands in the Bering Sea.

Migratory birds reach Alaska from every continent but Europe. Arctic terns travel up to 22,000 miles on their round-trip each year from Antarctica. Others come from South America, Hawaii, the South Pacific islands and Asia.

Each May one of the world's largest concentrations of shorebirds funnels through the Copper River Delta near

Cordova. Waterfowl such as trumpeter swans and the world's entire population of dusky Canada geese breed there.

More than 100 species of birds can be spotted in the Seward area. Other key waterfowl habitats include the Yukon–Kuskokwim Delta, Yukon Flats, Innoko Flats, Minto Lakes and the vast wetlands of the western Arctic Alaska south of Barrow. During migration, huge flocks gather at Egegik, Port Heiden, Port Moller, Izembek Bay, Chickaloon Flats, Susitna Flats and Stikine Flats.

Raptors, led by the bald eagle, range throughout the state. The largest gathering of eagles in the world takes place in Alaska each year between October and February. In 1982, the Alaska Chilkat Bald Eagle Preserve was set aside to protect the 3,000-plus eagles that assemble at the site along the Chilkat River near Haines.

Alaska has three subspecies of peregrine falcon: Arctic, American and Peale's. The Eskimo curlew, Steller's eider, spectacled eider and short-tailed albatross are on the federal endangered or threatened species list for the state. The Aleutian Canada goose was removed in 2001.

Following is a list of some geographically restricted birds, as well as a few of the state's more well-known species:

Arctic tern near the Mendenhall Glacier, Juneau. From *Alaska's Birds* by Robert H. Armstrong.

Aleutian Tern. Breeds in coastal areas, marshes, islands, lagoons, rivers and inshore marine waters. Nests in Alaska on the ground in matted, dry grass. Casual sightings in southeastern Alaska in spring and summer, and in northern Alaska in summer.

Arctic Tern. Breeds in tidal flats, beaches, glacial moraines, rivers, lakes and marshes. Nests in colonies or scattered pairs on sand, gravel, moss or in rocks. The Arctic tern winters in Antarctica, bypassing the Lower 48 in its 20,000-mile round-trip migration. Common sightings in southeastern, south coastal and western Alaska in spring, summer and fall, and in southwestern Alaska in spring and fall.

Arctic Warbler. Nests on the ground in grass or moss in willow thickets. Common sightings in the Alaska Range, the Seward Peninsula and the Brooks Range in spring, summer and fall.

Bald Eagle. Found in coniferous forests, deciduous woodlands, rivers and streams, beaches and tidal flats, rocky shores and reefs. Nests in old-growth timber along the coast and larger mainland rivers. In treeless areas, nests on cliffs or on the ground. There are more bald eagles in Alaska than in all the other states combined, and sightings commonly occur in southeastern, south coastal and southwestern Alaska year-round.

Bluethroat. Nests on the ground in shrub thickets in the uplands and the foothills of western and northern Alaska. Casual sightings in southwestern Alaska in spring and fall.

Emperor Goose. Nests near water in grassy marsh habitat on islands or banks or in large tussocks. The bulk of the world's population nests in the Yukon–Kuskokwim Delta, with a few others nesting farther north to Kotzebue Sound and a few more in eastern Siberia. Rarely is an emperor goose seen east or south of Kodiak. Common sightings in southwestern Alaska in spring, fall and winter, and in western Alaska in spring, summer and fall.

Horned Puffin. Nests on sea islands in rock crevices or in burrows among boulders, on sea cliffs and on grassy slopes. Breeds inshore, in marine waters and on islands. Common sightings in southwestern and western Alaska in spring, summer and fall.

NUGGETS

Ketchikan homeowner Jean Stack was lying awake in bed one morning when she heard a tremendous crash. Stack ran into the living room and saw glass shattered across her floor, feathers strewn about the room and a huge fish carcass lying where her dog normally slept.

Her neighbor reported that he'd seen a group of eagles fighting and thrashing around the nearby trees. Then one eagle, apparently bearing a fish carcass, made a beeline for Stack's bay window, crashed through, then reappeared and flew away (minus the fish and with fewer feathers). A local biologist remarked that while window strikes are common with smaller birds, it's surprising behavior for eagles.

—1998 *The Alaska Almanac*®

NUGGETS

A three-day howling winter storm hit the remote village of Kaktovik (population 300) on the Beaufort Sea in January 2005. Temperatures lingered at −20°F and winds at 70 mph. Then the power went out, plunging residents into a four-day deep freeze. Two days into the ordeal, Air National Guard helicopters were finally able to begin delivering help and supplies.

—*2005 The Alaska Almanac*®

Pacific Loon. Breeds on lakes in coniferous forests or on tundra lakes, and nests on projecting points or small islands. Folklore credits the loon with magical powers and several legends abound. Common sightings in southeastern and southcentral Alaska in spring, fall and winter, and in southwestern, central, western and northern Alaska in spring, summer and fall.

Red-faced Cormorant. Habitat includes inshore marine waters. Nests in colonies on ledges of sea cliffs, small piles of rocks and shelves on volcanic cinder cones. In North America this bird appears only in Alaska. Common sightings in south coastal and southwestern Alaska year-round.

Red-legged Kittiwake. Breeds in the Pribilof Islands, and on Buldir and Bogoslof Islands in the Aleutians. Nests on cliff ledges and cliff points. Common sightings near breeding areas in southwestern Alaska in summer.

Whiskered Auklet. A small, gray diving seabird with white whiskers. It nests only in the Aleutians, particularly at the eastern end of Unalaska Island and on the nearby Baby Islands.

White Wagtail. Found in open areas with short vegetation usually along the Seward Peninsula coast. Nests near or on the ground in crevices or niches in old buildings. Casual sightings in central Alaska

in spring, and in southwestern Alaska in spring and summer.

About 10 million **swans, geese** and **ducks** also nest in Alaska each year, making the state critical habitat for many of the continent's waterfowl. In North America some species and subspecies use Alaska as exclusive nesting grounds, while more than half the North American population of other species nests in the state.

Audubon Alaska (715 L St., Suite 200, Anchorage 99501; www.audubonalaska.org) is the Alaska State Office of the National Audubon Society. Six local chapters are based in Alaska: the Anchorage Audubon Society (P.O. Box 101161, Anchorage 99510), the Juneau Audubon Society (P.O. Box 021725, Juneau 99802), the Arctic Audubon Society (P.O. Box 82098, Fairbanks 99708), the Kodiak Audubon Society (P.O. Box 1756, Kodiak 99615), the YK Delta Audubon Society (P.O. Box 605, Bethel 99559), and the Prince William Sound Audubon Society (P.O. Box 2511, Cordova 99579). These local chapters coordinate some of the more than 20 annual Christmas bird counts around the state.

Bird-watchers gather during the first week of May for the Copper River Delta Shorebird Festival in Cordova and the Kachemak Bay Shorebird Festival in Homer. Ketchikan holds an annual rufous hummingbird festival in April. The Bald Eagle Festival is held in Haines each November.

The Alaska Department of Fish and Game encourages the enjoyment of Alaska's birds through its "Wings Over Alaska" program. Participants are awarded various levels of free certificates for bird species seen in Alaska. Additional information is available at www.wildlife.alaska.gov/index.cfm?adfg=birding.main.

BLANKET TOSS

As effective as a trampoline, the blanket toss (or *nalukataq*) features a walrus-hide blanket grasped by a number of people in a circle. They toss a person on the blanket as high as possible for as

Valdez Harbor holds pleasure craft as well as commercial fishing vessels and tour boats.
Photo by Tricia Brown.

long as that person can remain upright. Every true Eskimo festival and many non-Native occasions include the blanket toss, which originally was used to allow Eskimo hunters to spot game such as walrus and seal in the distance. Depending on the skill of the person being tossed and the number of tossers, a medium-weight person might typically go 20 feet in the air.

BOATING (See also Baidarka; Cruises; Ferries) Travel by boat is an important means of transportation in Alaska where highways serve only about one-third of the state. Until the advent of the airplane, boats often were the only way to reach many parts of Alaska. Most of Alaska's supplies still arrive by water and in Southeast—where precipitous terrain and numerous islands make road building impossible—water travel is essential.

In January 2001, vessel registration was transferred from the U.S. Coast Guard to the Alaska Division of Motor Vehicles. The division reported that there were 69,090 vessels registered in the state as of December 2006.

Moorage. This fleet is accommodated by rental slips, most of which are managed by public harbormasters. In a system called "hot berthing," the harbormaster may assign an empty, available slip to a transient user for a limited time. Many harbors also have the capacity to "double park" in certain fairways. About 20 moorage facilities are in remote locations with no other services available.

Local governments have the major responsibility for operating public floats, grids, docks, launch ramps and associated small-boat harbor facilities throughout the coastal areas of the state. Moorage facilities constructed by the state are intended for boats up to a maximum of 100 feet, with a limited number of facilities for larger vessels where large boats are common. With the exception of Ketchikan, Sitka and Juneau, there are no private marine facilities.

Recreational Boating. Alaska has thousands of miles of lakes, rivers and sheltered seaways. For information about boating within national forests, parks, monuments, preserves and wildlife refuges, contact the appropriate federal agency. For travel by boat in southeastern Alaska's Inside Passage and the sheltered seaways of Southcentral Alaska's Prince William Sound—or elsewhere in Alaska's coastal waters—NOAA nautical charts, pilot guides and tidal current tables are available. (See Information Sources)

Sea kayakers from around the world are drawn to Alaska to paddle its sheltered waterways and challenge its open coast. Kayakers in Alaska may visit tidewater glaciers and natural hot springs, meeting whales and sea otters along the way.

Inland boaters will find hundreds of river and lake systems suitable for traveling by boat, raft, kayak or canoe.

Canoe routes have been established on the Kenai Peninsula (contact Kenai National Wildlife Refuge, P.O. Box 2139, Soldotna 99669-2139; (907) 262-7021); in Nancy Lake State Recreation Area (Ranger Station, P.O. Box 10, Willow 99688; (907) 495-6273); and on rivers in the Fairbanks and Anchorage areas (contact Bureau of Land Management, 1150 University Ave., Fairbanks 99709; (907) 474-2200, and 222 W. Seventh Ave., Suite 13, Anchorage 99513; (907) 271-5960).

Travel by water in Alaska requires extra caution. Weather changes rapidly and is often unpredictable; it's important to be prepared for the worst. Even in mid-summer, Alaska waters are cold. A person falling overboard may become immobilized by the cold water in only a few minutes. And since many of Alaska's water routes are far from civilization, help may be a long way off.

Persons inexperienced in traveling Alaska's waterways might consider hiring a charter boat operator or outfitter. Guides offer local knowledge and provide all necessary equipment. For information on such services, contact the chamber of commerce or the convention and visitors bureau for an area. A listing of these agencies is given at www.travelalaska.com.

Recreation information on both state and federal lands is available at the four Alaska Public Lands Information Centers: 605 W. Fourth Ave., Suite 105, Anchorage 99501, (907) 271-2737; 250 Cushman St., Suite 1A, Fairbanks 99701, (907) 456-0527; P.O. Box 359, Tok 99780, (907) 883-5667; and 50 Main St., Ketchikan 99901, (907) 228-6220. Web site: www.nps.gov/aplic.

BORE TIDE (See also Tides) A "bore" is an abrupt rise of tidal water moving rapidly inland from the mouth of an estuary into a constricted inlet; the term derives from the Middle English word for "wave."

Cook Inlet has one of the largest fluctuating tides in the world. Maximum tidal range here approaches 40 feet. Incoming tides are further compressed in the narrowing of Knik and Turnagain Arms and tidal bores are commonly seen. One- to 2-foot bores are common, but spring tides in Turnagain Arm in particular can produce spectacular bores up to 6 feet high, running at speeds of up to 10 knots. Good spots to view Turnagain's bore tides are along the Seward Highway, between 26 and 37 miles south of Anchorage. They arrive there about 2 hours and 15 minutes later than the tide book prediction for low tide at Anchorage.

A dangerous, yet growing, extreme sport is surfing the bore tides in the choicest locations around the world, among them Turnagain Arm, England's Severn Bore, and Brazil's Amazon Basin.

BREAKUP (See also Nenana Ice Classic) Breakup occurs when warming temperatures and melting snows raise the level of ice-covered streams and rivers sufficiently to cause the ice to break apart and float downstream. Breakup is one of two factors determining the open-water season for river navigation, the second being the depth of the river. Peak water conditions occur just after breakup.

The navigable season for the Kuskokwim and Yukon Rivers is June 1 through Sept. 30; the Nushagak River, June 1 through Aug. 31; and the Noatak River, late May through mid-September.

Breakup is a spectacular sight-and-sound show. Massive pieces of ice crunch and pound against one another as they push their way downriver racing for the sea, creating noises not unlike many huge engines straining and grating. The spine-tingling sound can be heard for miles. It marks the finale of winter and the arrival of spring in Alaska.

Sometimes great ice jams occur, causing the water to back up and flood inhabited areas. Flooding occurred at Fort Yukon in spring 1982, at McGrath in 1990 and at Allakaket in 1993.

BUNNY BOOTS Bunny boots, also called vapor-barrier boots, are large, insulated rubber boots that protect feet from frostbite. Black bunny boots are generally rated to –20°F, while the more common white bunny boots are even warmer and have been used in the most extreme conditions, including the heights of Mount McKinley, even though they're cumbersome for climbing. They are no longer made but are still in demand. Used bunny boots can fetch $50 to $150 a pair.

BUSH Originally used to describe large expanses of wilderness beyond the fringes of civilization inhabited only by trappers and prospectors, Bush has come to stand for any part of Alaska not accessible by road. A community accessible only by air, water, sled or snowmachine is considered a Bush village and anyone living there is someone from the Bush. The Bush is home to most of Alaska's Native people and many non-Natives who live on homesteads, operate mines or work as guides, pilots, teachers, trappers or fishermen.

The term is also applied to the small planes and their pilots who service areas lacking roads. Bush planes are commonly equipped with floats and skis to match terrain and season. For their oft-courageous air service, Alaska Bush pilots have become modern frontier heroes.

BUS LINES AND SHUTTLES

Scheduled bus service is available to and within Alaska (primarily during summer), although buses don't run as frequently as in the Lower 48. Shuttle services operate from various Anchorage locations (including the airport) to outlying communities, as far north as Talkeetna, and south to Seward and Homer. Call for rates and seasons of operation.

Intrastate/Yukon

Alaska Direct Busline, P.O. Box 501, Anchorage 99501; (907) 277-6652 or (800) 770-6652; e-mail akdirectbus@msn.com. Provides service to Anchorage, Fairbanks, Glennallen, Tok, Delta, Dawson, Whitehorse, Skagway, Haines and all points in between.

Alaska Shuttle (Eagle River Shuttle), (907) 333-8888 Anchorage; (907) 694-8888 Eagle River; www.akshuttle.com. Operates

from Anchorage airport, north to Talkeetna, south to Seward and points in between.

The Alaska Park Connection, P.O. Box 22-1011, Anchorage 99522; (800) 266-8625; www.alaskacoach.com. Provides daily service between Anchorage, Seward and Denali National Park.

Alaska/Yukon Trails, P.O. Box 84608, Fairbanks 99708; (800) 770-7275; www.alaskashuttle.com. Provides daily service between Anchorage, Talkeetna, Denali Park, Fairbanks, Whitehorse and Dawson City.

Denali Overland Transportation Co., P.O. Box 330, Talkeetna 99676. (907) 733-2384; (800) 651-5221; www.denalioverland.com. Offers service (April 1–October 1) between Anchorage, Talkeetna and Denali Park.

Homer Stage Lines, 2607 Eagle St., Anchorage 99503; 1213 Ocean Dr., Homer 99603; Anchorage, (907) 868-3914; Seward, (907) 224-3608; Homer, (907) 235-2252; http://homerstageline.com. Offers service between Anchorage, Seward and Homer.

Seward Bus Lines, 3333 Fairbanks St., Suite B, Anchorage 99503; (907) 563-0800 Anchorage; (907) 224-3608 Seward; www.sewardbuslines.net. Provides daily service between Anchorage and Seward.

Shuttle Man, (907) 677-8537. Offers shuttle transportation between Anchorage, Talkeetna and Seward and points in between.

Talkeetna Shuttle Service, (888) 288-6008, (907) 733-1725; www.denalicentral.com. Offers service from Anchorage airport to Talkeetna.

Municipal Service

Anchorage. Anchorage People Mover, 3650A E. Tudor Road, Anchorage 99507-1252; Ride Line phone (907) 343-6543; www.muni.org/transit1/mapping. The People Mover bus stops every 30 minutes at Ted Stevens International Airport. Travelers may also call for shuttle service to the following communities: Eagle River, (907) 694-8888; Mat-Su Valley, (907) 373-4359; Talkeetna, (888) 288-6008.

Fairbanks. MACS (Metropolitan Area Commuter System), Fairbanks North Star Borough, P.O. Box 71267, Fairbanks 99707. Transit Park depot located on

Cushman Street between 5th and 6th in downtown Fairbanks; (907) 459-1011; www.co.fairbanks.ak.us/Transportation.

Juneau. CTS (Capital Transit System), 10099 Bentwood Place, Juneau 99801; (907) 789-6901; www.juneau.org/capitaltransit/.

Kenai Peninsula. Kasilof, Kenai, Nikiski, Soldotna and Sterling. CARTS (Central Area Rural Transit System), P.O. Box 993, Soldotna 99669; (907) 262-8900; www.ridesalaska.org.

Ketchikan. The Bus (Ketchikan Gateway Borough), 344 Front St., Ketchikan 99901; (907) 225-8726; http://borough.ketchikan.ak.us/works/bus_info.htm.

North Pole. MACS (Metropolitan Area Commuter System), Transit Park depot located on Cushman Street between 5th and 6th in downtown Fairbanks; (907) 459-1011; www.co.fairbanks.ak.us/Transportation.

Sitka. Community Ride Public Transit (Sitka Tribe of Alaska), 700 Katlian Street, Suite B, Sitka; (907) 747-7103; http://publictransit.sitkatribe.org.

Wasilla. MASCOT (Mat-Su Community Transportation), P.O. Box 871590, Wasilla 99687; phone (907) 376-5000; fax (907) 373-5999; www.matsutransit.com.

Cabbage grows to extra-large proportions under the Midnight Sun. Photo by Roy Corral.

Charter Service

A wide variety of charter bus services also are available throughout Alaska. For individual or group charters, please consult the Web, local telephone directories or the local chambers of commerce for a complete listing of charter service providers.

CABBAGE Meet the king of Alaska's

monster vegetables. Alaska's abundant summer sun, cool temperatures and rich soil make it possible for gardeners to grow colossal cold-weather vegetables, most notably cabbage. The Matanuska and Susitna valleys, north of Anchorage, are hotbeds of cabbage cultivation, where the biggest are grown not for eating but for glory and prize money. The Giant Cabbage Weigh-off is one of the highlights of the Alaska State Fair in Palmer. The winner collects a $2,000 prize. The U.S. record was set in 2000, when Barb Everingham of Wasilla grew a cabbage weighing 105.6 pounds. Other past winners include:
2002—Seth Dinkel, Wasilla, 89.9 pounds
2003—Brenna Dinkel, Wasilla, 77.6 pounds
2004—Scott Robb, Palmer, 90.5 pounds
2005—Brenna Dinkel, 85 pounds
2006—Brenna Dinkel, 73.4 pounds

CABIN FEVER Cabin fever is a state

of mind blamed on cold, dark, winter weather when people are often house-bound. It is characterized by depression, preoccupation, discontent and occasionally violence, and has been described as "a 12-foot stare in a 10-foot room." Today these symptoms are known as seasonal affective disorder, or SAD.

Cabin fever is commonly thought to afflict miners and trappers spending a lonely winter in the wilderness, but in truth, these people are active and outdoors enough to remain content. It is more likely to strike the snowbound city dwellers who do not ski or mush dogs, or the disabled. The arrival of spring or a change of scene usually relieves the symptoms.

CABINS (SEE ALSO Camping; National

Forests; State Park System) Rustic cabins in remote Alaska places can be rented from the USDA Forest Service, the Bureau of Land Management, the National Park

The Forest Service cabin at Paradise Lake on the Kenai Peninsula. From *Alaska's Kenai Peninsula: A Traveler's Guide.* Photo by Andromeda Romano-Lax.

Service, the Alaska State Parks and the U.S. Fish and Wildlife Service. The modest price ($15 to $65 a night per cabin) makes this one of the best vacation bargains in Alaska. Visitors should prepare for rigorous backcountry travel and be ready to seek emergency shelter should they be unable to reach their cabin.

More than 250 USDA Forest Service cabins are scattered through the Tongass and Chugach National Forests in Southeastern and Southcentral Alaska. Some are located on saltwater, others on freshwater rivers, streams or lakes. Some of the cabins can be reached by boat or trail but because of the cabins' remote locations, visitors frequently arrive by chartered aircraft.

The average cabin is 12 feet by 14 feet and is usually equipped with a table, an oil or wood stove and wooden bunks without mattresses. Most will accommodate a group of four to six. There is no electricity. Outhouses are within walking distance. Visitors should bring food, bedding, cooking utensils and stove fuel. It's advisable to have a gas or propane stove for cooking, a lantern and insect repellent. Firewood is scarce and often wet, so visitors should carry a supply of dry wood. Reservations may be made by phone or online. Payment can be by credit card; payments for reservations made more than 20 days in advance may be made by money order or cashier's check. Users will receive a confirmation number and letter as a permit to take to the cabin and should learn what type of heater the cabin has so they can bring appropriate fuel. Permits are issued on a first-come, first-served basis, up to 180 days in advance. Length of stay is normally limited to three days between May 1 and Sept. 30, and 7 days the rest of the year.

For general information on cabins in **Tongass National Forest** call (907) 225-3101. For information on cabins in Chugach National Forest call (907) 743-9500. To check availability and make reservations for either area: www.recreation.gov, (877) 444-6777 (toll free).

The National Park Service has three coastal cabins, open during summer months only, in Kenai Fjords National Park. One winter-only cabin is available at Exit Glacier. For information, contact the Alaska Public Lands Information Center, 605 W. Fourth Ave., Suite 105, Anchorage 99502; (907) 271-2742. Reservations may be made by phone, mail or in person.

(Continued on page 40)

Calendar of Annual Events 2008

For more information through community Web sites, see also **Chambers of Commerce** and **Convention and Visitors Bureaus and Information Centers.**

JANUARY

Anchorage—Great Alaska Beer and Barleywine Festival; Folk Festival.

Anchor Point—Cabin Fever Variety Show.

Bethel—Kuskokwim 300 Sled Dog Race.

Big Lake—Klondike 300 Sled Dog Derby.

Chistochina—Copper Basin 300 Sled Dog Race.

Glennallen—Copper Basin 300 Sled Dog Race.

Haines—Alcan 200 International Snowmachine Race.

Juneau—State Legislature convenes.

Kenai—Tustumena 200 Sled Dog Race; Annual Awards Ceremony; Peninsula Winter Games.

Kodiak—Russian Christmas and Starring; Russian New Year and Masquerade Ball.

Seward—Polar Bear Jump-Off Festival.

Sitka—Northwest Coast Arts Symposium; Russian Christmas and Starring.

Soldotna—Tustumena 200 Sled Dog Race; Ty Clark Memorial Sled Dog Race; Peninsula Winter Games.

Unalaska—Russian Orthodox Christmas Eve and Starring; Russian New Year's Eve; Qawalangin Tribe Masquerade Ball.

Willow—Winter Carnival.

FEBRUARY

Anchorage—Fur Rendezvous; Duct Tape Ball; World Championship Sled Dog Races; Ski for Women.

Anchor Point—Snow Rondi.

Big Lake—Tesoro Iron Dog Snowmachine Race; Eliminator K-400 Snowmachine Race; Susitna 100 Race and Little Su 50K.

Chistochina—Fun Days.

Cordova—Iceworm Festival.

Delta Junction—Festival of Lights with Fireworks Display; Polar Bear Plunge; Arts and Crafts Galleria.

Dillingham—Nushagak Classic Sled Dog Race.

Fairbanks—Tesoro Iron Dog Snowmachine Race; Yukon Quest International Sled Dog Race; Junior Yukon Quest; Yukon Quest 300.

Girdwood—Winterfest at Alyeska Resort.

Homer—Winter Carnival.

Kenai—Quilt Show (through April); Hospice Wine Tasting & Auction.

Ketchikan—Festival of the North.

Kodiak—Arts and Adventure Auction.

Naknek—Winterfest.

Nome—Tesoro Iron Dog Snowmachine Race.

Seldovia—Winter Carnival.

Sitka—Jazz Festival; Alaska Airlines Winter Classic Concert Series.

Tok—Trek Over the Top: Tok to Dawson International Poker Run (snowmachine).

Unalaska—Polar Bear Run.

Wasilla—Iditarod Days Festival; Iditasport; Tesoro Iron Dog Snowmachine Race.

Willow—Winter Carnival.

MARCH

Anchorage—Iditarod Trail Sled Dog Race; Tour of Anchorage Cross-Country Ski Race.

Big Lake—Klondike 150 Snowmachine Race.

Chatanika—Chatanika Days.

Chugiak/Eagle River—Iditarod Trail Sled Dog Race.

Dillingham—Beaver Roundup Festival.

Fairbanks—Festival of Native Arts; GCI Open North American Sled Dog Championships; Winter Carnival; World Ice Art Championships; Limited North American Sled Dog Championships; Art Expo.

Homer—Winter King Salmon Tournament.

Juneau—Gold Medal Basketball Tournament.

Kenai—Central Peninsula Writers' Night; Arctic Winter Games.

Ketchikan—An Evening of Dance.

Kodiak—Comfish Alaska; Pillar Mountain Golf Classic.

Nenana—Nenana Ice Classic Tripod Weekend.

Nome—Bering Sea Ice Golf Classic; Iditarod Trail Sled Dog Race; Miners and Mushers Ball; Nome-Golovin Snowmachine Race; Nome Council Sled Dog Race.

Palmer—Lions Club Gun Show.

Skagway—Buckwheat Ski Classic.

(continued)

More Calendar of Annual Events

MARCH *(continued)*

Soldotna—St. Patrick's Day Celebration.

Tok—Race of Champions (sled dog); Trek Over the Top: Tok to Dawson International Poker Run (snowmachine).

Trapper Creek—Cabin Fever Reliever.

Unalaska—USAFV Soup-off.

Valdez—Mayor's Cup Snowmachine Race.

Wasilla—Iditarod Trail Sled Dog Race Restart; Iditarod Days Festival.

APRIL

Anchorage—Anchorage Daily News Heart Run; Great Alaskan Sportsman Show; Native Youth Olympics.

Barrow—Spring Festival (Piuraagiaqta).

Bethel—Camai Dance Festival.

Big Lake—Annual Chamber Banquet and Auction.

Craig/Klawock—Salmon Derby (through July).

Fairbanks—Arctic Man Ski and Snow-Go Classic; Beat Beethoven 5K Run; International Curling Bonspiel.

Girdwood—Alyeska Spring Carnival and Slush Cup.

Homer—Sea to Ski Triathlon.

Juneau—Alaska Folk Festival.

Kodiak—Old Harbor Whaling Festival (through May); Whalefest—A Migration Celebration.

Ninilchik—King Salmon Derby.

Nome—Cannonball Run.

Skagway—International Mini Folk Festival.

Soldotna—Kenai Peninsula Sport Rec & Trade Show

Sutton—Annual Coalminers' Ball.

Tok—Tok Trot.

Valdez—Mountain Man Snowmobile Hill Climb Competition.

Wrangell—Garnet Festival.

MAY

Anchorage—Visitor Industry Charity Walk.

Anchor Point—King Salmon Saltwater Tournament.

Chugiak/Eagle River—Eagle River Nature Center Seymour Challenge.

Cordova—Copper River Delta Shorebird Festival.

Craig—Celebration by the Sea Quilt Show.

Delta Junction—Buffalo Wallow Square Dance Festival; Friendly Frontier Days.

Fairbanks—Chena River Run; Annual Harley Davidson Spring Run.

Haines—Great Alaska Craftbeer and Homebrew Festival; King Salmon Derby.

Hollis—Prince of Wales Island International Marathon, Hollis to Craig.

Homer—Kachemak Bay Shorebird Festival; Kachemak Bay Sea Festival; Jackpot Halibut Derby begins (summerlong); Quilt Show.

Juneau—Jazz and Classics Festival; Spring King Salmon Derby.

Ketchikan—Celebration of the Sea; Ballet Spring Gala.

Kodiak—Crab Festival; International Migratory Bird Day; Chad Ogden Ultramarathon.

Ninilchik—Memorial Day Pancake Breakfast.

Nome—Stroke and Croak Mini Triathlon.

Pelican—Boardwalk Boogie.

Petersburg—Little Norway Festival; Salmon Derby.

Seward—Seward Ocean Festival.

Sitka—Salmon Derby; Julie Hughes Triathlon.

Skagway—Skagway Film Festival.

Soldotna—State Parks Annual Kenai River Clean-Up.

Thorne Bay—Salmon Derby (through July).

Tok—Upper Tanana Migratory Bird Festival.

Unalaska—World Record Halibut Derby (through September); Annual Soap Box Derby.

Valdez—Halibut Derby; Sea Side Expo; May Day Fly-In.

Wasilla—Mat–Su King Salmon Derby (through July).

Wrangell—King Salmon Derby (through June).

JUNE

Anchorage—Mayor's Marathon and Half Marathon; AWAIC Summer Solstice Festival; Alaska Run for Women; Blues on the Green; Slam'n Salm'n King Derby; Three Barons Renaissance Fair.

Anchor Point—Kids All-American Fishing Derby.

Barrow—Nalukataq Whaling Festival.

Big Lake—Summer Solstice Festival; Triathlon; Lions' Mud Volleyball.

(continued)

More Calendar of Annual Events

JUNE (continued)

Chugiak/Eagle River—Alaskan Scottish Highland Games.

Cordova—Copper River Nouveau.

Dillingham—Wild Fish Festival.

Fairbanks—Midnight Sun Run; Midnight Sun Baseball Game; Midnight Sun Festival; Yukon 800 Boat Race; Summer Folk Fest.

Haines—Kluane to Chilkat International Bike Race; King Salmon Derby; Summer Solstice Celebration.

Homer—Kachemak Bay Writers' Conference; "Strut Your Mutt" Dog Walk; 10K Spit Run; Homer Yacht Club Regatta.

Juneau—Gold Rush Days.

Kenai—Kenai River Festival; Quilting on the Kenai.

Ketchikan—King Salmon Derby.

Kodiak—All-American Soap Box Derby.

Moose Pass—Summer Solstice Festival.

Nenana—River Daze.

Nikiski—Family Fun in the Midnight Sun.

Ninilchik—Halibut Derby (through September).

Nome—Midnight Sun Festival; River Raft Race; Polar Bear Swim in Bering Sea; Folk Festival.

Palmer—Colony Days; Friday Fling; Summer Market (through August).

Pelican—King Salmon Derby.

Seldovia—Summer Solstice Music Festival.

Seward—Jackpot Halibut Tournament (through August).

Sitka—Summer Music Festival; Fine Arts Camp.

Skagway—Summer Solstice.

Valdez—Last Frontier Theatre Conference.

Whittier—Walk to Whittier.

JULY

(In addition to these special events, July 4 celebrations take place in most communities.)

Anchorage—Governor's Picnic; Great Alaska Salmon Bake and Fly-by.

Anderson—Anderson Bluegrass Festival.

Chugiak/Eagle River—Bear Paw Festival.

Cordova—Wild Copper River Salmon Festival.

Dillingham—Salmon Bake.

Fairbanks—Golden Days; Fairbanks Summer Arts Festival; Fairbanks Summer Fine Arts Camp; World Eskimo–Indian Olympics; Midnight Sun Intertribal Powwow; Mutt March.

Girdwood—Forest Faire.

Haines—Southeast Alaska State Fair; Bald Eagle Music Festival.

Homer—Homer Street Fair; Concert on the Lawn; Summer String Festival; Halibut Tournament.

Hope—Wagon Trail Run Weekend; Pink Salmon Derby.

Ketchikan—Timber Carnival.

Kodiak—Bear Country Music Festival; Bear-Foot in the Park Quintathlon.

Ninilchik—Rodeo.

Naukati Bay—Skunk Cabbage Festival; Mud Bog Races.

Nome—Anvil Mountain Run; Poor Man's Paradise.

North Pole—Summer Festival and Parade; Santa Claus Half Marathon.

Palmer—Palmer Pride Picnic.

Petersburg—Canned Salmon Classic.

Seward—Mount Marathon Race.

Sitka—Island Institute's Sitka Symposium.

Skagway—Ducky Derby; International Softball Tournament; Soapy Smith's Wake; Craft Fair.

Soldotna—Dog Show; Progress Days; Creek Celebration.

Sutton—Old Timers' Picnic.

Talkeetna—Moose Dropping Festival.

Thorne Bay—Prince of Wales Island Fair and Logging Show.

Valdez—Silver Salmon Derby (through September).

AUGUST

Anchorage—Humpy's Marathon; Slam'n Salm'n Silver Derby; Galway Days on G Street.

Delta Junction—Deltana Fair.

Fairbanks—Tanana Valley State Fair; Tanana Valley Sandhill Crane Festival.

Girdwood—Alyeska Blueberry & Mountain Arts Festival.

Glennallen—Copper Valley Arts and Crafts Fair.

Homer—Homer Homes Tour.

(continued)

More Calendar of Annual Events

AUGUST *(continued)*

Houston—Founders' Day.

Juneau—Golden North Salmon Derby.

Kenai—Silver Salmon Derby; 10K Run for Women.

Ketchikan—Blueberry Arts Festival; Gigglefeet Dance Festival; CHARR Summer Beer Festival; Pennock Island Swim Challenge.

Kodiak—Kids' Pink Salmon Jamboree; Pilgrimage to St. Herman's Monks Lagoon; Silver Salmon Derby.

Naukati—Mud Bogg Races.

Nenana—Nenana Valley Fair.

Ninilchik—Kenai Peninsula State Fair.

Palmer—Alaska State Fair; Palmer Chamber State Fair Parade.

Seward—Silver Salmon Derby.

Skagway—Flower and Garden Show; Gamefish Derby.

Talkeetna—Bluegrass Festival.

Unalaska—Island Marathon.

Valdez—Gold Rush Days.

SEPTEMBER

Anchorage—Alaska Airlines Autumn Classic; Million Dollar Golf Classic.

Big Lake—Fall Festival/Chili Cook-Off.

Cold Bay—Russell Creek Silver Salmon Derby.

Fairbanks—Equinox Marathon; Tanana Valley Potato Extravaganza.

Haines—Labor Day Weekend Mardi Gras Party.

Homer—National Estuaries Day.

Hope—Coeur d'Alene Run/Walk.

Kenai—Lions Rubber Ducky Race.

Kodiak—State Fair and Rodeo.

Naukati Bay—Double Points Mud Bog Races.

Nome—Great Bathtub Race; Rubber Duck Race; Anvil Mountain 59 Minute 37 Second Challenge.

Seward—Blues Train.

Sitka—Running of the Boots.

Skagway—Klondike Road Relay.

Soldotna—Labor Day Picnic.

Unalaska—Blueberry Bash.

Whittier—Silver Salmon Derby; "Small Fry" Silver Salmon Derby.

OCTOBER

Anchorage—Make it Alaska Festival; Nye Frontier Hockey Classic; Halloween Family Concert; AlaskaFest.

Delta Junction—Halloween Bash.

Fairbanks—International Sled Dog Symposium; International Friendship Day; Cham Fashional.

Homer—National Wildlife Refuge Week.

Kenai—Chamber of Commerce Wine Tasting.

Ketchikan—Alaska Day Auction.

Kodiak—National Wildlife Refuge Week; Oktoberfest.

Petersburg—Oktoberfest Artshare.

Sitka—Alaska Day Festival.

Skagway—Southeast Alaska Quilt Retreat.

Soldotna—Pie Auction.

Valdez—Oktoberfest.

Wasilla—Wasilla Chamber "Murder on the Alaska Railroad" Excursion.

NOVEMBER

Anchorage—Carrs/Safeway Great Alaska Shootout Basketball Tournament; Crafts Emporium; Downtown for the Holidays.

Anchor Point—Holiday Happenings Craft Fair.

Fairbanks—Athabascan Fiddlers' Festival; BP Top of the World Classic; Yukon Title Cash Spiel, Rookie Spiel.

Haines—Bald Eagle Festival.

Homer—Putting on the Ritz.

Juneau—Public Market.

Kenai—Christmas Comes to Kenai (parade and fireworks); Arts and Crafts Fair.

Ketchikan—Winter Arts Faire.

Petersburg—Festival of Lights.

Sitka—WhaleFest; Native American Heritage Festival.

Soldotna—Craft Bazaars.

DECEMBER

Anchorage—Anchorage Film Festival; New Year's Fire and Ice Extravaganza; Anchorage Folk Festival.

(continued)

39

More Calendar of Annual Events

DECEMBER *(continued)*

Barrow—Qitik Games.

Big Lake—Tour of Lights.

Chugiak/Eagle River—Merry Merchant Munch; Community Tree Lighting.

Delta Junction—Holiday Decorating Contest; Children's Christmas Coloring Contest; Christmas Bazaar.

Fairbanks—Winter Solstice Celebration; "Sing-It-Yourself Messiah"; Ivory Jack's Invitational Golf Tournament.

Girdwood—Alyeska New Year's Eve Torchlight Parade and Fireworks Display.

Homer—The Nutcracker Ballet Performance and Craft Fair.

Juneau—Gallery Walk.

Ketchikan—Winter Art Walk; Winterfest.

Kodiak—Harbor Stars Boat Parade; Currier and Ives Old Fashioned Christmas.

Nome—Community Craft Bazaars; Firemen's Carnival.

North Pole—Candle and Lighting Ceremonies; Winter Festival.

Palmer—Colony Christmas Celebration and Parade of Lights; Triathlon and Crafts Fair.

Petersburg—Julebukking.

Seward—Holiday Train.

Skagway—Yuletide Celebration; Santa Train.

Soldotna—Tree Lighting Ceremony.

Talkeetna—Bachelor Society Ball and Wilderness Women Contest; Winterfest.

Unalaska—Museum of the Aleutians Annual Auction; New Year's Eve Fireworks.

Valdez—Ladies Annual Christmas Tea; Emblem Christmas Bazaar.

Willow—Holiday Dinner.

Wrangell—Midnight Madness and Christmas Tree Lighting.

(Continued from page 35)

The Bureau of Land Management has about a dozen public-use cabins in the White Mountains National Recreation Area east of Fairbanks, used primarily by winter recreationists. Only a few of the cabins are accessible during summer months. In addition one cabin near the roadside (not part of the White Mountains system) is available year-round. Cabins must be reserved prior to use and a fee is required. Contact the BLM Land Information Center, 1150 University Ave., Fairbanks 99709-3844; (907) 474-2200; www.blm.gov/ak/whitemountains/cabins.htm.

The U.S. Fish and Wildlife Service maintains eight public-use cabins within Kodiak National Wildlife Refuge, accessible only by floatplane or boat. Contact the refuge manager, 1390 Buskin River Road, Kodiak 99615; (907) 487-2600.

Alaska State Parks offers 56 public-use cabins throughout the state.

For reservations and information contact the Department of Natural Resources Public Information Center, 550 W. Seventh Ave., Suite 1260, Anchorage 99501-3557; (907) 269-8400; TDD (907) 269-8411; fax (907) 269-8901; ww.dnr.state.ak.us/parks/cabins/index.htm.

General information on all public-use cabins is available from the Alaska Public Lands Information Centers: 605 W. Fourth

Of all the states in the union, Alaskans rank number one in attainment of high school degrees, number one in ownership of Harley Davidson motorcycles, number one in consumption of ice cream, and Alaskans are the 2nd highest per capita consumers of Spam in the Nation. And to top it off, the makers of Itch-X anti-itch named Wasilla the "17th Itchiest City in the United States." Life is still good in Alaska!

Wood-Tikchik State Park's vast wilderness attracts kayakers, backpackers and anglers. From *Alaska's Accessible Wilderness* by Bill Sherwonit.

Ave., Suite 105, Anchorage 99501, (907) 271-2737; P.O. Box 359, Tok 99780, (907) 883-5667; 250 Cushman St., Suite 1A, Fairbanks 99701, (907) 456-0527; 50 Main St., Ketchikan 99901, (907) 228-6220; www.nps.gov/aplic.

CACHE Pronounced "cash," this small storage unit is built to be inaccessible to marauding animals. A cache traditionally is a miniature log cabin mounted on stilts. It is reached by a ladder that bears, dogs, foxes and other hungry or curious animals can't climb. Extra precautions include wrapping tin around the poles to prevent climbing by clawed animals and extending the floor a few feet in all directions from the top of the poles to discourage those clever enough to get that high. Squirrels are the most notorious of Alaska's cache-crashing critters.

To be truly animal-proof, a cache should be built in a clearing well beyond the 30-foot leaping distance a squirrel can manage from a treetop.

Bush residents use the cache as a primitive food freezer for game and fish in winter. A cache may also store furs from a trapline, extra fuel and bedding.

Size is determined by need. Sometimes a cache will be built between three or four straight trees growing close together.

Like mush *(marché),* the word *cache* is borrowed from French-Canadian voyageurs.

CAMPING (SEE ALSO Boating; Cabins; Chilkoot Trail; Hiking; National Forests; National Parks; National Wildlife Refuges; State Park System) Numerous public and privately operated campgrounds are found along Alaska's highways. Electrical hookups and dump stations are scarce.

The dump station at Russian River campground is available for Chugach National Forest visitors. Alaska's back-country offers virtually limitless possibilities for wilderness camping. Get permission before camping on private land. If the land is publicly owned, it's worthwhile to contact the managing agency for regulations and hiking/camping conditions.

The USDA Forest Service maintains 30 campgrounds in the Tongass and Chugach National Forests, most with tent and trailer sites and minimum facilities.

Since the late 1950s, the Forest Service has charged fees for using campgrounds.

Some campgrounds are now "fee demonstration projects," and at least 80 percent of the money collected is returned to the administering unit for maintenance and improvements at the site. Pack Creek Bear Viewing Area charges fees from early June through mid-September. Begich, Boggs Visitors Center charges no admission, but does charge for viewing the movie *Voices from the Ice.*

Most campgrounds are available on a first-come, first-served basis. Stays are limited to 14 days except in Russian River campground where the limit is 3 days during the salmon run. Campground fees are $6 to $24 per night depending upon facilities, which can include fire grates, pit toilets, garbage pickup, picnic tables and water. Most campgrounds are open from Memorial Day through Labor Day, weather permitting. For information on camping in the Chugach National Forest, contact 3301 C St., Suite 300, Anchorage 99503-3998, (907) 743-9500; www.fs.fed.us/r10/chugach. For information about camping in the Tongass National Forest, contact the Southeast Alaska Discovery Center, 50 Main St., Ketchikan 99901, (907) 228-6220; www.fs.fed.us/r10/tongass. Reservations may be made by calling the National Recreation Reservation Service, (877) 444-6777, or at www.recreation.gov.

The state's Division of Forestry requires permits for open burning in most areas of Interior and Southcentral Alaska. Permits are not required if fires are in approved burn barrels or are used for signaling.

The National Park Service at Denali National Park and Preserve operates five different campgrounds along the single road into the park. The campgrounds range in cost and comfort level, and advance reservations are recommended.

Private vehicle access on Denali Park Road is limited, so some campgrounds are accessible only by shuttle bus. Reservations and fee information for campsites or shuttle buses are available online (www.nps.gov/dena/planyourvisit/campground-reservations.htm); by fax at (907) 264-4684; by mail (Doyon/ARAMARK Joint Venture, 241 W. Ship Creek Ave., Anchorage 99501); or by calling (800) 622-7275. Anchorage and international callers should phone (907) 272-7275. Online reservations are available at www.reservedenali.com.

Except for the Riley Creek Campground, most camping areas are open from mid-May to mid-September, weather permitting.

Listed in order of the closest to the park entrance, the camping areas include:

• Riley Creek Campground, near the park entrance. Offers 153 sites for RVs and tents, flush toilets. Open year-round, with limited facilities September to May. Register at Wilderness Access Center or in advance by phone or online.

• Savage River Campground, Mile 13. Offers 33 sites for RVs and tents; water, flush toilets. Reserve in advance. Also, 3 sites for large groups; water, flush toilets. Reserve in advance. Valid Incidental Business Permit (IBP) required for commercial groups.

• Sanctuary River Campground, Mile 23. Offers 7 tent sites; accessible only by shuttle bus. Chemical toilets, no water available. Reserve at Wilderness Access Center (first-come, first-served basis).

• Teklanika River Campground, Mile 29. Offers 53 sites for RVs and tents; water, flush toilets. Reserve in advance or at Wilderness Access Center.

• Igloo Creek Campground, Mile 34 (currently closed due to wolf activity in the area). No vehicles allowed. Offers 7 tent sites; accessible only by shuttle bus. Chemical toilets. Reserve at Wilderness Access Center.

• Wonder Lake Campground, Mile 85. Offers 28 tent sites; accessible by shuttle bus only. Water, flush toilets available. Reserve in advance or at Wilderness Access Center. Open mid-June to mid-September.

> **The North American Butterfly Association's July 4 census showed Juneau to have the lowest number of butterflies in all of North America. Three counters spent 5 hours and saw only 8 butterflies!**

The Wilderness Access Center is located at Mile 1 on the Park Road. This center serves as the park's transportation hub, and is the place to go for campsite reservations, tickets for bus tours and shuttle bus trips into the park. It is open early June to mid-September, 5 A.M. to 8 P.M. Backcountry permits are available at the Backcountry Information Center, which is adjacent to the Wilderness Access Center. It is open daily from 9 A.M. to 6 P.M. during the peak summer season of early May to mid-September. The new Denali Visitor Center, Mile 1.5, is open from 8 A.M. to 6 P.M.

For further information, contact Denali National Park and Preserve, P.O. Box 9, Denali Park 99755, (907) 683-2294 or www.nps.gov/dena/planyourvisit/index.htm. Glacier Bay and Katmai National Parks each offers one campground for walk-in campers; Katmai requires reservations, which may be obtained in advance by calling (877) 444-6777; www.recreation.gov. Backcountry camping is permitted in Denali, Glacier Bay, Katmai and Klondike Gold Rush National Parks, as well as other national parks and monuments.

Alaska State Parks maintains the most extensive system of roadside campgrounds and waysides in Alaska. All are available on a first-come, first-served basis. Fees are charged, though free annual camping passes are issued to Alaskan veterans with service-connected disabilities. Contact Alaska State Parks, Public Information Center, 550 W. Seventh Ave., Suite 1260, Anchorage 99501-3557; (907) 269-8400; TDD: (907) 269-8411; fax (907) 269-8901; www.alaskastateparks.org.

The U.S. Fish and Wildlife Service has several wildlife refuges open to campers, although most are not accessible by highway (1011 E. Tudor Road, MS 225, Anchorage 99503; (907) 786-3354; fax (907) 786-3998; www.r7.fws.gov/nwr/nwr.htm). The Kenai National Wildlife Refuge has several campgrounds accessible from the Sterling Highway linking Homer and Anchorage (P.O. Box 2139 MS519, Soldotna 99669-2139; (907) 262-7021; fax (907) 262-3599; www.r7.fws.gov/nwr/kenai/index.htm).

The Bureau of Land Management maintains 14 campgrounds in Interior Alaska. In 1994, BLM opened its first fully developed campground on the Dalton Highway at Mile 180 (5 miles north of Coldfoot). Fees vary by location. Brochures describing the campgrounds are available. Contact BLM, 222 W. Seventh Ave., Suite 13, Anchorage 99513; (907) 271-5960; fax (907) 271-3684; www.ak.blm.gov.

Alaska Public Lands Information Centers provide information on all state and federal campgrounds in Alaska, along with state and national park passes and details on wilderness camping. Visit or contact one of the following centers: 605 W. Fourth Ave., Suite 105, Anchorage 99501, (907) 271-2737; P.O. Box 359, Tok 99780, (907) 883-5667; 250 Cushman St., Suite 1A, Fairbanks 99701, (907) 456-0527; 50 Main St., Ketchikan 99901, (907) 228-6220.

Private Campgrounds. For information, contact the Alaska Campground Owners Association, P.O. Box 111005 Anchorage, AK 99511-1005; (866) 339-9082; fax (907) 339-9082; www.alaskacampgrounds.net.

CHAMBERS OF COMMERCE

(SEE ALSO Convention and Visitors Bureaus)

Alaska State Chamber, 217 Second St., Suite 201, Juneau 99801; (907) 586-2323; fax (907) 463-5515. 601 W. Fifth Ave., Suite 700, Anchorage 99501; (907) 278-2722; fax (907) 278-6643; www.alaskachamber.com.

Anchor Point Chamber, P.O. Box 610, Anchor Point 99556; (907) 235-2600; www.anchorpointchamber.org.

Anchorage Chamber, 1016 W. Sixth Ave., Suite 303, Anchorage 99501; (907) 272-2401; fax (907) 272-4117; www.anchoragechamber.org.

Barrow, (City of), P.O. Box 629, Barrow 99723; (907) 852-5211; fax (907) 852-5871; www.cityofbarrow.org.

Bethel Chamber, P.O. Box 329, Bethel 99559; (907) 543-2911; fax (907) 543-3255; www.bethelakchamber.org.

Big Lake Chamber, P.O. Box 520067, Big Lake 99652; (907) 892-6109; fax (907) 892-6189; www.biglake-ak.com.

Chugiak/Eagle River Chamber, P.O. Box 770353, Eagle River 99577; (907) 694-4702; fax (907) 694-1205; www.cer.org.

Cooper Landing Chamber, P.O. Box 809, Cooper Landing 99572; (907) 595-8888 (phone/fax); www.cooperlandingchamber.com.

Copper Valley Chamber (Greater), P.O. Box 469, Glennallen 99588; (907) 822-5555; www.traveltoalaska.com.

Cordova Chamber, P.O. Box 99, Cordova 99574; (907) 424-7260; fax (907) 424-7259; www.cordovachamber.com.

Delta Junction Chamber, P.O. Box 987, Delta Junction 99737; (907) 895-5068; fax (907) 895-5141; www.deltachamber.org.

Denali Chamber (Greater Healy), P.O. Box 437, Healy 99743; (907) 683-4636; www.denalichamber.com.

Dillingham Chamber, P.O. Box 348, Dillingham 99576; (907) 842-5115; fax (907) 842-4097; www.dillinghamak.com.

Fairbanks Chamber (Greater), 100 Cushman St., Suite 102, Fairbanks 99701; (907) 452-1105; fax (907) 456-6968; www.fairbankschamber.org.

Girdwood Chamber, P.O. Box 1313, Girdwood 99587; (907) 222-7682; www.girdwoodchamber.com.

Haines Chamber, P.O. Box 1449, Haines 99827; (907) 766-2202; fax (907) 766-2271; www.haineschamber.org.

Homer Chamber, P.O. Box 541, Homer 99603; (907) 235-7740; fax (907) 235-8766; www.homeralaska.org.

Houston Chamber, P.O. Box 356, Houston 99694; (907) 892-6555, (907) 892-6716, (907) 895-0828; fax (907) 892-6566.

Juneau Chamber, 3100 Channel Drive, Suite 300, Juneau 99801; (907) 463-3488; fax (907) 463-3489; www.juneauchamber.com.

Kenai Chamber, 402 Overland St., Kenai 99611; (907) 283-7989; fax (907) 283-7183; www.kenaichamber.org.

Ketchikan Chamber (Greater), P.O. Box 5957, Ketchikan 99901; (907) 225-3184; fax (907) 225-3187; www.ketchikanchamber.com.

Kodiak Chamber, 100 E. Marine Way, Suite 300, Kodiak 99615; (907) 486-5557; fax (907) 486-7605; www.kodiak.org/chamber.html.

Kotzebue, (City of), P.O. Box 46, Kotzebue 99752; (907) 442-3401; http://kotzpdweb.tripod.com/city/.

Moose Pass Chamber, P.O. Box 147, Moose Pass 99631; www.moosepassalaska.com.

Nenana Valley Chamber, P.O. Box 124, Nenana 99760; (907) 832-5442; www.nenanahomepage.com.

Nikiski/North Peninsula Chamber, P.O. Box 8053, Nikiski 99635; (907) 283-3777.

Ninilchik Chamber, P.O. Box 39164, Ninilchik 99639; (907) 567-3571; fax (907) 567-1041; www.ninilchikchamber.com.

An Anchorage Safeway store advertised a Super Saver special on "Salad Bowels" for only $3.69 each!

Nome Chamber, P.O. Box 250, Nome 99762; (907) 443-3879; fax (907) 443-3892; www.nomechamber.org.

North Pole Community Chamber, P.O. Box 55071, North Pole 99705; (907) 488-2242; www.northpolechamber.com.

Palmer Chamber (Greater), 723 S. Valley Way, 99645; (907) 745-2880; fax (907) 746-4164; www.palmerchamber.org.

Pelican Chamber of Commerce, P.O. Box 737, Pelican 99832; (907) 735-2202; fax (907) 735-2258; www.pelican.net.

Petersburg Chamber, P.O. Box 649, Petersburg 99833; (907) 772-3646 (phone/fax); www.petersburg.org.

Prince of Wales Chamber, P.O. Box 490, Klawok 99925; (907) 755-2626; fax (907) 755-2627; www.princeofwalescoc.org.

Seldovia Chamber, Drawer F, Seldovia 99663; (907) 234-7612 (message); www.seldovia.com.

Seward Chamber, P.O. Box 749, Seward 99664; (907) 224-8051; (907) 224-5353; www.seward.com.

Sitka Chamber (Greater), P.O. Box 638, Sitka 99835; (907) 747-8604; fax (907) 747-7413; www.sitkacoc.com.

Skagway Chamber, P.O. Box 194, Skagway 99840; (907) 983-1898; fax (907) 983-2031; www.skagwaychamber.org.

Soldotna Chamber, 44790 Sterling Highway, Soldotna 99669; (907) 262-9814; fax (907) 262-3566; www.soldotnachamber.com.

Stewart and Hyder International Chamber, P.O. Box 306, Stewart B.C. V0T 1W0, Canada; (888) 366-5999; fax (250) 636-2199; www.stewart-hyder.com.

Talkeetna Chamber, P.O. Box 334, Talkeetna 99676; (907) 733-2330; www.talkeetna-chamber.com.

Tok Chamber, P.O. Box 389, Tok 99780; (907) 883-5775; fax (907) 883-3682; www.tokalaskainfo.com.

Wasilla Chamber (Greater), 415 E. Railroad Ave., Wasilla 99654; (907) 376-1299; fax (907) 373-2560; fax (907) 373-2560; www.wasillachamber.org.

Whittier Chamber (Greater), P.O. Box 607, Whittier 99693; www.whittieralaskachamber.org.

Willow Chamber, P.O. Box 183, Willow 99688-1083; (907) 495-6800 (phone/fax); www.willowchamber.org.

NUGGETS

There was no mail, groceries or supplies delivered during April 2004 to the 130 residents of Ekwok near Bristol Bay. The previous winter's colder weather and heavy snow accumulation led to the airstrip becoming a 2,700-foot river of mud during spring thaw. Everyone had to wait for a much-needed week of sun: dental patients, tobacco-less smokers, even the IRS. Completed tax returns were "in the mail."

—2004 *The Alaska Almanac*®

Wrangell Chamber, P.O. Box 49, Wrangell 99929; (907) 874-3901; fax (907) 874-3905; www.wrangellchamber.org.

CHEECHAKO Pronounced chee-CHA-ko, the word means tenderfoot or greenhorn. According to *The Chinook Jargon,* a 1909 dictionary of the old trading language used by traders from the Hudson's Bay Co. in the early 1800s, the word *cheechako* comes from combining the Chinook Indian word *chee,* meaning "new, fresh or just now," with the Nootka Indian word *chako,* which means "to come, to approach or to become."

CHILKAT BLANKET Dramatic, bilaterally symmetrical patterns, usually in black, white, yellow and blue, adorn these heavily fringed ceremonial blankets. The origin of the Chilkat dancing blanket is Tsimshian Indian. Knowledge of the weaving techniques apparently diffused north to the Tlingit, where blanket making reached its highest form among the Chilkat group. Visiting traders coined the blanket's name during the late 19th century.

Time, technical skill and inherited privileges were required to weave Chilkat blankets and other ceremonial garments. High-ranking men and women wore

Woman in Chilkat blanket, about 1900.
Picture Alaska Art Gallery. From *The Alaska Heritage Seafood Cookbook* by Ann Chandonnet.

Pass that winter. Those who reached Lake Bennett built boats to float down the Yukon River to Dawson City.

Today the steep and rocky Chilkoot Trail is part of Klondike Gold Rush National Historical Park and is climbed each year by approximately 3,000 backpackers.

The Chilkoot Trail begins about 9 miles from Skagway on Dyea Road. There are a dozen campgrounds along the trail and ranger stations on both the Alaska and British Columbia portions of the trail.

The trail crosses the international border at 3,525-foot Chilkoot Pass, 16.5 miles from the trailhead. Highlights of the area include Slide Cemetery near the remains of the town of Dyea; the Golden Stairs, a 45-degree climb to the summit; and numerous relics left by prospectors still visible along the trail. The trail ends at Bennett, 8 miles from the nearest roadway. For more information, contact Klondike Gold Rush National Historical Park, P.O. Box 517, Skagway 99840; (907) 983-2921; www.nps.gov/klgo.

CHITONS Chitons are oval-shaped marine mollusks with shells made up of eight overlapping plates. The gumboot and the Chinese slipper chiton are favorite Alaska edible delicacies. The gumboot, named for the tough, leathery, reddish brown covering that hides its plates, is the largest chiton in the world. It is prized as traditional food by southeastern Alaska Natives.

CLIMATE (See also Regions of Alaska; Winds) Alaska's climate zones are maritime, transition, continental and arctic.

the blankets as cloaks. Portions of worn blankets, or smaller weavings, were made into dance aprons and tunics.

Yarn for Chilkat dancing blankets was spun primarily from the wool of the mountain goat. Designs woven into Chilkat blankets are geometric totemic shapes that can be reproduced by the method known as twining. (Early blankets are unadorned or display geometric patterns lacking curvilinear elements.) Often totemic crests on painted house posts and the designs woven into garments were quite similar. Female weavers reused pattern boards of wood painted with a design by men. A few weavers are producing Chilkat blankets and the related Raven's Tail robes today.

CHILKOOT TRAIL (See also Gold; Skagway) The Chilkoot Trail, which spans 33 miles from Dyea, just north of Skagway, over Chilkoot Pass to Lake Bennett, British Columbia, was one of the established routes taken by prospectors to Yukon District goldfields during the Klondike gold rush of 1897–98. Thousands of stampeders climbed the tortuous trail over Chilkoot

NUGGETS

Residents of Sand Point, on the Alaska Peninsula, were treated to a rare sight for Alaska in August 2005. A tornado, verified by the National Weather Service, touched down on two uninhabited mountains on Unga Island, across Popof Strait from Sand Point.

—2006 *The Alaska Almanac®*

With the exception of the transition zone along Western Alaska, the zones are divided by mountain ranges that form barriers to shallow air masses and modify those deep enough to cross the ranges.

The Brooks Range inhibits southward movement of air from the Arctic Ocean, thus separating the arctic climate zone from the Interior. The Chugach, Wrangell, Aleutian and Alaska mountain ranges often limit northward air movement and dry the air before it reaches the Interior's continental zone.

Other meteorologic and oceanographic factors affecting Alaska's climate zones are air temperature, water temperature, cloud coverage and wind and air pressure. The amount of moisture that air can hold in a gaseous state is highly dependent on its temperature. Warm air can contain more water vapor than cold air. Therefore precipitation as rain or snow or in other forms is likely to be heavier from warm than from cold air. Water temperatures change more slowly and much less than land temperatures. Coastal area temperatures vary less than those farther inland.

Climate Zones. The maritime climate zone includes Southeast, the Northern Gulf Coast and the Aleutian Chain. Temperatures are mild—relatively warm in the winter and cool in summer. Precipitation ranges from 50 to 200 inches annually along the coast and up to 400 inches on mountain slopes. Storms are frequently from the west and southwest, resulting in strong winds along the Aleutian Islands and the Alaska Peninsula. Amchitka Island's weather station has recorded some of the windiest weather in the state, followed by Cold Bay. Frequent storms with accompanying high winds account for rough seas and occasional waves to 50 feet in the Gulf of Alaska, particularly in fall and winter.

The transition zone may be thought of as two separate zones. One is the area between the coastal mountains and the Alaska Range, which includes Anchorage and the Matanuska Valley. Summer temperatures are higher than those of the maritime climate zone, with colder winter temperatures and less precipitation. Temperatures however are not as extreme as in the continental zone.

Climate Records

Highest temperature:
100°F, at Fort Yukon, June 27, 1915.
Lowest temperature:
−80°F, at Prospect Creek Camp, Jan. 23, 1971.
Most precipitation in one year:
332.29 inches, at MacLeod Harbor (Montague Island), 1976.
Most monthly precipitation:
70.99 inches at MacLeod Harbor, November 1976.
Most precipitation in 24 hours:
15.2 inches, in Angoon, Oct. 12, 1982.
Least precipitation in a year:
1.61 inches, at Barrow, 1935.
Most snowfall in a season:
974.5 inches, at Thompson Pass, 1952–53.
Most monthly snowfall:
297.9 inches, at Thompson Pass, February 1953.
Most snowfall in 24 hours:
62 inches, at Thompson Pass, December 1955.
Least snowfall in a season:
3 inches, at Barrow, 1935–36.
Highest recorded snowpack
(also highest ever recorded in North America): 356 inches at Wolverine Glacier, Kenai Peninsula, after the winter of 1976–77.
Highest recorded wind speed:
143 mph, at Dutch Harbor, November 2000.

Another transition zone includes the western coast from Bristol Bay to Point Hope. This area has cool summer temperatures that are somewhat colder than those of the maritime zone, and cold winter temperatures similar to the continental zone. Cold winter temperatures are partly due to the sea ice in the Chukchi and Bering Seas.

The continental climate zone covers the majority of Alaska except the coastal fringes

(Continued on page 50)

Average Temperatures (Fahrenheit) and Precipitation (Inches)

	ANCHORAGE	BARROW	BETHEL	COLD BAY	FAIRBANKS	HOMER	JUNEAU
January							
Temperature	14.9	−13.4	6.7	28.6	−10.1	22.7	24.2
Precipitation	0.80	0.20	0.81	2.71	0.55	2.23	3.98
February							
Temperature	18.7	−17.8	6.0	27.4	−3.6	24.7	28.4
Precipitation	0.86	0.18	0.71	2.30	0.41	1.78	3.66
March							
Temperature	25.7	−15.1	13.3	29.9	11.0	28.0	32.7
Precipitation	0.65	0.15	0.80	2.19	0.37	1.57	3.24
April							
Temperature	35.8	−2.2	23.6	33.3	30.7	35.4	39.7
Precipitation	0.63	0.20	0.65	1.90	0.28	1.27	2.83
May							
Temperature	46.6	19.3	39.9	39.6	48.6	42.8	47.0
Precipitation	0.63	0.16	0.83	2.40	0.57	1.07	3.46
June							
Temperature	54.4	34.0	50.5	45.7	59.8	49.3	53.0
Precipitation	1.02	0.36	1.29	2.13	1.29	1.00	3.02
July							
Temperature	58.4	39.3	55.0	50.5	62.5	53.4	56.0
Precipitation	1.96	0.87	2.18	2.50	1.84	1.63	4.09
August							
Temperature	56.3	37.9	52.9	51.5	56.8	53.3	55.0
Precipitation	2.31	0.97	3.65	3.71	1.82	2.56	5.10
September							
Temperature	48.4	30.5	45.2	47.7	46.5	47.6	49.4
Precipitation	2.51	0.64	2.58	4.06	1.02	2.96	6.25
October							
Temperature	36.6	13.5	29.4	39.6	25.1	37.5	42.2
Precipitation	1.86	0.51	1.48	4.45	0.81	3.41	7.64
November							
Temperature	21.2	−1.7	16.8	34.4	2.7	28.6	33.0
Precipitation	1.08	0.27	0.98	4.33	0.67	2.74	5.13
December							
Temperature	16.3	−11.2	8.5	31.0	−6.5	24.3	27.1
Precipitation	1.06	0.17	0.95	3.16	0.73	2.71	4.48
Annual							
Temperature	35.9	9.4	29.0	38.3	26.9	37.4	40.6
Precipitation	15.37	4.67	16.90	35.84	10.37	24.93	52.86
Mean Seasonal Snowfall (inches)	69.0	28.0	47.0	62.0	68.0	58.0	100.0

KETCHIKAN	KING SALMON	KODIAK	MCGRATH	NOME	PETERSBURG	VALDEZ	
							January
33.9	14.9	29.9	–8.7	7.0	27.6	20.5	Temperature
14.01	1.11	9.52	0.81	0.88	9.31	5.63	Precipitation
							February
38.9	14.8	30.5	–2.6	3.9	31.1	24.1	Temperature
12.36	0.82	5.67	0.74	0.56	7.85	5.08	Precipitation
							March
38.9	22.4	32.9	10.2	8.6	34.7	29.2	Temperature
12.22	1.06	5.16	0.75	0.63	7.19	4.06	Precipitation
							April
42.8	30.2	37.5	26.5	17.6	40.4	37.1	Temperature
11.93	1.07	4.47	0.73	0.67	6.94	2.89	Precipitation
							May
48.6	42.4	43.5	44.5	35.6	47.2	45.2	Temperature
9.06	1.25	6.65	0.84	0.58	5.92	2.74	Precipitation
							June
54.0	50.0	49.6	55.3	45.9	53.0	51.8	Temperature
7.36	1.54	5.72	1.56	1.14	5.00	2.64	Precipitation
							July
58.0	54.7	54.4	58.7	51.5	55.8	54.9	Temperature
7.80	2.10	3.80	2.16	2.18	5.36	3.77	Precipitation
							August
58.4	53.9	55.2	54.3	50.2	55.0	53.5	Temperature
10.60	2.96	4.03	2.87	3.20	7.57	5.73	Precipitation
							September
53.6	47.2	50.0	44.2	42.5	50.3	47.2	Temperature
13.61	2.75	7.18	2.19	2.59	11.15	7.99	Precipitation
							October
46.3	32.4	40.7	24.7	28.0	43.5	38.1	Temperature
22.55	1.98	7.85	1.24	1.38	16.83	8.23	Precipitation
							November
39.0	22.0	34.4	4.4	15.9	35.6	27.4	Temperature
17.90	1.45	6.89	1.18	1.02	11.99	6.09	Precipitation
							December
35.4	15.9	30.8	–6.0	7.3	30.5	22.9	Temperature
15.82	1.19	7.39	1.12	0.82	10.66	6.65	Precipitation
							Annual
45.5	33.5	40.8	25.5	26.2	42.1	37.7	Temperature
155.22	19.28	74.33	16.18	15.64	105.77	61.50	Precipitation
							Mean Seasonal
37.0	46.0	80.0	93.0	56.0	102.0	320.0	**Snowfall (inches)**

(Continued from page 47)

and the Arctic Slope. It has extreme temperatures and low precipitation. There are fewer clouds in the continental zone than elsewhere, so there is more warming by the sun during the long days of summer and more cooling during the long nights of winter. Precipitation is light because air masses affecting the area lose most of their moisture crossing the mountains to the south. The Arctic north of the Brooks Range has cold winters, cool summers and desertlike precipitation. Prevailing winds are from the northeast off the arctic ice pack, which never moves far offshore. Summers are generally cloudy, the winters are clear and cold. The cold air allows little precipitation and inhibits evaporation. Because continuous permafrost prevents the percolation of water into the soil, the area is generally marshy with numerous lakes. (SEE ALSO Permafrost)

The two-page chart that accompanies this entry shows normal average monthly temperatures and precipitation for 14 communities in Alaska. Included are annual temperatures, precipitation and mean seasonal snowfall. The chart is based on data from NOAA and the Alaska state climatologist. You may also refer to the Web site of the National Weather Service Forecast Office in Anchorage: www.arh.noaa.gov.

COAL (SEE ALSO Minerals and Mining) About half of the coal resources of the United States are believed to lie in Alaska. The demonstrated coal reserve base of the state is over 6 billion short tons, identified coal resources are about 160 billion short tons and hypothetical and speculative resource estimates range upward to 6 trillion short tons. The regions containing the most coal are northwestern Alaska, Cook Inlet–Susitna Lowland and the Nenana Trend. Geologists estimate that perhaps 80 percent of Alaska's coal underlies the 23-million-acre National Petroleum Reserve on the North Slope. Although the majority of the coals are of bituminous and subbituminous ranks, anthracite coal does occur in the Bering River and Matanuska fields. In addition to the vast resource base and wide distribution, the important selling points for Alaska coal are its extremely low sulfur content and access to the coast for shipping.

Exploration, technology and economics will ultimately determine the marketability of Alaska's coal. Large-scale exploration programs have been conducted in most of Alaska's coalfields by private industry and state and federal governments.

Alaska's production of coal in 2006 was 1.4 million short tons and came exclusively from the Usibelli Coal Mine near Healy. Of that amount, nearly two-thirds were burned in Interior Alaska power plants and the remainder was shipped to South Korea and South America.

CONK Alaskans apply this term to a type of bracket fungus. The platelike conks grow on dead trees. When dry and hard, conks are snapped off and painted by artists or burned as mosquito repellent.

CONSTITUTION OF ALASKA
One of the most remarkable achievements in the long battle for Alaska statehood was the creation of the state's constitution in the mid-1950s. Statehood supporters believed that a constitution would demonstrate Alaska's maturity and readiness for statehood, so in 1955 the territorial legislature appropriated $300,000 to convene a Constitutional Convention in Fairbanks.

For 73 days in 1955–56, a total of 55 elected delegates from all across the territory met in the new Student Union Building (now called Constitution Hall) on the University of Alaska campus. William A. Egan, a territorial legislator and former mayor of Valdez, who later became the first governor of the state of Alaska, was president of the convention. Under his leadership, the disparate group of Alaskans hammered out a document that is considered a model state constitution.

The National Municipal League calls the brief 14,000-word document drafted by the convention delegates "one of the best, if not the best, state constitutions ever written." By an overwhelming margin Alaskans approved the new constitution at the polls in 1956, paving the way for the creation of the 49th state in 1959.

A copy of the constitution is available on the Internet through the lieutenant governor's office at http://ltgov.state.ak.us/constitution.php.

CONTINENTAL DIVIDE (See also Mountains)

The Continental Divide extends into Alaska. Unlike its portions in the Lower 48, which divide the country into east–west watersheds, the Continental Divide in Alaska trends through the Brooks Range, separating watersheds that drain north into the Arctic Ocean and west and south into the Bering Sea.

Alaska Science Nuggets says that geologists once regarded the Brooks Range as a structural extension of the Rocky Mountains. Recent thinking assesses the range as 35 million to 200 million years older than the Rockies. The Alaska Range is comparatively young—only about 5 million years old.

CONVENTION AND VISITORS BUREAUS AND INFORMATION CENTERS

Anchorage Convention and Visitors Bureau, 524 W. Fourth Ave., Anchorage 99501-2122; (907) 276-4118; fax (907) 278-5559; www.anchorage.net.

Anchor Point Visitors Information Center, 34175 Sterling Hwy., Anchor Point 99556; (907) 235-2600.

Barrow, City of, P.O. Box 629, Barrow 99723; (907) 852-5211; fax (907) 852-5871; www.cityofbarrow.org.

Begich, Boggs Visitors Center, P.O. Box 129, Girdwood 99587; (907) 783-2326; www.fs.fed.us/r10/chugach/chugach_pages/bbvc.html.

Copper Valley (Greater) Visitor Information Center, P.O. Box 469, Glennallen 99588; (907) 822-5555; www.traveltoalaska.com.

Fairbanks Convention and Visitors Bureau, 550 First Ave., Fairbanks 99701-4790; (907) 456-5774; (800) 327-5774; fax (907) 452-4190; www.explorefairbanks.com.

Gustavus Visitors Association, P.O. Box 167, Gustavus 99826; (907) 697-2454; www.gustavusak.com.

Haines Convention and Visitors Bureau, P.O. Box 530, Haines 99827; (800) 458-3579, (907) 766-2234; fax (907) 766-3155; www.haines.ak.us.

Homer Visitors Information Center, P.O. Box 541, Homer 99603; (907) 235-7740; fax (907) 235-8766; www.homeralaska.org.

Juneau Convention and Visitors Bureau, One Sealaska Plaza, Suite 305, Juneau 99801; (800) 587-2201; (907) 586-1737; fax (907) 586-1449; www.traveljuneau.com.

Kenai Convention and Visitors Bureau, 11471 Kenai Spur Highway, Kenai 99611; (907) 283-1991; fax (907) 283-2230; www.visitkenai.com.

Ketchikan Visitors Bureau, 131 Front St., Ketchikan 99901; (800) 770-3300; (907) 225-6166; fax (907) 225-4250; www.visit-ketchikan.com.

Kodiak Island Convention and Visitors Bureau, 100 Marine Way, Suite 200, Kodiak 99615; (907) 486-4782; (800) 789-4782; fax (907) 486-6545; www.kodiak.org.

Kotzebue, City of, P.O. Box 46, Kotzebue 99752; (907) 442-3401; http://kotzpdweb.tripod.com/city/index.html.

Matanuska–Susitna Convention and Visitors Bureau, 7744 E. Visitors View Ct., Palmer 99645; (907) 746-5000; fax (907) 746-2688; www.alaskavisit.com.

Nenana, City of, P.O. Box 70, Nenana 99760; (907) 832-5441; fax (907) 832-5503.

Nome Convention and Visitors Bureau, P.O. Box 240 H-P, Nome 99762; (907) 443-6624; fax (907) 443-5832; www.nomealaska.org.

Palmer Visitor Information Center, 723 S. Valley Way, Palmer 99645; (907) 745-2880; fax (907) 746-4164.

Petersburg Visitor Information, P.O. Box 649, Petersburg 99833; phone/fax: (907) 772-4636; (866) 484-4700; www.petersburg.org.

Seward Visitor Information Cache, P.O. Box 749, Seward 99664; (907) 224-8051; www.seward.com.

Sitka Convention and Visitors Bureau, P.O. Box 1226, Sitka 99835; (907) 747-5940; fax (907) 747-3739; www.sitka.org.

Skagway Convention and Visitors Bureau, P.O. Box 1029, Skagway 99840; (907) 983-2854; fax (907) 983-3854; www.skagway.com.

Tok Main Street Visitor Center, P.O. Box 389, Tok 99780; (907) 883-5775; www.tokalaskainfo.com.

Unalaska/Port of Dutch Harbor Convention and Visitors Bureau, P.O. Box 545, Unalaska 99685; (877) 581-2612; (907) 581-2612; fax (907) 581-2613; www.unalaska.info.

Valdez Convention and Visitors Bureau, P.O. Box 1603, Valdez 99686; (907) 835-2984; fax (907) 835-4845; www.valdezalaska.org.

Whittier (City of) Visitors Center, P.O. Box 608, Whittier 99693; (907) 472-2327; fax (907) 472-2404; www.ci.whittier.ak.us.

COOK, CAPT. JAMES James Cook

(1728–79) went to sea as an apprenticed seaman, entering the British Royal Navy at the age of 27. He rose in rank by merit and was sent on two scientific expeditions—the first to the South Pacific (1768–71) and the second to Antarctica (1772–75).

In July 1776, the British Admiralty instructed Cook to proceed to the northwest coast of North America and attempt to find the Northwest Passage, a hoped-for sea link from the Pacific to the Atlantic.

The *Resolution* and *Discovery* sailed from Plymouth via Cape of Good Hope,

A statue of Captain Cook overlooks Cook Inlet in Anchorage. Photo by Tricia Brown.

New Zealand, Tahiti and the Hawaiian Islands, arriving at Nootka Sound on Vancouver Island on March 30, 1778.

From then until Oct. 3, Cook cruised north and west to the Arctic Ocean, sketching the chief features of the coast, practically unknown to Europeans before Cook's historic voyage. He named many features of the coast, including Turnagain Arm, where land blocked his ships and they were forced to "turn again."

Failing to find the Northwest Passage, Cook left Unalaska in the Aleutians on Oct. 27. Cook returned to Hawaii's Big Island, where he was killed by local residents on Feb. 14, 1779. His accounts of the voyage were published in 1784–85 in three volumes and a large atlas.

This pioneering navigator and explorer is commemorated in Alaska by Cook Inlet and Mount Cook. A statue of Cook stands in Anchorage, facing the inlet named for him.

COPPERS (SEE ALSO Potlatch) Coppers

(tinnehs) are beaten copper plaques that were important symbols of wealth among the Pacific Northwest Coast Natives.

Coppers are shaped something like a keyhole or a shield, are usually 2 feet to 3 feet long and weigh approximately 40 pounds. Coppers varied in value from tribe to tribe.

Early coppers were made of ore from the Copper River area, although western traders quickly made sheet copper available. Some scholars believe that Tlingit craftsmen shaped placer copper into the desired form themselves, while others maintain that coppers were forged by Athabascans. The impressive plaques were engraved or carved in relief with totemic crests.

The value of coppers increased as they were traded or sold, and their transfer implied that a potlatch would be given by the new owner. Coppers were given names, such as "Cloud," "Point of Island" or "Killer Whale," and were spoken of in respectful terms. They were thought of as powerful and their histories were as well known as those of the noblest families.

Coppers were often broken and destroyed during public displays and distribution of wealth. Some parts of the coppers were valued nearly as much as the whole.

To this day, certain coppers that were part of museum collections for years are still valued highly by some tribes, and are displayed as symbols of wealth and prestige during marriage ceremonies and potlatches.

COST OF LIVING Determining how expensive it is to live in Alaska not only depends on whom you ask, but how. Labor economists hired by the state to track cost-of-living data rely on several indexes, each with its own methods, focus and results.

For a comparison among cities, the American Chamber of Commerce Researchers Association (ACCRA) offers valuable data, as does Runzheimer International, a private research group under contract to the state. To learn how prices have changed in a particular place over time, the Consumer Price Index is a useful gauge of inflation.

One way to unlock cost-of-living data in Alaska is to look at a map of the state's roads. Where there are fewer roads and fewer people, costs are generally higher. That's contrary to other states, where cost of living tends to be higher in cities. But because transportation to and within Alaska figures into the price of everything from a can of corn to roofing material, costs tend to be far lower in urban centers such as Anchorage and Fairbanks, where highways and economies of scale are factors.

Alaska has only limited agriculture and manufacturing, so most goods and foods must be shipped in at added cost. Highest food costs are found in isolated communities dependent on airfreight.

Remembering the Pipeline Days

As of October 1975, costs of food, clothing, housing and gasoline were 15 to 40 percent higher than in the Lower 48 states.

Sample Anchorage prices back then were:

Man's haircut: $5

Woman's cut, shampoo, set: $8 to $18

Premium gas: 71.9 to 79.9 cents per gallon

Unleaded gas: 69.9 to 78.9 cents per gallon

Regular gas: 69.9 to 76.9 cents per gallon

Steak dinner (New York cut): $7.50 to $12.90

Coffee: 15 to 35 cents a cup

Tuna sandwich: $1.35 to $2.10

Deluxe hamburger: $1.90 to $2.25

Ham and eggs: $3 to $3.25

1-bedroom apartment: $150 to $325

2-bedroom apartment: $300 to $420

3-bedroom apartment: $400 to $600

Furnished apartments: Add $50

Buy 2-bedroom home: $23,000 to $65,000 ($55,154 average)

Buy 3-bedroom home: $50,000 to $78,000 ($69,119 average)

Beer (Budweiser), per case: $8.93

Beer, per glass (bar): $1 to $1.25

Wine (bottle of least expensive red): $1.75

Bourbon (Jim Beam), per fifth: $6.25

Scotch and water (bar): $1.25 to $1.50

—1976 *The Alaska Almanac*®

Some studies overlook distinctive elements of Alaska life that play a role in the cost of living. For instance, Alaska is among the few places without a state income tax. A factor unique to Alaska is the state's annual distribution from its oil wealth savings account, the Permanent Fund Dividend. In 2006 a dividend of $1,106.96 was paid to every qualified resident.

The ACCRA data places Alaska cities among the most expensive in the nation. The study attempts to duplicate spending of a mid-management executive's household. It focused on four Alaska cities in 2006: Anchorage, Fairbanks, Kodiak and Juneau.

The ACCRA study found the cost of living in Anchorage was 23 percent higher than the national average, Fairbanks was nearly 25 percent higher, Kodiak was 21 percent higher and Juneau was 29 percent higher.

The data compiled by Runzheimer International show a much smaller cost-of-living differential between Alaska and the rest of the nation. This is because Runzheimer studies the cost of living for a family of four that earns $32,000—a lower-income group than in the ACCRA study. In addition, Runzheimer includes the effect of taxes on consumer spending.

Runzheimer found that for 2004, cost of living exceeded the national average by 15 percent in Anchorage, 8 percent in Fairbanks and 26 percent in Juneau. (The State of Alaska obtains information from Runzheimer International every three years.)

Inflation. While the cost of living in Alaska may be higher than in the Lower 48, consumer prices in Alaska have generally increased more slowly than in the rest of the nation, according to the U.S.

Department of Labor's Bureau of Labor Statistics. However, consumer prices in Anchorage rose 3.2 percent in 2006, matching the 3.2 percent gain nationally. Anchorage is the only Alaska city for which the bureau tracks consumer prices.

Food. Economists have long relied on the Cost of Food at Home study prepared by the University of Alaska Fairbanks' Cooperative Extension Services to track food prices around the state. This study has its limitations. Many grocery items that can be purchased in larger cities are not available in rural communities.

In addition, the market basket of foods tracked by the university in each community is identical, despite dramatic differences in buying habits among communities. But the university's quarterly survey is the only study to offer a comparative measure among 20 Alaska communities, and it has been produced consistently for many years.

In December 2006, the study found that the lowest food prices were in Fairbanks, where it cost $113.97 to feed a family of four at home for a week. The Palmer/Wasilla area was second, with a cost of $114.20. Kotzebue's food prices were highest, where it cost $224.98. Kotzebue is located on the Baldwin Peninsula in Kotzebue Sound, some 549 air miles northwest of Anchorage, and 26 miles above the Arctic Circle.

Housing. The state Labor Department monitors housing costs by studying rental markets in 10 communities statewide. Costs vary widely depending on the local economy, vacancy rates and demographics.

In 2006, the median adjusted monthly rent (including utilities) was highest in Juneau, where the cost of a two-bedroom apartment was $1,073. Kodiak followed with a monthly rent of $1,070. Anchorage was fifth at $945, and Fairbanks ranked sixth at $940. The lowest monthly rent was found in Wrangell/Petersburg at $693.

The rental market for a three-bedroom home in 2006 was most expensive in Valdez/Cordova with a monthly rent of $1,720. Juneau was second at $1,711, and Fairbanks was third at $1,565. The least expensive was in the Wrangell-Petersburg Census Area, in Southeast Alaska, with a monthly rental of $881.

> *Alaska* **magazine reported that "Real Alaskans know the ideal time to till your garden, plant the seeds, and harvest the vegetables falls on the same day."**

Personal income. Preliminary figures for 2006 compiled by the Federal Bureau of Economic Analysis show that annual per capita personal income for Alaska was $37,271, positioning the state 16th among the states. The nation's per capita income in 2006 was $36,276.

For more cost-of-living information, write the Alaska Department of Labor, Research and Analysis section, P.O. Box 21149, Juneau 99802-1149. The department's cost-of-living data can be found at http://almis.labor.state.ak.us.

COURTS
The Alaska court system operates at four levels: the supreme court, court of appeals, superior court and district court. The Alaska judiciary is funded by the state and administered by the supreme court.

The five-member supreme court, established by the Alaska Constitution in 1959, has final appellate jurisdiction over all actions and proceedings in lower courts. It sits monthly in Anchorage, approximately quarterly in Juneau and Fairbanks, and occasionally in other court locations.

The three-member court of appeals was established in 1980 to relieve the supreme court of some of its ever-increasing caseload.

The supreme court retained its ultimate authority in all cases, but concentrated its attention on civil appellate matters, giving authority in criminal and quasi-criminal matters to the court of appeals. The court of appeals has appellate jurisdiction in certain superior court proceedings and jurisdiction to review district court decisions. It meets regularly in Anchorage and travels occasionally to other locations.

The superior court is the trial court with original jurisdiction in all civil and criminal matters and appellate jurisdiction over all matters appealed from the district court. The superior court has exclusive jurisdiction in probate and in cases concerning minors. There are 40 superior court judges.

The district court has jurisdiction over misdemeanor violations and violations of ordinances of political subdivisions. In civil matters, the district court may hear cases for recovery of money, damages or specific

NUGGETS

The Alaska Supreme Court in a unanimous ruling said the Dalton Highway—the state's only road heading north to the Arctic coast—can be opened to the public, but only after the state reveals the costs of opening the road. Opponents feared the unrestricted use would damage the environment and impose a financial burden on municipal emergency response.

—1994 *The Alaska Almanac*®

personal property if the amount does not exceed $100,000.

The district court may also inquire into the cause and manner of death, as well as issue summonses, writs of habeas corpus and search and arrest warrants. District court criminal decisions may be appealed directly to the court of appeals or the superior court. There are 21 district court judges.

Administration of the superior and district courts is divided by region into four judicial districts: First Judicial District, Southeast; Second Judicial District, Nome–Barrow–Kotzebue; Third Judicial District, Anchorage–Kodiak–Kenai; and Fourth Judicial District, Fairbanks.

District magistrates serve rural areas and help ease the workload of district courts in metropolitan areas. In criminal matters, magistrates may enter judgment of conviction upon a plea of guilty to any state misdemeanor and may try state misdemeanor cases if defendants waive their right to a district court judge. Magistrates may also hear municipal ordinance violations and state traffic infractions without the consent of the accused. In civil matters, magistrates may hear cases for recovery of money, damages or specific personal property if the amount does not exceed $10,000.

Selection of Justices, Judges and Magistrates.

Supreme court justices and judges of the court of appeals, superior court and district court are appointed by the governor from candidates submitted by the Alaska Judicial Council.

The chief justice of the supreme court, selected by majority vote of the justices, serves a three-year term and may not serve consecutive terms.

Each supreme court justice and each judge of the court of appeals is subject to approval or rejection by a majority of the voters of the state on a nonpartisan ballot at the first general election held more than three years after appointment. Thereafter, each justice must participate in a retention election every 10 years. A court of appeals judge must participate every eight years.

Superior court judges are subject to approval or rejection by voters of their judicial district at the first general election held more than three years after appointment. Thereafter, it is every sixth year. District court judges must run for retention in their judicial

districts in the first general election held more than two years after appointment. Thereafter, it is every fourth year. District magistrates are appointed for an indefinite period by the presiding superior court judge of the judicial district in which they will serve.

Additional information about the court system is available at www.state.ak.us/courts.

Alaska State Supreme Court, 1960–2007: Justices and Tenure.

Current Justices:

Alexander O. Bryner, 1997–
   Chief Justice, 2003–2006
Dana Fabe, 1996–
   Chief Justice, 2000–2003; 2006–
Walter L. Carpeneti, 1998–
Robert L. Eastaugh, 1994–
Warren W. Matthews, 1977–
   Chief Justice, 1987–90; 1997–2000

Former Justices:

Harry O. Arend, 1960–65
George F. Boney, 1968–72
   Chief Justice, 1970–72
Robert Boochever, 1972–80
   Chief Justice, 1975–78
Edmond W. Burke, 1975–93
   Chief Justice, 1981–84
Allen T. Compton, 1980–98
   Chief Justice, 1996–97
Roger G. Connor, 1968–83
John H. Dimond, 1959–71
Robert C. Erwin, 1970–77
James M. Fitzgerald, 1972–75
Walter H. Hodge, 1959–60
Daniel A. Moore Jr., 1983–95
   Chief Justice, 1992–96
Buell A. Nesbett, 1959–70
   Chief Justice, 1959–70
Jay A. Rabinowitz, 1965–97
   Chief Justice, 1972–75; 1978–81; 1984–87; 1990–92

Alaska State Court of Appeals, 1980–2007: Judges and Tenure.

Current Judges:

Robert G. Coats, 1980–
   Chief Judge, 1997–
David Mannheimer, 1990–
David C. Stewart, 1997–

Former Judges:

Alexander O. Bryner, 1980–97
   Chief Judge, 1980–97
James K. Singleton Jr., 1980–90

CRUISES <small>(SEE ALSO Boating; Ferries)</small> There
are many opportunities for cruising Alaska
waters aboard charter boats, scheduled
boat excursions or luxury cruise ships.

Charter boats are readily available in
Southeast and Southcentral Alaska. Charter
boat trips range from daylong fishing and
sightseeing trips to overnight and longer
customized trips or package tours. There
is a wide range of charter boats, from
simple fishing boats to sailboats, yachts
and mini-class cruise ships.

In summer, scheduled boat excur-
sions—from day trips to overnight
cruises—are available: Ketchikan (Misty
Fiords); Sitka (harbor and area tours);
Bartlett Cove and Gustavus (Glacier Bay);
Juneau (Lynn Canal); Valdez and Whittier
(Columbia Glacier, Prince William Sound);
Seward (Resurrection Bay, Kenai Fjords);
Homer (Kachemak Bay); and Fairbanks
(Chena and Tanana Rivers).

For details and additional information on
charter boat operators and scheduled boat
excursions, contact the Alaska Travel Industry
Association at www.travelalaska.com.

From May through September, cruise
lines that carry visitors to Alaska via the Inside
Passage include Carnival, Princess, Holland
America, Cruise West, Majestic America Line,
Norwegian Cruise Line, Royal Caribbean,

**Cruise-ship travel allows close-up views of
Glacier Bay's tidewater glaciers.** Photo by
Tricia Brown.

Celebrity, Regent Seven Seas and Lindblad.
For the phone number of a particular company, contact Cruise Lines International,
(754) 224-2200 or www.cruising.org. Both
round-trip and one-way cruises are available,
or a cruise may be sold as part of a package
tour that includes air, rail and/or motorcoach
transportation. (SEE Bus Lines)

The cost for a 7- to 11-day Inside
Passage cruise can vary depending on
cabin location and cruise line. Booking
by Feb. 14 or just prior to the date of
departure can yield substantial savings.
The cruise industry in Alaska waters
continues to thrive. A passenger capacity
of one million is expected during the
summer of 2007, a number comparable
with 2006 actual arrivals. Because of the
wide variety of cruise trip options, it is
wise to work with a travel agent. For
additional information on cruises go to
www.claalaska.com.

DALTON HIGHWAY <small>(SEE ALSO</small>
Highways) The 416-mile-long Dalton
Highway begins at Milepost 73.1 on the
Elliott Highway.

This all-weather, mostly gravel road
bridges the Yukon River, crosses the Arctic
Circle at Mile 115.4 and climbs the Brooks
Range. At Atigun Pass (Mile 247.5) it
crosses a continental divide, the highest
highway pass in Alaska (elevation 4,800

The 2,290-foot E. L. Patton Bridge spans the Yukon River at the Dalton Highway in Alaska. From *Two in a Red Canoe* by Matt Hage and Megan Baldino.

feet). Then the road passes through tundra plains before ending at the Prudhoe Bay oil fields at Deadhorse, nine miles from the coast of the Arctic Ocean.

Public travel for the final nine miles is restricted to commercial tours. As of 2006, the state had paved 93 miles of the Dalton Highway, with a goal of eventually paving the entire route.

The highway was named for James Dalton, a post–World War II explorer who played a large role in the development of North Slope oil and gas industries. It was built as a haul road for supplies and to provide access to the northern half of the 800-mile trans-Alaska oil pipeline during construction. Originally called the North Slope Haul Road, it is still often referred to as the Haul Road.

About 16 miles north of Fairbanks, the Hilltop Truck Stop and Café on the Elliott Highway is the last-chance dining and gas for many miles. The Dalton Highway is open to all vehicles and is maintained year-round. Services are limited to Yukon River Camp (Mile 56), Hot Spot Cafe (Mile 60) and Coldfoot Services (Mile 175). The Arctic Getaway, a family-run B&B in Wiseman (Mile 188), accommodates visitors year-round. Current driving, construction and weather conditions information is available by calling 511 (within Alaska) or (866) 282-7577 (toll free, outside of Alaska); or http://511.alaska.gov.

DAYLIGHT HOURS
(See also Arctic Circle)

Maximum (at Summer Solstice, June 20 or 21)

	Sunrise	Sunset	Hours of Daylight
Adak	6:27 A.M.	11:10 P.M.	16:43 hrs
Anchorage	3:21 A.M.	10:42 P.M.	19:21 hrs
Barrow	May 10	Aug. 2	84 days continuous
Fairbanks	1:59 A.M.	11:48 P.M.	21:49 hrs
Juneau	3:51 A.M.	10:09 P.M.	18:18 hrs
Ketchikan	4:04 A.M.	9:33 P.M.	17:29 hrs

Minimum (at Winter Solstice, Dec. 21 or 22)

	Sunrise	Sunset	Hours of Daylight
Adak	10:52 A.M.	6:38 P.M.	7:46 hrs
Anchorage	10:14 A.M.	3:42 P.M.	5:28 hrs
Barrow	*	*	0:00 hrs
Fairbanks	10:59 A.M.	2:41 P.M.	3:42 hrs
Juneau	9:46 A.M.	4:07 P.M.	6:21 hrs
Ketchikan	9:12 A.M.	4:18 P.M.	7:06 hrs

* From Nov. 18 through Jan. 24—a period of 67 days—there is no daylight in Barrow.

DIAMOND WILLOW Fungi,
particularly *Valsa sordida Nitschke,* can create diamond-shaped patterns in the wood grain of some willow trees. There are 33 varieties of willow in Alaska, at least five of which can develop diamonds. They are found throughout the state but are most plentiful in river valleys. Diamond willow, stripped of bark, is used to make lamps, walking sticks and novelty items.

DOG MUSHING (See also Calendar of
Annual Events; Iditarod Trail Sled Dog Race; Yukon Quest International Sled Dog Race) In many areas of the state where snowmachines had nearly replaced the working dog team, the sled dog has returned, due in part to a rekindled appreciation of the reliability of nonmechanical transportation. In addition to working and racing dog teams, many people keep 2 to 20 sled dogs for recreational mushing.

Sled-dog racing is Alaska's official state sport. Races ranging from local club meets

Open World Championship Sled Dog Race, Anchorage

Scheduled during Fur Rendezvous in February. Best elapsed time in three heats over three days, 25 miles each day. Purse is split among the top 15 finishers. Winners since 1995:

Year Winner	Elapsed Time (minutes:seconds)				
	Day 1	Day 2	Day 3	Total	Purse
1995 Ross Saunderson	84:19	88:57	85:07	258:23	45,000
1996 Canceled due to lack of snow					
1997 Axel Gasser	95:47	99:09	102:03	296:59	45,000
1998 Ross Saunderson	96:12	99:20	101:28	291:00	50,000
1999 Egil Ellis	84:02	90:28	88:33	263:03	20,000
2000 Egil Ellis	84:42	90:26	90:59	266:07	38,400
2001 Canceled due to lack of snow					
2002 Egil Ellis	85:47	91:29	88:13	265:29	*60,000
2003 Canceled due to lack of snow					
2004 Blayne Streeper	85:18	85:42	87:27	258:27	40,000
2005 Egil Ellis	90:09	88:16	90:34	240:29	60,000
2006 Canceled due to lack of snow					
2007 Blayne Streeper	83.36	86.06	86.07	255:49	35,000

* Purse amount does not include Dodge truck.

Open North American Sled Dog Race Championship, Fairbanks

Held in March. Best elapsed time in three heats over three days; 20 miles on Days 1 and 2; 30 miles on Day 3. (Times have been rounded off.) In 1998, the Day 3 heat was shortened to 20 miles. Purse is split among the top 15 finishers. Winners since 1995:

Year Winner	Elapsed Time (minutes:seconds)				
	Day 1	Day 2	Day 3	Total	Purse
1995 Amy Streeper	61:42	65:29	94:48	221:59	46,940
1996 Amy Streeper	68:58	63:17	90:29	222:45	32,500
1997 Neil Johnson	64:06	64:53	94:25	223:24	22,500
1998 Michi Konno	70:05	69:41	67:00	206:47	40,000
1999 Egil Ellis	**	63:07	91:46	154:52	46,300
2000 Egil Ellis	59:58	61:08	90:40	211:46	40,000
2001 Egil Ellis	58:52	59:36	88:46	207:14	50,000
2002 Egil Ellis	63:25	66:15	95:14	224:55	35,000
2003 Buddy Streeper	62:42	63:32	90:39	216:54	37,000
2004 Egil Ellis	58:38	59:30	88:46	206:54	35,000
2005 Egil Ellis	61:16	61:42	87:58	210:56	35,000
2006 Egil Ellis	59:26	60:21	88:56	208:43	20,000
2007 Blayne Streeper	58:00	59:56	86:52	204:47	20,000

** No first-day time as trail was blocked.

Source: Alaska Dog Mushers Association

to world championships are held throughout the winter.

Championship speed races are usually run over two or three days, with the cumulative time for the heats deciding the winner. Distances for the heats vary from about 5 to 30 miles. The size of dog teams also varies, with mushers using anywhere from 4 to 20 dogs in their teams. Since racers are not allowed to replace dogs in the team, most finish with fewer than they started with. Attrition may be caused by anything from tender feet to sore muscles.

Sprint mushing is divided into limited and open classes. Limited class ranges from 3 to 10 dogs and from 3 to 12 miles a day. Open-class racing has no limit on the number of dogs and ranges from 10 to 30 miles a day.

Long-distance racing (the Yukon Quest; the Iditarod) pits racers not only against one another but also against the elements. Sheer survival can quickly take precedence over winning when a winter storm catches a dog team in an exposed area. Stories abound of racers giving up their chance to finish "in the money" to help out another musher who has gotten into trouble. Besides the weather, long-distance racers also have to contend with moose attacks on the dogs, sudden illness, straying off the trail and sheer exhaustion. With these and other challenges to overcome, those who finish have truly persevered against the odds.

Prizes range from trophies to cash from a purse that is split among the finishers. The richest purse in sled-dog racing is the Iditarod, which paid a record total of $824,172 in March 2007.

For information about dog mushing: www.mushing.com; www.sleddog.org; www.iditarod.com.

See charts on previous page for statistics on two of the biggest championship sprint races. Other major races around the state follow.

Copper Basin 300, Glennallen. Covers 300 miles over two to three days. Held in January; www.cb300.com.

Don Bowers Memorial Race, Willow. Covers a 200-mile loop. Held in January; Montana Creek Mushers' Association; www.mcdma.org.

GCI Open North American Sled Dog Race Championship, Fairbanks. First run in 1946; now the oldest continuously run sled-dog race of any kind in the world. Best elapsed time in three heats over three days; 20 miles on Days 1 and 2; 30 miles on Day 3. Held in March; www.sleddog.org.

Iditarod Trail Sled Dog Race. (SEE Iditarod Trail Sled Dog Race) www.iditarod.com.

Junior North American Championships, Fairbanks. For youth under 18. Three heats, one- to eight-dog classes. Held in March; www.sleddog.org.

Junior Iditarod Trail Sled Dog Race, Wasilla. For youth under 18. Willow to Yentna Station and back. Held in February; www.jriditarod.com.

Junior World Championship Race, Anchorage. Three heats in three days. Held in February. Alaska Sled Dog and Racing Association; www.asdra.org.

Klondike 300, Big Lake. Loop 150 miles out and back on Iditarod Trail. Held in January; http://klondike300.org.

Kobuk 440, Kotzebue to Kobuk and back. Held in April; Kotzebue Dog Mushers' Association, www.kotzdogmushers.org.

Kusko 300, Bethel to Aniak. Held in January; www.k300.org/bethelinfo.htm.

Limited North American Championships, Fairbanks. Three heats over three days; one-, two- and three-dog skijoring. Held in March; www.sleddog.org.

Open World Championship Sled Dog Race, Anchorage. Three heats in three days, 25 miles each day. Held in February; Alaska Sled Dog and Racing Association; www.asdra.org.

Tok Race of Champions, Tok. Two heats in two days, 20.5 miles a day. Held in March; http://tokdogmushers.org.

Women's World Championship Race, Anchorage. Three heats in three days, 12 miles each day. Held in February; Alaska Sled Dog and Racing Association; www.asdra.org.

Yukon Quest International Sled Dog Race. (SEE Yukon Quest International Sled Dog Race); www.yukonquest.com.

EARTHQUAKES (SEE ALSO Waves)

Alaska is the most seismic of the 50 states, and the most seismically active part of the state is the Aleutian Islands arc system. Seismicity related to this system extends into the Gulf of Alaska and northward into Interior Alaska as far as Mount McKinley. These earthquakes are largely the result of underthrusting of the North Pacific Plate beneath the North American plate. Many earthquakes resulting from this subduction occur in Cook Inlet—particularly near Mount Iliamna and Mount Redoubt—and near Mount McKinley. North of the Alaska Range, in the central Interior, most earthquakes are of shallow origin.

Ten great earthquakes have occurred along the Aleutian trench since 1900 that equaled or exceeded a magnitude of 8 on the Richter scale. Alaska averages one M8 earthquake every 13 years, one M7 every year and a yearly average of one thousand M3.5 or greater events. In February 2004 alone, the Alaska Earthquake Information Center detected and located 2,964 events in Alaska. The largest of these measured 5.5 and was located in the Kenai Peninsula region.

The world's strongest earthquake for 2002, and the strongest ever recorded in Alaska's Interior, occurred on Nov. 3 that year. Centered in a sparsely populated area about 90 miles south of Fairbanks, this M7.9 shock was comparable in size and type to the 1906 San Francisco quake, but caused little structural damage and no deaths. The trans-Alaska oil pipeline suffered damage to support structures, but not to the actual pipeline. The quake triggered countless landslides as well as severe road damage to the portion of the Glenn Highway known as the Tok Cutoff.

The West Coast/Alaska Tsunami Warning Center is responsible for warning coastal residents of Alaska, Washington, Oregon, California and British Columbia about any earthquake that could generate a tsunami, a seismic sea wave. According to the Center, Alaska's earthquake activity typically follows the same pattern from month to month, interspersed with sporadic swarms, or groups of small

Earthquake damage in downtown Anchorage, 1964. Special Collections Division, UW Libraries. From *Alaska's History* by Harry Ritter.

earthquakes, and punctuated every decade or so by a great earthquake and its aftershocks.

The earthquake that created the highest seiche, or splash wave, ever recorded occurred on the evening of July 9, 1958, when a quake with a magnitude of 7.9 on the Richter scale rocked the Yakutat area. A landslide containing approximately 40 million cubic yards of rock plunged into Gilbert Inlet at the head of Lituya Bay. The gigantic splash resulting from the slide sent a wave 1,740 feet up the opposite mountainside, denuding it of trees and soil down to bedrock. It then fell back and swept through the length of the bay and out to sea. One fishing boat anchored in Lituya Bay at the time was lost with its crew of two; another was carried over a spit of land by the wave and soon after foundered, but its crew was saved. A third boat anchored in the bay miraculously survived intact.

The most destructive earthquake to strike Alaska occurred at 5:36 P.M. on Good Friday, March 27, 1964. Registering between 8.4 and 8.6 on the Richter scale in use at the time, its equivalent moment magnitude has since been revised upward to 9.2, making it the strongest earthquake ever recorded in North America. With its primary epicenter deep beneath Miners Lake in northern Prince William Sound, the earthquake spread shock waves that were felt 700 miles away. The earthquake and seismic waves that followed killed 131 people, including 115 Alaskans. Of the 131 deaths, 119 were caused by the tsunami generated by the earthquake.

The 1964 earthquake released 10 million times more energy than the atomic bomb that devastated Hiroshima in World War II, and 80 times the energy of the San Francisco earthquake of 1906. It also moved more earth farther, both horizontally and vertically, than any other earthquake ever recorded except the 1960 (9.4) Chilean earthquake. In the 69-day period after the main quake, there were 12,000 jolts of 3.5 magnitude or greater.

The highest sea wave caused by the 1964 earthquake occurred when an undersea slide near Shoup Glacier in Port Valdez triggered a wave that toppled trees 100 feet above tidewater and deposited silt and sand 220 feet above salt water.

During June 1996, the Alaska Earthquake Information Center located 567 earthquakes in or near Alaska. The largest of these was a major earthquake on June 9 in the Aleutian Island chain with a magnitude of 7.9, the largest earthquake to have occurred in North America in more than 10 years. The earthquake was felt sharply at Adak and Atka; minor damage was reported at Adak. This quake generated minor tsunamis in Alaska and other locales in the Pacific Basin.

To learn more about earthquakes, visit the University of Alaska Fairbanks Web site at www.aeic.alaska.edu/seis.

Frayed Nerves

Intense episodes of quakes on March 10–11 and March 13–14, 1996, alarmed residents when Akutan Volcano, one of the liveliest peaks in the Aleutian Chain, rattled the island of Akutan. As a result, ceilings cracked, scientists arrived to install seismometers and beer consumption skyrocketed on the island. More than 800 small earthquakes a day occurred on March 13 and 14. Half of the 100 residents of the town of Akutan and some seasonal cod fishery processors boarded amphibious planes for Dutch Harbor.

—1996 The Alaska Almanac®

ECONOMY (SEE ALSO Cost of Living; Employment) Alaska's economy is driven by several basic sectors: exports, including petroleum, mining, seafood and forest products; tourism; international air cargo; the military; and state and federal governments.

No single factor figures more prominently into Alaska's economic scene than the price of crude oil. The higher the price of oil, the more incentive big oil companies like British Petroleum, ConocoPhillips and ExxonMobil have to explore and drill. Activity within the big companies, in turn, stimulates oil-field service industries—all of which generate jobs and income for Alaskans.

The price of oil also affects the level of state revenues. Oil taxes and royalties fund over 80 percent of the state's unrestricted general-purpose revenue. Fluctuations in oil prices—the price per barrel bounced from a low of $9.39 in 1998 to more than $72 in May 2006—result in huge fluctuations in state revenue from year to year. The largest single factor in the projected decrease in state revenues, however, is declining production from North Slope oil fields. Alaska state government spending per capita is also higher than the national average, resulting in a large influence on the total economy.

Another factor influencing state revenue is the Permanent Fund. In 1976, a constitutional amendment established a trust fund for all Alaskans. A percentage of all mineral lease rentals, royalties, royalty sales proceeds, federal mineral revenue-sharing payments and bonuses are placed in the Permanent Fund. Qualifying residents receive a dividend payment from the investment income generated by the fund—a check that pumps close to a billion dollars into the hands of Alaska's resident consumers each year.

Tourism continues to be an important industry in Alaska, with the state attracting more than 1.6 million summer visitors in 2006. The tourism industry is one of Alaska's largest private-sector employers. Travel concerns related to terrorism and recession have not lessened the lure of visiting the state.

The bountiful waters off Alaska's coast bring in an annual fishing harvest of nearly 6 billion pounds of seafood. Growing consumer preference for the health benefits of wild Alaska seafood led to a 3 percent growth in seafood exports, a record total of more than $2 billion, in 2006.

Growing world demand, technological advances and rising commodity prices are fueling growth in the mining industry. Like the development of other natural resources in Alaska, mining involves the high cost of building infrastructure at remote sites, as well as the cost of transporting goods long distances to market. In 2006, some $176.5 million was spent on mineral exploration and $331.0 million on mine development, with mineral production value of $2,752 million from Alaska's metal (lode and placer), coal and industrial minerals (rock, sand and gravel) mines, according to the Alaska Division of Geological and Geophysical Surveys.

International air cargo is one sector that shows promise in diversifying the state's economy. Cargo operations have expanded rapidly at Ted Stevens Anchorage International Airport as well as in Fairbanks. Anchorage was ranked as the busiest cargo airport in the nation in 2006, based on all-cargo aircraft landed weight. Alaska is well positioned to play an important role in growing trans-Pacific markets.

The military also figures prominently in the economy of Alaska. The number of soldiers stationed in the state has risen dramatically in recent years with the

When a customer complained about an account error to the First National Bank in Anchorage, a manager wrote her a letter apologizing "for any *incontinence* or hardship this may have caused." The woman leaked the story to us.

arrival of the 4th Brigade Combat Team (Airborne), the 25th Infantry Division (Light) at Fort Richardson and the 1st Striker Brigade Combat Team, 25th Infantry Division at Fort Wainwright. Significant construction activity at these installations as well as on Elmendorf Airforce Base in Anchorage and Eielson Air Force Base in Fairbanks, have greatly increased military spending in Alaska. Tension in many parts of the world has substantially increased the number of troops stationed in Alaska. While Alaska's resource-dependent economy has been characterized by boom and bust cycles, overall growth has been positive since statehood in 1959. For more information about Alaska's economy check the following Web sites:

Dept. of Community and Economic Development: www.dced.state.ak.us.

Dept. of Labor and Workforce Development: www.labor.state.ak.us.

Institute of Social & Economic Research, University of Alaska, Anchorage: www.iser.uaa.alaska.edu.

EDUCATION (See also Universities and Colleges)

According to the 2006-07 Alaska Education Directory, Alaska has 504 public schools. The Bureau of Indian Affairs operated some rural schools in Alaska until 1985.

The State Board of Education and Early Development has seven members appointed by the governor. (In addition, two non-voting members are appointed by the board to represent the military and public school students.) The board is responsible for setting policy for education in Alaska schools and appoints a commissioner of Education and Early Development to carry out its decisions. The public schools are controlled by 53 school districts, and each school district elects its own school board. Nineteen Regional Education Attendance Areas oversee education in rural areas outside the 34 city and borough school districts.

Any student in grades kindergarten through 12 may choose to study at home through the several school districts that operate distance-learning correspondence programs, which serve traveling students and students living in remote areas. Home study has been an option for Alaska students since 1939.

The state Department of Labor and Workforce development operates the Alaska Vocational Technical Center at Seward, which offers a number of other education programs ranging from adult basic education to literacy skills.

Alaskans between 7 and 16 years old are required to attend school. The Alaska Legislature passed a law in 1997 requiring the development of the Alaska High School Graduation Qualifying Examination. Beginning with the class of 2004, students must pass the exam and earn 21 credits to receive a high school diploma. The State Board of Education and Early Development has stipulated that four credits must be earned in language arts, three in social studies, two each in math and science and one in physical education or health. Local school boards set the remainder of the required credits. Those students who meet local requirements but do not pass the test will receive a certificate of achievement.

Since 1976 the state has provided secondary school programs to any community in which an elementary school is operated and one or more children of high school age wish to attend high school. This mandate was the result of a class action suit initiated on behalf of Molly Hootch, a high school–age student. Prior to the Molly Hootch settlement (the Tobeluk Consent Decree), high school–age students in villages without a secondary school attended high school outside their village. Of the 127 villages originally eligible for high school programs under the Molly Hootch Decree, only a few remain without one.

There were 8,856 teachers and administrators in the public schools and 134,840 students enrolled in PE–12 in public schools in 2006-07. The size of schools in Alaska varies greatly, from a 2,198-student high school in Anchorage to one-room schools, with one or two teachers, in remote rural areas.

Nearly 62 percent of the school districts' operating fund is provided by the state, about 29 percent by local governments and about 9 percent by the federal government. Alaska's average salary for classroom teachers is among the highest in the nation, with the statewide average in 2006-07 at $54,678.

EMPLOYMENT (See also Economy)

For the nineteenth consecutive year, Alaska enjoyed employment growth in 2006—a remarkable feat, especially considering the two national recessions, declining North Slope oil production and oil prices that dipped lower than $15 per barrel during those same years. Preliminary statewide employment numbers from the Alaska Department of Labor show a growth rate of 1.5 in 2006, compared to 1.9 in 2005. The service-providing sector led the way with a total increase of 3,500 jobs.

The oil and gas industry continued its impressive gains in 2006, resulting in an 11.5 percent increase from 2005. There's growing consensus that the year's record high oil prices, which have invigorated exploration activity and boosted industry employment, are likely to remain high for the foreseeable future. The state added 1,000 new oil and gas jobs in 2006, reminiscent of industry employment levels of the early 1990s. Total oil revenue in fiscal year 2006 was about $3.7 billion, and the

Alaska Department of Revenue expects that number to grow to $4.3 billion in 2007.

Minerals and mining enjoyed another strong year in 2006, adding 1,200 new jobs due, primarily, to the increased prices for gold (36 percent), silver (16 percent), lead (35 percent) and zinc (233 percent). Alaska is one of the richest depositories of mineral wealth in the world; therefore the current market trend is expected to continue.

The construction industry added to its remarkable stretch of stability with an additional 200 jobs during 2006. However, following a decade of strong growth, the industry is expecting a slight reduction in future jobs as large, publicly funded projects of recent years are completed.

Retail employment experienced an increase of 700 new jobs in the past year, while the visitor industry, following a solid year in 2005, added 500 jobs within the leisure and hospitality segment (a 1.6 percent gain). Cruise ship travel to Alaska seems to have increased somewhat during the year, while independent travel has remained steady.

Following consistent declines from the late 1990s to the early 2000s, the economic health of Alaska's fisheries has improved slightly in 2006. While competition from farmed salmon remains challenging, the state's fisheries are expected to contribute economic stability—if not strong growth—over the next two years.

The government sector saw mixed results in 2006, with a decrease of 300 federal jobs (–1.8 percent), and an

A nationwide survey by the prestigious Morgan Quitno Press showed that Alaska is the 44th Smartest State in the U.S.A. Bumper stickers immediately appeared proclaiming: "What's the problem? What's the fuss? There's six states that are dumber than us!"

Alaska Average Annual Employment 1993–2006

Employees (in thousands)

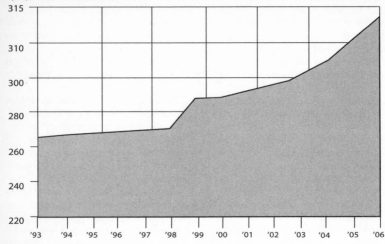

Source: Alaska Department of Labor

Alaska Employment by Month 2002–2006

Employees (in thousands)

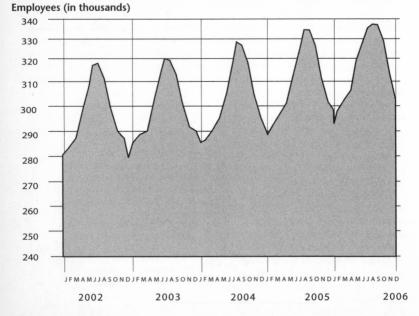

Source: Alaska Department of Labor

increase of 300 (1.2 percent) at the state, and 400 (1.0 percent) at the local government levels.

Unemployment January 2006

Area	Percent
Statewide	6.7
Anchorage	5.3
Fairbanks North Star Borough	5.8
Juneau Borough	4.9
Ketchikan Gateway Borough	6.2
Nome	12.1
Bristol Bay Borough	5.5
Kodiak Island Borough	7.7

Source: Alaska Department of Labor and Workforce Development

Wage and Salary Employment by Industry 2006

Industry	Percent
Government (federal, state, local)	26
Educational and Health Services	12
Professional/Business Services	8
Other Services	4
Trade/Transportation/Utilities	20
Leisure and Hospitality	10
Manufacturing	4
Construction	6
Natural Resources and Mining	4
Financial Activities	5
Information	2

Source: Alaska Department of Labor and Workforce Development

Alaska's unemployment rate fluctuates seasonally. Tourism and commercial fishing jobs drive down unemployment in summer, while decreased business activity in winter prompts rates to rise. Employment prospects also vary widely depending on region; some rural areas have high unemployment rates because paying jobs are scarce and there is greater reliance on subsistence hunting and fishing.

In 2006, Alaska recorded a 0.1 percent decrease in unemployment, resulting in a total rate of 6.7 percent. Residents of other states hoping to find work in Alaska are strongly advised to make a visit and gauge job prospects for themselves. Consolidation in petroleum has largely meant an end to the state's fabled big-money oil jobs. In the populous Railbelt region between Seward and Fairbanks, job seekers will find housing, taxes and food costs more in line with prices in the West, a departure from just a few decades ago when Alaska prices were far higher.

State employment information is available from the Alaska Department of Labor, Alaska State Employment Service, P.O. Box 3-7000, Juneau 99802; www.jobs.state.ak.us. A Labor Department publication, *Alaska Economic Trends,* is an excellent monthly compilation of state workforce issues; look for it at http://almis.labor.state.ak.us.

ENERGY AND POWER When it comes to power use, Alaska can be divided into three major regions, each having similar energy patterns, problems and esources: the Extended Railbelt region, the Southeast region and the Bush region. The Extended Railbelt consists of major urban areas linked by the Alaska Railroad (Seward, Anchorage and Fairbanks). The southcentral area of this region uses relatively inexpensive natural gas from Cook Inlet and hydroelectric power plants for electrical production and heating. The Fairbanks–Tanana Valley area uses primarily coal and oil to meet its electrical needs. Future electrical demand for the Extended Railbelt region will be met by a combination of hydropower and coal- and gas-fired generators. The Southeast region relies on hydropower for much of its electrical generation. Most of the existing hydroelectric power projects in Alaska are located in the Southeast region. In the smaller communities, diesel generators are used.

The Bush region includes all communities that are remote from the major urban areas of the Extended Railbelt and Southeast regions. Electricity in Bush communities is typically provided by small diesel generators. Where wind projects are feasible, such as at Lolo Bay and Unalakleet, wind power can be a viable, fuel-saving alternative to diesel-powered generators. Bush residents rely heavily on heating oil. Wood and kerosene heaters are used to a limited extent. Natural gas is available in Barrow.

Skiing with Wolves

As Alan Kendall skied alone up the frozen Tanana River from Nenana to Fairbanks in April 2006, he was reveling at his good fortune of being in a beautiful wilderness setting at sunrise all by himself—or so he thought. Rounding a bend, Kendall, 57, saw what looked like a couple of dogs loping toward him.

As Kendall continued to ski, the number of animals increased to seven. By the time they numbered 10, he realized they were wolves trotting toward him. When the wolves spotted him, they froze in their tracks. Kendall knew he shouldn't turn his back on them. He had always read that wolves wouldn't attack humans, but standing there, alone and unarmed in the middle of a vast windswept, frozen river, those stories became meaningless.

After considering his limited options, Kendall charged toward the wolves as fast as he could, yelling at the top of his lungs. The animals immediately peeled off and ran into the woods, circling around behind Kendall. Kendall skied on, hard, constantly glancing over his shoulder. Though the wolves loped along behind him for a while, he had no further encounters with them.

—2006 *The Alaska Almanac*®

ESKIMO ICE CREAM
Also called *akutak* (the Yup'ik Eskimo word for Eskimo ice cream), this classic Native delicacy, popular throughout Alaska, is traditionally made of whipped berries, seal oil and freshly fallen snow. Sometimes shortening, raisins and sugar are added. Ingredients vary by region and may include whitefish. One recipe uses the soopalallie berry, *Shepherdia canadensis* (also called soapberry), a bitter species that forms a frothy mass like soapsuds when beaten.

Soapberry. From *Alaska Wild Berry Guide and Cookbook.*

EXPORTS
(SEE ALSO Economy) Alaska exports seafood, minerals, petroleum products, fertilizer, wood, precious metals and animal feed. Japan is Alaska's largest trading partner, buying nearly $1.1 billion in Alaskan exports last year. Alaska's other export markets include South Korea, Canada, China, Germany and, to a lesser extent, The Netherlands, Switzerland, Mexico, Singapore, Spain, Belgium and Hong Kong.

Alaska's exports totaled $4.0 billion in 2006, an increase of more than $453 million from 2005.

Seafood remained Alaska's largest export, topping $2 billion last year, and accounting for half of total exports. In 2006, $1.5 billion in seafood exports went to Asia, $461 million to Europe.

The current high prices of gold, silver and especially zinc have increased the profitability of existing mines and encouraged the development of future projects. In 2006, minerals were Alaska's second-highest international export, totaling $1.1 billion, a record high for the state.

Exports from the energy sector are now focused on refined petroleum products. Though Alaska no longer exports crude oil, this does not significantly affect the state's economy since prices are similar whether the oil goes overseas or to West Coast refineries. The value of Alaska's total energy exports dropped $72 million in 2006, a 21 percent decrease, for a total of $263 million. Fertilizer exports totaled $163 million, down 40 percent from 2006. Seafood, minerals, energy and fertilizer products accounted for nearly 88 percent of all international exports.

FAIRBANKS Nicknamed "The Golden Heart City," Fairbanks is located in Alaska's Interior, 200 miles south of the Arctic Circle and 100 miles north of Denali National Park and Preserve.

Long before European explorers and trappers came to the area, Athabascan Indians lived, fished and hunted in the Tanana Valley, site of the present-day city.

Fairbanks was founded through the misadventure of Ohio trader E. T. Barnette, who never intended to establish a town on the Chena River. Barnette and his $20,000 worth of trading goods had set out from St. Michael in late August 1901, bound to establish a trading post at the village of Tanacross, where the Valdez Trail crossed the Tanana River. After Barnette's own stern-wheeler was wrecked, he hired Charles Adams, part owner of the *Lavelle Young*, to take him to Tanacross. Once again Barnette ran into trouble when the 150-foot *Lavelle Young* could not ascend the Tanana past the sandy shallows called the Bates Rapids, a few miles above the mouth of the Chena River. In hopes that the Chena would meet up with the Tanana, Barnette persuaded Adams to carry him up the Chena until the boat ran into shallow water. Adams left Barnette, his party and his goods on the banks of the Chena River near what is now First Avenue and Cushman Street in Fairbanks.

Things were looking bleak for Barnette until Felix Pedro struck gold about 16 miles away on July 22, 1902. Barnette took this opportunity to expand his trading goods business and immediately dispatched Jujiro Wada, a Japanese employee, to Dawson City to spread the good news of a gold strike in the Tanana Valley. Soon the community became the new hub of the Alaska gold rush. A friend of Barnette's, Judge James Wickersham, suggested Fairbanks as the name for the new town, in honor of Indiana Sen. Charles Fairbanks. In exchange, Wickersham agreed to move the seat of the District Court from Eagle to Fairbanks, thus ensuring that the latter town would further flourish.

By 1908, Fairbanks was the largest, busiest city in the territory, boasting electric lights, city sewer, fire and police protection,

The "Unknown First Family" is a Fairbanks landmark. From *Fairbanks: Alaska's Heart of Gold* by Tricia Brown (text) and Roy Corral (photographs).

a courthouse and jail, a hospital, school, library and three newspapers.

Today Fairbanks is Alaska's second-largest city, home to 30,552 residents, and the service and supply center for Interior and Arctic industries. About 87,849 people live in the Fairbanks North Star Borough. Government, oil, mining, construction and tourism are important elements in the Fairbanks economy, as is Fort Wainwright, the first Army airfield in Alaska, and Eielson Air Force Base. The University of Alaska Fairbanks campus overlooks the city.

The bumper-sticker-of-the-year award in Interior Alaska goes to the driver whose car proclaimed: "Support Bacteria—they're the only culture in Fairbanks."

Summer temperatures average 59.5°F, often ranging into the 70s and 80s, with nearly 24 hours of daylight at the solstice (June 20 or 21), when a Midnight Sun Baseball Game is played after 10:30 P.M. with no artificial lighting. Winter temperatures range from 7.6°F to –19.2°F with the lowest-ever temperature recorded at –66°F in 1934. The winter snowfall averages 68.9 inches.

Winter attractions include the World Ice Art Championships, sled-dog races and northern lights viewing. Fairbanks is considered one of the best places on earth to view the northern lights. Summer activities include the Golden Days celebration, Tanana Valley Fair (the state's oldest) and the World Eskimo–Indian Olympics held annually in July. (See World Eskimo–Indian Olympics)

Pioneer Park is a 44-acre attraction featuring a gold rush town, historic buildings, food, small shops, entertainment and tours of the historic, dry-docked stern-wheeler, the SS *Nenana*.

Fairbanks also offers canoeing and kayaking, stern-wheeler riverboat tours, gold rush sites and dog mushing, and is a favorite jumping-off spot for the Alaska Railroad, Denali National Park and Preserve, Alaska's Interior and the Arctic.

For information, contact the Fairbanks Convention and Visitors Bureau, 550 First Ave., Fairbanks 99701-4790; (800) 327-5774 or (907) 456-5774; www.explorefairbanks.com.

FERRIES (See also Boating; Cruises) The Alaska Marine Highway System, within the state Department of Transportation and Public Facilities, provides year-round

NUGGETS

Fairbanks area electrical workers, stringing new power lines, were shocked to find a live moose suspended—fifty feet in the air—from a wire they were attempting to tighten. The moose was lowered to the ground, and then destroyed by Fish and Game officials who believed it most likely would not survive the stress of the ordeal.

—2005 *The Alaska Almanac*®

scheduled ferry service for passengers and vehicles to communities in Southeast and Southcentral Alaska and seasonal service in Southwestern Alaska. Twice-monthly sailings in the summer connect the Southeast ferry system with Southcentral, and regularly scheduled service is available between the Southcentral system and Kodiak, of the Southwestern system.

A fleet of seven ferries on the southeastern system connects Bellingham, Wash., and Prince Rupert, British Columbia, with the southeastern Alaska ports of Ketchikan, Metlakatla, Petersburg, Wrangell, Kake, Sitka, Angoon, Pelican, Hoonah, Tenakee Springs, Juneau, Haines and Skagway. These southeastern communities (with the exception of Haines and Skagway) are accessible only by boat, ferry or airplane. The seven vessels of the southeastern system are the *Lituya, Fairweather, Columbia, LeConte, Malaspina, Matanuska* and *Taku*.

The fast vehicle ferry, *Fairweather*, provides dayboat service between Juneau, Haines, Skagway and Sitka. The *LeConte* offers dayboat service to Juneau, Hoonah, Angoon, Tenakee and Haines.

Southwestern and Southcentral Alaska are served by four ferries. The *Tustumena* and the *Kennicott* serve Whittier, Port Lions, Kodiak, Homer and Seldovia, with limited summer service to Valdez, Chignik, False Pass, Akutan, Sand Point, King Cove, Cold Bay and Dutch Harbor. The *Aurora* and

Fairbanks' Tanana Valley State Fair has always taken the prize for its yearly themes, which have included "And the Beet Goes on" as well as "Lettuce Entertain You." The 1998 theme tops them all with "Strawberry Fields for Heifer."

the new *Chenega* provide service between Valdez and Cordova with summer service to Whittier and year-round whistle-stops at Chenega Bay and Tatitlek.

Scheduled state ferry service to southeastern Alaska began in 1963; ferry service to Kodiak Island began in 1964. The first three ferries of the Alaska ferry fleet were the *Malaspina, Matanuska* and *Taku.*

Reservations are required for all sailings. Rates for senior citizens and for passengers with disabilities are available. Contact the Alaska Marine Highway System, 6858 Glacier Highway, Juneau 99801-7909; (800) 642-0066; (907) 465-3941; www.ferryalaska.com; or read the *Marine Highway News,* published May 1.

Nautical Miles Between Ports

Southeastern System

Bellingham–Ketchikan	595
Prince Rupert–Ketchikan	91
Ketchikan–Metlakatla	16
Hollis–Petersburg	123
Hollis–Wrangell	100
Ketchikan–Wrangell	89
Wrangell–Petersburg	41
Petersburg–Kake	65
Kake–Sitka	115
Sitka–Angoon	67
Angoon–Tenakee	35
Tenakee–Hoonah	49
Angoon–Hoonah	63
Hoonah–Juneau (Auke Bay)	48
Sitka–Hoonah	115
Hoonah–Pelican via South Pass	64
Hoonah–Juneau	48
Haines–Skagway	13
Juneau (Auke Bay)–Haines	68
Petersburg–Juneau (Auke Bay)	123
Petersburg–Sitka	156
Juneau (Auke Bay)–Sitka	132
Juneau–Yakutat	234

Southwestern System

Cordova–Valdez	74
Valdez–Whittier	78
Kodiak–Port Lions	48
Kodiak–Homer	136
Homer–Seldovia	17
Kodiak–Sand Point via Sitkinak Strait	353
Yakutat–Valdez	286

Alaska State Ferry Boats

Aurora (235 feet, 14.5 knots): 300 passengers, 34 vehicles, no cabins. Began service in 1977.

Chenega (235 feet, 32 knots): 250 passengers, 36 vehicles, no cabins. Began service in 2005.

Columbia (418 feet, 17.3 knots): 499 passengers, 134 vehicles, 103 cabins. Began service in 1974.

Fairweather (235 feet, 32 knots): 250 passengers, 36 vehicles, no cabins. Began service in 2004.

Kennicott (382 feet, 16.75 knots): 499 passengers, 80 vehicles, 104 cabins. Began service in 1998.

LeConte (235 feet, 14.5 knots): 300 passengers, 34 vehicles, no cabins. Began service in 1974.

Lituya (180 feet, 12 knots): 149 passengers, 18 vehicles, no cabins. Began service in 2004.

Malaspina (408 feet, 16.5 knots): 499 passengers, 88 vehicles, 72 cabins. Began service in 1963 and was lengthened and renovated in 1972.

Matanuska (408 feet, 16.5 knots): 499 passengers, 88 vehicles, 105 cabins. Began service in 1963.

Taku (352 feet, 16.5 knots): 370 passengers, 69 vehicles, 42 cabins. Began service in 1963 and was renovated in 1981.

Tustumena (296 feet, 13.5 knots): 174 passengers, 36 vehicles, 29 cabins. Began service in 1964 and was renovated in 1969.

The ferry *Aurora*, and a commercial fishing boat. Alaska Division of Tourism.

Embarking Passengers and Vehicles on Alaska Mainline Ferries*

Southeastern System			Southwestern System		
Year	Passengers	Vehicles	Year	Passengers	Vehicles
1994	348,000	90,800	1994	48,500	15,200
1995	332,200	88,900	1995	45,400	15,100
1996	318,900	87,900	1996	46,100	14,800
1997	300,600	82,400	1997	49,400	15,800
1998	303,600	84,300	1998	48,300	16,500
1999	323,500	88,100	1999	45,500	17,000
2000	301,200	82,600	2000	50,000	17,500
2001	270,900	76,400	2001	48,400	17,600
2002	263,000	74,400	2002	51,400	18,000
2003	245,800	72,400	2003	52,100	18,600
2004	240,700	70,000	2004	50,000	18,600
2005	233,677	67,938	2005	48,509	18,580
2006	237,965	71,609	2006	69,255	25,461

* Numbers rounded off. Mainline ports for the Southeastern system are Bellingham, Prince Rupert, Ketchikan, Wrangell, Petersburg, Sitka, Juneau, Haines and Skagway. Mainline ports for the Southwestern system are Cordova, Valdez, Whittier, Homer, Seldovia, Kodiak and Port Lions.

FISHING

Commercial Fishing. Alaska's abundant and pristine fishing grounds have provided a harvest of more than 50 billion pounds of seafood over the last decade, accounting for nearly 52 percent of all domestically produced seafood. The staggering volume is almost four times more than the next-largest seafood-producing state. Commercial fishing's ripple effect is felt beyond the generations of coastal families that have made their living from the sea. Seafood is Alaska's largest export, representing more than half of Alaska's total exports.

Value and Volume of Alaska Fish and Shellfish Landings

Year	Value	Volume
1995	$1.40 billion	5.3 billion lbs.
1996	$1.19 billion	5.0 billion lbs.
1997	$1.22 billion	4.2 billion lbs.
1998	$1.18 billion*	5.1 billion lbs.*
1999	$1.21 billion	4.9 billion lbs.
2000	$883 million	4.5 billion lbs.
2001	$1.12 billion	5.0 billion lbs.
2002	$955 million	5.0 billion lbs.
2003	$1.1 billion	5.3 billion lbs.
2004	$1.2 billion	5.4 billion lbs
2005	$1.3 billion	5.4 billion lbs
2006	$1.3 billion	5.9 billion lbs

Sources: National Marine Fisheries Service, U.S. Department of Commerce; * Alaska Department of Fish and Game

The state's seafood industry is one of the most important private-sector industries in Alaska, both in terms of employment and income. More than 6 percent of the private-sector jobs rely on commercial fishing

NUGGETS

The Alaska Marine Highway System, an extraordinarily breathtaking 3,500-nautical-mile stretch of waterways traversed daily by Alaska's ferries, was designated as an All-American Road in the fall of 2005. The Federal Highway Administration award has been given to only 27 highways in the country, among them the Seward Highway in Southcentral Alaska.

—2006 The Alaska Almanac®

Anglers flock to the Kenai River for the challenge of king fishing. From *Alaska's Kenai Peninsula: A Traveler's Guide* by Andromeda Romano-Lax. Photo by Bill Sherwonit.

or seafood processing. In many small coastal and river towns, commercial fishing is the primary source of income. Cities and boroughs receive one-half of the state's fisheries business tax, an important element in many smaller communities' tax base.

The preliminary ex-vessel value of Alaska's commercial fisheries has remained constant over the last four years with nearly $1.3 billion in 2006, the second-highest value in the last 10 years. This increase was due in part to the continued increase in salmon and groundfish ex-vessel values.

Salmon. Five species of Pacific salmon inhabit Alaska waters and are commercially harvested: chinook (also known as king); coho (silver); pink (humpback); sockeye (red); and chum (dog) salmon.

The preliminary ex-vessel value of Alaska's commercial salmon harvest in 2006 was $309 million, down from $334 million in 2005. In 2006 the total catch of all these species of salmon was 142 million fish. The pink salmon harvest was the largest (73,348,000), followed by sockeye (41,860,000), chum (21,458,000), coho (4,263,000) and chinook (618,000).

Shellfish. Alaska's commercial shellfish harvest includes king crab, Dungeness crab, Tanner crab, snow crab, Korean hair crab, shrimp, scallops and clams.

The ex-vessel value of Alaska's crab industry declined in 2006, largely due to the Barents Sea crab impact on the domestic market and continued effects on the fishery from crab rationalization. The preliminary ex-vessel value of the state's shellfish harvest in 2006 was $148 million, down from $150 million in 2005. In contrast, the harvest in 1999 was worth $310 million.

Herring. Much of Alaska's commercial herring is harvested as sac roe, a longtime delicacy in Japan. The preliminary ex-vessel value of the 2006 sac roe fishery totaled more than $6 million, down from $11 million in 2005. In addition to sac roe, preliminary ex-vessel value for Alaska's herring spawn on kelp was $2.3 million in 2006. Relied on by the earliest Natives for food, herring are found in commercial quantities from Dixon Entrance in the southeast as far north as Norton Sound. Most of Alaska's commercial herring is harvested in the Togiak region of Bristol Bay. Traditional dried herring is still savored in some Bering Sea villages; Southeast Alaska Natives consume herring eggs.

Halibut. Alaska's commercial halibut harvest is federally regulated and runs from March 15 through November 15. A quota program imposed in 1995 limited the number of halibut permit holders and ended "derby style" fishing that had boats awaiting numerous openings of just 24 to 48 hours.

> In the last three years, the average amount of money Alaskan anglers have spent has risen from $150.80 to $213.00 *per fish caught!* The price of bribing a legislator is now less than 10 fish. Speakers and Presidents of the House or Senate, however, may run slightly higher.

Ex-vessel Value of Alaska's Commercial Fisheries
(in millions of dollars)

Species	1999	2000	2001	2002	2003	2004	2005*	2006*
Salmon	$383	$272	$229	$160	$210	$272	$334	$309
Shellfish	310	133	129	143	164	170	150	148
Halibut	145	112	121	129	171	175	169	164
Herring	17	7	14	12	12	15	15	6
Groundfish	503	323	632	553	560	565	660	760

* Preliminary figures

Source: Alaska Department of Fish and Game, www.cf.adfg.state.ak.us

2006 Final Commercial Salmon Harvest*
(in thousands of fish)

Region	King	Sockeye	Coho	Pink	Chum	Total
Southeast	355	1,330	2,054	11,650	13,931	29,320
Central (Prince William Sound, Cook Inlet)	51	4,962	884	24,160	2,565	32,621
AYK (Norton Sound/Kotzebue, Yukon, Kuskokwim)	71	149	421	1	510	1,151
Western (Kodiak, Chignik, Alaska Peninsula, Bristol Bay)	141	35,419	905	37,537	4,452	78,453
Total	618	41,860	4,264	73,348	21,458	141,548

* Preliminary figures

Figures may not total exactly or match figures from other summary tables due to rounding or differing methods of calculation.

Source: Alaska Department of Fish and Game, www.cf.adfg.state.ak.us

Halibut are targeted in three zones: the Bering Sea; Southeast Alaska; and the Gulf of Alaska, which accounts for most of the catch. The preliminary ex-vessel value in 2006 came to $164 million, down from $169 million in 2005.

Groundfish. Commercially harvested groundfish in Alaska include Pacific cod, rockfish, sablefish and walleye pollock. The largest of these fisheries is regulated by the National Marine Fisheries Service.

By far, the largest catch is pollock, much of it taken in the Bering Sea. Pollock is the mild white fish used to make fish sticks and fillets found in fast-food restaurants around the world. It's also used to make surimi, the fish paste that is fashioned into imitation crab and other products. The 2006 preliminary ex-vessel value of groundfish was $760 million, up from $660 million in 2005.

For more information on commercial fishing in Alaska, see the Department of Fish and Game's Web site: www.cf.adfg.state.ak.us.

Sportfishing. The Alaska Department of Fish and Game has established five regulatory zones, each with its own sportfishing rules. Anglers are advised to consult the Alaska Sport Fishing Regulations summary for areas they plan to fish at P.O. Box 5526, Juneau 99802-5526; www.sf.adfg.state.ak.us/statewide/reghome.cfm. The Alaska Department of Fish and Game advises that Emergency Orders always supersede published regulations. Anglers are urged to check the above Web site for any Emergency Orders before finalizing plans.

Regulations are grouped into these zones: Bristol Bay; Southcentral; Interior (Arctic, Yukon, Kuskokwim); Kodiak; Southeast.

Alaska State Record Trophy Fish

Species	Min. Wt.	Lbs./oz.	Year	Location	Angler
Arctic Char/					
Dolly Varden	10 lbs.	27/6	2002	Wulik River	Mike Curtiss
Brook Trout*	3 lbs.				
Burbot	8 lbs.	24/12	1976	Lake Louise	George R. Howard
Chum Salmon	15 lbs.	32/0	1985	Caamano Point	Frederick Thynes
Coho Salmon	20 lbs.	26/0	1976	Icy Strait	Andrew Robbins
Cutthroat Trout	3 lbs.	8/6	1977	Wilson Lake	Robert Denison
Grayling	3 lbs.	4/13	1981	Ugashik Narrows	Paul F. Kanitz
Halibut	250 lbs.	459/0	1996	Unalaska Bay	Jack Tragis
King Salmon (Kenai River)	**	97/4	1985	Kenai River	Lester Anderson
Lake Trout	20 lbs.	47/0	1970	Clarence Lake	Daniel Thorsness
Lingcod	55 lbs.	81/6	2002	Monty Island	Charles Curny
Northern Pike	15 lbs.	38/0	1991	Innoko River	Jack Wagner
Pink Salmon	8 lbs.	12/9	1974	Moose River	Steven A. Lee
Rainbow Trout/					
Steelhead	15 lbs.	42/3	1970	Bell Island	David White
Rockfish	18 lbs.	38/11	2001	Prince William Sound	
					Rosemary Roberts
Sheefish	30 lbs.	53/0	1986	Pah River	Lawrence E. Hudnall
Sockeye Salmon	12 lbs.	16/0	1974	Kenai River	Chuck Leach
Whitefish	4 lbs.	9/0	1989	Tozitna River	Al Mathews

* This species was added in 1995; no entries to date
** King salmon minimum weight for Kenai River is 75 lbs.; for rest of state, 50 lbs.
  Source: Alaska Department of Fish and Game Trophy Fish Program

Regulations. A sportfishing license is required for residents and nonresidents 16 years of age or older. Alaska residents age 60 or older who have been resident one year or more do not need a sportfishing license as long as they remain residents. A special identification card is issued for this exemption.

Anglers rarely fish all of Alaska in a lifetime; the state has more coastline than all of the Lower 48 states and millions of lakes. Alaska's salmon sportfishing is deservedly renowned, although some urban Alaska streams have seen reductions in recent years. Conservation-minded anglers should note that while many stocks of Pacific salmon are in trouble in other states, all five species found in Alaska are at healthy levels. In general, king salmon fishing occurs in spring and ends in mid-summer; sockeye, pink and chum seasons are next, followed by silver salmon in late summer and fall. Out-of-state anglers may call (907) 465-4180 for Alaska information.

Resident sportfishing licenses cost $24, valid for the calendar year issued (nonresident, $145; 1-day nonresident, $20; 3-day nonresident, $35; 7-day nonresident, $55; 14-day nonresident, $80). A resident is a person who, for the preceding 12 consecutive months, has maintained a home in Alaska, with the intent to stay, and who is

The Alaska Sportfishing Association newsletter contained the following offer for speakers: "We have participants who will offend meetings in Anchorage, Juneau and Fairbanks."

not claiming residency elsewhere. Military personnel on active duty permanently stationed in the state, and their dependents, can purchase a nonresident military sport-fishing license ($24).

An additional stamp is required for those wishing to fish for king salmon. Cost for residents is $10. Nonresidents may purchase a king stamp that's good for the calendar year for $100. Other options are: 1-day nonresident, $10; 3-day nonresident, $20; 7-day nonresident, $30; 14-day non-resident, $50; military, $20.

Nearly all sporting goods stores and many grocery stores in Alaska sell fishing licenses. They are also available by mail from the Alaska Department of Fish and Game, Licensing Section, P.O. Box 115525, Juneau 99811-5525; (907) 465-2376; www.admin.adfg.state.ak.us/license.

FISH WHEEL
The fish wheel is a handcrafted, wooden device fastened to a river bank, propelled by current, that floats on a log raft and scoops up fish heading upstream to spawn. Widely used for subsistence salmon fishing along stretches of Alaska's largest rivers during most of the past century, the fish wheel provides an efficient way of catching salmon. Non-Natives first introduced the fish wheel on the Tanana River in 1904. Soon after, it appeared on the Yukon River, where both settlers and Natives made use of fish wheels. It first appeared on the Kuskokwim in 1914, when prospectors introduced it for catching salmon near Georgetown.

Fish wheel on the Tanana River.
Photo by Ann Chandonnet.

Top Ten Trophy King Salmon

1. 97 lbs., 4 oz. (Kenai River, 1985)
2. 95 lbs., 10 oz. (Kenai River, 1990)
3. 92 lbs., 4 oz. (Kenai River, 1985)
4. 91 lbs., 10 oz. (Kenai River, 1988)
5. 91 lbs., 4 oz. (Kenai River, 1987)
6. 91 lbs. (Kenai River, 1995)
7. 90 lbs., 4 oz. (Kenai River, 1995)
8. 89 lbs., 4 oz. (Kenai River, 2002)
9. 89 lbs., 3 oz. (Kenai River, 1989)
10. 89 lbs., 1 oz. (Kenai River, 1995)

Source: Alaska Department of Fish and Game Trophy Fish Program

Fish wheels are currently used by Alaskan families to harvest subsistence salmon.

Today, subsistence fishing using fish wheels is allowed on the Upper Copper River, Kuskokwim River and the Yukon River, including the Tanana River and other tributaries. Fish wheels are only rarely used on the Kuskokwim River. On the upper Yukon River—the only river where both commercial and subsistence fishermen use fish wheels—up to 165 limited-entry permits are issued annually for use of fish wheels by commercial salmon fishermen; the upper Yukon area remained closed to all commercial fishing, including fish wheel use, in the 2000 and 2001 seasons due to poor salmon runs. Limited commercial fishing was allowed in 2002 through 2006.

Prior to its appearance in Alaska, the fish wheel was used on the East Coast, on the Sacramento River in California and on the Columbia River in Washington and Oregon.

Salmon in Lemon Sauce

1 red or silver salmon, filleted	1 tablespoon Worcestershire
1 stick butter	2 to 3 tablespoons chopped
Juice of 1 lemon	fresh or dried chives

Place salmon fillets on foil and put in shallow dish. Cover tightly and bake at 450°F until milk comes to top. (Or before you bake, measure the thickest point of the fillet and allow 10 minutes cooking time per inch.) Melt butter, add lemon juice, chives and Worcestershire. Remove cover from fish, pour on sauce and finish baking uncovered, basting occasionally with sauce.

—Belva Hamilton, Cooper Landing, *Cooking Alaskan*

FURS AND TRAPPING

The major sources of harvested Alaska furs are the Yukon and Kuskokwim River Valleys.

The Arctic provides limited numbers of arctic fox, wolverine and wolf but the Gulf Coast areas and Southeast are more productive. Southeast Alaska is a good source of mink and otter.

Trapping is seasonal work, and most trappers work summers at fishing or other employment. Licenses are required for trapping. (SEE Hunting for license fees.) State-regulated furbearers are beaver, coyote, arctic fox (includes white or blue), red fox (includes cross, black or silver color phases), lynx, marmot, marten, mink, muskrat, river (land) otter, squirrel (parka or ground, flying and red), weasel, wolf and wolverine. Very little harvest or use is made of parka squirrels and marmots.

Prices for raw skins are widely variable and depend on the buyer, quality, condition and size of the fur. Pelts accepted for purchase are beaver, coyote, lynx, marten, mink, muskrat, otter, red and white fox, red squirrel, weasel (ermine), wolf and wolverine.

GEOGRAPHY (SEE map, pages 6–7. SEE ALSO Glaciers and Ice Fields; Lakes; Mountains; Populations and Zip Codes; Regions of Alaska; Rivers)

State capital: Juneau.
State population: 670,053.
Land area: 570,374 square miles, or about 365 million acres—largest state in the Union; one-fifth the size of the Lower 48. Alaska is larger than the three next largest states combined.

Area per person: About 0.9 square mile.
Diameter: East to west 2,400 miles; north to south 1,420 miles.
Coastline: 6,640 miles, point to point; as measured on the most detailed maps available, including islands, Alaska has 33,904 miles of shoreline—twice the length of the Lower 48. Estimated tidal shoreline, including islands, inlets and shoreline to head of tidewater, is 47,300 miles.
Adjacent salt water: North Pacific Ocean, Bering Sea, Chukchi Sea, Arctic Ocean.
Alaska–Canada border: 1,538 miles long: length of boundary between the Arctic Ocean and Mount St. Elias,

In March 2007, the Alaska Board of Game opened portions of Chugach State Park to trapping of wolverines even though biologists reported that there might only be 11 to 23 of the animals in the entire park. One Board member justified his vote by saying that wolverines have no value as "viewable wildlife" because they are so rare that no one ever sees them anyway.

647 miles; Southeast border with British Columbia and Yukon Territory, 710 miles; water boundary, 181 miles.

Geographic center: 63°50' north, 152° west, about 60 miles northwest of Mount McKinley.

Northernmost point: Point Barrow, 71°23' north.

Southernmost point: Tip of Amatignak Island, Aleutian Chain, 51°15' north.

Easternmost and westernmost points: It all depends on how you look at it. The 180th meridian—halfway around the world from the prime meridian at Greenwich, England, and the dividing line between east and west longitudes— passes through Alaska. According to one view, Alaska has both the easternmost and westernmost spots in the country!

The westernmost is Amatignak Island, 179°06' west; and the easternmost, Pochnoi Point, 179°46' east. But on the other hand, if you are facing north, east is to your right and west to your left. Therefore, the westernmost point in Alaska is Cape Wrangell, Attu Island, 172°27' east; and the easternmost point in Alaska is near Camp Point, in southeastern Alaska, 129°59' east.

Tallest mountain: Mount McKinley, 20,320 feet, and the tallest mountain in North America. Alaska has 39 mountain ranges, containing 17 of the 20 highest peaks in the United States.

Largest natural freshwater lake: Iliamna, 1,150 square miles. Alaska has at least 2 million lakes that are 20 acres (or larger) in size.

Longest river: Yukon, 1,875 miles in Alaska; 2,298 total. There are more than 3,000 rivers in the state. The Yukon River ranks third in length of U.S. rivers, behind the Mississippi and Missouri Rivers.

Largest island: Kodiak, in the Gulf of Alaska, 3,588 square miles. There are 1,800 named islands in the state, 1,000 of which are located in Southeast Alaska.

Largest city in population: Anchorage, population 282,813.

Largest city in area: Sitka, with 4,710 square miles, 1,816 square miles of which is water. Juneau is second, with 3,108 square miles.

GLACIERS AND ICE FIELDS

The greatest concentrations of glaciers are in the Alaska Range, Wrangell Mountains and the coastal ranges of the Chugach, Coast, Kenai and St. Elias mountains, where annual precipitation is high. All of Alaska's well-known glaciers fall within these areas. The distribution of glacier ice is shown on the map on page 79.

Glaciers cover approximately 29,000 square miles—or 3 percent—of Alaska, which is 128 times more area covered by glaciers than in the rest of the United States. There are an estimated 100,000 glaciers in Alaska, ranging from tiny cirque glaciers to huge valley glaciers.

Glaciers are formed over a number of years at elevations where more snow falls than melts. Alaska's glaciers fall roughly into five general categories: alpine, valley, piedmont, ice fields and ice caps. Alpine (mountain and cirque) glaciers head high on the slopes of mountains and plateaus. Valley glaciers are an overflowing accumulation of ice from mountain or plateau basins. Piedmont glaciers result when one or more glaciers join to form a fan-shaped ice mass at the foot of a mountain range. Ice fields develop when large valley glaciers interconnect, leaving only the highest peaks and ridges to rise above the ice surface. Ice caps are smaller glaciers perched on plateaus.

Alaska's better-known glaciers accessible by road are Worthington (Richardson Highway), Matanuska (Glenn Highway), Exit (Seward Highway), Portage (Seward Highway) and Mendenhall (Glacier Highway). In addition, Childs and Sheridan Glaciers may be reached by car

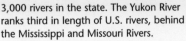

The menu of the Easy Street Café in Bowling Green, Ohio, lists a Friday special of "Alaskan Walleye." The last time we checked, there wasn't a Walleye within 1,000 miles of here, but there's no such thing as bad publicity.

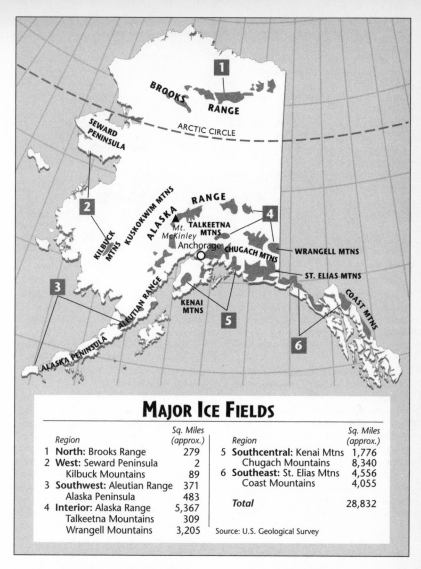

Major Ice Fields

Region	Sq. Miles (approx.)	Region	Sq. Miles (approx.)
1 **North:** Brooks Range	279	5 **Southcentral:** Kenai Mtns	1,776
2 **West:** Seward Peninsula	2	Chugach Mountains	8,340
Kilbuck Mountains	89	6 **Southeast:** St. Elias Mtns	4,556
3 **Southwest:** Aleutian Range	371	Coast Mountains	4,055
Alaska Peninsula	483		
4 **Interior:** Alaska Range	5,367	**Total**	28,832
Talkeetna Mountains	309		
Wrangell Mountains	3,205	Source: U.S. Geological Survey	

from Cordova, and Valdez Glacier is also accessible by car and only a few miles from the town of Valdez. The sediment-covered terminus of Muldrow Glacier in Denali National Park and Preserve is visible at a distance along several miles of the park road.

Many spectacular glaciers in Glacier Bay National Park and Preserve, in Kenai Fjords and in Prince William Sound are visible from tour boats or by flightseeing.

Some glacier facts:

• Glacier ice often appears blue to the eye because it absorbs all the colors of the spectrum except blue, which is scattered back.

• About three-fourths of all the freshwater in Alaska is stored as glacial ice. This is many times greater than the volume of water stored in all the state's lakes, ponds, rivers and reservoirs.

• Longest tidewater glacier in North America is Hubbard, 76 miles long (heads

The Matanuska Glacier is visible from the Richardson Highway. Photo by Tricia Brown.

in Canada). In 1986, the Hubbard rapidly advanced and blocked Russell Fiord near Yakutat. Later in the year, the ice dam gave way. In July of 2002, the glacier again advanced, blocking Russell Fiord until Aug. 14.

• Longest glacier in Alaska is Bering (including Bagley Icefield), more than 100 miles long.

• Southernmost active tidewater glacier in North America is LeConte.

• Greatest concentration of tidewater-calving glaciers is in Prince William Sound, with 20 active tidewater glaciers.

• Largest piedmont lobe glacier is Malaspina, 850 square miles; the Malaspina Glacier complex (including tributary glaciers) is approximately 2,000 square miles in area.

• The largest glacier is the Bering Glacier complex, about 2,250 square miles in size, which includes Bagley Icefield.

• La Perouse Glacier in Glacier Bay National Park is the only calving glacier in North America that discharges icebergs directly into the open Pacific Ocean.

• There are more than 750 glacier-dammed lakes in Alaska; the largest at present is 28-square-mile Chakachamna Lake west of Anchorage.

• Variegated Glacier, at Russell Fiord in Yakutat Bay, is the most studied glacier in the world. The glacier, which extends

10 miles from its head to its foot, surprised scientists in 1995 by surging (a rise in forward movement) four years ahead of schedule. By the end of summer 1995, the glacier had moved hundreds of yards. Scientists attribute the surge to the movement of water beneath the glacier rather than climatic conditions.

GOLD (See also Gold Strikes and Rushes; Minerals and Mining) The largest gold nugget ever found in Alaska was discovered in the summer of 1998. The nugget, weighing 294 troy ounces (24.5 pounds), was found in the Ruby District of Northern Alaska.

The second-largest nugget, weighing 155 troy ounces (12.9 pounds), was found Sept. 29, 1903, at the Discovery Claim on Anvil Creek, Nome District. The nugget was 7 inches long, 4 inches wide and 2 inches thick.

Four other large nuggets have been found in Alaska, one of which also came from the Discovery Claim on Anvil Creek in 1899. It was the largest Alaska nugget found up to that time, weighing 82.1 troy ounces, and was 6¼ inches long, 3¼ inches wide, ⅜ inch thick at one end and ½ inch thick at the other.

In 1914 the third-largest nugget mined, weighing 138.4 troy ounces, was found near the Discovery Claim of Hammond River in the Koyukuk–Nolan District.

Three of the top five nuggets have been discovered since 1984, including one from Lower Glacier Creek, Kantishna District, in 1984, weighing 91.8 troy ounces, and the other from Ganes Creek, Innoko District, in 1986, weighing 122 troy ounces. In 2003, a miner found a 40.9 troy ounce nugget on his placer mining claim near Nome.

If you are interested in gold panning, sluicing or suction dredging in Alaska—for fun or profit—you'll have to know whose land you are on and familiarize yourself with current regulations.

Panning, sluicing and suction dredging on private property, established mining claims and Native lands is considered trespassing unless you have the consent of the owner. On state and federal lands, contact the managing agency for current restrictions on mining. On Native-owned lands, contact the tribal council of the village or the Native corporation well in advance of your visit. (SEE Native Regional Corporations on page 157.)

You can pan for gold for a small fee by visiting one of the gold-panning attractions in Alaska. Commercial resorts rent gold pans and let you try your luck on gold-bearing creeks and streams on their property. If you want to stake a mining claim, call the Department of Natural Resources in Anchorage, (907) 269-8400, or Fairbanks, (907) 451-2705, for further information. A general government source for information about mining claims and property in Alaska is www.dnr.state.ak.us.

Gold lured thousands to the Northland in the last century but precious few got rich.
From *The World-Famous Alaska Highway* by Tricia Brown.

The following chart shows the fluctuation in the price of gold (1994–2006) after the gold standard was lifted in 1967. These are average annual prices and do not reflect the yearly high or low prices.

Average Annual Price of Gold, per Troy Ounce

1934 to 1967	$ 35.00
1994	$386.00
1995	$395.00
1996	$387.60
1997	$330.76
1998	$293.88
1999	$278.70
2000	$279.10
2001	$271.04
2002	$310.06
2003	$363.58
2004	$409.72
2005	$444.74
2006	$603.46

Source: Alaska Division of Geological and Geophysical Survey's annual *Alaska Mineral Industry* reports

Gold Production in Alaska, 1995–2006

Year	Vol. (in troy oz.)	Value
1995	141,882	$56.0 million
1996	161,565	$62.6 million
1997	590,516	$207.3 million
1998	594,111	$174.6 million
1999	509,000	$144.9 million
2000	551,982	$154.0 million
2001	550,644	$149.2 million
2002	562,094	$174.3 million
2003	528,191	$191.9 million
2004	456,508	$192.3 million
2005	427,031	$189.9 million
2006	574,818*	$336.1 million

* Preliminary

GOLD STRIKES AND RUSHES

1848—First Alaska gold discovery at Russian River on Kenai Peninsula

1861—Stikine River near Telegraph Creek, British Columbia; Wrangell

1872—Cassiar district in Canada (Stikine headwaters country)

1872—Near Sitka

1874—Windham Bay near Juneau

1880—Gold Creek at Juneau
1886—Fortymile discovery
1887—Yakutat areas and Lituya Bay
1893—Mastodon Creek, starting in Circle City
1895—Sunrise district on the Kenai Peninsula
1896—Klondike strike, Bonanza Creek, Yukon Territory, Canada
1896—Council (Seward Peninsula)
1898—Anvil Creek near Nome; Atlin district
1898—Hope and Sunrise on Turnagain Arm

1898—British Columbia
1899—Nome beaches
1900—Porcupine rush out of Haines
1902—Fairbanks (Felix Pedro, Upper Goldstream Valley)
1905—Kantishna Hills
1906—Innoko
1907—Ruby
1908—Iditarod
1913—Chisana
1913—Marshall
1914—Livengood

Sourdough Marriage Contract

Ten miles from the Yukon
On the banks of this lake
A partner to Koyukuk
McGillis, I take;
We have no preacher –
We have no ring –
It makes no difference
It's all the same thing.
AGGIE DALTON

I swear by my Gee-pole,
Under this tree
A faithful husband to Aggie
I always will be;
I'll love and protect her
This maiden so frail,
From the Sourdough bums
On the Koyukuk Trail.
FRANK McGILLIS

For two dollars apiece
In "cheechako" money
I unite this couple
In matrimony;
He be a rancher
She be a teacher
I do up the job
Just as well as a preacher.
FRENCH JOE

—From Ruth Allman's *Alaska Sourdough*, first published by Alaska Northwest Books® in 1976. This message was carved on a birch tree during one of the early Alaskan gold stampedes.

GOLF The Municipality of Anchorage maintains two golf courses—the Anchorage Golf Course on O'Malley Road, an 18-hole all-grass course offering views of the Chugach Range, the city and, on a clear day, Mount McKinley; and a 9-hole course (artificial turf greens) at Russian Jack Springs located at Boniface Parkway and Debarr Road. Another option, Tanglewood Lakes Golf Club, offers a 9-hole all-grass course.

Two military courses are open to the public—Eagle Glen Golf Course (18 holes) at Elmendorf Air Force Base, and the 18-hole Moose Run Golf Course (the oldest golf course in Alaska) at Fort Richardson.

Palmer Municipal Golf Course (18 holes) has a driving range, clubhouse and rental clubs and carts.

Fairbanks offers the 9-hole Fairbanks Golf and Country Club west of the downtown area, the 9-hole Chena Bend Golf Course at Fort Wainwright, and North Star Golf Club at 4.5 Mile Steese Highway, north of Fairbanks.

Mendenhall Golf Course in Juneau (9 holes) has a driving range, rental clubs and glacier views.

Every March, Kodiak holds the Pillar Mountain Golf Classic, an irreverent par-70, 1-hole match up the side of 1,400-foot Pillar Mountain.

Muskeg Meadows, opened in 1998 in Wrangell, is a 9-hole, 36-acre regulation course and driving range. A tournament is held there annually in April.

During the summer months, golfers in Fairbanks may tee off 24 hours a day.

Die-hard golfers play in the winter using brightly painted balls. At the annual Lake Louise winter game in Wasilla, played on lake ice, golfers use orange balls that are highly visible on the snow and ice. Nome hosts the Bering Sea Ice Classic Golf Tournament in March and additional golf tournaments in September.

Alaska's northernmost golf course is in Coldfoot, featuring three holes, a driving range and rental clubs. Herds of musk oxen are allowed to "play through."

Other golf courses can be found throughout the state, including Birch Ridge in Soldotna and Settlers Bay in Knik. An occasional private campground will offer putting greens or mini-golf for guests.

GOVERNMENT (SEE ALSO Courts; Government Officials) Alaska is represented in the U.S. Congress by two senators and one representative. The capital of Alaska is Juneau.

A governor and lieutenant governor are elected by popular vote for four-year terms on the same ticket. The governor is given extensive powers under the constitution, overseeing 15 major departments: Administration, Commerce and Economic Development, Community and Regional Affairs, Corrections, Education, Environmental Conservation, Fish and Game, Health and Social Services, Labor, Law, Military and Veterans Affairs, Natural Resources, Public Safety, Revenue and Transportation and Public Facilities.

The Legislature is bicameral, with 20 senators elected from a total of 20 senate districts for 4-year terms, and 40 representatives from 27 election districts for 2-year terms. Under the state constitution, redistricting is done every 10 years, after the reporting of the decennial federal census. The judiciary consists of a state supreme court, court of appeals, superior court, district courts and magistrates.

Alaska is unique among the 50 states in not having most of its land mass organized into political subdivisions equivalent to the county form of government. Local government is by a system of organized boroughs, much like counties in other states. Several areas of the state are not included in any borough because of sparse population. Boroughs generally provide a more limited number of services than cities.

There are two classes of boroughs. First- and second-class boroughs have three mandatory powers: education, land use planning and tax assessment and collection. The major difference between the two classes is in how they may acquire other powers. Both classes have separately elected borough assemblies and school boards. All boroughs may assess, levy and collect

Governor Sarah Palin.
Photo by Jeff Schultz.

83

real and personal property taxes. They may also levy sales taxes.

Incorporated cities are small units of local government, serving one community. There are two classes. First-class cities, generally urban areas, have six-member councils and a separately elected mayor. Taxing authority is somewhat broader than for second-class cities and responsibilities are broader. A first-class city that has adopted a home rule charter is called a home rule city; adoption allows the city to revise its ordinances within lawful limits. Second-class cities, generally places with fewer than 400 people, are governed by a seven-member council, one of whom serves as mayor. Taxing authority is limited. A borough and all cities located within it may unite in a single unit of government called a unified municipality.

There are 246 federally recognized tribal governments in Alaska and one community (Metlakatla, originally an Indian reservation) organized under federal law.

In 2007, there were 16 organized boroughs: 3 unified home-rule boroughs (unified municipalities), 6 non-unified home rule boroughs and 7 second-class boroughs.

Alaska's 149 incorporated cities include 12 home-rule cities, 20 first-class cities and 116 second-class cities.

Alaska's Boroughs

Aleutians East Borough, P.O. Box 349, Sand Point 99661; (907) 383-2699; fax (907) 383-3496; www.aleutianseast.org.

> A proud club member gave us a copy of the Palmer Kiwanis Club newsletter dated August 1978. The epistle stated, "Recently the Palmer police were called to investigate a dope ring. It turned out to be six politicians standing in a circle." Time marches on, but politics remains the same.

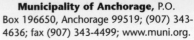

Municipality of Anchorage, P.O. Box 196650, Anchorage 99519; (907) 343-4636; fax (907) 343-4499; www.muni.org.

Bristol Bay Borough, P.O. Box 189, Naknek 99633; (907) 246-4224; fax (907) 246-6633; www.theborough.com.

Denali Borough, P.O. Box 480, Healy 99743; (907) 683-1330; fax (907) 683-1340; www.denaliborough.govoffice.com.

Fairbanks North Star Borough, P.O. Box 71267, Fairbanks, 99707; (907) 459-1000; fax (907) 459-1102; www.co.fairbanks.ak.us.

Haines Borough, P.O. Box 1209, Haines, AK 99827; (907) 766-2231; fax (907) 766-2716; www.hainesborough.us.

City and Borough of Juneau, 155 S. Seward St., Juneau 99801; (907) 586-5240; fax (907) 586-5385; www.juneau.org.

Kenai Peninsula Borough, 144 North Binkley St., Soldotna, AK 99669; (800) 478-4441, (907) 262-4441; fax (907) 262-1892; www.borough.kenai.ak.us.

Ketchikan Gateway Borough, 344 Front St., Ketchikan, 99901; (907) 228-6625; fax (907) 247-6625; www.borough.ketchikan.ak.us.

Kodiak Island Borough, 710 Mill Bay Road, Kodiak 99615; (907) 486-9301; fax (907) 486-9374; www.kodiakak.us.

Lake and Peninsula Borough, P.O. Box 495, King Salmon 99613; (800) 764-3421, (907) 246-3421; fax (907) 246-6602; www.lakeandpen.com.

Matanuska–Susitna Borough, 350 E. Dahlia Ave., Palmer 99645; (907) 745-4801; fax (907) 745-9845; www.co.mat-su.ak.us.

North Slope Borough, P.O. Box 69, Barrow 99723; (907) 852-2611; fax (907) 852-5989; www.co.north-slope.ak.us.

Northwest Arctic Borough, P.O. Box 1110, Kotzebue 99752; (800) 478-1110, (907) 442-2500; fax (907) 442-2930; www.nwabor.org.

City and Borough of Sitka, 100 Lincoln St., Sitka 99835; (907) 747-3294; fax (907) 747-7403; www.cityofsitka.com.

City and Borough of Yakutat, P.O. Box 160, Yakutat 99689; (907) 784-3323, fax (907) 784-3281; www.yakutatak.govoffice2.com.

GOVERNMENT OFFICIALS

Russian Alaska

Emperor Paul of Russia granted the Russian-American Company an exclusive trade charter in Alaska.

Chief Manager	Dates Served
Alexander Andreyevich Baranov	1799–1818
Leonti Andreanovich Hagemeiste	January–October 1818
Semen Ivanovich Yanovski	1818–1820
Matxei I. Muravief	1820–1825
Peter Egorovich Chistiakov	1825–1830
Baron Ferdinand P. von Wrangell	1830–1835
Ivan Antonovich Kupreanof	1835–1840
Adolph Karlovich Etolin	1840–1845
Michael D. Tebenkof	1845–1850
Nikolai Y. Rosenberg	1850–1853
Alexander Ilich Rudakof	1853–1854
Stephen Vasili Voevodski	1854–1859
Ivan V. Furuhelm	1859–1863
Prince Dmitri Maksoutoff	1863–1867

Territory of Alaska

The United States purchased Alaska from Russia in 1867; U.S. Army was given jurisdiction over Department of Alaska.

Army Commanding Officers	Dates Served
Bvt. Maj. Gen. Jefferson C. Davis	Oct. 18, 1867–Aug. 31, 1870
Bvt. Lt. Col. George K. Brady	Sept. 1, 1870–Sept. 22, 1870
Maj. John C. Tidball	Sept. 23, 1870–Sept. 19, 1871
Maj. Harvey A. Allen	Sept. 20, 1871–Jan. 3, 1873
Maj. Joseph Stewart	Jan. 4, 1873–April 20, 1874
Capt. George R. Rodney	April 21, 1874–Aug. 16, 1874
Capt. Joseph B. Campbell	Aug. 17, 1874–June 14, 1876
Capt. John Mendenhall	June 15, 1876–March 4, 1877
Capt. Arthur Morris	March 5, 1877–June 14, 1877

U.S. Army troops left Alaska in 1877; the highest-ranking federal official left in Alaska was the U.S. collector of customs. The Department of Alaska was put under control of the U.S. Treasury Department.

U.S. Collectors of Customs	Dates Served
Montgomery P. Berry	June 14, 1877–Aug. 13, 1877
H. C. DeAhna	Aug. 14, 1877–March 26, 1878
Mottrom D. Ball	March 27, 1878–June 13, 1879

In 1879 the U.S. Navy was given jurisdiction over the Department of Alaska.

Navy Commanding Officers	Dates Served
Capt. L. A. Beardslee	June 14, 1879–Sept. 12, 1880
Comdr. Henry Glass	Sept. 13, 1880–Aug. 9, 1881
Comdr. Edward Lull	Aug. 10, 1881–Oct. 18, 1881
Comdr. Henry Glass	Oct. 19, 1881–March 12, 1882

```
Comdr. Frederick Pearson ............................ March 13, 1882–Oct. 3, 1882
Comdr. Edgar C. Merriman ........................... Oct. 4, 1882–Sept. 13, 1883
Comdr. Joseph B. Coghlan .......................... Sept. 15, 1883–Sept. 13, 1884
Lt. Comdr. Henry E. Nichols ........................ Sept. 14, 1884–Sept. 15, 1884
```

Congress provided civil government for the new District of Alaska in 1884; on Aug. 24, 1912, territorial status was given to Alaska. The U.S. president appointed territorial governors.

Presidential Appointment	Dates Served
John H. Kinkead (President Arthur)	July 4, 1884–May 7, 1885
Alfred P. Swineford (President Cleveland)	May 7, 1885–April 20, 1889
Lyman E. Knapp (President Harrison)	April 20, 1889–June 18, 1893
James Sheakley (President Cleveland)	June 18, 1893–June 23, 1897
John G. Brady (President McKinley)	June 23, 1897–March 2, 1906
Wilford B. Hoggatt (President Theodore Roosevelt)	March 2, 1906–May 20, 1909
Walter E. Clark (President Taft)	May 20, 1909–April 18, 1913
John F.A. Strong (President Wilson)	April 18, 1913–April 12, 1918
Thomas Riggs Jr. (President Wilson)	April 12, 1918–June 16, 1921
Scott C. Bone (President Harding)	June 16, 1921–Aug. 16, 1925
George A. Parks (President Coolidge)	Aug. 16, 1925–April 19, 1933
John W. Troy (President Franklin Roosevelt)	April 19, 1933–Dec. 6, 1939
Ernest Gruening (President Franklin Roosevelt)	Dec. 6, 1939–April 10, 1953
B. Frank Heintzleman (President Eisenhower)	April 10, 1953–Jan. 3, 1957
Mike Stepovich (President Eisenhower)	April 8, 1957–Aug. 9, 1958

In 1906, Congress authorized Alaska to send a voteless delegate to the House of Representatives.

Delegate to Congress	Dates Served
Frank H. Waskey	1906–1907
Thomas Cale	1907–1909
James Wickersham	1909–1917
Charles A. Sulzer	1917–contested election
James Wickersham	1918, seated as delegate
Charles A. Sulzer	1919, elected; died before taking office
George Grigsby	1919, elected in a special election
James Wickersham	1921, seated as delegate, having contested election of Grigsby
Dan A. Sutherland	1921–1930
James Wickersham	1931–1933
J. Dimond	1933–1944
E. L. Bartlett	1944–1958

Alaska sent unofficial delegates to Congress to promote statehood, elected under a plan first devised by Tennessee. The Tennessee Plan delegates were not seated by Congress but did serve as lobbyists.

Senator	Dates Served
William Egan	1956–1958
Ernest Gruening	1956–1958

Representative	Dates Served
Ralph Rivers	1956–1958

State of Alaska

Alaska became a state Jan. 3, 1959, and sent two senators and one representative to the U.S. Congress.

Governor	Dates Served
William A. Egan	Jan. 3, 1959–Dec. 5, 1966
Walter J. Hickel*	Dec. 5, 1966–Jan. 29, 1969
Keith H. Miller*	Jan. 29, 1969–Dec. 7, 1970
William A. Egan	Dec. 7, 1970–Dec. 2, 1974
Jay S. Hammond	Dec. 2, 1974–Dec. 6, 1982
Bill Sheffield	Dec. 6, 1982–Dec. 1, 1986
Steve Cowper	Dec. 1, 1986–Dec. 3, 1990
Walter J. Hickel	Dec. 3, 1990–Dec. 5, 1994
Tony Knowles	Dec. 5, 1994–Dec. 2, 2002
Frank Murkowski	Dec. 2, 2002–Dec. 4, 2006
Sarah Palin	Dec. 4, 2006–

*Hickel resigned before completing his first full term as governor to accept the position of secretary of the interior. He was succeeded by Miller.

Addresses

Gov. Sarah Palin, Office of the Governor, P.O. Box 110001, Juneau 99811-0001; www.gov.state.ak.us.

Lt. Gov. Sean Parnell, Office of the Lieutenant Governor, P.O. Box 110015, Juneau 99811-0015; www.gov.state.ak.us/ltgov.

U.S. Congressional Delegation

Senator	Dates Served
E. L. Bartlett	1958–1968
Ernest Gruening	1958–1968
Mike Gravel	1968–1980
Ted Stevens	1968–
Frank H. Murkowski	1980–2002
Lisa Murkowski	2003–

Representative	Dates Served
Ralph Rivers	1958–1966
Howard Pollock	1966–1970
Nicholas Begich	1970–1972
Donald E. Young	1972–

Addresses

Sen. Ted Stevens, U.S. Senate, 522 Hart Senate Office Bldg., Washington, D.C. 20510-0201; (202) 224-3004; fax (907) 224-2354; stevens.senate.gov.

Sen. Lisa Murkowski, U.S. Senate, 709 Hart Senate Office Bldg., Washington, D.C. 20510-0202; (202) 224-6665; fax (202) 224-5301; murkowski.senate.gov.

Rep. Donald E. Young, House of Representatives, 2111 Rayburn House Office Bldg., Washington, D.C. 20515-0201; (202) 225-5765; fax (202) 225-0425; http://donyoung.house.gov.

Alaska State Legislature

During sessions, members of the legislature receive mail at the State Capitol, Juneau 99801-1182. Direct e-mail to a specific legislator by typing Senator OR Representative_First name_Lastname@legis.state.ak.us. The legislature's Web site is www.legis.state.ak.us.

House of Representatives

District 1: Kyle Johansen (R)
District 2: Peggy Wilson (R)
District 3: Beth Kerttula (D)
District 4: Andrea Doll (D)
District 5: Bill Thomas Jr. (R)
District 6: Woodie Salmon (D)
District 7: Mike Kelly (R)
District 8: David Guttenberg (D)
District 9: Scott Kawasaki (D)
District 10: Jay Ramras (R)
District 11: John Coghill Jr. (R)
District 12: John Harris (R)

District 13: Carl Gatto (R)
District 14: Vic Kohring* (R)
District 15: Mark Neuman (R)
District 16: Bill Stoltze (R)
District 17: Anna Fairclough (R)
District 18: Nancy Dahlstrom (R)
District 19: Bob Roses (R)
District 20: Max Gruenberg (D)
District 21: Harry Crawford (D)
District 22: Sharon Cissna (D)
District 23: Les Gara (D)
District 24: Berta Gardner (D)
District 25: Mike Doogan (D)
District 26: Lindsey Holmes (D)
District 27: Bob Buch (D)
District 28: Craig Johnson (R)
District 29: Ralph Samuels (R)
District 30: Kevin Meyer (R)
District 31: Bob Lynn (R)
District 32: Mike Hawker (R)
District 33: Kurt Olson (R)
District 34: Mike Chenault (R)
District 35: Paul Seaton (R)
District 36: Gabrielle LeDoux (R)
District 37: Bryce Edgmon (D)
District 38: Mary Nelson (D)
District 39: Richard Foster (D)
District 40: Reggie Joule (D)
*Vic Kohring resigned in June 2007

Alaska Senate

District A: Bert Stedman (R)
District B: Kim Elton (D)
District C: Albert Kookesh (D)
District D: Joe Thomas (D)
District E: Gary Wilken (R)
District F: Gene Therriault (R)
District G: Lyda Green (R)
District H: Charlie Huggins (R)
District I: Fred Dyson (R)
District J: Bill Wielechowski (D)
District K: Bettye Davis (D)
District L: Johnny Ellis (D)
District M: Hollis French (D)
District N: Lesil McGuire (R)
District O: John Cowdery (R)
District P: Con Bunde (R)
District Q: Thomas Wagoner (R)
District R: Gary Stevens (R)
District S: Lyman Hoffman (D)
District T: Donald Olson (D)

HIGHWAYS (SEE ALSO Alaska Highway; Dalton Highway) As of December 2005, the state Department of Transportation and Public Facilities estimated total public road mileage in Alaska at 14,788 center-line miles. This total includes state, borough, city and federal roads that are open to

Major Highways in Alaska

Route/ Highway	Number	Year Opened	Total Length (miles) in Alaska		
			Paved	Gravel	Open
Alaska*	2	1942	198		All year
Copper River**	10		12	38	Apr.–Oct.
Dalton	11	1974	93	321	All year
Denali	8	1957	21.4	113	Apr.–Oct.
Edgerton	10	1923	33		All year
Elliott	2	1959	30	122	All year
George Parks	3	1971	324		All year
Haines*	7	1947	44		All year
Klondike*	2	1978	15		All year
Richardson	4	1923	363		All year
Seward/Glenn	9&1	1951	305		All year
Steese	6	1928	44	112	All year
Sterling	1	1950	138		All year
Taylor	5	1953	23	135	Apr.–Oct.
Tok Cutoff	1	1940	122		All year

 * Most of the highway lies within Canada.

** Construction of the Copper River Highway, which was to link up with Chitina on the Edgerton Highway, was halted by the 1964 Good Friday earthquake, which damaged the Million Dollar Bridge.

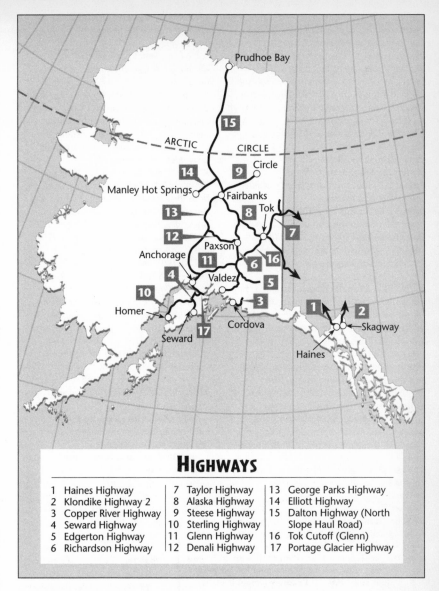

HIGHWAYS

1 Haines Highway	7 Taylor Highway	13 George Parks Highway
2 Klondike Highway 2	8 Alaska Highway	14 Elliott Highway
3 Copper River Highway	9 Steese Highway	15 Dalton Highway (North
4 Seward Highway	10 Sterling Highway	Slope Haul Road)
5 Edgerton Highway	11 Glenn Highway	16 Tok Cutoff (Glenn)
6 Richardson Highway	12 Denali Highway	17 Portage Glacier Highway

the public. The state also operates 2,860 miles of ferry routes within Alaska, and an additional 624 miles from Bellingham, WA, to the Alaska border.

Highways in Alaska range from six-lane paved freeways to one-lane dirt and gravel roads.

Approximately 33 percent of the roads in the Alaska highway system are paved.

The following major highways are all or partially gravel: Steese (Alaska Route 6), Taylor (Alaska Route 5), Elliott (Alaska Route 2), Dalton (Alaska Route 11) and Denali (Alaska Route 8). Alaska's relative lack of roadways is accentuated by a comparison to Austria, a country only one-eighteenth the size of Alaska but with nearly twice as many miles of road.

The youngest highway in the state system, Portage Glacier Highway, connects the Seward Highway south of Anchorage with the town of Whittier on Prince William Sound. In May 2002, a revised toll was instituted for the highway's Anton Anderson Memorial Tunnel—at 2.5 miles long, North America's longest highway tunnel. Passenger vehicles without trailers and RVs under 28 feet in length are charged $12; RVs and vehicles with trailers pay a $20 to $35 toll, depending on length.

Although cruise traffic to Alaska continues to grow, road traffic from Outside remains relatively steady.

Current driving, construction and weather conditions information is available by calling 511 (within Alaska) or (866) 282-7577 (toll-free, outside of Alaska); or at http://511.Alaska.gov.

HIKING
Developed trails suitable for all ability levels may be found near Alaska's larger cities and towns. However most of Alaska's public recreation lands are wilderness. Trails are nonexistent and hikers must chart their own course using topographic maps and a compass. Using both maps and tide tables, it is also possible to hike along ocean shorelines at low tide.

Hikers in Alaska must plan for cold, wet and rapidly changing weather. Take rain gear. If staying overnight in the backcountry, carry a tent, backpacking stove, first-aid kit and emergency flares. Snow can be encountered in any season.

Plan to bring everything you need with you. Some businesses rent canoes and kayaks, but few rent personal gear such as backpacks. Backcountry guides often furnish equipment on escorted expeditions.

Bears inhabit most of Alaska. Read all bear safety information and follow safe procedures for camping and hiking in bear country. You must be completely self-sufficient and responsible for your own safety. (SEE Bears)

Information on hiking in Alaska's national parks and monuments is available from the Alaska Public Lands Information Centers: 605 W. Fourth Ave., Suite 105, Anchorage 99501, (907) 271-2737; 250 Cushman St., Suite 1A, Fairbanks 99701, (907) 456-0527; P.O. Box 359, Tok 99780, (907) 883-5667; and 50 Main St., Ketchikan 99901, (907) 228-6220; www.nps.gov/aplic; or from park headquarters for the area you're interested in. (SEE National Parks, Preserves and Monuments) The Alaska Division of Parks (SEE State Park System) has information on hiking on the lands managed by that agency; www.dnr.state.ak.us/parks/aktrails/ats.htm.

HISTORY (SEE ALSO Gold Strikes and Rushes; Russian Alaska)

11,000–6,000 years ago—Humans inhabit southeastern, Aleutians, Interior and northwestern Arctic Alaska.

6,000 years ago—Most recent migration from Siberia across the land bridge. Earliest migration believed to have taken place 20,000 or more years ago.

5,000–3,000 years ago—Humans inhabit the Bering Sea Coast.

1725—Vitus Bering sent by Peter the Great to explore the North Pacific.

1741—On a later expedition, Bering and Alexei Chirikov, in separate ships, sight Alaska. Georg Steller goes ashore on Kayak Island, becoming the first European known to have set foot on Alaska soil.

1743—Russians begin concentrated hunting of sea otter, continuing until the species is almost decimated.

When Mr. Whitekeys' Fly By Night Club closed its doors, Anchorage Mayor Mark Begich declared September 9th as "Mr. Whitekeys Day." The problem was that I didn't know about it until 10:30 at night so I really only got "Mr. Whitekeys Hour and a Half." If I'd known about it earlier, I wouldn't have eaten dinner over the kitchen sink!

1772—A permanent Russian settlement is established at Unalaska.

1774–94—Explorations of Alaska waters by Juan Perez, James Cook and George Vancouver.

1784—Kodiak Island's first Russian settlement is established at Three Saints Bay.

1794—George Vancouver sights Mount McKinley.

1799—Alexander Baranov establishes the Russian post known today as Old Sitka. A trade charter is granted to the Russian–American Co.

1821—Russians prohibit trading in Alaska waters by other nations, making the Russian–American Co. the sole trading firm.

1824–42—Russian exploration of the mainland leads to the discovery of the Kuskokwim, Nushagak, Yukon and Koyukuk Rivers.

1837—Father Herman, last survivor of the original Russian missionaries to Alaska, dies on Spruce Island near Kodiak.

1845—The Missionary School at Sitka opens, offering the study of the Aleut, Tlingit and Eskimo languages, medicine and Latin.

1847—Fort Yukon is established by Hudson's Bay Co.

1848—American whalers first enter the Arctic Ocean through Bering Strait.

1853—Russian explorer-trappers find the first oil seeps in Cook Inlet.

1855—The U.S. Navy explores the North Pacific around the Aleutian Islands and the Bering Sea.

1859—Baron Edouard de Stoeckl, minister and chargé d'affaires of the Russian delegation to the United States, is given authority to negotiate the sale of Alaska.

1860—Russians estimate Native Alaskan Christians at 12,000, with 35 chapels, 9 churches, 17 schools and 3 orphanages in 43 communities.

1866—Alaska's first newspaper, the *Esquimeaux,* is published in manuscript at Libbyville.

1867—United States under President Andrew Johnson buys Alaska from Russia for $7.2 million; the treaty is signed March 30 and formal transfer takes place Oct. 18 at Sitka. Fur seal population begins to stabilize. U.S. Army is given jurisdiction over the Department of Alaska.

1869–70—The *Alaska Times,* the first newspaper to be printed in Alaska, is published in Sitka.

1872—Gold is discovered near Sitka.

1878—First salmon canneries established at Klawock and Old Sitka.

1882—First commercial herring fishing begins. U.S. Navy destroys the Tlingit village of Angoon.

1883—Lt. Frederick Schwatka conducts a military reconnaissance of the Yukon River from source to mouth.

1884—An Organic Act gives Alaska its first civil government.

1885—Lt. Henry Allen explores the Copper River.

1891—First oil claims staked in Cook Inlet area.

1897–1900—Klondike gold rush in Yukon Territory; heavy traffic through Alaska on the way to the goldfields.

1898—Gold is discovered on Nome beaches. Frank Reid shoots and kills con artist Soapy Smith in Skagway. U.S. Geological Survey begins mapping Alaska.

1902—First oil production, at Katalla. Telegraph from Eagle to Valdez is completed.

1906—Peak gold production year. Alaska is granted a nonvoting delegate to Congress. Governor's office moves from Sitka to Juneau.

1911—Copper production begins at Kennicott.

1912—Territorial status for Alaska; first territorial Legislature is convened the following year. Mount Katmai erupts.

1913—First airplane flight in Alaska, at Fairbanks. First automobile trip from Fairbanks to Valdez.

1914—President Woodrow Wilson authorizes construction of the Alaska Railroad.

1916—First bill proposing Alaska statehood is introduced in Congress. Peak copper production year.

1917—Creation of Mount McKinley National Park. Founding of Wasilla.

1918—Worldwide epidemic of Spanish flu decimates Alaska's Native population. Creation of Katmai National Monument.

1922—First pulp mill starts production at Speel River near Juneau.

1923—President Warren Harding drives spike completing the Alaska Railroad.

1930—The first "talkie" motion picture is shown in Fairbanks, featuring the Marx Brothers in *The Cocoanuts.*

1935—Matanuska Valley Project, which moves farming families to Alaska, begins. First Juneau-to-Fairbanks flight.

1936—All-time record salmon catch in Alaska—126.4 million fish. Black Rapids Glacier advances 3 miles in three months, coming within a half mile of the Richardson Highway.

1937—Nell Scott is the first woman appointed to the Alaska Legislature.

1940—Military buildup in Alaska; Fort Richardson, Elmendorf Air Force Base are established. Alaska's population includes about 32,000 Natives and 40,000 non-Native Alaskans. Pan American Airways inaugurates twice-weekly service between Seattle, Ketchikan and Juneau, using Sikorsky flying boats.

1942—Dutch Harbor is bombed and Attu and Kiska Islands are occupied by Japanese forces. Alaska Highway is built—first overland connection to Lower 48.

1943—Japanese forces are driven from Alaska.

1953—Oil well is drilled near Eureka, on the Glenn Highway, marking the start of modern oil history.

1957—Kenai oil strike.

1958—Congress passes Alaska statehood measure; statehood is proclaimed officially on Jan. 3, 1959; first general election is held.

1963—State ferry service to Southeast Alaska begins.

1964—Good Friday earthquake of March 27 causes heavy damage throughout the Gulf Coast region; 131 people are killed.

1967—Fairbanks flood.

1968—Oil and gas discoveries at Prudhoe Bay on the North Slope; $900 million North Slope oil lease sale the following year; pipeline proposal follows.

1970—Federal government sets aside 500,000 acres for Chugach State Park.

1971—Congress approves Alaska Native Claims Settlement Act, granting title to 40 million acres of land and providing $962.5 million in payment to Alaska Natives.

1973—The first 1,100-mile sled dog race begins March 3, following part of an old dog team mail route blazed in 1910; it's called the Iditarod Trail Sled Dog Race.

1974—Trans-Alaska pipeline receives final approval; construction buildup begins.

1975—Population and labor force soar with construction of pipeline. Alaska gross product hits $5.8 billion—double the 1973 figure.

1976—Voters select Willow area for new capital site.

1977—Completion of the trans-Alaska oil pipeline from Prudhoe Bay to Valdez; shipment of first oil by tanker from Valdez to Puget Sound.

1978—A 200-mile offshore fishing limit goes into effect. President Jimmy Carter withdraws 56 million acres of federal lands in Alaska to create 17 new national monuments. Congress designates the Iditarod as a National Historic Trail.

1979—State of Alaska files suit to halt the withdrawal of 56 million acres of Alaska land by President Carter under the Antiquities Act.

1980—Alaska Legislature votes to repeal the state income tax and establishes Permanent Fund as a repository for one-fourth of all royalty oil revenues for future generations. Census figures show Alaska's population grew by 32.4 percent during the 1970s. The Alaska National Interest Lands Conservation Act of 1980 puts 53.7 million Alaska acres into the national wildlife refuge system, parts of 25 rivers into

NUGGETS

A much-forgotten part of Alaska history lay entombed in a nondescript World War II Army bunker just south of the Sitka airport. Inside the bunker were 188 bodies of tuberculosis victims—mostly Native children—who were sent to the federal Bureau of Indian Affairs Mount Edgecumbe Hospital from the mid-1940s to the early 1960s.

—1990 *The Alaska Almanac*®

Dog teams served an important role in the gold rushes of the North. Courtesy of William F. Berry. From *Gold Rush Dogs* by Claire Rudolf Murphy and Jane G. Haigh.

the national wild and scenic rivers system, 3.3 million acres into national forest lands and 43.6 million acres into national park land.

1981—Secretary of the Interior James Watt initiates plans to sell oil and gas leases on 130 million acres of Alaska's nonrestricted federal land and to open 16 offshore areas of Alaska to oil and gas development.

1982—Voters turn down authorization of funds to move the state capital from Juneau to Willow, leaving the capital at Juneau. First Permanent Fund dividend checks of $1,000 each are mailed to every six-month resident of Alaska.

1983—All Alaska, except westernmost Aleutian Islands, moves to Alaska Standard Time, one hour ahead of Pacific Standard Time. Record-breaking salmon harvest in Bristol Bay. Building permits set a record at just under $1 billion.

1984—State of Alaska celebrates its 25th birthday.

1985—Anchorage receives the U.S. bid for the 1994 Winter Olympics. Iditarod Trail Sled Dog Race is won by Libby Riddles, the first woman to win in the history of the race.

1986—Mount Augustine in lower Cook Inlet erupts. World Championship Sled Dog Race held during Fur Rendezvous is canceled for the first time for lack of

snow. Iditarod Trail Sled Dog Race is again won by a woman, Susan Butcher of Manley.

1987—*AlaskaMen* magazine launches, profiling Alaska's available bachelors.

1988—Susan Butcher wins the Iditarod Trail Sled Dog Race for the third year in a row. Anchorage loses to Norway in its bid for the 1994 Winter Olympics.

1989—Worst oil spill in U.S. history occurs in Prince William Sound when the *Exxon Valdez* runs aground. Record-breaking cold hits entire state, lasting for weeks. Soviets visit Alaska, and the Bering Bridge Expedition crosses the Bering Strait by dogsled and skis.

1990—Valdez sets a new record for snowfall. Susan Butcher wins her fourth Iditarod Trail Sled Dog Race. Election upset as Walter J. Hickel becomes governor.

1991—Fairbanks sets a new record for snowfall. Rick Swenson claims fifth Iditarod win.

1992—Alaska celebrates 50th anniversary of the Alaska Highway. One of Alaska's oldest newspapers, the *Anchorage Times,* shuts down. Mount Spurr erupts.

1993—The Department of Fish and Game announces a plan to allow aerial hunting of wolves.

1994—Diseased herring appear in Prince William Sound for the second season. Exxon is found guilty of recklessness in the 1989 oil spill in Prince William Sound. Alaska skier Tommy Moe is a gold medalist at the Olympic Games in Norway.

1995—Two Anchorage residents are killed by a grizzly along a trail in a popular hiking area of Chugach State Park.

1996—Princess Tours' Denali Lodge burns down in March but is rebuilt by June. Alaska's worst wildfire destroys $8.8 million in homes and other buildings.

1997—Legislature approves 71-cent tax increase per cigarette pack. Arco Alaska and British Petroleum announce plans to develop two more North Slope oil fields.

1998—Falling oil prices force state to use budget reserve funds.

1999—BP–Amoco buys out competitor Arco Alaska. Joe Redington Sr., "Father" of the Iditarod Trail Sled Dog Race, dies at his home in Knik.

2000—Alaskans vote down a statewide cap on property taxes and a measure to legalize marijuana. Banker and philanthropist Elmer Rasmuson dies at 91.

2001—Fifteen crewmen aboard the *Arctic Rose* die when the 92-foot vessel sinks in the Bering Sea on April 2. Delegates from 62 Alaska tribes sign an agreement formalizing tribal relations with the state.

2002—An arctic version of the perfect storm slams into Anchorage in March, dumping 28.7 inches of snow in a 24-hour period, nearly doubling the record of 15.6 inches. The U.S. Congress defeats an amendment to open the Arctic National Wildlife Refuge to oil development. Alaska's congressional delegation vows to continue the fight to access the oil.

2003—As of Jan. 1, Alaska's minimum wage is raised $1.50 to a new level of $7.15 per hour, transforming Alaska's minimum wage rate from the lowest to the highest on the West Coast.

2004—Between June and October, 6.7 million acres burn during a record wildland fire season.

NUGGETS

There is no free land in Alaska. None. Zero. Zip. But no matter how often officials say it, the calls and letters keep coming from dreamers in the Lower 48 who want some of that land. And some can't resist getting on the road to the Last Frontier to find it.

—1995 *The Alaska Almanac*®

2005—Oil prices reach all-time high of nearly $70 per barrel.

2006—Alaska voters elect the state's first female governor, Sarah Palin.

HOLIDAYS IN 2008

New Year's Day	Jan. 1
Martin Luther King Day	Jan. 21
Presidents' Day	
—holiday	Feb. 18
—traditional	Feb. 22
Seward's Day*	March 31
Memorial Day	
—holiday	May 26
—traditional	May 30
Independence Day	July 4
Labor Day	Sept. 1
Alaska Day**	Oct. 18
Veterans Day	Nov. 11
Thanksgiving Day	Nov. 27
Christmas Day	Dec. 25

* Seward's Day commemorates the signing of the treaty by which the United States bought Alaska from Russia, signed on March 30, 1867.

** Alaska Day is the anniversary of the formal transfer of the territory and the raising of the U.S. flag at Sitka on Oct. 18, 1867.

HOMESTEADING (See also Land Use)

Until 1995, any Alaska resident of at least one year, 18 years or older and a U.S. citizen, had a chance to receive up to 40 acres of nonagricultural land or up to 160 acres of agricultural land nearly free. To receive title the homesteader was required to pay a $10 application fee and either survey or reimburse the state for survey costs, brush and stake the parcel boundary, build a dwelling and occupy and improve the land in certain ways within specific time frames. This is called "proving up" on the homestead. The last available parcel was won in a lottery in early 1997.

Many of the original homesteaders were veterans who came to Alaska during the late 1940s and early 1950s. They had to brush up their boundaries within 90 days after issuance of the entry permit, complete an approved survey of the land within two or five years (depending on purchase option), erect a habitable permanent dwelling on the homestead within three years and live on the parcel for 25 months within five years. If the parcel was classified for agricultural use, homesteaders labored mightily to clear and put into production or cultivation 25 percent of the land within five years.

All laws related to homesteading on federal land (as opposed to state land) in Alaska were repealed as of 1986. Federal land is not available for homesteading or trade and manufacturing sites. However, following are the two programs currently used for the sale of state land.

Auction. Alaska has been selling land by public auction since statehood. The state may sell full surface rights, lease of surface or subsurface rights or restricted title at an auction. There is a minimum bid of fair market value and the high bidder is the purchaser. Participants must be Alaska residents for a period of at least one year immediately preceding the date of auction and be at least 18 years old. All lands not taken at auction are granted "over-the-counter" status, making them available to residents and non-residents alike for purchase at fair market value.

Remote Recreational Cabin Sites. In 1997, the Alaska legislature passed a new law to let Alaskans who have been residents for at least one year immediately before the date of the lottery and are at least 18 years old, stake remote recreational cabin sites on state land. Similar to the state's open-to-entry, remote parcel and early homestead programs of the 1970s and 1980s, this program allows individuals to stake a parcel of state land for a cabin site in a designated remote settlement area, obtain a lease for the land for a limited time and then purchase the land at fair market value. The remote recreational cabin sites are from 5 to 20 acres, and are mostly accessible by all-terrain vehicle, snowmachine, floatplane or boat. Under state law, the state has no legal obligation to build roads or provide services to or within these areas. Cabin site leases allow for recreational use only while under the lease. Once the land is under purchase contract or conveyed into private ownership, these restrictions do not apply. There are no building or "prove-up" requirements with this program. Qualifying veterans are entitled to a once-in-a-lifetime discount of 25 percent on the purchase price of state land exclusive of survey, platting and other reimbursable costs. Veterans must be at least 18 years old on the date of sale, have been an Alaska resident for at least one year immediately preceding the date of sale, have served on active duty for at least 90 days and have received an honorable discharge or general discharge under honorable conditions.

When the state offers land, it advertises statewide and publishes a brochure titled *Land for Alaskans*. The brochure contains information about available

> A nationwide study listed Alaskans as among the most overweight people in the country. During the same period of time, an ad for the Anchorage Yamaha dealer offered to sell a 2,000 lb. *wench* for only $69.95! I would gladly pay $69.95 for a 2,000 lb. wench!

parcels, minimum-opening bids, residency requirements, the bidding process and other general information. For additional information, contact one of the Alaska Department of Natural Resources Public Information Centers at 605 W. Fourth Ave., Suite 105, Anchorage 99501, (907) 271-2737; P.O. Box 359, Tok 99780, (907) 883-5667; 250 Cushman St., Suite 1A, Fairbanks 99701, (907) 456-0527; 50 Main St., Ketchikan 99901, (907) 228-6220; www.nps.gov/aplic; or go to www.dnr.state.ak.us/mlw/landsale/index.htm.

HOOLIGAN
Smelt, also known as eulachon or candlefish, are "ooligan" in southeastern Alaska. The Tlingit dried these oily little fish, inserted a twisted spruce bark wick and used them as candles. The Tlingit caught the 9-inch fish in great numbers, ripened them for several days to speed the release of the oil from the flesh and then rendered their oil in baskets or cooking pots. The flavor and color of the oil, or "grease," were determined by the length of time the fish ripened. The oil was stored in bulb kelp "jars" corked with wooden plugs or in bentwood boxes. Some of the oil was traded with Interior people by packing it over timeworn paths that became known as grease trails. The Tlingit considered hooligan vital to their diet and gallons of the oil were consumed during the winter as a nutritious dip for dried foods.

Hooligan, now considered a subsistence or sport catch only, are caught by dip-netting as they travel upriver to spawn. Hooligan resemble trout in general structure and have a distinctive odor and taste. The flesh is ivory colored, extremely perishable and should be cooked or pickled the same day it is caught.

HOSPITALS AND HEALTH FACILITIES
(SEE ALSO Pioneers' Homes)
Alaska has numerous hospitals, nursing homes and other health care facilities.

For a list of emergency medical services, contact the Office of Emergency Medical Services, Division of Public Health, Dept. of Health and Social Services, P.O. Box 10616, Juneau 99811-0616.

Municipal, Private and State Facilities

Anchorage: Alaska Psychiatric Institute (80 beds), 2800 Providence Drive, 99508; Alaska Regional Hospital (250 beds), 2801 DeBarr Road, P.O. Box 143889, 99514-3889; North Star Hospital (74 beds), 2530 DeBarr Road, 99508; Providence Alaska Medical Center (326 beds), 3200 Providence Drive, P.O. Box 196604, 99519-6604.

Cordova: Cordova Community Medical Center (23 beds), 602 Chase Ave., P.O. Box 160, 99574.

Fairbanks: Fairbanks Memorial Hospital (152 beds), 1650 Cowles St., 99701.

Glennallen: Cross Roads Medical Center, Mile 187 Glenn Hwy, P.O. Box 5, 99588.

Homer: South Peninsula Hospital (47 beds), 4300 Bartlett St., 99603.

Juneau: Bartlett Regional Hospital (71 beds), 3260 Hospital Drive, 99801; Rainforest Recovery Center (16 beds), 3250 Hospital Drive, 99801.

Ketchikan: Ketchikan General Hospital (68 beds), 3100 Tongass Ave., 99901.

Kodiak: Providence Kodiak Island Medical Center (44 beds), 1915 E. Rezanof Drive, 99615.

Palmer: Mat-Su Regional Medical Center (74 beds), 2500 S. Woodworth Lp., P.O. Box 1687, 99645.

Petersburg: Petersburg Medical Center (27 beds), 103 Fram St., P.O. Box 589, 99833.

Seward: Providence Seward Medical & Care Center (6 beds), 417 First Ave., P.O. Box 365, 99664.

Sitka: Sitka Community Hospital (27 beds), 209 Moller Ave., P.O. Box 500, 99835.

Soldotna: Central Peninsula General Hospital (62 beds), 250 Hospital Place, 99669.

Valdez: Providence Valdez Medical Center (21 beds), 911 Meals Ave., P.O. Box 550, 99686.

Wrangell: Wrangell Medical Center (22 beds), 310 Bennett St., P.O. Box 1081, 99929.

Sweetwater, Alaska

The 660 villagers from the Western Alaska community of Kipnuk enjoy the best-tasting water in all of rural America, according to national competition sponsored in April 2005 by the National Rural Water Association. This came as something of a surprise to the local residents of a village with no running water and no indoor plumbing. In winter, Kipnuk villagers travel by snowmachine across the flat, treeless tundra, past nearby rivers full of brackish seawater, to freshwater ponds. Using axes, they chop ice chunks, then load them onto sleds and haul them back home. Summer rain falling on rooftops is caught in gutters for drinking and household uses. Sewage is carried in "honey buckets" to a sewage lagoon.

The water sample entered in the contest, however, came from the Kipnuk School, which—like many rural Alaska schools—has a water filtration system of its own, with water supplied from a tundra pond. The water sample was chilled to a steady 34 degrees for the overnight express shipment to Washington, D.C., where judges at the Hyatt Regency Hotel pronounced it to be the winner among entries from 47 other states.

"Water," according to one of the judges, "should have no taste . . . no smell . . . (and) should be a clean, refreshing taste on the palate. This one did. It was desirable."

—2003 *The Alaska Almanac*®

Tribal Health Facilities

Tribal organizations oversee a variety of health facilities in villages and urban centers.

Anchorage: Alaska Native Medical Center (156 beds), 4315 Diplomacy Drive, 99508.

Barrow: Samuel Simmonds Memorial Hospital (14 beds), P.O. Box 29, 99723-0029.

Bethel: Yukon–Kuskokwim Regional Hospital (50 beds), P.O. Box 287, 99559.

Dillingham: Bristol Bay/Kanakanak Hospital (16 beds), 6000 Kanakanak Rd., P.O. Box 130, 99576.

Fairbanks: Chief Andrew Isaac Health Center, 1638 Cowles St., 99701.

Juneau: SEARHC Medical Clinic, 3245 Hospital Drive, 99801.

Ketchikan: KIC Tribal Health Clinic, 2960 Tongass Ave., 99901-5742.

Kodiak: Kodiak Community Health Center, 1915 E. Rezanof Drive, 99615.

Kotzebue: Maniilaq Health Center (17 beds), P.O. Box 43, 99752.

Metlakatla: Annette Island Service Unit, P.O. Box 439, 99926.

Nome: Norton Sound Regional (33 beds), 306 W. Fifth Ave., P.O. Box 966, 99762.

Sitka: SEARHC Mount Edgecumbe Hospital (27 beds), 222 Tongass Drive, 99835.

Military Hospitals

Anchorage: Alaska VA Healthcare System, 2925 DeBarr Road, 99508-2989.

Eielson Air Force Base: Eielson Air Force Base Clinic, 2630 Central Ave., Eielson AFB 99702.

Elmendorf Air Force Base: Headquarters Third Medical Group, 5955 Zeamer Ave., Elmendorf AFB, 99506-3240.

Fort Richardson: U.S. Army Troop Medical Clinic, 604 Richardson Drive, 99505.

Fort Wainwright: Bassett Army Community Hospital, 1060 Gaffney Road, Building 7400, 99703-7400.

Ketchikan: Coast Guard Dispensary, 1300 Stedman St., 99901.

Kodiak: USCG Integrated Support Command, Rockmore–King Medical Clinic, P.O. Box 195002, 99619-5002.

Sitka: U.S. Coast Guard Air Station, 611 Airport Road, 99835-6500.

Nursing Homes

Anchorage: Mary Conrad Center (90 beds), 9100 Centennial Drive, 99504; Providence Extended Care Center (224 beds), 4900 Eagle St., 99503.

Cordova: Community Medical Center LTC (10 beds), 602 Chase Ave., P.O. Box 160, 99574.

Fairbanks: Denali Center LTC (90 beds), 1510 19th Ave., 99701.

Homer: South Peninsula Hospital LTC (25 beds), 4300 Bartlett St., 99603.

Juneau: Wildflower Court (49 beds), 2000 Salmon Creek Lane, 99801.

Ketchikan: General Hospital LTC (29 beds), 3100 Tongass Ave., 99901.

Kodiak: Providence Kodiak Island Medical Center (19 beds), 1915 E. Rezanof Drive, 99615.

Nome: Quyanna Care Center (15 beds), P.O. Box 966, 99762.

Petersburg: Petersburg Medical Center LTC (15 beds), P.O. Box 589, 99833.

Seward: Providence Seward Medical & Care Center (43 beds), 431 First Ave., P.O. Box 430, 99664.

Sitka: Sitka Community Hospital LTC (15 beds), 209 Moller Ave., 99835.

Soldotna: Heritage Place (60 beds), 232 Rockwell Ave., 99669.

Valdez: Providence Valdez Medical Center (10 beds) 911 Meals Ave., P.O. Box 550, 99686.

Wrangell: Wrangell Medical Center (14 beds), 310 Bennett St., P.O. Box 1081, 99929.

Chemical Dependency Centers

Alaska has 52 chemical dependency treatment centers, located in various communities throughout the state. For online details, go to http://dasis3.samhsa.gov/; or call the Alaska State Medical Association at (907) 562-0304.

HOSTELS Cities throughout Alaska offer

private hostel accommodations. Check online listings or purchase a copy of *The Hostel Handbook* at http://hostelhandbook.com. There are no longer any member hostels of Hostelling International in Alaska at the time of this printing. Alaska hostels have opted, instead, to join together in a state organization, the Alaska Hostel Association, which can guide you to comfortable, inexpensive lodgings that may not be included on *The Hostel Handbook*'s online listings:

Alaska Hostel Association, P.O. Box 92422, Anchorage, 99509-2422; www.alaskahostelassociation.org.

HOT SPRINGS The Alaska Division

of Geological and Geophysical Surveys identifies 124 geothermal areas in the state that include hot springs, fumaroles, geothermal wells or a combination of these. Most geothermal areas (56) occur along the Aleutian volcanic arc, 19 are located in the Southeast panhandle and 49 are scattered throughout mainland Alaska. Most are inaccessible by automobile.

Only 19 of these geothermal areas have experienced any sort of development, and only three hot spring areas provide resort facilities. A resort with swimming pools, changing rooms, restaurants and lodging is found at Chena Hot Springs (a 62-mile drive east from Fairbanks). Less developed is Manley Hot Springs in the small community

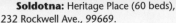

A Willow resident made the police blotter by becoming intoxicated and shooting himself with a small caliber handgun *in both arms!* After months of yoga, I've failed to find a position that will make such an act possible. They always say that the Eskimos have a hundred different words for "Snow." In English we only have a handful of words for "Stupid," but they seem to work in almost any situation.

of the same name at the end of Elliott Highway (160 miles west of Fairbanks). The hot springs are privately owned and a primitive bathhouse is used primarily by local residents and occasional visitors. The resort itself is no longer in operation, although guests can stay at the Manley Roadhouse or a local B&B. Ophir Hot Springs (about 50 miles southwest of Aniak) has a private hunting camp with accommodations and an aboveground hot pool.

There are 11 additional springs with cabins and/or bathing tubs and changing facilities. Most of these are accessible only by boat, plane, snowmobile, dog team, ATV or on foot. Among them is the community of Tenakee Springs on Chichagof Island in southeastern Alaska, which maintains an old bathhouse near the waterfront for public use.

The Alaska Marine Highway System provides ferry service to Tenakee Springs. Chief Shakes Hot Springs, near Wrangell, and White Sulfur Hot Springs and Goddard Hot Springs, both near Sitka, all have Forest Service cabins and are accessible by boat or floatplane. Tolovana Hot Springs, 45 miles northwest of Fairbanks, features two cabins and a hot tub. Reservations are required. Visitors can soak and photograph the old buildings that were once an orphanage at Pilgrim Hot Springs, 60 miles from Nome, accessible by road in summer only. Also on the Seward Peninsula is Serpentine Hot Springs, a winter destination by snowmobile from Nome.

Other springs include Baranof Hot Springs on Baranof Island. Kanuti Hot Springs is about 10 miles west of the Dalton Highway near Caribou Mountain. These springs are used primarily by skiers and mushers in the winter.

A map featuring most of the thermal areas in Alaska can be purchased for $5 from the Alaska Division of Geological and Geophysical Surveys, 3354 College Road, Fairbanks 99709-3707; (907) 451-5000; fax (907) 451-5050; www.dggs.dnr.state.ak.us.

HUNTING
Alaska is divided into 26 game management units with a wide variety of seasons and bag limits. Current copies of Alaska State Hunting Regulations with maps showing game unit boundaries are available from the Alaska Department of

Chena Hot Springs lies about an hour northeast of Fairbanks. Photo by Roy Corral.

Fish and Game (P.O. Box 115526, Juneau 99811), from Fish and Game offices and sporting goods stores throughout the state or at www.wildlife.alaska.gov.

Regulations. A hunting or trapping license is required for all residents and nonresidents with the exception of Alaska residents under 16 or older than 60. A special identification card is issued for the senior citizen exemption.

A resident hunting license (valid for the calendar year) costs $25; trapping license (valid until Sept. 30 of the year following the year of issue), $15; hunting and trapping license, $39; hunting and sportfishing license, $48; hunting, trapping and sport-fishing license, $62; low income license, $5; waterfowl stamps, $5.

A nonresident (U.S. citizen) hunting license (valid for the calendar year) costs $85; hunting and sportfishing license, $230; hunting and trapping license, $250. Non-U.S. citizens pay $300 for a big-game hunting license.

Military personnel permanently stationed in Alaska for the preceding 12 months are considered residents, and must have the appropriate resident licenses, harvest tickets, permits and tags to hunt anywhere in Alaska. Those who have been on duty for less than 12 months are considered nonresidents when hunting on nonmilitary land in Alaska. Licenses may be obtained from any designated issuing agent, online at www.admin.adfg.state.ak.us/license, or by mail from the Alaska Department of Fish and Game, Licensing Division, P.O. Box 115525, Juneau 99811; (800) 478-2376, (907) 465-2376.

Big-game tags and fees are required for residents hunting musk oxen and brown/grizzly bear and for nonresidents and noncitizens hunting any big-game animal. These nonrefundable, nontransferable, locking tags (valid for the calendar year) must be purchased prior to the taking of the animal. A tag may be used for any species for which the tag fee is of equal or less value. Fees quoted below are for each animal.

All residents (regardless of age), nonresidents and aliens intending to hunt brown/grizzly bear must purchase tags (resident, $25; nonresident, $500; alien, $650). Residents, nonresidents and aliens are also required to purchase musk oxen tags (resident, $500 each bull and $25 each cow taken on Nunivak Island, $25 each bull or cow from Nelson Island; nonresident, $1,100; alien, $1,500).

Nonresident tag fees for other big-game animals: deer, $150; wolf, $30; black bear, $225; elk or goat, $300; caribou, $325; moose, $400; bison, $450; sheep, $425; and wolverine $175.

Nonresident alien tag fees for other big-game animals: deer, $200; wolf, $50; black bear, $300; elk or goat, $400; caribou, $425; moose, $500; bison, $650; sheep, $550; and wolverine $250. Nonresidents hunting brown/grizzly bear, Dall sheep or mountain goat are required to have a registered guide or be accompanied by an Alaska resident relative over 19 within the second degree of kinship (includes parents, children, sisters or brothers). Nonresident aliens hunting big game must have a guide. A list of registered Alaska guides is available for $5 from the Department of Commerce, Community and Economic Development, Division of Corporate, Business and Professional Licensing, P.O. Box 110806, Juneau 99811-0806; www.commerce.state.ak.us/occ/apps/ODQuery.cfm.

Residents and nonresidents 16 or older hunting waterfowl must have a signed federal migratory bird-hunting stamp (duck stamp). A signed state waterfowl conservation stamp is also required, though Alaska residents 60 years or older, qualifying disabled veterans and low-income hunters are exempted. Alaska duck stamps are available from agents who sell hunting licenses, by mail from the Alaska Department of

Moose Mayhem

Two Anchorage policemen responded to a call in January that a moose was causing a nuisance in an Anchorage neighborhood. An officer found the moose near a house, frightening the homeowner. The officer tried to coax the female moose away from the house. She turned and charged him, chasing him 25 yards and coming within 3 feet of him, before his partner turned on the police siren.

The moose ran off at the noise, and the partner had a good laugh inside the patrol car, but his laughter was short-lived. A second moose crashed through the brush and walked onto the hood of the patrol car. The officer lay down on the seat and waited for a hoof to go through the windshield.

The car sustained about $1,000 damage. The officers were not injured.

—1991 *The Alaska Almanac*®

Both male and female Dall sheep grow horns. From *Alaska's Mammals* by Dave Smith (text) and Tom Walker (photographs).

Fish and Game, Licensing Section or at www.admin.adfg.state.ak.us/license.

Trophy Game. World's record big game in Alaska as recorded by the Boone and Crockett Club (www.boone-crockett.org).

Brown bear (coastal region): Score $30\frac{12}{16}$; skull $17\frac{15}{16}$ inches long (without lower jaw), $12\frac{13}{16}$ inches wide; Kodiak Island; Roy Lindsley (1952).

Grizzly bear: Score $27\frac{13}{16}$; skull $17\frac{4}{16}$ inches long, $10\frac{9}{16}$ inches wide; Lone Mountain (picked up); Gordon Scott (1976).

Polar bear: Score $29\frac{15}{16}$; skull $18\frac{8}{16}$ inches long (without lower jaw), $11\frac{7}{16}$ inches wide; Kotzebue; Shelby Longoria (1963). It is illegal for anyone but an Alaska Eskimo, Aleut or Indian to hunt polar bear in Alaska.

Barren Ground caribou: Score 477; Right beam $55\frac{5}{8}$ inches, 17 points; left beam $57\frac{7}{8}$ inches, 25 points; inside spread $38\frac{3}{8}$ inches; right brow point length $22\frac{5}{8}$ inches, width $4\frac{5}{8}$ inches; left brow point length $23\frac{2}{8}$ inches, width $18\frac{5}{8}$ inches; Iliamna Lake; Daniel L. Dobbs (1999).

Moose (Alaska–Yukon): Score $261\frac{5}{8}$; right palm length $54\frac{4}{8}$ inches, width $22\frac{2}{8}$ inches; left palm length $53\frac{6}{8}$ inches, width $21\frac{4}{8}$ inches; right antler 19 points, left 15 points; circumference of beam at smallest place, right 8 inches, left 8 inches; greatest spread $65\frac{1}{8}$ inches; Fortymile River; John A. Crouse (1994).

Dall sheep: Score $189\frac{6}{8}$; right horn $48\frac{5}{8}$ inches long, base circumference $14\frac{5}{8}$ inches, third quarter circumference $6\frac{5}{8}$ inches; left horn $47\frac{7}{8}$ inches long, base circumference $14\frac{6}{8}$ inches, third quarter circumference $6\frac{7}{8}$ inches; greatest spread $34\frac{3}{8}$ inches; tip to tip $34\frac{3}{8}$ inches; Wrangell Mountains; Harry L. Swank Jr. (1961).

Walrus: Score $147\frac{4}{8}$; entire length of loose tusk, right $37\frac{7}{8}$ inches; left $36\frac{7}{8}$ inches; base circumference right $9\frac{7}{8}$ inches; left $9\frac{7}{8}$ inches; Bristol Bay (picked up); Ralph Young (1997).

HYPOTHERMIA

(SEE ALSO Windchill Factor) Hypothermia develops when the body is exposed to cold and cannot maintain normal temperatures. In an automatic survival reaction, blood flow to the extremities is shut down in favor of preserving warmth in the vital organs. As internal temperature drops, judgment and coordination become impaired. Hypothermia leads to stupor, collapse and death. Immersion hypothermia occurs in cold water.

Hypothermia can occur at any season. To prevent hypothermia, always bring warmer clothing, even in relatively warm summer months. Dress in layers, including inner layers that give warmth even when wet. Keep your energy up by eating snacks and drinking warm beverages. Travel outdoors with a partner, or in groups, to watch one another for early signs of hypothermia such as shivering, fatigue, stumbling, aimless wandering or irrationality. Victims of hypothermia should be sheltered from wind and weather and brought indoors as soon as possible.

At the retirement party for a Department of Fish and Game biologist, three different people gave testimonials about times he threw anchors overboard from a Fish and Game boat and the anchor ropes were not even attached to the boat!

ICE (See Glaciers and Ice Fields; Icebergs; Ice Fog; Iceworms; Nenana Ice Classic)

ICEBERGS (See also Glaciers and Ice Fields)

Icebergs are formed in Alaska wherever glaciers reach salt water or a freshwater lake. Some accessible places to view icebergs include Glacier Bay, Icy Bay, Yakutat Bay, Taku Inlet, Endicott Arm, portions of northern Prince William Sound (College Fiord, Barry Arm, Columbia Bay), Mendenhall Lake and Portage Lake.

If icebergs contain little or no sediment, approximately 75 percent to 80 percent of their bulk may be underwater. The more sediment an iceberg contains, the greater its density, and an iceberg containing large amounts of sediment will float slightly beneath the surface. Glaciologists of the U.S. Geological Survey believe that some of these "black icebergs" may actually sink to the bottom of a body of water. Since salt water near the faces of glaciers may be liquid to temperatures as low as 28°F, and icebergs melt at 32°F, some of these underwater icebergs may remain unmelted indefinitely.

Alaska's icebergs are small compared to the icebergs found near Antarctica and Greenland. One of the largest icebergs ever recorded in Alaska was formed in May 1977, in Icy Bay. Glaciologists measured it at 346 feet long, 297 feet wide and 99 feet above the surface of the water.

Sea Ice. Seawater typically freezes at −1.8°C or 28.8°F. The first indication that seawater is freezing is the appearance of frazil—tiny needlelike crystals of pure ice—in shallow coastal areas of low current or areas of low salinity such as near the mouths of rivers. Continued freezing turns the frazil into a soupy mass called grease ice and eventually into an ice crust approximately 4 inches thick. More freezing, wind and wave action thicken the ice and break it into ice floes ranging from a few feet to several miles across. In the Arctic Ocean, ice floes can be 10 feet thick. Most are crisscrossed with 6- to 8-foot-high walls of ice caused by the force of winds.

Sea salt that is trapped in the ice during freezing is leached out over time, making the oldest ice the least saline. Meltwater forming in ponds on multiyear-old ice during summer months is a freshwater source for native marine life.

Refreezing of meltwater ponds and the formation of new ice in the permanent ice pack (generally north of 72° north latitude) begins in mid-September. While the ice pack expands southward, new ice freezes to the coast (shorefast ice) and spreads seaward. Where the drifting ice pack grinds against the relatively stable shorefast ice, tremendous walls or ridges of ice are formed, some observed to be 100 feet thick and grounded in 60 feet of water. They are impenetrable by all but the most powerful icebreakers.

By late March the ice cover has reached its maximum extent, approximately from Port Heiden on the Alaska Peninsula in the south to the northern Pribilof Islands and northwestward to Siberia. In Cook Inlet, sea ice usually no more than 2 feet thick can extend as far south as Anchor Point and Kamishak Bay on the east and west sides of the inlet, respectively. The ice season usually lasts from mid-November to April.

The Navy began observing and forecasting sea ice conditions in 1954 during construction of defense sites along the Arctic coast. In 1969, the National Weather Service began a low-profile sea ice reconnaissance program, which expanded greatly during the summer of 1975 when, during a year of severe ice, millions of dollars of materials had to be shipped to Prudhoe Bay. Expanded commercial fisheries in the Bering Sea also heightened the problem of sea ice for crabbing and bottom-fish trawling operations. In 1976, headquarters for a seven-days-a-week ice watch was established at Fairbanks; it was moved to Anchorage in 1981.

The National Weather Service operates a radio facsimile broadcast service that makes current ice analysis charts, special oceanographic charts and standard weather charts available to the public via standard radios equipped with "black box" receivers. Commercial fishing operators, particularly in the Bering Sea, use the radio-transmitted charts to steer clear of problem weather and troublesome ice formations. More information is available from the National Weather Service in Kodiak or Anchorage; www.arh.noaa.gov.

Warming Trend. The Environmental Protection Agency continues to monitor climate changes that indicate a loss of sea ice in polar regions. The EPA reports that Alaska has warmed by an average of 4°F since the 1950s, a subtle change with significant results. After several decades of studying the thickness of Arctic sea ice in late summer and early autumn, researchers report that the ice has thinned by about 40 percent. For more EPA studies on global warming, see http://epa.gov/climatechange/index.html.

ICE FOG
Ice fog develops when air just above the ground becomes so cold it can no longer retain water vapor and tiny, spherical ice crystals form. Ice fog is most common in arctic and subarctic regions in winter when clear skies create an air inversion, trapping cold air at low elevations. It is most noticeable when pollutants are suspended in the air inversion.

ICEWORMS
Although often regarded as a hoax, iceworms actually exist. These small, threadlike, segmented black worms, usually less than one inch long, thrive in temperatures just above freezing. Observers as far back as the 1880s reported that at

dawn or dusk, or on overcast days, the tiny worms, all belonging to the genus *Mesenchytraeus,* may literally carpet the surface of glaciers. When sunlight strikes them, ice worms burrow back down into the ice; temperatures above 75°F kill them.

The town of Cordova commemorates its own version of the iceworm each February with an Iceworm Festival when a 100-foot-long, multilegged "iceworm" leads a parade down Main Street. Other activities include an arts and crafts show, ski events, contests, dances and honorary king and queen.

IDITAROD TRAIL SLED DOG RACE (SEE ALSO Dog Mushing; Yukon Quest International Sled Dog Race)
Two of the longest sled-dog races in the world take place in Alaska: the Yukon Quest and the Iditarod. The earliest version of today's Iditarod Trail Sled Dog Race, conceived and organized by the late Joe Redington Sr., of Knik, and the late Dorothy Page, of Wasilla, was run in 1967 and covered only 56 miles.

The race was lengthened in 1973, and the first-ever 1,100-mile sled dog race began in Anchorage on March 3, 1973, and ended April 3 in Nome. Of the 34 who started the race, 22 finished. The Iditarod has been run every year since. In 2007, the Iditarod Trail Sled Dog Race marked its 35th anniversary.

In 1976, Congress designated the Iditarod as a National Historic Trail. The official length of the Iditarod National Historic Trail System, including northern and southern routes, is 2,350 miles.

Following the old dog-team mail route blazed in 1910 from Knik to Nome, the race route crosses two mountain ranges, follows the Yukon River for about 150 miles, runs through several Bush villages and crosses the pack ice of Norton Sound.

Strictly a winter trail because the ground is mostly spongy muskeg swamps, the route attracted national attention in 1925 when sled dog mushers, including the famous Leonhard Seppala, relayed 300,000 units of life-saving diphtheria serum to

NUGGETS

A moose that had broken through the ice in Soldotna was rescued when a local biologist and some electrical workers wrapped a rope around a utility pole and used a truck to hoist the angry, half-ton animal back to solid ground.

—1997 *The Alaska Almanac*®

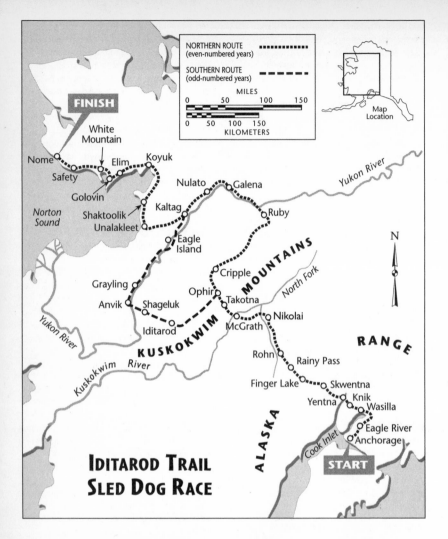

NORTHERN ROUTE (even-numbered years)

SOUTHERN ROUTE (odd-numbered years)

MILES
0   50   100   150

0   50   100   150
KILOMETERS

Map Location

FINISH

White Mountain

Nome
Safety
Elim
Koyuk
Golovin

Norton Sound

Nulato
Galena

Kaltag
Ruby

Shaktoolik
Unalakleet

Eagle Island

Cripple

Grayling
Ophir
Takotna

Anvik
Shageluk
McGrath
Nikolai

Iditarod

North Fork

KUSKOKWIM MOUNTAINS

Yukon River

N

KUSKOKWIM River

RANGE

Rohn
Rainy Pass

Finger Lake
Skwentna

Yentna
Knik
Wasilla

Eagle River
Anchorage

Cook Inlet

ALASKA

START

**IDITAROD TRAIL
SLED DOG RACE**

---

epidemic-threatened Nome. As the airplane and snowmobile replaced the sled dog team, the trail fell into disuse. Thanks to Redington and Page, the trail has been assured a place in Alaska history.

The Iditarod alternates a portion of the route each year, using the northern route in even-numbered years and the southern route in odd-numbered years (SEE accompanying map). The Iditarod is traditionally described as 1,049 miles long (the last part of the number selected because Alaska is the 49th state), but the actual distance run each year is close to 1,100 miles.

The purse for 2007 Iditarod champion Lance Mackey was $69,000 and a new Dodge truck.

For more information contact the Iditarod Trail Committee, P.O. Box 870800, Wasilla 99687; www.iditarod.com.

IGLOO (SEE ALSO Barabara) The word *igloo,* meaning snowhouse, is from northern and eastern Eskimo (Iñupiaq *iglu,* or "house").

The stereotypical igloo is a snow-block structure that could be built quickly as a temporary trail shelter for arctic Alaska and

Iditarod Trail Sled Dog Race 2007 Results

Place	Musher	Days	Hrs.	Min.	Day	Arrival Time
1.	Lance Mackey	9	5	9	3/13	20:08:41
2.	Paul Gebhardt	9	7	28	3/13	22:28:12
3.	Zack Steer	9	12	46	3/14	03:46:07
4.	Martin Buser	9	13	7	3/14	04:07:04
5.	Jeff King	9	15	5	3/14	06:05:17
6.	Ed Iten	9	16	34	3/14	07:34:10
7.	Ken Anderson	9	18	29	3/14	09:28:48
8.	John Baker	9	18	36	3/14	09:36:22
9.	Mitch Seavey	9	19	30	3/14	10:30:23
10.	Tollef Monson	9	21	32	3/14	12:31:40
11.	Cim Smyth	10	2	17	3/14	17:16:40
12.	Robert Sorlie	10	4	35	3/14	19:34:34
13.	Aaron Burmeister	10	6	12	3/14	21:12:20
14.	Jason Barron	10	6	38	3/14	21:38:15
15.	Hans Gatt	10	7	58	3/14	22:58:17
16.	Ramey Smyth	10	10	20	3/15	01:20:18
17.	Ray Redington Jr.	10	12	43	3/15	03:43:10
18.	Ryan Redington	10	12	46	3/15	03:46:00
19.	Hugh Neff	10	13	5	3/15	04:05:15
20.	Sigrid Ekran (r)	10	13	21	3/15	04:21:07
21.	Jessie Royer	10	15	25	3/15	06:25:05
22.	Sebastian Schnuelle	10	15	38	3/15	06:37:45
23.	Louis Nelson Sr.	10	18	23	3/15	09:23:55
24.	Sonny Lindner	10	18	28	3/15	09:28:05
25.	Rick Swenson	10	18	43	3/15	09:42:49
26.	Silvia Willis (r)	10	18	43	3/15	09:42:51
27.	Jim Lanier	10	19	02	3/15	10:01:56
28.	Aliy Zirkle	10	19	57	3/15	10:57:07
29.	Matt Hayashida	11	1	59	3/15	16:58:46
30.	Gerry Willomitzer (r)	11	2	54	3/15	17:54:08

* Time rounded to nearest minute

(r) indicates rookie status

Canada Eskimos. Igloos are constructed in a spiral with each tier leaning inward at a greater angle. The entrance is a tunnel with a cold trap. A sleeping platform raises sleepers off the cold floor, while a vent at the top allows fresh air for ventilation and an ice window admits light.

Most Alaska indigenous dwellings were sod igloos, dome- or Quonset-shaped structures with roofs supported by wood or whalebones and covered with insulating sod.

INFORMATION SOURCES

Agriculture. State Division of Agriculture, 1800 Glenn Highway, Suite 12, Palmer 99645-6736; (907) 745-7200; fax (907) 745-7112; www.dnr.state.ak.us/ag.

Alaska Natives. Alaska Federation of Natives, 1577 C St., Suite 300, Anchorage 99501; (907) 274-3611; fax (907) 276-7989; www.nativefederation.org.

Boating, Canoeing and Kayaking. Alaska Department of Transportation and Public Facilities, 3132 Channel Drive, Juneau 99801; (907) 465-6977; www.dot.state.ak.us; Alaska Division of Parks and Outdoor Recreation, 550 W. Seventh Ave., Suite 1260, Anchorage 99501-3557; (907) 269-8400;

fax (907) 269-8901; www.dnr.state.ak.us/parks/boating/index.htm.

Business. Alaska Department of Commerce, Community and Economic Development, P.O. Box 110800, Juneau 99811-0800; (907) 465-2500; fax (907) 465-5442; www.dced.state.ak.us; State Chamber of Commerce, 217 Second St., Suite 201, Juneau 99801; (907) 586-2323; fax (907) 463-5515; www.alaskachamber.com.

Census Data. Alaska Department of Labor and Workforce Development, Research and Analysis, P.O. Box 115501, Juneau 99811-5501; (907) 465-2439; fax (907) 465-4506; http://almis.labor.state.ak.us.

Customs. U.S. Customs, 1910 Alex Holden Way, Juneau 99801; (907) 586-7211; fax (907) 586-9309.

Directory Assistance. (907) 555-1212.

Disabled Access. Challenge Alaska, 3350 Commercial Drive, Suite 208, Anchorage 99501; (907) 344-7399; fax (907) 344-7349; www.challenge.ak.org. Outdoor recreation programs for persons with disabilities; sea kayaking, adaptive skiing. Access Alaska, 121 W. Fireweed Lane, Suite 105, Anchorage 99503; (907) 248-4777, (800) 770-4488; fax (907) 248-0639; TT (907) 248-8799; www.accessalaska.org.

Dog Mushing. Alaska Dog Mushers Association, P.O. Box 70662, Fairbanks 99707; (907) 457-6874; www.sleddog.org. Alaska Sled Dog and Racing Association, P.O. Box 110569, Anchorage 99511; Tozier Track: (907) 562-2235; www.asdra.org.

Education. Alaska Department of Education and Early Development, 801 W. 10th St., Suite 200, Juneau 99801-1878;

> Snowmobilers breaking trail for the Iditarod Trail Sled Dog Race discovered that if they wired a can of SPAM® to their exhaust manifold, they had a perfect hot meal in 50 miles!

(907) 465-2800; fax (907) 465-4156; TTD (907) 465-2815; www.eed.state.ak.us.

Elderly. Division of Senior and Disabilities Service, 3601 C St., Suite 310, Anchorage 99503-5984; (800) 478-9996; (907) 269-3666; fax (907) 269-3688; www.hss.state.ak.us/dsds.

Environmental Conservation. Department of Environmental Conservation, 410 Willoughby Ave., Suite 303, Juneau 99801-1795; (907) 465-5010; fax (907) 465-5097; www.dec.state.ak.us.

Ferry System. Alaska Marine Highway, P.O. Box 112505 Juneau 99811-2505; (800) 642-0066, (907) 465-3941; fax (907) 465-8824; www.ferryalaska.com.

Gold Panning. Alaska Miners Association, 3305 Arctic Blvd., Suite 105, Anchorage 99503; (907) 563-9229; fax (907) 563-9225; www.alaskaminers.org.

Health. State Department of Health and Social Services, Division of Public Health, P.O. Box 110610, Juneau 99811-0610; (907) 465-3030; fax (907) 465-3068; TDD/TTY 586-4265; www.hss.state.ak.us.

Highway Information. Alaska State Troopers (for nonemergencies), (907) 269-5511; for current driving, construction and weather conditions, call 511 (within Alaska) or (866) 282-7577 (from outside of Alaska); http://511.alaska.gov/.

Historical Archives. Alaska State Archives, 141 Willoughby Ave., Juneau 99801; (907) 465-2270; fax (907) 465-2465; www.archives.state.ak.us; National Archives, 654 W. Third Ave., Anchorage 99501-2145; (907) 261-7820; fax (907) 261-7813; www.archives.gov/pacific-alaska/anchorage/index.html; Consortium Library, 3211 Providence Drive, Anchorage 99508; (907) 786-1849; fax (907) 786-1845; www.lib.uaa.alaska.edu/archives.

Housing. Association of Alaska Housing Authorities, 4300 Boniface Parkway Anchorage 99504; (907) 338-3970; fax (907) 338-4904; www.alaska.net/~aaha.

Hunting and Fishing Regulations. State Department of Fish and Game, P.O. Box 115525, Juneau 99811-5525; (907) 465-4100; www.adfg.state.ak.us.

Job Opportunities. Job Service, 3301 Eagle Street, Anchorage 99503; (907) 269-

Three Cheers for Haines!
(Quiet, please!)

There isn't a small-town library in the country that does a better job serving its community than the Haines Borough Public Library, according to the judges of *Library Journal*. The Haines library was named the best small library in America in the February 2005 issue. Haines won the award based on its "steady progress, commitment to community and excellent services." Haines is located in Southeast Alaska, and has a well-read population of 2,245.

—2005 *The Alaska Almanac®*

4800; fax (907) 269-4825; Alaska Job Centers, 10002 Glacier Highway, Suite 200, Juneau 99801-8569; (907) 465-4562; fax (907) 465-2984; www.jobs.state.ak.us.

Job Opportunities for People with Disabilities. ASSETS, Inc., 2330 Nichols St., Anchorage 99508-3495; (907) 279-6617; fax (907) 274-0636; TTY (907) 278-8766; www.assetsinc.org.

Labor. State Department of Labor, P.O. Box 111149, Juneau 99802-1149; (907) 465-2700; fax (907) 465-2784; www.labor.state.ak.us.

Land. Alaska Public Lands Information Centers, 605 W. Fourth Ave., Suite 105, Anchorage 99501, (907) 271-2737; 250 Cushman St., Suite 1A, Fairbanks 99701, (907) 456-0527; P.O. Box 359, Tok 99780, (907) 883-5667; 50 Main St., Ketchikan 99901, (907) 228-6220; www.nps.gov/aplic; Bureau of Land Management, 222 W. Seventh Ave., Suite 13, Anchorage 99513; (907) 271-5960; fax (907) 271-3684; www.ak.blm.gov.

Law. Department of Law, P.O. Box 110300, Juneau 99811-0300; (907) 465-2133; (907) 465-2075; www.law.state.ak.us.

Legal Assistance. Alaska Legal Services, 1016 W. Sixth Ave., Suite 200, Anchorage 99501; (907) 272-9431; (888) 478-2572; fax (907) 279-7417; www.alsc-law.org.

Legislature. Legislative Information Office, 716 W. Fourth Ave., Suite 200, Anchorage 99501-2133; (907) 269-0111, fax (907) 269-0229, TDD (907) 269-0260; www.legis.state.ak.us.

Libraries. Alaska State Library, 333 Willoughby Avenue, 8th Floor State Office Building, Juneau 99811; (907) 465-1301; www.library.state.ak.us.

Maps (topographic). U.S. Geological Survey, 4230 University Drive, Suite 101, Anchorage 99508; (907) 786-7011; http://alaska.usgs.gov.

Military. Department of the Air Force, Headquarters, Alaskan Command, 9480 Pease Ave., Suite 224, Elmendorf Air Force Base 99506; (907) 552-2341; fax (907) 552-5411; www.elmendorf.af.mil; Department of the Army, Headquarters, U.S. Army Alaska, 600 Richardson Drive, No. 5900, Fort Richardson 99505-5900; (907) 384-1542; fax (907) 384-2060; www.usarak.army.mil; State Department of Military and Veterans Affairs, Box 5800, Camp Denali, Fort Richardson 99505-5800; (907) 428-6031; fax (907) 428-6035; www.ak-prepared.com/dmva; U.S. Coast Guard, 17th Coast Guard District, P.O. Box 25517, Juneau 99802-5517; (907) 463-2065; fax (907) 388-2072; www.uscg.mil/d17.

Mines and Petroleum. Alaska Miners Association, 3305 Arctic Blvd., Suite 105, Anchorage 99503; (907) 563-9229; fax (907) 563-9225; www.alaskaminers.org; State Division of Geological and Geophysical Surveys, 3354 College Road, Fairbanks 99709; (907) 451-5000; fax (907) 451-5050; www.dggs.dnr.state.ak.us.

Natural Resources. Department of Natural Resources, Public Information Center, 400 Willoughby Ave., Juneau 99801; (907) 465-3400; fax (907) 586-2954; www.dnr.state.ak.us/pic.

Permanent Fund Dividend. Permanent Fund, 333 Willoughby Ave.,

11th Floor, State Office Bldg., Juneau 99811; (907) 465-2326; fax (907) 465-3470; www.pfd.state.ak.us.

Public Safety. Department of Public Safety, State Troopers, 450 Whittier St., P.O. Box 111200, Juneau 99811-1200; (907) 465-4336; fax (907) 465-5500; www.dps.state.ak.us.

Revenue. Department of Revenue, P.O. Box 110410, Juneau 99811-0410; (907) 465-2300; fax (907) 465-2389; www.revenue.state.ak.us.

River Running. Bureau of Land Management, 222 W. Seventh Ave., Suite 13, Anchorage 99513; (907) 271-5960; fax (907) 271-3684; www.ak.blm.gov; National Park Service, 240 W. Fifth Ave., Suite 114, Anchorage 99501; (907) 644-3510; www.nps.gov; Alaska Public Lands Information Center (SEE Land).

Road Conditions. Alaska Department of Transportation and Public Facilities, Alaska Road Traveler. For current driving, construction and weather conditions, call 511 (within Alaska) or (866) 282-7577 (from outside of Alaska); http://511.alaska.gov/.

Stranded Residents. Association for Stranded Rural Alaskans in Anchorage, 2606 C St., Suite 2B, Anchorage 99503; (907) 272-0643; fax (907) 272-5728; www.lssalaska.org.

Tourism Information. Alaska Travel Industry Association, 2600 Cordova St., Suite 201, Anchorage 99503; (907) 929-2842; fax (907) 561-5727; www.alaskatia.org; Alaska Visitor Information, www.travelalaska.com.

Veterans Affairs. (SEE Military).

Weather Information. National Weather Service, Alaska Region Headquarters, 222 West Seventh Ave., Suite 23, Anchorage 99513-7575, (907) 271-5088; fax (907) 271-3711; recorded, statewide weather forecasts (800) 472-0391; www.arh.noaa.gov.

INSIDE PASSAGE The meandering, protected waterway that threads between the mainland and the coastal islands of Southeast Alaska and British Columbia is called the Inside Passage.

From the head of Washington's Puget Sound to Skagway at the head of Lynn Canal, the route is about 1,000 miles long. It is a transportation corridor for fishing boats, barges, cruise ships and state ferries and a lifeline for Southeast Alaska communities inaccessible by road.

The route passes through the Tongass National Forest, the largest national forest in the United States. The spectacular scenery and wildlife found in the Inside Passage make it a popular tourist route. From the deck of a cruise ship, visitors can see misty bays, islands dense with towering spruce and hemlock trees, mountains, glaciers, bears, whales and eagles.

INUIT CIRCUMPOLAR CONFERENCE Started in Barrow in 1977, the Inuit Circumpolar Conference brings together Inuit from Greenland, Canada, Alaska and Chukotka (Russia) to address common concerns regarding environment, human rights, health and economic development.

The ICC is prominent in national and international arenas, including the United Nations and circumpolar initiatives such as the eight-nation Arctic Environmental Protection Strategy. In Alaska, the ICC has supported international Native-to-Native agreements on managing shared wildlife resources such as polar bears.

National offices in each of the four countries represented by the ICC carry on the work of the organization.

NUGGETS

In June 2006, biologists recovered the carcass of an 8-foot-long beluga whale from the shore of the Tanana River, 15 miles upstream from Nenana and 1,000 miles from the Bering Sea. The whale, believed to be a 2-year-old, offered the first tangible evidence that these marine mammals venture upriver far into Alaska's Interior. Scientists examined the whale to try and determine where it came from and how it died.

—2006 *The Alaska Almanac*®

General assemblies are held every four years at sites that rotate among the countries. The assembly in Canada in 2002 brought together more than 1,500 Inuit from around the Arctic. The 2006 general assembly was held in Barrow, Alaska.

ISLANDS

Southeast Alaska contains about 1,000 of the state's 1,800 named islands, rocks and reefs; several thousand remain unnamed. The Aleutian Island chain, stretching southwest from the mainland, is comprised of more than 200 islands.

Of the state's 10 largest islands, 6 are in southeastern Alaska. Of the remainder, Unimak is in the Aleutians, Nunivak and St. Lawrence are in the Bering Sea off the western coast of Alaska, and Kodiak is in the Gulf of Alaska (See map, pages 6–7). The state's 10 largest islands, according to the U.S. Geological Survey, are:

1. Kodiak, 3,588 sq. mi.
2. Prince of Wales, 2,731 sq. mi.
3. Chichagof, 2,062 sq. mi.
4. St. Lawrence, 1,780 sq. mi.
5. Admiralty, 1,709 sq. mi.
6. Baranof, 1,636 sq. mi.
7. Nunivak, 1,600 sq. mi. (estimate)
8. Unimak, 1,600 sq. mi.
9. Revillagigedo, 1,134 sq. mi.
10. Kupreanof, 1,084 sq. mi.

IVORY

Eskimos traditionally carved sea mammal ivory to make such implements as harpoon heads, dolls and *ulu* (fan-shaped knife) handles. For the past century, however, most carvings were made to sell. Etching on ivory originally was done with hand tools and the scratched designs were filled in with soot. Today power tools supplement the hand tools and carvers may color the etching with India ink, graphite, hematite or commercial coloring.

The large islands of the Bering Sea—St. Lawrence, Little Diomede and Nunivak—are home to the majority of Alaska's ivory carvers. Eskimos from King Island, renowned for their carving skill, now live in Nome. The bulk of the ivory used today comes from walrus tusks and teeth seasoned for a few months. Old walrus ivory, often mistakenly called fossil ivory, also is used. This ivory has been buried in the ground or left on beaches for years; contact

with various minerals has changed it from white to tan or any of a multitude of colors. Some highly prized old ivory exhibits rays of deep blue or areas of brown and gold that shine. Most old ivory comes from ancient sites or beaches on St. Lawrence Island and is sold by the pound to non-Native buyers, generally for use in some kind of artwork.

Mastodon tusks are often unearthed in the summer by miners or found eroding on river cutbanks where they  have been buried for thousands of years. Although these tusks are enormous and their colorations often beautiful, the material cannot be used efficiently because it dries and then separates into narrow ridges.

Various federal prohibitions govern the collection of old walrus, mammoth and mastodon ivory. These materials may be gathered from private or reservation lands, but may not be traded or sold if found on public lands. The taking of fresh walrus ivory is illegal for non-Natives, in accordance with the Marine Mammal Protection Act of 1972.

Walrus may be taken only by Alaska Natives (Aleuts, Eskimos and Indians) who dwell on the coast of the North Pacific Ocean or the Arctic Ocean and rely on the animals for subsistence or for the creation and sale of Native handicrafts or clothing.

Raw walrus ivory and other parts can be sold only by an Alaska Native to an Alaska Native within Alaska, or to a registered agent for resale or transfer to an Alaska Native within the state. Only authentic Native-processed ivory articles of handicrafts or clothing may be sold or

> The owners of Alaska's largest Moose Nugget Jewelry manufacturing company explained that they gather the best nuggets in fall, winter and early spring. Quality is a problem once the rainy season starts because, "You don't want dirty poop."

transferred to a non-Native, or sold in interstate commerce.

Beach ivory, which is found on the beach within one-quarter mile of the ocean, may be kept by anyone. This ivory must be registered by all non-Natives with the U.S. Fish and Wildlife Service (USFWS) or the National Marine Fisheries Service within 30 days of discovery. Beach-found ivory must remain in the possession of the finder even if carved or scrimshawed.

Carved or scrimshawed walrus ivory (authentic Native handicraft) or other marine mammal parts made into clothing or other authentic Native handicrafts may be exported from the United States to a foreign country, but the exporter must first obtain a permit from the USFWS. Even visitors from the Lower 48 simply traveling through or stopping in Canada on their way home are required to have a USFWS export and/or transit permit if their souvenirs contain whale parts. The permit will cost $100, and take 4 to 6 weeks to process. Mailing the carved ivory home will avoid the need for an export/transit permit. Importation of walrus or other marine mammal parts is illegal except for scientific research purposes or for public display once a permit is granted. Because of ecological sensitivity to the use of elephant ivory, many carvers are switching to whalebone, recycled from the skeletons of harvested species.

For further information contact Import/Export Office, U.S. Fish and Wildlife Service, located in the Ted Stevens International Airport; P.O. Box 190045, Anchorage 99519; (907) 271-6198; or Resident Agent in Charge, U.S. Fish and Wildlife Service, 1412 Airport Way, Fairbanks 99701, (907) 456-2335.

The Corporate Policy of the Year Award goes to the Red Dog Saloon in Juneau, which displays a sign reading "If our food, drink, and service aren't up to your standards, please lower your standards!"

JADE Most Alaska jade is found near the Dall, Shungnak and Kobuk Rivers, and Jade Mountain, all north of the Arctic Circle. The stones occur in various shades of green, brown, black, yellow, white and even red. The most valuable are those that are marbled black, white and green. Gem-quality jade, about one-fourth of the total mined, is used in jewelry making. Fractured jade is used for clock faces, tabletops, bookends and other items. Jade is the Alaska state gem.

JUNEAU Located on scenic Gastineau Channel, Juneau is the capital of Alaska. Established in 1880 as a mining camp, it was originally called Harrisburg after Richard Harris, who with his partner, Joseph Juneau, discovered gold and staked their claim in 1880. The camp quickly boomed.

Under Russian rule, the seat of government was at Sitka—with no official capital. In 1900 Congress moved this seat to Juneau, but Juneau did not become the capital (that is, where the legislature convenes) until 1912. In 1974, Alaskans voted to move the state capital closer to the state's population center, selecting a site between Anchorage and Fairbanks at Willow. Juneau remained the capital after funding for the transfer of government to Willow was defeated by voters in 1982. Of Southeast Alaska's 60,000 residents, half live in Juneau, Alaska's third-largest city.

Juneau is accessible only by boat, ferry or plane. No roads lead into or out of town. Often called "a little San Francisco," Juneau is tucked at the foot of Mount Juneau. The climate is wet and mild, with summer average daily maximum temperatures of 63°F and winter average daily minimum temperatures of 20°F. Average annual snowfall is about 92 inches in the downtown area.

Sights include the historic shopping district, the Red Dog Saloon, the State and City Museum, the Macaulay Salmon Hatchery, the State Office Building and the Governor's Mansion. Helicopter tours of the Juneau Icefield and tours to Glacier Bay National Park are popular activities, as are kayaking, fishing, hiking and Inside Passage cruises.

Juneau's cruise passenger arrivals for 2006 was 951,000 visitors. A popular attraction in the city is the Mount Roberts Tramway, a 2,000-foot scenic ride in a spacious gondola.

Additional information is available from the Juneau Convention and Visitors Bureau, Centennial Hall Visitor Center, 101 Egan Drive, Juneau 99801; (907) 586-2201; www.traveljuneau.com. For a free Juneau travel planner, call (888) 581-2201.

KENNECOTT, KENNICOTT

Kennicott Glacier in the Wrangell Mountains was named for explorer and geologist Robert Kennicott.

The Kennecott Mines Co. was formed in 1906 to exploit the rich copper ore deposits nearby. The mining company was supposed to be named after the glacier, but the name was misspelled with a second "e" and the error stuck.

The mining town of Kennicott took its name from the glacier. The mine closed down in 1938. But the timeworn ghost town of Kennicott still stands and is a National Historic Landmark.

KODIAK (See ALSO Islands) Kodiak, the oldest European settlement in Alaska, is located on Kodiak Island in the Gulf of Alaska, 252 air miles south of Anchorage. The 100-mile-long island, second only to Hawaii's Big Island in size in the United States, is known as Alaska's "Emerald Isle." The island and its main city are accessible only by boat, ferry or plane.

After 7,500 years of occupation by the Alutiiq people, Kodiak Island was "discovered" by Russian explorer Stephen Glotov in 1763. The town of Kodiak served as Russian Alaska's first capital city until 1804. In 1912, Kodiak was caught in drifting ash from the eruption of Novarupta Volcano on the Alaska Peninsula, which buried the town under 18 inches of pumice. The 9.2-magnitude earthquake that struck Alaska on March 27, 1964, set off a tsunami (a seismic sea wave) that virtually destroyed downtown Kodiak, its fishing fleet, processing plants and more than 150 homes.

Today, over 13,000 residents inhabit the Kodiak Island Borough. As homeport to more than 700 commercial fishing vessels, Kodiak is the state's largest fishing port and consistently ranks among the top three commercial fishing ports in the United

Remains of the Kennecott Copper Mine. From *Picture Journeys in Alaska's Wrangell–St. Elias* by George Herben.

States, based on value. Timber activities and tourism are also important segments of the local economy. Kodiak is home to the U.S. Coast Guard's base for North Pacific operations, the nation's largest.

The city of Kodiak has three museums: the Baranov Museum, the Kodiak Military History Museum and the Alutiiq Museum and Archaeological Repository. The Baranov Museum displays many items from the Russian era. The Kodiak Military History Museum exhibits include military memorabilia from 1911 to the present.

The Alutiiq Museum chronicles the history of the indigenous Alutiiq people and the advent of the Russian fur trade. Icons, rare paintings and handmade brassworks can be seen at the Russian Orthodox Church. Visitors are asked to respect the schedule of religious services.

It is estimated that more than 3,000 Kodiak bears, largest of the state's brown/grizzly bears, inhabit the island. Kodiak National Wildlife Refuge (accessible only by floatplane or boat) was established in 1941 to preserve the natural habitat of the bears. Bears can be observed feeding on salmon in summer in remote parts of the refuge.

For maps, brochures and hunting and fishing information, contact the Kodiak Island Convention and Visitors Bureau, 100 Marine Way, Suite 200, Kodiak 99615; (907) 486-4782; www.kodiak.org.

KUSPUK A *kuspuk* is an Eskimo woman's parka, often made with a loosely cut back so that an infant may be carried piggyback-style.

Parkas are made from seal, marmot, ground squirrel, rabbit or fox skins; traditionally, the fur lining faced inward. The ruffs are generally made of wolverine or wolf fur. A cloth outer shell, the *qaspeg,* was worn over a fur parka to keep it clean and to reduce wear. This outer shell was usually made of brightly colored corduroy, cotton print or velveteen-like material trimmed with rickrack. In warmer months, many women wear a cotton *kuspuk* with long pants as daily, informal wear.

LABOR AND EMPLOYER ORGANIZATIONS
Alaska has local branches of dozens of unions, including unions for longshoremen, carpenters, restaurant employees, pulp and paper workers, electrical workers, aerospace workers, firefighters, teachers and others. For details, consult the Alaska Labor Union Directory of the Alaska State AFL-CIO; (907) 258-6284.

LAKES
There are 94 lakes with surface areas of more than 10 square miles among Alaska's more than 3 million lakes.

According to the U.S. Geological Survey, the 10 largest natural freshwater lakes are:
1. Iliamna, 1,150 sq. mi.
2. Becharof, 458 sq. mi.
3. Teshekpuk, 315 sq. mi.
4. Naknek, 242 sq. mi.
5. Tustumena, 117 sq. mi.
6. Clark, 110 sq. mi.
7. Dall, 100 sq. mi.
8. Upper Ugashik, 75 sq. mi.
9. Lower Ugashik, 72 sq. mi.
10. Kukaklek, 72 sq. mi.

Spenard Builders Supply in Homer sponsored a duct tape sculpture contest. The coveted prize was a trip to Anchorage. Sculpture entries included hockey players on the ice, Cinderella's pumpkin coach, a bouquet of roses, and "a whole lot of duct tape bikinis."

LAND USE
(SEE ALSO Highways; Homesteading; National Forests; National Parks; National Wild and Scenic Rivers; National Wilderness Areas; National Wildlife Refuges; Native Peoples; State Park System)
At first glance it seems odd that such a huge area as Alaska has not been more heavily settled. Thousands of acres of forest and tundra, miles and miles of rivers and streams, hidden valleys, bays, coves and mountains are spread across an area so vast that it staggers the imagination. Yet more than two-thirds of the population of Alaska remains clustered around two major centers of commerce, Anchorage and Fairbanks.

Visitors flying over the state are impressed by immense areas showing no sign of humanity. Current assessments indicate that approximately 160,000 acres of Alaska have been cleared, built on or otherwise directly altered by people, either by settlement or resource development, including mining, pipeline construction and agriculture. In comparison to the 365 million acres of land that make up the total of the state, the settled or altered area amounts to less than one-twentieth of 1 percent.

There are several reasons for this lack of development. Frozen for long periods in the Arctic, much of the land cannot support quantities of people or industry. Where the winters are "warm," the mountains, glaciers, rivers and oceans prevent easy access for commerce and trade.

In most places, the free market affects patterns of land ownership, but in Alaska all land ownership patterns until recent decades were the result of a century-long process of a single landowner, the United States government.

The Statehood Act in 1958 signaled the beginning of a dramatic shift in land ownership patterns. It authorized the state to select 104 million of the 365 million acres of land and inland waters in Alaska. (Under the Submerged Lands Act, the state has title to submerged lands under navigable inland waters.)

In passing the Statehood Act, Congress cited economic independence and the need to open Alaska to economic development as the primary purposes for large Alaska land grants.

Canoeists glide across Wonder Lake in Denali National Park and Preserve.
Photo by Roy Corral.

Alaska Native Claims Settlement
Act. The issue of Native claims in Alaska was resolved with the passage of the Alaska Native Claims Settlement Act (ANCSA) on Dec. 18, 1971. This act of Congress provided for the creation of Alaska Native village and regional corporations and gave Alaska Eskimos, Aleuts and Indians $962.5 million and the right to select 44 million acres from a land pool of some 115 million acres.

Immediately after the settlement act passed, and before Native lands and National Interest Lands were selected, the state filed to select an additional 77 million acres of land. In September 1972, the litigation initiated by the state was resolved by a settlement affirming state selection of an additional 41 million acres.

The settlement act, in addition to establishing a Joint Federal–State Land Use Planning Commission, directed the secretary of the interior to withdraw from public use up to 80 million acres of land in Alaska for study as possible national parks, wildlife refuges, national forests and wild and scenic rivers. These were the National Interest Lands Congress was to decide upon by Dec. 18, 1978. The U.S. House of Representatives passed a bill (HR39) that would have designated 124 million acres of national parks, forests and wildlife refuges, and designated millions of acres of these and existing parks, forests and refuges as wilderness. Although a bill was reported out of committee, it failed to pass the Senate before Congress adjourned.

In November 1978, the secretary of the interior published a draft environmental impact supplement, which listed the actions that the executive branch of the federal government could take to protect federal lands in Alaska until the 96th Congress could consider the creation of new parks, wildlife refuges, wild and scenic rivers and national forests. In keeping with this objective, the secretary of the interior, under provisions of the 1976 Federal Land Policy and Management Act, withdrew about 114 million acres of land in Alaska from most public uses. On Dec. 1, 1978, President Jimmy Carter, under the authority of the 1906 Antiquities Act, designated 56 million acres of these lands as national monuments.

In February 1980, the House of Representatives passed a modified HR39.

In August 1980, the Senate passed a compromise version of the Alaska lands bill that created 106 million acres of new conservation units and affected 131 million acres in Alaska. In November 1980, the House accepted the Senate version of the Alaska National Interest Lands Conservation Act (ANILCA), which President Carter signed into law Dec. 2, 1980.

Land use in Alaska continues to be a complex subject. Distribution of land ownership from the federal government to the state of Alaska, Native village and regional corporations and private citizens has required considerable time. Debate continues over issues such as Native sovereignty and subsistence hunting and fishing rights.

Acquiring Land for Private Use.
The easiest and fastest way to acquire land for private use is by purchase from the private sector, through real estate agencies or directly from individuals. Because of speculation, land claim conflicts and delays

involving Native, state and federal groups, however, private land may be expensive and in short supply.

Private land in Alaska, excluding land held by Native corporations, is estimated at 2.7 million acres, but less than 1 percent of the state. Much of this land passed into private hands through the federal Homestead Acts and other public land laws, as well as land disposal programs of the state, boroughs or communities. Most private land is located along Alaska's limited road network. Compared to other categories of land, it is highly accessible and constitutes some of the prime settlement land.

Remote Recreational Cabin Sites.

(SEE ALSO Homesteading) Alaska residents also have an opportunity to lease (for a limited time) and then purchase remote recreational cabin sites on state lands through a state-run lottery. Those entering the lottery must meet age, residency and some land use requirements.

For additional information, contact one of the Alaska Department of Natural Resources Public Information Centers at 605 W. Fourth Ave., Suite 105, Anchorage 99501, (907) 271-2737; P.O. Box 359, Tok 99780, (907) 883-5667; 250 Cushman, Suite 1A, Fairbanks 99701, (907) 456-0527; 50 Main St., Ketchikan 99901, (907) 228-6220; www.nps.gov/aplic; or go to www.dnr.state.ak.us/mlw/landsale/index.htm.

Following is the amount of land owned by various entities as of September 2006:

A spokesman for an Anchorage garden center reports that bottled wolf urine is now quite a popular deterrent for urban moose who eat ornamental shrubs. The store could increase its sales but "we couldn't stand the smell of it any more." Does it work? "Nobody's ever brought it back to us."

Alaska Land Ownership

Owner	Acreage (in millions)
State	91.7
U.S. Bureau of Land Management	83.5
U.S. Fish and Wildlife Service	70.6
National Park Service	54.0
Native	38.1
U.S. Forest Service	22.0
Military and other federal	2.0
Other Private (besides Native)	2.7

Source: U.S. Bureau of Land Management (as of 2006)

LANGUAGES (SEE ALSO Igloo; Masks; Native Peoples; Parka)

Besides English, Alaska's languages include 20 Native American languages.

The Eskimo language group—Central Yup'ik, Siberian Yupik and Iñupiaq—is widely spoken by many Natives in Western and Northern Alaska.

Most of these Native languages are at risk of extinction. They include Han, Haida, Eyak, Tanana, Tlingit, Dena'ina (or Tanaina), Ahtna, Ingalik, Holikachuk, Tsimshian, Koyukon, Upper Kuskokwim, Upper Tanana, Gwich'in and Aleut.

MAMMALS (SEE ALSO Bears; Musk Oxen; Whales; Whaling)

Large Land Mammals

Black Bear. Highest densities are found in Southeast, Prince William Sound and Southcentral coastal mountains and lowlands. Black bears also occur in Interior and Western Alaska, but are absent from Southeast islands north of Frederick Sound (primarily Admiralty, Baranof and Chichagof) and the Kodiak archipelago. They are not commonly found west of about Naknek Lake on the Alaska Peninsula, in the Aleutian Islands or on the open tundra sloping into the Bering Sea and Arctic Ocean. (SEE ALSO Bears)

Brown/Grizzly Bear. These large omnivores are found in most of Alaska except for Southeast islands south of Frederick Sound or in the Aleutians (except for Unimak Island). (SEE ALSO Bears)

Polar Bear. There are two groups in Alaska's Arctic rim: an eastern group found largely in the Beaufort Sea and a western

Did You See That?

Residents of Barrow were amazed when a shaggy musk ox wandered into town in November 2005, apparently on vacation from its herd in the Arctic National Wildlife Refuge. While sightings of musk oxen are not unheard of as far north as Kaktovik or Point Lay, seeing the Ice Age–looking creature dodging traffic in Barrow created quite a stir. State biologist Geoff Carroll explained that the musk ox was likely exiled from his herd. "When the subdominant males get bumped," Carroll stated, "they'll often go on a walkabout for years, and then they'll go back and recruit a female, and that's how they expand their territory."

—2006 *The Alaska Almanac®*

group found in the Chukchi Sea between Alaska and Siberia. The latter group includes the largest polar bears in the world. Old males can exceed 1,500 pounds. (SEE ALSO Bears)

American Bison. In 1928, 23 bison were transplanted from Montana to Delta Junction to restore Alaska's bison population, which had died out some 500 years before. Today, several hundred bison graze near Delta Junction; other herds range at Farewell, at Chitina and along the lower Copper River.

Barren Ground Caribou. There are at least 13 distinct caribou herds, with some overlapping ranges: Adak, Alaska Peninsula, Arctic, Beaver, Chisana, Delta, Kenai, McKinley, Mentasta, Mulchatna, Nelchina, Porcupine and Fortymile. Porcupine and Fortymile herds range into Canada. The Western Arctic herd numbers about 450,000, the state's largest. Hunters of the 50 villages along its migration route take about 20,000 caribou annually for meat.

Sitka Black-tailed Deer. These deer range the coastal rain forests of southeastern Alaska. They have been successfully transplanted to the Yakutat area, Prince William Sound and Kodiak and Afognak islands.

Roosevelt Elk. Alaska's only elk occur on Raspberry and Afognak Islands, the result of a 1928 transplant of 105 Roosevelt elk from the Olympic Peninsula in Washington State. Other transplant attempts have failed.

Moose. Moose occur from the Unuk River in Southeast to the Arctic Slope, but are most abundant in second-growth birch forests, on timberline plateaus and along major rivers of Southcentral and Interior. They are not found on islands in Prince William Sound or the Bering Sea, on most major islands in Southeast or on Kodiak or the Aleutians groups.

Mountain Goat. These white-coated animals are found in mountains throughout Southeast, and north and west along coastal mountains to Cook Inlet and Kenai Peninsula. They have been successfully transplanted to Kodiak and Baranof Islands.

Musk Oxen. These shaggy, long-haired mammals were eliminated from Alaska by hunters by 1865. The species was reintroduced and first transplanted to Nunivak Island, and from there to the Arctic Slope around Kavik, Seward Peninsula, Cape Thompson and Nelson Island. (SEE also Musk Oxen)

Reindeer. Introduced from Siberia just before the 20th century, reindeer roamed much of the Bering Sea Coast region but are now confined to St. George and Nunivak Islands and the Seward Peninsula.

Dall Sheep. The only white, wild sheep in the world, Dall sheep are found

Caribou calf. From *Caribou: Wanderer of the Tundra* by Tom Walker.

in all major mountain ranges in Alaska except the Aleutian Range south of Iliamna Lake.

Wolf. Wolves are protected and managed as big game and valuable furbearers. Wolves are found throughout Alaska except Bering Sea islands, some Southeast and Prince William Sound islands and the Aleutian Islands. The wolf succeeds in a variety of climates and terrains. Because some biologists believe wolves must be culled to maintain caribou herd populations, controversial wolf kills, in which wolves are hunted by air, have taken place.

Wolverine. Shy, solitary creatures, wolverines are found throughout Alaska and on some Southeast islands. They are not abundant in comparison with other furbearers.

Furbearers

Beaver. These large vegetarian rodents are found in most of mainland Alaska from the Brooks Range to the middle of the Alaska Peninsula. Abundant in some major mainland river drainages in the Southeast and on Yakutat Foreland, they have also been successfully transplanted to the Kodiak area. Beaver dams are sometimes destroyed to allow salmon upstream; however, beavers can rebuild their dams quickly and usually do so on the same site.

Coyote. The coyote is a relative new-comer to Alaska, showing up shortly after the turn of the 20th century, based on reports from old-timers and records. They are not abundant statewide, but are common in Tanana, Copper, Matanuska and Susitna River drainages and on Kenai Peninsula. The coyote is found as far west as Alaska Peninsula and the north side of Bristol Bay. Coyotes are increasingly seen near Anchorage.

Fox. *Arctic* (white and blue phases): Arctic foxes are found almost entirely along the Arctic coast as far south as the north-western shore of Bristol Bay. They have been introduced to the Pribilof and Aleutian Islands, where the blue color phase, most popular with fox farmers, predominates. The white color phase occurs naturally on St. Lawrence and Nunivak Islands.

Red: Its golden fur coveted by trappers, the red fox is found throughout Alaska except for most areas of Southeast and around Prince William Sound.

Lynx. These shy night-prowlers' main food source is the snowshoe hare. The lynx is found throughout Alaska, except on the Yukon–Kuskokwim Delta, southern Alaska Peninsula and along coastal tidelands. It is relatively scarce along the northern Gulf Coast and in southeastern Alaska.

Hoary Marmot. Present throughout most of the mountain regions of Alaska and along the Endicott Mountains east into Canada, the hoary marmot lives in the high country, especially the warm slopes near and above timberline.

Marten. The marten must have climax spruce forest to survive; its habitat ranges throughout timbered Alaska, except north of the Brooks Range, on treeless sections of the Alaska Peninsula and on the Yukon–Kuskokwim Delta. It has been successfully introduced to Prince of Wales, Baranof, Chichagof and Afognak Islands.

Muskrat. Muskrats are found in greatest numbers around lakes, ponds, rivers and marshes throughout all of main-land Alaska south of the Brooks Range except for the Alaska Peninsula west of the Ugashik lakes. They were introduced to Kodiak, Afognak and Raspberry Islands. Muskrats were traditionally an important early spring subsistence food for Native Alaskans.

River Otter. A member of the weasel family, the river otter occurs throughout the state except on the Aleutian Islands, Bering Sea islands and the Arctic coastal plain east of Point Lay. It is most abundant in southeastern Alaska, in Prince William Sound coastal areas and on the Yukon–Kuskokwim Delta. It is sometimes called the "land otter" to distinguish it from the sea otter.

Raccoon. The raccoon is not native to Alaska and is considered an undesirable addition because of its impact on native wildlife. It is found on the west coast of Kodiak Island, on Japonski and Baranof Islands and on other islands off Prince of Wales Island in Southeast.

Squirrel. *Northern flying:* These small nocturnal squirrels are found in Interior, Southcentral and Southeast Alaska where coniferous forests are sufficiently dense to provide suitable habitat. *Red:* These tree squirrels inhabit spruce forests, especially along rivers, from Southeast north to the Brooks Range. They are not found on the Seward Peninsula, Yukon–Kuskokwim Delta and Alaska Peninsula south of Naknek River.

Weasel. Least weasels and short-tailed weasels are found throughout Alaska, except for the Bering Sea and Aleutian Islands. Short-tailed weasels are brown with white underparts in summer, becoming snow-white in winter (designated ermine).

Other Small Mammals

Bat. Alaska has five common bat species.

Northern Hare (Arctic Hare or **Tundra Hare).** This large hare inhabits western and northern coastal Alaska, weighs 12 pounds or more and measures 2½ feet long.

Snowshoe Hare (or **Varying Hare**). In winter, these animals become pure white; in summer, their coats are grayish to brown. The snowshoe hare occurs throughout Alaska except for the lower portion of Alaska Peninsula, the Arctic coast and most islands; it is scarce in southeastern Alaska. Cyclic population highs and lows of hares occur roughly every 10 years. Their big hind feet, covered with coarse hair in winter, act as snowshoes for easy travel over snow.

Brown Lemming. Lemmings are found throughout Northern Alaska and the Alaska Peninsula; they are not present in Southeast, Southcentral or the Kodiak archipelago.

Collared Lemming. Resembling large meadow voles, collared lemmings range from the Brooks Range north and from the lower Kuskokwim River drainage north.

Northern Bog Lemming (sometimes called **Lemming Mouse**). These tiny mammals, rarely observed, are in meadows and bogs across most of Alaska.

Deer Mouse. These rodents inhabit timber and brush in southeastern Alaska.

House Mouse. Extremely adaptive, familiar house mice are found in Alaska seaports and large communities in Southcentral Alaska.

Meadow Jumping Mouse. These mice can jump 6 feet and are found in the southern third of Alaska from the Alaska Range to the Gulf of Alaska.

Collared Pika. Members of the rabbit family, pikas are found in central and southern Alaska; they are most common in the Alaska Range.

Porcupine. These slow-moving rodents prefer forests and inhabit most wooded regions of mainland Alaska.

Norway Rat. The Norway rat came to Alaska on whaling ships in the mid-1800s, thriving in Aleutian ports (the Rat Islands group is named for the Norway rats). They are now found in virtually all Alaska seaports, and in Anchorage and Fairbanks and other population centers with open garbage dumps.

Shrew. Seven species of shrew range in Alaska.

Meadow Vole (or Meadow Mouse). Extremely adaptive, there are seven species of meadow vole attributed to Alaska that range throughout the state.

Red-backed Vole. The red-backed vole prefers cool, damp forests and is found throughout Alaska from Southeast to Norton Sound.

Woodchuck. These large, burrowing squirrels, also called groundhogs, are found in the eastern Interior between the Yukon and Tanana Rivers, from east of Fairbanks to the Alaska-Canada border.

Bushy-tailed Woodrat. Commonly called Pack Rats because they tend to carry off objects to their nests, woodrats are found along the mainland coast of southeastern Alaska.

In March, a Southeast Alaska Fish & Game biologist shot a tranquilizer dart at a moose from a helicopter. The angry ungulate charged the helicopter, hit it, and caused it to crash! The last time we checked, the Acme Helicopter instruction manual still contained the statement, "Warning—Do not fly this helicopter low enough to be hit by a freakin' moose!"

Marine Mammals

Marine mammals found in Alaska waters are **dolphin** (Grampus, Pacific white-sided and Risso's); **Pacific walrus; porpoise** (Dall and harbor); **sea otter; seal** (harbor, larga, northern elephant, northern fur, Pacific bearded or *oogruk*, ribbon, ringed and spotted); **Steller sea lion;** and **whale** (Baird's beaked or giant bottlenose, beluga, blue, narwhal, bowhead, Cuvier's beaked or goosebeaked, fin or finback, gray, humpback, killer, minke or little piked, northern right, pilot, sei, sperm and Bering Sea beaked or Stejneger's beaked). (SEE Whales; Whaling)

The U.S. Fish and Wildlife Service (Department of the Interior) is responsible for the management of polar bears, sea otters and walrus in Alaska. The National Marine Fisheries Service (Department of Commerce) is responsible for the management of all other marine mammals.

MASKS (SEE ALSO Native Arts and Crafts)

Masks are integral to the cultures of the Eskimos, coastal Indians and Aleuts of Alaska.

Eskimo. Eskimo masks rank among the finest tribal art in the world. Ceremonialism and the mask-making that accompanied it were highly developed and practiced widely by the time the first Russians established trading posts in southeastern Alaska in the early 1800s.

Shamans used masks during certain ceremonies, sometimes in conjunction with wooden puppets, in ways that frightened and entertained participants. Dancers wore religious masks in festivals that honored the spirits of animals and birds to be hunted or that needed to be appeased. Each spirit was

Walrus. From *Alaska's Mammals* by Dave Smith (text) and Tom Walker (photographs).

Scary Swim Buddies

A 12-year-old Ketchikan boy, Ellis Miller, had a shocking encounter with a 30-foot killer whale as he paddled around in 6 feet of water in Helm Bay, jut north of Ketchikan. It was the summer of 2005, and Miller was with his family and friends on a weekend outing at a Forest Service cabin. Diving under the surface, Miller suddenly saw the enormous whale next to him, the 8-foot dorsal fin close to his head. The whale bumped Ellis on the shoulder, then abruptly turned away. A few seconds later, six more orcas surfaced just a few feet offshore. The pod paraded past four times, slapping their fins on the water.

—2006 *The Alaska Almanac*®

interpreted in a different mask and each mask was thought to have a spirit, or *inua,* of its own. This *inua* tied the mask to the stream of spiritual beliefs present in Eskimo religion. Not all masks were benign; some were surrealistic pieces that represented angry or dangerous spirits. Some had moving parts.

In 1996, the Anchorage Museum of History and Art held a notable exhibit, "Agayuliyararput Our Way of Making Prayer: The Living Tradition of Yup'ik Masks," to demonstrate the interest of Yup'ik people in preserving their past and carrying the vital tradition of mask-making into the future. The exhibit went on to tour the Lower 48 in 1997.

Indian. Several types of masks existed among the Tlingit and other coastal Indians of Alaska, including simple single-face masks, occasionally having an elaborately carved totemic border; a variation of the face mask with the addition of moving parts; and transformation masks, which have several faces concealed within the first.

Masked dancers were accompanied by a chorus of tribal singers who sang songs associated with the masks and reflecting the wealth of the host. Masks were the critical element in portraying the relationship of the tribe with spirits and projecting their power to spellbind their audiences.

Masks were always created to be worn, but not all members of the tribe held sufficient status or power to wear them. Ceremonial use of masks generally took place in the fall or winter, when the spirits of the other world were said to be nearby.

Northwest Coast Indian mask-makers primarily used alder, though red and yellow cedar were used at times.

Aleut. Examples of masks used on various islands of the Aleutian Chain for shamanistic and ceremonial purposes are reported as early as the mid-18th century. Some of these early masks represented animals. Many were apparently destroyed after use. Aleut legends maintain that some masks were associated with ancient inhabitants of the region.

On the Shumagin Islands, a group of cavelike chambers yielded important examples of Aleut masks late in the 19th century. A number of well-preserved masks, apparently associated with the burials of Aleut whalers, were found. All of them had once been painted. Some of them had attached ears and tooth grips. Pegs were used for inserting feathers or carved wooden appendages similar to those of Eskimo masks of southern Alaska today. Fragments of composite masks, those decorated with feathers, appendages or movable parts, have been found on Kagamil Island with earlier remains.

Early accounts of masked Aleut dances say each dance was accompanied by special songs. Most masks were apparently hidden in caves or secret places when the ceremony ended.

Today, modern Aleut mask-makers study the old traditions and reproduce masks from museum collections or create contemporary variants in clay, glass and even chrome.

McNEIL RIVER STATE GAME SANCTUARY

Photographers, naturalists, wildlife enthusiasts and researchers come to McNeil River State Game Sanctuary in Southwestern Alaska for the opportunity to view the world's largest concentration of brown bears in their natural habitat. The Alaska Department of Fish and Game manages the sanctuary's unique bear-viewing program, which allows visitors to watch the brown bears as they congregate to feed on migrating salmon. Small groups are escorted to a viewing area by a department guide and are limited to 10 visitors a day. Despite the number of bears and the presence of humans, there have been no injuries to bears or humans through more than two decades of the program's operation.

All visitors must apply for a permit to visit the sanctuary. A maximum of 13 nontransferable viewing permits are in effect each day from June 7 to Aug. 25, and are awarded by lottery. Applications are now available online (www.wildlife.alaska.gov/mcneil/index.cfm) and must be submitted online or postmarked by March 1 for the upcoming visitor season. Contact the Alaska Department of Fish and

Bears and Salmon

The two are as synonymous as Alaska and winter. Both Alaska brown bears, *Ursus arctos,* and American black bears, *Ursus americanus,* catch and eat salmon, but rarely do the two species coexist on the same watercourse. Black bears enjoy exclusive use of only a few streams; most are dominated by their larger cousins. A brown bear may kill and eat any black bear it catches.

—*Alaska's Wildlife* by Tom Walker

Game, Division of Wildlife Conservation, 333 Raspberry Road, Anchorage 99518-1599, Attention: McNeil River; (907) 267-2257; www.adfg.state.ak.us.

Statistics on bears in the sanctuary have been compiled since 1976:

- Most bears seen at one time at McNeil Falls—72
- Most bears seen in one day at McNeil Falls—126
- Most salmon seen caught in one day by one bear—90
- Most salmon seen caught in one year by one bear—1,012
- Most salmon seen caught in one year at McNeil Falls—15,455

MEDAL OF HEROISM By a law
enacted in 1965, the Alaska governor is authorized to award, in recognition of valorous and heroic deeds, a state medal of heroism to those who have saved a life or, at risk to their lives, have served the state or community on behalf of the health, welfare or safety of others. The heroism medal is not necessarily given every year, and may be awarded post-humously. In 2002, author Nancy Warren Ferrell profiled the medal winners in a book titled *Alaska's Heroes*. Following are recipients and year of the award of the State of Alaska Award for Bravery-Heroism:

Albert Rothfuss (1965), Ketchikan. Rescued a child from drowning in Ketchikan Creek.

Randy Blake Prinzing (1968), Soldotna. Saved two lives at Scout Lake.

Nancy Davis (1971), Seattle. A flight attendant who convinced a hijacker to surrender.

Jeffrey Stone (1972), Fairbanks. Saved two youths from a burning apartment.

Gilbert Pelowook (1975), Savoonga. An Alaska state trooper who aided plane crash victims on St. Lawrence Island.

Residents of Gambell (1975), Provided aid and care for plane crash victims on St. Lawrence Island.

George Jackinsky (1978), Kasilof. Rescued two persons from a burning plane.

Mike Hancock (1980), Lima, Ohio. Rescued a victim of a plane crash that brought down high-voltage lines.

David Graham (1983), Kenai. Rescued a person from a burning car.

John Stimson (1983), Cordova. A first sergeant in the Division of Fish and Wildlife Protection who died in a helicopter accident during an attempt to rescue others.

Robert Larson (1983), Anchorage. An employee of the Department of Public Safety who flew through hazardous conditions to rescue survivors of the crash that took John Stimson's life.

Esther Farquhar (1984), Sitka. Tried to save other members of her family from a fire in their home; lost her life in the attempt.

Darren Olanna (1984), Nome. Died while attempting to rescue a person from a burning house.

Billy Westlock (1986), Emmonak. Rescued a youngster from the Emmonak River.

Lt. Cmdr. Whiddon, Lt. Breithaupt, ASM2 Tunks, AD1 Saylor and AT3 Milne (1987), Sitka. U.S. Coast Guard personnel rescued a man and his son from their sinking boat during high seas.

The Army and Air National Guard (1988), Gambell, Savoonga, Nome and Shishmaref. Searched for seven missing walrus hunters from Gambell.

Evans Geary, Johnny Sheldon, Jason Rutman, Jessee Ahkpuk Jr. and Carl Hadley (1989), Buckland. Youths rescued two friends who, while skating on a frozen pond, had fallen through the ice.

Robert Cusack (1991), Lake Iliamna. Rescued a woman and a child who were trapped inside a floatplane that had crashed and sunk in Lake Iliamna.

Clifford Comer, Robert Yerex, Gary Strebe, David Schron and Jeffery Waite (1992), Air Station Kodiak. Coast Guard members rescued a four-man fishing crew in 45-knot winds and 35-foot seas.

Clyde Aketachunak (1994), Kotlik. Awarded posthumously after Aketachunak died in an attempt to save six-year-old Jennifer Prince from drowning in Kotlik Slough.

Sgt. David Lancaster (1994), formerly of Fort Richardson, and Tom Burgess (1994), North Pole. Saved the lives of passengers on a tour bus that was involved in a head-on collision on the Parks Highway.

METRIC CONVERSIONS (approximate)

	When you know:	You can find:	If you multiply by:
Length	inches	millimeters	25.4
	feet	centimeters	30.5
	yards	meters	0.9
	miles	kilometers	1.6
	millimeters	inches	0.04
	centimeters	inches	0.4
	meters	yards	1.1
	kilometers	miles	0.6
Temperature	degrees Fahrenheit	degrees Celsius	5/9 (after subtracting 32)
	degrees Celsius	degrees Fahrenheit	9/5 (then add 32)

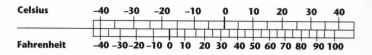

Celsius −40 −30 −20 −10 0 10 20 30 40

Fahrenheit −40 −30 −20 −10 0 10 20 30 40 50 60 70 80 90 100

Eric Pentilla, Randy Oles, Walter Greaves and Jerry Austin (1994). Helped rescue seven missionaries whose plane crashed in the Bering Sea when returning from Russia.

Travis Bennett (1994), North Pole. At the age of 14, waded into the Chena River to save the life of Debbie Peterson, who was drowning.

Mike Olsen, Rusty Shaub, Kevin Kramer and George Coulter (1994). Rescued the survivors of an airplane crash in Taku Inlet.

(Louis R.) Rick Gottwald (1995), Juneau. Swam to a burning boat in Juneau's Harris Harbor and saved an intoxicated man who was on board.

Rose Edgren (1995), Delta Junction. A state trooper who pushed her partner to safety when they were fired upon, shot the attacker and then administered lifesaving first aid.

Sam Hoger (1996), Eagle River. While visiting New Orleans, rescued a 10-year-old boy from drowning.

Timothy Eldridge and Billy Luce (1997), Anchorage. Entered an apartment on the third floor of a burning building in Anchorage, dragged the occupant to safety and doused the flames.

Gene Snell (2000), Shishmaref. Rescued a snowmachine rider who had fallen through the ice and was clinging to his floating sled.

Rick Siangco (2000), Juneau. Fisherman and his crew rescued two fishermen whose boat had capsized in 10-foot seas near Juneau.

Larry Erickson (2002), Fairbanks. A state trooper who dove into the Chena River to rescue a baby from a submerged automobile.

Keira Lestina (2003), Mile 73 Seward Highway. Rescued a mother and her six-year-old daughter from an overturned motor home that, moments later, exploded in flames.

MICROBREWERIES

As in many parts of the United States, limited-edition stouts, ales and beers are a trend in Alaska. Many of the breweries offer dining and window observation of the brewing process. Others offer tours and samples. For more details, browse online at www.brewpubzone.com/States/Alaska.html.

Alaskan Brewing & Bottling Co., 5429 Shaune Drive, Juneau 99801.

Glacier Brewhouse, 737 W. Fifth Ave., Suite 110, Anchorage 99501.

MILEAGE CHART

Driving Mileage Between Principal Points	Anchorage, AK	Dawson City, YT	Dawson Creek, BC	Fairbanks, AK	Haines, AK	Homer, AK	Prince Rupert, BC	Seattle, WA	Skagway, AK	Valdez, AK	Whitehorse, YT
Anchorage, AK		515	1608	358	775	226	1605	2435	832	304	724
Dawson City, YT	515		1195	393	578	741	1192	2022	435	441	327
Dawson Creek, BC	1608	1195		1486	1135	1834	706	827	992	1534	884
Fairbanks, AK	358	393	1486		653	584	1483	2313	710	284	602
Haines, AK	775	578	1135	653		1001	1132	1962	359	701	251
Homer, AK	226	741	1834	584	1001		1831	2661	1058	530	950
Prince Rupert, BC	1605	1192	706	1483	1132	1831		1033	989	1531	881
Seattle, WA	2435	2022	827	2313	1962	2661	1033		1819	2361	1711
Skagway, AK	832	435	992	710	359	1058	989	1819		758	108
Valdez, AK	304	441	1534	284	701	530	1531	2361	758		650
Whitehorse, YT	724	327	884	602	251	950	881	1711	108	650	

Great Bear Brewing Co., 238 N. Boundary St., Wasilla 99654.

Haines Brewing Co., 108 White Fang Way (Dalton City), Haines 99827.

Homer Brewing Co., 1411 Lake Shore, Homer 99603.

Kassik's Kenai Brew Stop, 47160 Spruce Haven Street, Kenai 99611.

Kenai River Brewing Company, 241 North Aspen Drive, Suite 100, Soldotna 99669.

Kodiak Island Brewing Company, 338 Shelikof Avenue, Kodiak 99615.

Midnight Sun Brewing Co., 7329 Arctic Blvd., Anchorage 99518.

The Moose's Tooth Pub & Pizzeria, 3300 Old Seward Highway, Anchorage 99503.

Regal Eagle Brewing Co., 11501 Old Glenn Highway, Eagle River 99577.

Silver Gulch Brewing & Bottling, 2195 Old Steese Highway, Fairbanks 99701.

Snow Goose Restaurant/Sleeping Lady Brewing Co., 717 W. Third Ave., Anchorage 99501.

MILITARY
Congress saw little need for a strong military presence in the Territory of Alaska until the rapid escalation of World War II. Spurred by the realization that Alaska could be a strategic location both defensively and offensively, the government built and still maintains units of the Air Force, Army, Navy and Coast Guard at dozens of installations across the state.

Joint Service Commands. Alaskan Command (ALCOM), the senior military command in Alaska, integrates, expedites and coordinates military efforts both within Alaska and beyond. The combined forces of ALCOM include nearly 29,000 Air Force, Army, Navy, Coast Guard personnel, guardsmen and reservists. The Air National Guard and Army National Guard Units have roles at both federal and state levels. Total military economic impact within Alaska was $1.8billion in fiscal year 2006.

U.S. Army. U.S. Army Alaska (USARAK) occupies two posts, Fort Richardson, near Anchorage, and Fort Wainwright, near Fairbanks. USARAK is commanded by a major general stationed at Fort Richardson.

U.S. Army Alaska consists mainly of three brigades: the 1-25th Stryker Brigade Combat Team and Aviation Task Force 49 at Fort Wainwright and the 4-25th Airborne Brigade Combat Team at Fort Richardson.

Other USARAK subordinate units include:
• The 17th Combat Support Sustainment Brigade at Fort Richardson, made up of engineering, chemical and maintenance units;

- The 164th Military Police Battalion at both posts, providing law enforcement and security;
- Medical Activity Command and Dental Activity Command at both posts, providing healthcare services;
- The 59th Signal Battalion at Fort Richardson, overseeing all Army communications at both posts;
- The Northern Warfare Training Center at Fort Wainwright, training Department of Defense personnel in arctic combat and survival; and
- The Cold Regions Test Center at Fort Wainwright, testing Department of Defense equipment for cold-weather use.

USARAK totals nearly 12,000 soldiers and 14,000 family members and employs more than 3,600 civilians, with a total payroll of $676 million. The training lands on both posts total 1.7 million acres. The Alaska District of the U.S. Army Corps of Engineers designs and constructs buildings, runways, roads, utilities and related facilities for the Army, Air Force and other defense agencies. The Corps also operates and maintains 52 river and navigation projects, regulates aquatic resources and is involved with environmental restoration.

U.S. Air Force. The 11th Air Force helps maintain air superiority in Alaska, supports Alaska-based ground forces and air forces and prepares air forces for deployment to worldwide locations. The largest units are the 3rd Wing at Elmendorf Air

NUGGETS

In June 2002, construction began at Fort Greely, near Delta Junction, on six interceptor missile silos as part of the United States national defense program. On December 17, President Bush announced plans to add 10 more ground-based interceptors at Greeley by the end of 2005.

—2003 *The Alaska Almanac*®

Force Base near Anchorage and the 354th Fighter Wing at Eielson Air Force Base near Fairbanks. The 3rd Wing contains the 12th, 19th and 90th fighter squadrons as well as the 517th airlift squadron and the 962nd airborne warning and control squadron. The wing currently has the F-15 C/D, the C-12, and the E-3 Sentry and will be gaining the C-17 and F-22 in summer of 2008. The 354th Fighter Wing uses the F-16 and OA-10 Thunderbolt II.

Remote locations of the 11th Air Force include Galena and King Salmon airports, Eareckson Air Force Station on Shemya Island, and a network of 18 Air Force radar sites throughout Alaska.

U.S. Navy and Marine Corps. A small contingent of U.S. Navy officers and enlisted personnel are assigned as staff to the Alaskan Command headquarters and the U.S. Naval Forces Alaska. The Navy and Marine Corps have commands and detachments in Anchorage.

U.S. Coast Guard. The U.S. Coast Guard has been a part of Alaska since the mid-1800s, when it patrolled Alaska's coastline with the wooden sailing and steamships of its predecessor, the Revenue Cutter Service. Since those early days, the service has changed names and today's fleet of ships, boats and aircraft has replaced wooden ships.

The 17th Coast Guard District encompasses the entire state of Alaska, with a coastline far longer than that of all other states combined. The Coast Guard performs its missions in Alaska with nearly 2,000 active-duty members and reservists, along with 237 civilian employees. The district headquarters is located in Juneau. The Air Station Kodiak is the largest in the country.

Among the Coast Guard's missions in Alaska are homeland defense, port security, the enforcement of fisheries laws, search and rescue, marine safety and marine environmental protection. The service also maintains navigation aids, including six Long Range Navigation (LORAN) stations.

Alaska National Guard. The Alaska Army National Guard and the Air National Guard perform a wide range of missions, including security, search and rescue, airlift, transportation, aerial refueling, space surveillance, drug interdiction and youth support. Guard units also respond to emergencies and natural disasters.

From the Joint Forces Headquarters at Camp Denali, on Fort Richardson located just outside of Anchorage, the Alaska National Guard manages some 4300 soldiers and airmen.

The Army Guard, some 2000 soldiers strong, is participating in Operation Enduring Freedom in Afghanistan and Operation Iraqi Freedom in Iraq and Kuwait. Soldiers are providing security forces at forward operating bases in Iraq and Kuwait. C-23B Sherpa aviators are in Iraq flying cargo, equipment and people throughout the Iraqi theater. A contingent of Alaska Army National Guard members has also embedded with the Afghan National Army for training and support purposes.

In addition, the Army Guard has about 200 soldiers stationed at Fort Greely operating the Missile Defense system. These soldiers are some of the most highly trained men and women in their field.

The 2,300 members of the Air Guard are participating in multiple exercises around the world, in addition to Operation Enduring Freedom and Operation Iraqi Freedom. These airmen lead airlift missions, provide security forces for base installations, and are the first responders for rescue operations in the state. The Alaska Air National Guard continues to evolve, creating innovative ways to improve airdrops of needed supplies to troops on the front lines.

Military Population. Military services are a major component of Alaska's economy. The total population of the military in Alaska as of September 2006 was approximately 28,900 service members, plus more than 37,000 family members.

MINERALS AND MINING

(SEE ALSO Coal; Gold; Oil and Gas; Rocks and Gems)
The total value of Alaska's mineral industry in 2006 was $3.26 billion, the eleventh billion-dollar year in a row and a new record. Exploration investment was about $176.5 million, development investment was about

NUGGETS

The Greens Creek mine on Admiralty Island is expected to become the top-producing silver mine in the United States, its owners say.

—1988 *The Alaska Almanac*®

$331 million and the total production value of all minerals was about $2,752.6 million.

Development investment amounting to $331 million for 2006 showed a slight decrease from the 2005 level of $347.9 million This investment primarily funded work at the Teck Pogo project, new construction at Coeur Alaska Inc.'s Kensington gold project in southeastern Alaska and NovaGold Resources, Inc.'s Rock Creek gold project near Nome. Mystery Creek Resources, Inc. rehabilitated the historic Nixon Fork Mine and mill, and began stockpiling ore. Other significant investments took place at the Fort Knox Mine, the Greens Creek Mine and the Chuitna coal project.

Production values amounting to $2,752.6 million for 2006 almost doubled the 2005 value of $1401.6 million due to improved metal prices, especially zinc prices.

Production volumes were down compared to 2005 for all materials except gold and lead, though metal price improvements clearly overcame production shortfalls. Gold prices were 35.7 percent higher in 2006 at $603.46 per ounce, silver 16.4 percent higher at $11.35 per ounce, lead 34.9 percent higher at $0.58 per pound, and zinc 233 percent higher at $1.47 per pound. Hard-rock metal production values were up for all commodities; placer gold production may be down, but information was incomplete at the time of this printing. Metals (gold, silver, lead and zinc) accounted for $2,653 million or 96 percent of the total production value, coal and peat for $49.8 million, and industrial minerals for $49.9 million.

The giant Red Dog Mine north of Kotzebue produces zinc, lead and silver, and is not only the world's largest zinc mine, but also the largest reserve of zinc in the world. Red Dog Mine produced 614,538 tons of zinc, along with lead and silver, worth $1.54 billion. Greens Creek Mine near Juneau produces zinc, lead, silver, gold and minor copper. It is one of the world's largest silver producers, with 8.8 million ounces of silver produced in 2006. The Fort Knox Mine near Fairbanks produced 333,383 ounces of gold from the 14.8 million tons of ore that were milled in 2006. Pogo gold production began in February 2006 with 112,500 ounces produced in 2006. Red Dog Mine reported an operating profit of $268 million on 3.4 million tons of lead zinc ore. About 50 placer gold mines statewide produced over 21,000 ounces of gold.

The Usibelli Coal Mine near Healy slightly decreased production for 2006 from its Two Bull Ridge pit with an output of 1,397,500 short tons of subbituminous coal. The mine supplied six power plants in Interior Alaska, and exported coal to Korea and Chile through the port of Seward.

Exploration expenditures in Alaska were more than $176.5 million, 70 percent higher than the $103.9 million spent in 2005. Exploration occurred across Alaska, but more than $122.8 million (or 70 percent of the exploration funds) were spent in southwestern Alaska. At least 23 exploration projects in Alaska spent more than $1 million in 2006. Two advanced exploration projects accounted for most of the exploration expenditures and drill footage. One notable is Northern Dynasty Minerals Ltd.'s Pebble copper–gold project; another is the 23-million-ounce Donlin Creek intrusion-hosted gold project in southwestern Alaska, a project of Barrick Gold Corp., NovaGold Resources, Inc., and Calista Corp. Significant exploration also continued at Kennecott Mineral's Greens Creek Mine near Juneau, at the Pogo and LMS properties in eastern Alaska, the Niblack project in southeastern Alaska, the Rock Creek and Ambler projects in western Alaska, and the Lucky Shot property in southcentral Alaska.

The Pebble property, near Iliamna in southwestern Alaska, was Alaska's largest exploration project in 2006. Recent discoveries of copper, gold and molybdenum metal resources at the Pebble property have outlined a possible open-pit resource at the Pebble West Deposit and a likely underground resource at the Pebble East Deposit. Exploration in 2006 concentrated on drilling the Pebble East deposit. Announced metal resources for the Pebble deposit total 67 billion pounds of copper, 82 million ounces of gold, and 5.2 billion pounds of molybdenum, making this the second-largest "porphyry copper" deposit in the world.

MOSQUITOES
Alaska's ubiquitous mosquito is sometimes jokingly referred to as the state bird. At least 25 species of mosquito are found in Alaska (the number may be as high as 40). The females of all species feed on people, other mammals or birds. Males and females eat plant sugar, but only the females suck blood, which they use for egg production. The itch that follows the bite comes from an anti-coagulant injected by the mosquito. No Alaska mosquitoes carry diseases. As of February 2007, there have been no reported cases of West Nile virus in Alaska.

The insects are present from April through September in many areas of the state. Out in the Bush they are often at their worst in June, tapering off in July. The mosquito menace usually passes by late August and September. From Cook Inlet south, the bugs concentrate on coastal flats and forested valleys. In the Aleutian Islands, mosquitoes are absent or present only in small numbers. The most serious mosquito infestations occur

(Continued on page 128)

Researchers on the northern tundra reported up to 9,000 mosquito bites per minute. At that rate, a person would lose half of his blood supply in 2 hours!

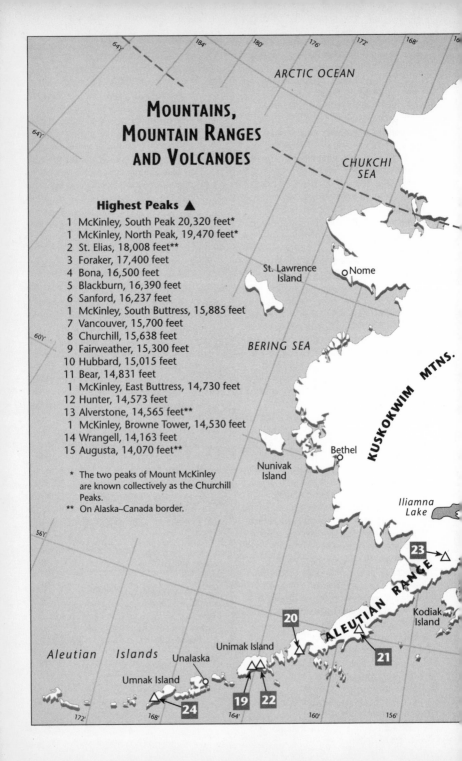

MOUNTAINS, MOUNTAIN RANGES AND VOLCANOES

Highest Peaks ▲

1 McKinley, South Peak 20,320 feet*
1 McKinley, North Peak, 19,470 feet*
2 St. Elias, 18,008 feet**
3 Foraker, 17,400 feet
4 Bona, 16,500 feet
5 Blackburn, 16,390 feet
6 Sanford, 16,237 feet
1 McKinley, South Buttress, 15,885 feet
7 Vancouver, 15,700 feet
8 Churchill, 15,638 feet
9 Fairweather, 15,300 feet
10 Hubbard, 15,015 feet
11 Bear, 14,831 feet
1 McKinley, East Buttress, 14,730 feet
12 Hunter, 14,573 feet
13 Alverstone, 14,565 feet**
1 McKinley, Browne Tower, 14,530 feet
14 Wrangell, 14,163 feet
15 Augusta, 14,070 feet**

 * The two peaks of Mount McKinley
    are known collectively as the Churchill
    Peaks.
 ** On Alaska–Canada border.

ARCTIC OCEAN

CHUKCHI SEA

St. Lawrence Island

Nome

BERING SEA

KUSKOKWIM MTNS.

Bethel

Nunivak Island

Iliamna Lake

ALEUTIAN RANGE

Kodiak Island

Aleutian Islands

Unalaska

Unimak Island

Umnak Island

23

20

21

19 22

24

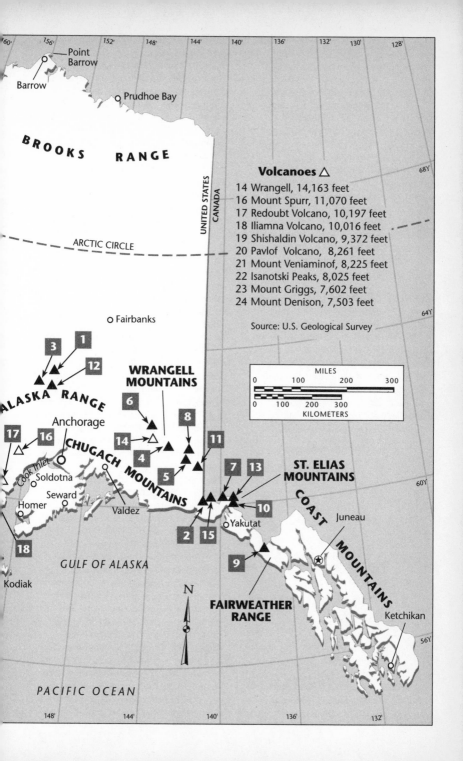

Volcanoes △

14 Wrangell, 14,163 feet
16 Mount Spurr, 11,070 feet
17 Redoubt Volcano, 10,197 feet
18 Iliamna Volcano, 10,016 feet
19 Shishaldin Volcano, 9,372 feet
20 Pavlof Volcano, 8,261 feet
21 Mount Veniaminof, 8,225 feet
22 Isanotski Peaks, 8,025 feet
23 Mount Griggs, 7,602 feet
24 Mount Denison, 7,503 feet

Source: U.S. Geological Survey

MILES
0   100   200   300

KILOMETERS
0   100   200   300

Point Barrow
Barrow
Prudhoe Bay

BROOKS   RANGE

UNITED STATES
CANADA

ARCTIC CIRCLE

Fairbanks

WRANGELL MOUNTAINS

ALASKA RANGE

Anchorage
CHUGACH MOUNTAINS

Cook Inlet
Soldotna
Seward
Homer
Valdez

ST. ELIAS MOUNTAINS

Yakutat

COAST MOUNTAINS

Juneau

GULF OF ALASKA

Kodiak

N

FAIRWEATHER RANGE

Ketchikan

PACIFIC OCEAN

(Continued from page 125)

in moist areas of slow-moving or standing water, such as fields, bogs and forests of Interior Alaska, from Bristol Bay eastward. Mosquitoes are most active at dusk and dawn; low temperatures and high winds decrease their activity. Mosquitoes can be controlled by draining their breeding areas or spraying with approved insecticides. When traveling in areas of heavy mosquito infestations, it is wise to wear protective clothing, carefully screen living areas and tents, and use a good insect repellent.

MOUNTAINS Of the 20 highest
mountains in the United States, 17 are in Alaska, which has 19 peaks over 14,000 feet. (See map on pages 126–27)

MOUNT McKINLEY in the Alaska
Range is the highest mountain on the North American continent. The South Peak is 20,320 feet high; the North Peak has an elevation of 19,470 feet. The mountain was named in 1896 for William McKinley of Ohio, who was the Republican candidate for president.

An earlier name had been Denali, an Athabascan word meaning "the high one." The state of Alaska officially renamed the

Photographers hope for a shot like this; McKinley is often shrouded in clouds.
Photo by Roy Corral.

mountain Denali in 1975, and the state Geographic Names Board claims the proper name for the mountain is Denali. However, the federal Board of Geographic Names has not taken any action, and congressional legislation was introduced to retain the name McKinley in perpetuity.

Mount McKinley is within Denali National Park and Preserve. The park entrance is about 237 miles north of Anchorage and 121 miles south of Fairbanks via the George Parks Highway.

A 90-mile gravel road runs west from the highway through the park; vehicle traffic on the park road is limited. The park is also accessible via the Alaska Railroad and by aircraft.

The mountain and its park are among the top tourist attractions in Alaska. The finest times to see McKinley up close are on summer mornings. August is best, according to statistics based on 13 summers of observation by park ranger Rick McIntyre. The mountain is rarely visible the entire day.

The best view is from Eielson Visitor Center, about 66 miles from the park entrance and 33 miles northeast of the summit. The aging center was closed, however, after the 2004 visitor season, and construction of a new facility should be completed in time for the 2008 season. During the closure, shuttle bus service is available to Fish Creek, which also offers an excellent view of the mountain. The fee for the eight-hour round-trip bus ride to Fish Creek is $28.75, and $39.75 to Wonder Lake. Discounts are available for ages 15 to 17; children under 15 are free. Denali Park Resorts information is available by calling (800) 622-7275 or (907) 272-7275.

Eleven climbers perished on Mount McKinley in May 1992, making it the deadliest climbing season in the mountain's history. The 11 climbers, including one American mountaineering guide, died in five separate incidents on the mountain. Since 1932, when the National Park Service began keeping records of climbers attempting to reach the summit of Mount McKinley, 98 climbers have been killed on the mountain. Among the deadliest years on the mountain were 1981 and 1989, when six mountaineers were killed each of those two years; 1967 and 1980, when eight mountaineers were killed each year; and 1992, when 11 died.

Of the 1,154 climbers taking part in the 2006 mountaineering season, 582, or 50 percent, reached the summit. Climbers came from 38 countries. The average expedition lasted 17.8 days, and the average age of the climbers was 37 years old. June was the busiest summit month, with 315 climbers reaching the top.

The Park Service requires climbers to register 60 days before a planned climb. In 2005, climbers planning to scale the mountain had to pay an increased special-use fee, now $200.

Information on climbing Mount McKinley is available at (907) 733-2231 and www.nps.gov/dena/planyourvisit/mountaineering.htm.

Mount McKinley Firsts

1896: Prospector William Dickey names the prominent peak Mount McKinley.

1902: Alfred H. Brooks, leader of a U.S. Geological Survey party, is the first white man to set foot on McKinley's slopes.

1903: Judge James Wickersham and four others from Fairbanks make the first attempt on the peak.

1910: The Sourdough Expedition makes an attempt; two members reach the summit of the North Peak.

1913: Hudson Stuck's expedition is the first to reach the South Peak.

1932: Bush pilot Joe Crosson makes the first glacier landing on Muldrow Glacier for the Allen Carpé Expedition.

1947: Barbara Washburn is the first woman to reach the summit.

1967: Ray Genet, Dave Johnston and Art Davidson make the first winter ascent.

1979: Mushers Joe Redington, Sr., and Susan Butcher mush a team of sled dogs to the summit.

1984: Japanese explorer Naomi Uemura makes the first winter solo ascent but dies during his descent.

1988: Vern Tejas makes the first complete winter solo climb.

NUGGETS

Fifty-four-year-old Joni Phelps, blind since the age of 30, scaled Mount McKinley. According to the National Park Service, she is the first blind woman to reach the summit. She was accompanied by her two 29-year-old sons. Phelps has traveled the world enjoying scuba, rock climbing and kayaking.

—1999 *The Alaska Almanac*®

1993: Joni Phelps, 54, is the first blind woman to reach the summit; Mike Jacober is the first to fly an ultralight over the summit.

1995: Merrick Johnston, 12, is the youngest female climber.

1999: Highest short-haul rescue by the National Park Service Lama helicopter is made from 19,500 feet.

2001: Galen Johnston, 11, (son of Dave Johnston, but no relation to Merrick Johnston) holds the new record as youngest male climber.

2001: Oldest woman to reach summit, Toshiko Uchida, age 70.

2002: First use of Clean Mountain Cans (for removal of solid human waste) by more than 500 climbers from 20 different countries.

2005: Sadao Hoshiko, age 74, of Oita-shi, Japan, became the oldest man to summit Mount McKinley.

MUKLUKS Mukluks are lightweight boots designed to provide warmth in extreme cold. Eskimo mukluks are traditionally made with *oogruk* (bearded seal) skin soles and leg uppers of caribou trimmed with fur. Athabascan mukluks are traditionally made of moose hide and trimmed with fur and beadwork. Hay inner soles add insulation. The mukluks may be either calf-height or knee-height, with a leather drawstring in a casing around the top to keep out the wind and snow.

Eskimos of long ago sewed all their own clothing, mainly from the skins of

129

The Sourdough Expedition

In 1906 explorer Frederick Cook announced that he and a companion had conquered Mount McKinley. Cook provided detailed reports of the alleged climb, as well as a photograph of himself at the summit. He was hailed by the gullible New York press [as] a celebrity. Cook's claims did not play well in the saloons of Fairbanks where, in late 1909, a group of miners led by Tom Lloyd decided no Easterner should be first to reach Denali's summit. Thus arose the "Sourdough Expedition." Lloyd and six partners—none with climbing experience—set off in the dead of winter. Before they reached the mountain a fist fight broke out, and three turned back. The remaining four began their assault in March 1910, without ropes and carrying a 14-foot flagpole to plant at the top. In a remarkable sustained climb of 18 hours, two of the party negotiated the final 9,000-foot ascent of McKinley's north peak, planted their pole, and came down—unaware that the south peak was actually 850 feet higher. Their exploit is still considered one of mountaineering's most astonishing feats.

—Harry Ritter, *Alaska's History*

animals and seabirds. These mukluks were not worn in winter unless the weather was warm, for they were made from seal leather with the hair removed and *oogruk* soles. The *oogruk* was oiled very heavily to be water-resistant and no fur trim was used on the "water mukluks," as they were called. The skins of large fish, including salmon, were also used to make the water-resistant mukluks.

Any mukluks that have been exposed to water or dampness should be hung in a cool place to dry slowly; sudden heat could shrink them out of shape and make them hard and stiff.

MUKTUK This Eskimo delicacy consists of outer skin layers and attached blubber of a whale. The two species of whale from which muktuk is most often sliced are the bowhead and the beluga, or white whale. The outer skin layers consist of a corky protective layer, the true skin and the blubber. In the case of beluga muktuk, the outer layer is white, the next layer is black and the blubber is pink. It may be eaten fresh, frozen, boiled or fermented.

MUSEUMS, CULTURAL CENTERS, EXHIBITS, HISTORIC PARKS, HISTORICAL SOCIETIES AND REPOSITORIES

Visiting any of the following museums, historic sites, notable exhibits, archives or other repositories offers a look into the rich diversity of Alaska culture and history. Many of the smaller museums are open only June through September. Information is available at www.museums.state.ak.us and www.museumsalaska.org.

Anaktuvuk Pass: Simon Paneak Memorial Museum, P.O. Box 21085, Anaktuvuk Pass 99721-0085; (907) 661-3413; www.north-slope.org/nsb/55.htm. Display of hunting tools and a description of the Paleo–Indian people who occupied the Mesa Site in the Brooks Range more than 11,000 years ago.

Anchorage: Alaska Aviation Heritage Museum, 4721 Aircraft Drive, Anchorage 99502; (907) 248-5325; www.home.gci.net/~aahm. On the south shore of Lake Hood. Features 30 vintage aircraft, video and a military aviation gallery. Watch takeoffs and landings from the largest floatplane base in the world.

Alaska Collection, Z. J. Loussac Library, 3600 Denali St., Anchorage 99503; (907) 343-2975; http://anchoragelibrary.org. Rare books, reference books, state records, microfilm of newspapers, catalogs of photographs at other archives in the state.

Alaska Museum of Natural History, 201 N. Bragaw, 99508; (907) 274-2400; www.alaskamuseum.org. Museum focuses on Alaska's unique geological, cultural and ecological history. Exhibits include dinosaurs of Alaska.

Alaska Native Heritage Center, 8800 Heritage Center Drive, Anchorage 99506; (907) 330-8000; www.alaskanative.net. Welcome House, contemporary culture and traditional village exhibits, theater and Native Tradition Bearers.

Alaska Public Lands Information Center, 605 W. Fourth Ave., Anchorage 99501; (907) 271-2737 (866) 869-6887 (U.S. only); www.nps.gov/aplic/center. Displays and information on refuges, forests, parks and outdoor recreation lands in Alaska. Video programs and computers permit self-help trip planning.

Alaska Resources Library and Information Services, Library Building, University of Alaska, 3211 Providence Drive, Anchorage 99508; (907) 272-7547; www.arlis.org. Information on archaeology, Native land claims, environmental and natural resources of Alaska, ornithology and wildlife biology, fisheries biology and cold-regions engineering.

Alaska State Troopers Museum, 245 West Fifth, P.O. Box 100280, Anchorage 99510-0280; (800) 770-5050; (907) 279-5054; www.alaskatroopermuseum.com. Exhibits, memorabilia and photographs detailing Alaska law enforcement history.

Alaska Zoo, 4731 O'Malley Road, Anchorage 99507; (907) 346-2133; www.alaskazoo.org. Exhibits the wildlife of the Arctic and Subarctic in a natural setting.

Anchorage Museum at Rasmuson Center, 121 W. Seventh Ave., Anchorage 99501; (907) 343-4326; www.anchoragemuseum.org. Alaska Gallery dioramas depict 10,000 years of Alaska history. Guided tours with docents available. "Art of the Far North" contains early engravings by artists who accompanied 18th-century explorers and features works of art from travelers, adventurers, early residents and Natives.

Elmendorf Air Force Base Wildlife Museum, Building 8414 19th St., Elmendorf AFB 99506; (907) 552-2436. Enter base through Boniface Parkway Gate. Habitat displays of Alaska wildlife: bear, musk oxen, Dall sheep, small mammals, extensive displays of fish.

Fourth Avenue Theatre, 630 W. Fourth Ave., Suite 300, Anchorage 99501; (907) 263-2787. Art deco building from the 1940s houses museum photo display of old Anchorage on the lower level. On the main level, free Alaska-theme movies on the big screen. Dinner theater during the summer. Departure point for one-hour trolley tours of Anchorage.

Heritage Library and Museum (Wells Fargo Bank Heritage Library), 301 W. Northern Lights Blvd., Anchorage 99503; (907) 265-2834; www.wellsfargohistory.com/museums/alaska.html. Native baskets, ivory and artifacts, photos, hunting implements, rare books and paintings.

Imaginarium Science Discovery Center, 737 W. Fifth Ave., Suite G, Anchorage 99501; (907) 276-3179; www.imaginarium.org. Hands-on scientific displays for children, planetarium bubble show, polar bear lair, arctic ecology. Monthly rotating exhibits.

National Archives, Pacific Alaska Region, 654 W. Third Ave., Anchorage 99501-2145; (907) 261-7820; fax (907) 261-7813; www.archives.gov/pacific-alaska/anchorage/index.html. Historical records including photographs, maps and architectural drawings, dating from 1867 to the present. Both original records and microfilm are available for research.

Oscar Anderson House, 420 M St., Anchorage 99501; (907) 274-2336; www.alaskan.com/akencinfo/oscar.html. The city's first wood-frame house, built in 1915 by Swedish immigrant Oscar Anderson, was completely restored in 1982. Swedish Christmas celebration.

Potter Section House and Historic Park, Mile 115 Seward Highway, HC52, Box 8999, Indian 99540; (907) 345-5014. Alaska Railroad historic site. Chugach

State Park headquarters; maps, brochures, interpretive display, rotary snowplow, railroad cars.

University of Alaska Archives and Manuscripts, Consortium Library, University of Alaska, 3211 Providence Drive, Anchorage 99508; (907) 786-1849. Historic and contemporary papers, records, photographs; some artifacts. Open by appointment to researchers. Catalog of holdings available.

Anvik: **Anvik Historical Society and Museum,** P.O. Box 110, Anvik 99558; (907) 663-6366. Displays archaeology and history of lower Yukon Athabascan village.

Barrow: **Iñupiat Heritage Center,** 5421 North Star St., P.O. Box 749, Barrow 99723; (907) 852-0422; www.nps.gov/inup. Cultural collection, library, storage areas for artifacts; unusual aspects include a Traditional Room for an Elders-in-Residence program and a Skinning Room.

Bethel: **Yupiit Piciryarait ("People's Lifeways") Culture Center and Museum,** 420 Chief Eddie Hoffman Highway, P.O. Box 219, Bethel 99559; (907) 543-1819. Artifacts from the region such as masks, drums, parkas, tools and a kayak.

Central: **Circle Historical Museum,** Mile 127.7 Steese Highway, P.O. Box 31893, Central 99730; (907) 520-1893. Displays include a period cabin of the mining camps, the first printing press north of Juneau, equipment used in early day mining and trapping, Yukon Quest Sled Dog Race sled display, research library with archives and photograph collection.

Copper Center: **Copper Center Lodge,** Drawer J, Copper Center 99573; (907) 822-3245, (866) 330-3245; www.coppercenterlodge.com/museum. Historic roadhouse opened in 1898. Museum exhibits, operating fish wheel.
George I. Ashby Memorial Museum/ Copper Valley Historical Society, P.O. Box 84, Copper Center 99573; (907) 822-5285. Early mining of gold and copper, church and Native artifacts. Information about the stampeders who unsuccessfully tried to take the Valdez Glacier "All-Alaska" Trail to the Klondike in 1898.

Cordova: **Cordova Historical Museum,** P.O. Box 391, Cordova 99574; (907) 424-6665; www.cordovamuseum.org. Exhibits of art, geology, fisheries and marine articles.

Ilanka Cultural Center and Museum, 110 Nicholoff Way, P.O. Box 322, Cordova 99574; (907) 424-7903. Historical and contemporary exhibits of the Native peoples and cultures of the Copper River and Prince William Sound area.

Delta Junction: **Alaska Homestead and Historical Museum,** Milepost 1415.4 Alaska Highway, P.O. Box 389, Delta Junction 99737; (907) 895-4431. Large collection of historical farming equipment; guided tours of authentic homestead farm.
Delta Historical Society, Mile 275 Richardson Highway, P.O. Box 1089, Delta Junction 99737; (907) 895-4555. Provides exhibits at Rika's Roadhouse and Sullivan Roadhouse:
Rika's Roadhouse, Mile 275 Richardson Highway, P.O. Box 1229, Delta Junction 99737; (907) 895-4201; www.rikas.com. Offers a glimpse of life in Interior Alaska, 1904–47. Built in 1910 and restored in 1986, Rika's Roadhouse was an important way station on the Valdez to Fairbanks Trail. Features sod-roofed museum, ferryman's cabin and other historic structures. Guides are in period costumes.
Sullivan Roadhouse, Mile 267 Richardson Highway, P.O. Box 987, Delta Junction 99737; (907) 895-5068; www.deltachamber.org/sullivan.html. Visitor center and historic buildings with photos and displays depicting the winter Valdez to Fairbanks Trail. Oldest roadhouse in Interior Alaska.

Dillingham: **Samuel K. Fox Museum** (Dillingham Heritage Museum), corner of Seward and D Streets, P.O. Box 273, Dillingham 99576; (907) 842-5610 (Chamber of Commerce). Ethnohistory museum featuring Yup'ik Eskimo culture of Southwestern Alaska through contemporary and traditional arts, crafts and artifacts.

The UA Museum in Fairbanks draws crowds for its arctic wildlife display, prehistoric mastodon tusks, hefty gold nuggets and more. Photo by Roy Corral.

Eagle: **Eagle Historical Society and Museum,** P.O. Box 23, Eagle 99738; (907) 547-2325; www.eagleak.org. Restored courthouse, customs house and several Fort Egbert buildings. Daily walking tours and historical movies.

Eagle River: **Eagle River Nature Center,** 32750 Eagle River Road, Eagle River 99577; (907) 694-2108; www.ernc.org. Interpretive displays, programs, guided daily hikes, outdoor telescopes, spectacular views. Entrance to walkable section of scenic Iditarod Trail.

Eklutna Historical Park and Heritage House Museum, 16515 Centerfield Drive, Suite 201, Eagle River 99577; (907) 696-2828. Located 25 miles north of Anchorage on the Glenn Highway. The park offers 30-minute tours and information about the blending of Athabascan and missionary cultures. Historic photos and objects. Unique grave monuments called spirit houses, and St. Nicholas Russian Orthodox Church.

Elfin Cove: **Elfin Cove Museum.** P.O. Box 36, Elfin Cove 99825; (907) 239-2222. A beginning collection featuring small displays of local history and artifacts.

Ester: **Ester Gold Camp,** P.O. Box 109-F, Ester 99725; (800) 354-7274; www.akvisit.com/ester.html. Ester Camp was built in 1936 by the Fairbanks Exploration Co. to support a large-scale gold-dredge operation; reopened in 1958 as a tourist attraction and is on the National Register of Historic Places.

Fairbanks: **Alaska Public Lands Information Center,** 250 Cushman St., Suite 1A, Fairbanks 99701; (907) 456-0527; www.nps.gov/aplic/center. Information on Alaska's state parks, national parks, national forests and wildlife refuges. Free museum featuring films on Alaska, interpretive programs, lectures, exhibits, artifacts, photographs and short video programs on each region of the state.

Dog Mushing Museum, P.O. Box 80136, Fairbanks 99708; (907) 456-6874. Dog sleds, mushing paraphernalia.

El Dorado Gold Mine, 1975 Discovery Drive, Fairbanks 99709; (866) 479-6673. Located at Mile 1.3 Elliott Highway, just past Fox, 9 miles north of Fairbanks; www.eldoradogoldmine.com. Tour of a working gold mine, permafrost tunnel, sluice box, assay office, gold panning.

Fairbanks Community Museum, 410 Cushman St., Suite 225, Fairbanks, 99701; (907) 457-3669; www.fairbankscommunitymuseum.com.

Details the history of Fairbanks via interpretive displays of the gold rush era through the great floods of the 1960s. Dog mushing memorabilia.

Fairbanks Historic Exploration Inn, 505 Illinois St., Fairbanks 99701; (907) 451-

 1920. Four houses for miners built in 1916 serve as an inn. Visitors may watch gold pans being manufactured and see a machine shop complex where "time stands still."

Gold Dredge No. 8, 1755 Old Steese Highway N., Fairbanks 99712-1014; (907) 457-6058; www.golddredgeno8.com. Millions of ounces of gold have been extracted by this dredge since 1928—one of two gold dredges in Alaska open to the public. Listed in the National Register of Historic Sites. Exhibits include mastodon and woolly mammoth bones and tusks.

Historic Hall, 825 First Ave., Fairbanks 99701; (907) 452-2013. A museum of Alaskan memorabilia and ephemera housed in 1907 building that was once the First Avenue Bathouse and later the Oddfellows Hall. Open 1:30-8 P.M. most summer days; other times by appointment; no admission charge.

Museum of the North, University of Alaska, 907 Yukon Drive, Box 756960, Fairbanks 99775-6960; (907) 474-7505; www.uaf.edu/museum. Five galleries display Alaska's history, Native culture, art, natural phenomena, wildlife, birds, geology and prehistoric past, including the mummy of a 36,000-year-old Steppe bison, and a display on the northern lights. Sculptures, totem poles, a Russian blockhouse and a nature trail; many special programs.

Pioneer Air Museum, Pioneer Park, Airport Way, Box 70437, Fairbanks 99707-0437; (907) 451-0037; www.akpub.com/akttt/aviat.html. Located behind Civic Center. Antique aircraft and stories of their Alaska pilots, with displays from 1913–48.

Pioneer Park, Airport Way and Peger Road, P.O. Box 71267, Fairbanks 99707-1267; (907) 459-1087. Guided historical walking tours, upon request. Features Kitty Hensley house, Judge Wickersham house, first Presbyterian Church (1906); re-created Native village, gold rush town and paddle-wheel riverboat.

Pioneers of Alaska Museum, Pioneer Park, Airport Way and Peger Road, Fairbanks 99707; www.akpub.com/akttt/pione.html; (907) 456-8579. Photos and artifacts of Fairbanks and the Fairbanks mining district from 1902 through World War II. Also features The Big Stampede, portraying the great gold rush to the Klondike and to Fairbanks.

Rasmuson Library, University of Alaska, 310 Tanana Drive, Fairbanks 99775-6800; (907) 474-7481; www.uaf.edu/library. Extensive Alaska and Arctic archives and photograph collection available to researchers.

SS *Nenana*/Fairbanks Historical Preservation Foundation, Pioneer Park, 2300 Airport Way, Cabin No. 1876, Box 70552, Fairbanks 99707; (907) 456-8848. A restored river steamer, a National Historic Landmark. Compelling 300-foot diorama takes visitors on a 2,400-mile voyage through the years 1847–1932 along the Yukon River system.

Girdwood: **Crow Creek Mine,** Mile 3.1 Crow Creek Road, Girdwood 99587; (907) 278-8060. National historic site with eight original, fully restored buildings from 1898; daily gold panning, tools.

Haines: **Alaska Indian Arts,** P.O. Box 271, Haines 99827; (907) 766-2160; www.alaskaindianarts.com. Workshop with totem carvers, silversmiths and printmakers.

American Bald Eagle Foundation, Haines Highway and Second Street, P.O. Box 49, Haines 99827; (907) 766-3094; www.baldeagles.org. Programs and lectures explain how birds interact with the environment.

Hammer Museum, 108 Main St., P.O. Box 702, Haines 99827; (907) 766-2374; www.hammermuseum.org. A collection of approximately 1,200 different types of hammers representing various trades.

Sheldon Museum and Cultural Center, P.O. Box 269, Haines 99827; (907) 766-2366; www.sheldonmuseum.org. Exhibits on the Dalton Trail, the overland freight route used to Fort Selkirk in the Klondike, Tlingit culture, Chilkat blankets, pioneer history.

Homer: Alaska Islands and Ocean Visitor Center, 95 Sterling Highway, Homer 99603; (907) 235-6961; www.islandsandocean.org. An interpretive educational and research facility dedicated to the understanding and conservation of the marine environment.

Pratt Museum, 3779 Bartlett St., Homer 99603; (907) 235-8635; www.prattmuseum.org. Natural and cultural history of Kenai Peninsula. Displays include Eskimo, Indian and Aleut tools and clothing dioramas, whale skeletons; marine aquarium; botanical garden.

Hoonah: Hoonah Cultural Center/Hoonah Indian Association, P.O. Box 602, Hoonah 99829; (907) 945-3545. History and culture of local Tlingit Indians; displays of Tlingit art and artifacts, totem poles, guided tours.

Hope: Hope and Sunrise Historical and Mining Museum, Second Street, P.O. Box 88, Hope 99605; (907) 782-3740; www.advenalaska.com/hope. Historic buildings; gold rush, mining and home-steading memorabilia.

Hyder: Hyder Community Association, Main St., P.O. Box 149, Hyder 99638; (250) 636-9148. Small museum with historical artifacts, photos and a collection of local wildlife.

Juneau: Alaska State Archives, 141 Willoughby Ave., Juneau 99801-1720; (907) 465-2270; www.archives.state.ak.us. Photographs, documents, state government records.

Alaska State Museum, 395 Whittier St., Juneau 99801-1718; (907) 465-2901; www.museums.state.ak.us. Collections on Alaska Natives, art, natural history, gold rush days, archaeology, botany, contemporary gold-mining issues, geology and paleontology. Lectures, guided tours, workshops, films and demonstrations.

House of Wickersham/Tanana Yukon Historical Society, 213 Seventh St. (mailing address: 400 Willoughby Ave., Suite 500), Juneau 99801; (907) 586-9001; www.dnr.state.ak.us/parks/units/wickrshm.htm. Built in 1898, the house was the residence of one of Alaska's first federal judges, James Wickersham. Educational tours and permanent collections.

Juneau–Douglas City Museum, 155 S. Seward St., Juneau 99801; (907) 586-3572; www.juneau.org/parksrec/museum. Videos and exhibits highlight Juneau's colorful history and gold-mining heritage; historic walking tour.

Last Chance Mining Museum, 1001 Basin Road, Juneau 99801; (907) 586-5338. Historic gold rush mining building listed on National Register of Historic Places.

Kenai: K'beq Kenaitze Indian Tribe, P.O. Box 988, Kenai 99611-0988; (907) 283-3633. Archives of Kenai branch of Cook Inlet Athabascan Indians.

Kenai Visitors and Cultural Center, 11471 Kenai Spur Highway, P.O. Box 1991, Kenai 99611; (907) 283-1991; www.visitkenai.com. Houses all the exhibits from Fort Kenay, plus a large eagle display.

Ketchikan: Saxman Totem Park and Tribal House, P.O. Box 8558, Ketchikan 99901. Historic site, 2.5 miles south of town. Park includes totems such as the famous Lincoln Pole, a carving center and Tlingit tribal house. Guided tours available.

Southeast Alaska Discovery Center, 50 Main St., Ketchikan 99901; (907) 228-6220; www.fs.fed.us/r10/tongass/districts/discoverycenter. Exhibits and videos about public lands and mining; crystals and marble mined from southeastern Alaska; historic gold rush photos.

Tongass Historical Museum, 629 Dock St., Ketchikan 99901; (907) 225-5600; www.city.ketchikan.ak.us/departments/museums/tongass.html. Collection of Alaskana, Northwest Coast Native materials, photo archives and maritime history displays. Summer exhibit features the historic cannery town of Loring.

Totem Heritage Center, 601 Deermont St. (mailing address: 629 Dock St.), Ketchikan 99901; (907) 225-5900; www.city.ketchikan.ak.us/departments/museums/totem.html. Large collection of original Tsimshian, Haida and Tlingit totems from the surrounding islands.

Klawock: **Klawock Totem Park/City of Klawock,** P.O. Box 469, Klawock 99925. Historic site on west coast of Prince of Wales Island. Reached by air, private boat, state ferry. Park contains 21 totems—both replicas and originals—from the abandoned village of Tuxekan.

Kodiak: **Alutiiq Museum and Archaeological Repository (Kodiak Museum),** Kodiak Area Native Association, 215 Mission Road, Suite 101, Kodiak 99615; (907) 486-7004; www.alutiiqmuseum.com. Repository holds 100,000 artifacts, historic photos and archival documents about Alutiiq culture.

Baranov Museum (Erskine House)/Kodiak Historical Society, 101 Marine Way, Kodiak 99615; (907) 486-5920; www.baranov.us. Closed in February. Former Russian fur warehouse from early 1800s, oldest wooden building on the West Coast of the United States. Exhibits offer an overview of Alutiiq, Russian and early American history. National historic landmark.

Kodiak Maritime Museum, P.O. Box 1876, Kodiak 99615; (907) 486-0384; www.kodiakmaritimemuseum.org. Displays on Alaska's commercial fishing industry and maritime heritage.

Kodiak Military History Museum, Fort Abercrombie State Historical Park, 1623 Mill Bay Road, Suite 5, Kodiak 99615; (907) 486-7015; www.kadiak.org. Collection consists of communication equipment, artillery, accessories, uniforms, artwork, photographs and documents from World War I, World War II and later in Kodiak and the Aleutians. Spans 1911 to present.

Kodiak Museum of the History of the Orthodox Church in Alaska, St. Herman's Russian Orthodox Theological Seminary, 414 Mission Road, Kodiak 99615; (907) 486-3524. Archive of personal items belonging to Ivan Veniaminov (later Bishop Innocent); papers and documents, many in Russian, about Russian America and the Orthodox church in Russian America.

Kotzebue: **NANA Museum of the Arctic,** 100 Shore Ave., Kotzebue (mailing address: Tour Arctic, 1001 E. Benson Blvd., Third Floor, Anchorage 99508); (907) 265-4157. Collections reflect Eskimo ethnology and natural history of northwestern Alaska; wildlife exhibits, slide show; cultural heritage demonstrations such as skin sewing, ivory carving, Eskimo dancing, Eskimo blanket toss. Winter hours by appointment.

McCarthy: **Kennecott Mine,** Wrangell–St. Elias National Park, P.O. Box 439, Copper Center 99573-0439; (907) 822-5234. An abandoned copper mine with many buildings perched on steep slopes. Kennicott-McCarthy Wilderness Guides conduct historical tours of the mine and town, which ceased operating in 1938.

Metlakatla: **Duncan Cottage Museum,** Duncan Street, P.O. Box 8, Metlakatla 99926; (907) 886-8687; www.metlakatlatours.net. Tsimshian bentwood boxes, antiques, books, photographs.

Nenana: **Alfred Starr Nenana Cultural Center,** 415 Riverfront, P.O. Box 1, Nenana 99760; (907) 832-5520. Ice Classics, boat racing, Native land claims and Episcopal Church exhibits. Features Athabascan history and traditions.

Nome: **Carrie M. McLain Memorial Museum,** 223 Front Street, P.O. Box 53, Nome 99762; (907) 443-6630; www.nomealaska.org/museum. Artifacts, photos and treasures; exhibits include the Nome gold rush featuring more than 6,000 gold rush photos, Eskimo culture and the Bering Land Bridge. Videos on the history of Nome shown during the summer season.

Nome Historical Park, c/o Nome Convention and Visitors Bureau, P.O. Box 240H-P, Nome 99762; (907) 443-6624; fax (907) 443-5832. Contains a nonworking gold dredge and mining equipment from the gold rush era.

Palmer: **Colony House Museum/ Palmer Historical Society,** 316 E. Elmwood Ave., P.O. Box 1935, Palmer 99645-1935; (907) 745-1935. Original "Colony Farm House," built as part of the New Deal resettlement project in 1935.

Independence Mine State Historical Park, Hatcher Pass, near Palmer 99645; (907) 745-2827. Restored gold-mine buildings, mining machinery and a visitor center in spectacular mountain setting. Recreational gold panning permitted.

Palmer Museum, 723 S. Valley Way, Palmer 99645; (907) 746-7668. Colony items, farm implements, flowers and vegetables that thrive in the North.

Petersburg: **Clausen Memorial Museum,** 203 Fram Street, P.O. Box 708, Petersburg 99833; (907) 772-3598; www.clausenmuseum.net. Photos, Norwegian family items, cannery and fisheries items, fox farming, world's record king salmon and other artifacts from area's past.

Portage: **Portage Glacier/Begich, Boggs Visitor Center,** P.O. Box 129, Girdwood 99587; (907) 783-2326; www.fs.fed.us/r10/chugach/chugach_pages/ bbvc/bbvc.htm. Located 55 miles south of Anchorage off the Seward Highway. Exhibits on glaciers and ice caves. Theater shows 20-minute documentary *Voices from the Ice.* Interpretive programs during the summer.

Prince of Wales Island: **Kasaan Totem Park,** east side of Prince of Wales Island. Reached by charter plane or private boat. Part of a government-sponsored totem restoration program begun in 1937. Contains some examples moved from the Haida village of Old Kasaan.

Seward: **Alaska SeaLife Center,** 301 Railway Ave., P.O. Box 1329, Mile 0 Seward Highway, Seward 99664; (800) 224-2525; (907) 224-6300; www.alaskasealife.org. Live marine mammals and seabirds in habitat exhibits. Aquarium, research center and rehab center for marine mammals and seabirds.

Chugach Museum and Institute of History and Art, Third and Washington Street, Orca Building, Seward 99664; www.chugachmuseum.org. Only museum dedicated solely to the history and culture of the Chugach region's Native people.

Marine Education Center, Third and Railway, P.O. Box 730, Seward 99664; (907) 224-5261. Interpretive displays about northern seas, Resurrection Bay, marine animals; live saltwater tanks; movies feature whales, salmon and other marine subjects. Operated by the University of Alaska.

Seward Museum/Resurrection Bay Historical Society, 336 Third Ave., P.O. Box 55, Seward 99664-0055; (907) 224-3902. Depicts Seward's history through photographs, artifacts and documents. Native baskets and ivory carvings on display.

Sitka: **Isabel Miller Museum/ Sitka Historical Society,** 330 Harbor Drive, Sitka 99835; (907) 747-6455; www.sitkahistory.org/museum.shtml. In the Centennial Building near the cruise ship lightering dock, exhibits include Tlingit baskets and carvings; the New Archangel Russian dancers and Noow Tlien Native dancers perform; research library of manuscripts and photographs.

Russian Bishop's House, P.O. Box 738, Sitka 99835; (907) 747-0130; www.nps.gov/sitk. Located on Lincoln Street, a restored residence built in 1842 with private chapel. One of only four Russian log structures remaining in North America. Both a unit of the Sitka National Historical Park and a National Historic Landmark. Exhibits describe Russian America.

Sheldon Jackson Museum, 104 College Drive, Sitka 99835-7657; (907) 747-8981; www.museums.state.ak.us/sjhome.html. On the campus of Sheldon Jackson College, Alaska's oldest museum has exhibits of Tlingit artifacts, clothing, beadwork, art and carvings.

Sitka National Historical Park Visitor Center, 106 Metlakatla St., Sitka 99835; (907) 747-0110; www.nps.gov/sitk. Tlingit history, totems, artifacts. Totem pole collection contains both original pieces collected 1901–03 and copies of originals.

Southeast Alaska Indian Cultural Center, 106 Metlakatla St., Sitka 99835;

Alaska Money

In Tok, Alaska's Mainstreet Visitor Center is housed in a beautiful log structure at the junction of two highways. At the center, you can learn about Tok's strategic role during the building of the Alaska Highway and about area wildlife, events and attractions.

Say hello to Sid Venne, who greets visitors, offers directions and enjoys answering questions, even the most bizarre ones. In her self-published humor book *If It's Tourist Season, Why Can't We Shoot Them?* Venne tells about the man who gave her a $20 bill and asked for change in "Alaskan money." She said OK, opened her register, and handed over a ten, a five and five ones. He pocketed the money and walked away satisfied.

—Tricia Brown, *The World-Famous Alaska Highway*

(907) 747-8061; www.nps.gov/sitk/parkmgmt/southeast-alaska-indian-cultural-center.htm. Housed in the Sitka National Park Visitor Center; visitors may talk to Native artists at work: beadworkers, carvers, printmakers, silversmiths.

Skagway: Klondike Gold Rush National Historical Park, P.O. Box 517, Skagway 99840; (907) 983-2921; www.nps.gov/klgo. An unusual unit of this park is the Chilkoot Trail, a 33-mile trek through history, sometimes called "the longest museum in the world." Hundreds of relics such as wagon wheels and coffeepots left behind by the stampeders of '98 remain on the trail.

Skagway Museum and Archives, P.O. Box 521, Skagway 99840; (907) 983-2420; www.skagwaymuseum.org. On Broadway. Gold rush artifacts, all once used by stampeders, and some personal belongings of notorious con man Soapy Smith. Photographs, historical records.

Soldotna: Soldotna Historical Society and Museum, P.O. Box 1986, Soldotna 99669; (907) 262-3756. Wildlife museum and historic log village, including last territorial school (1958). Homesteading artifacts and photos.

Sutton: Alpine Historical Park, Centennial Park Road, P.O. Box 266, Sutton 99674, access via Elementary School Road from Glenn Highway; (907) 745-7000. Open-air museum featuring the concrete

ruins of the Sutton Coal Washery (1920–22), historical buildings, perennial gardens and picnic and playground facilities.

Talkeetna: Talkeetna Historical Society Museum, P.O. Box 76, Talkeetna 99676; (907) 733-2487. Located one block off Main Street, the Talkeetna Townsite Historic District contains buildings reflecting a small 1917–40 gold-mining community. Museum portrays lives of gold miners, early aviators and climbers of Mount McKinley.

Tok: Alaska Public Lands Information Center, Mile 1314 Alaska Highway, P.O. Box 359, Tok 99780; (907) 883-5667; www.nps.gov/aplic/center.

Mukluk Land, Tok Chamber of Commerce, P.O. Box 90, Tok 99780; (907) 833-2571; www.muklukland.com. A summer display of early mining equipment, some actually operating Alaska Road Commission machinery, old snowmobile collection and gold panning.

Tok Main Street Visitor Center, P.O. Box 389, Tok 99780; (907) 883-5775; fax (907) 883-5887. At the junction of Alaska and Glenn Highways, displays of Dall sheep, waterfowl, wolf, caribou, fossils and minerals. Open May to October.

Trapper Creek: Trapper Creek Museum, Mile .6, (west of Parks Highway) on Petersville Road, P.O. Box 13011, Trapper Creek 99683; (907) 733- 2557; www.trappercreekmuseum.com. Highlights history of Trapper Creek, Cache Creek Mining District and Petersville Road. Includes maps, photographs and artifacts of the gold rush.

Unalaska: **Museum of the Aleutians,** P.O. Box 648, Unalaska 99685-0648; (907) 581-5150; www.aleutians.org. Preserves and shares the cultural and artistic heritage of the Aleutian Islands area. Volunteers and students are welcome to participate in annual archaeological fieldwork.

Valdez: **Maxine and Jesse Whitney Museum,** 303 Airport Road, P.O. Box 97, Valdez 99686; (907) 834-1614; fax (907) 835-8933; www.pwscc.edu/museum.shtml. Reportedly the world's largest collection of Native Alaskan art and artifacts, from prehistory to modern day.

Valdez Museum and Historical Archive, 217 Egan St., Valdez 99686-0008; (907) 835-2764; www.valdezmuseum.org. Permanent exhibits celebrate the 1898 gold rush route across Valdez Glacier. Restored 1907 Ahrens steam fire engine, log cabin, original Cape Hinchinbrook lighthouse lens, exhibits on the 1964 earthquake, the trans-Alaska oil pipeline and the 1989 *Exxon Valdez* oil spill cleanup.

Wasilla: **Dorothy Page Museum and Old Wasilla Townsite Park,** 323 North Main St., Wasilla 99654; (907) 373-9071; also Wasilla–Knik–Willow Creek Historical Society; www.cityofwasilla.com/museum. Historic buildings, including first schoolhouse (1917). Eskimo and Athabascan exhibits, gold-mining exhibits, "Flying Dentist's" office.

Iditarod Trail Sled Dog Race Headquarters and Museum, Mile 2.2 Knik Goose Bay Road, P.O. Box 870800, Wasilla 99687; (907) 376-5155; www.iditarod.com. Memorabilia, mushing films, full-size replica of checkpoint cabin and cache; the sleds that Susan Butcher and Joe Redington Sr. used to mush to the top of Mount McKinley.

Knik Museum, Mile 13.9 Knik Road (mailing address: 300 N. Boundary St., Suite B), Wasilla 99654; (907) 376-2005. Restored pool hall houses exhibits about fish camps, gold mines, dog mushers.

Museum of Alaska Transportation and Industry, off Mile 47 Parks Highway, Wasilla 99687-0646; (907) 376-1211; www.museumofalaska.org. Planes, trains, vehicles, tractors, tools.

Wrangell: **Tribal House of the Bear,** Front Street, P.O. Box 868, Wrangell 99929; (907) 874-3747. Replica of a traditional tribal house constructed by the CCC during the Roosevelt administration. Exhibits include a "spruce canoe," baskets and totem poles.

Wrangell Museum, 296 Outer Drive, P.O. Box 1050, Wrangell 99929; (907) 874-3770; www.wrangell.com/visitors/attractions/history/museum. Housed in Wrangell's oldest building, displays include items from Wrangell history, Tlingit artifacts and petroglyphs including the oldest known Tlingit houseposts.

MUSHROOMS

More than 500 species of mushrooms grow in Alaska and while most are not common enough to be seen and collected readily by the amateur mycophile (mushroom hunter), many edible and choice species shoot up in any available patch of earth. Alaska's giant arc of mushrooms extends from Southeast's panhandle through Southcentral, the Alaska Peninsula and the Aleutian Chain and is prime mushroom habitat. Interior, Western and Northern Alaska also support mushrooms in abundance.

Mushroom seasons vary considerably according to temperature, humidity and available nutrients but most occur from June through September. In a particularly cold or dry season, the crop will be scant.

There are relatively few poisonous mushrooms considering the number of species that occur throughout Alaska. Potentially fatal mushrooms, some of which occur in populated areas, include fly agaric *(Amanita muscaria),* poison pax *(Paxillus involutus)* and false morels.

Easy-to-identify edible species include hedgehogs *(Hydnum repandum)* and shaggy manes *(Coprinus comatus).* Even edible mushrooms may disagree with one's digestion; the only test for an inedible or poisonous mushroom is positive identification. If you can't identify it, don't eat it.

MUSKEG
Muskegs are bogs where little vegetation can grow except for sphagnum moss, black spruce, Sitka spruce, dwarf birch, tussocks and a few other shrubby plants. Such swampy areas cover much of Alaska. Nearly half of Alaska—175 million acres—is classified as wetlands.

With nearly two-thirds of the nation's wetlands within its borders, Alaska boasts many of the most diverse wildlife habitats in North America. Waterfowl, muskrats, moose and many species of insect depend on wetlands for survival.

MUSK OXEN
Musk oxen are stocky, shaggy, long-haired mammals of the extreme northern latitudes. They remain in the open through Alaska's long winters. Their name is misleading, for they have no musk gland and are more closely related to sheep and goats than to cattle. Adult males may weigh 500 to 900 pounds, females 300 to 700 pounds. Both sexes have horns that droop down from their forehead and curve back up at the tips.

When threatened by wolves or other predators, musk oxen form circles or lines with their young in the middle. These defensive measures did not protect them from hunters and their guns.

Musk oxen were eliminated from Alaska in about 1865, when hunters shot and killed the last herd of 13. The species was reintroduced to the territory in the 1930s when 34 musk oxen were purchased from Greenland and brought to the University of Alaska Fairbanks. In 1935–36, the 31 remaining musk oxen at the university were shipped to Nunivak Island in the Bering Sea, where the herd eventually thrived. Animals from the Nunivak herd have been transplanted to areas along Alaska's western and northern coasts; at least five wild herds—approximately 3,000 musk oxen—exist in the state.

The soft underhair of musk oxen is called *qiviut* and grows next to the skin, protected by long guard hairs. It is shed naturally every spring. The Musk Ox Development Corp. maintains a herd in Palmer and collects *qiviut* for the Oomingmak Cooperative. The hair is spun into yarn in Rhode Island and sent back to Alaska, where the cooperative arranges for knitters in villages in Western Alaska, where jobs are scarce, to knit the yarn into clothing at their own pace.

Each village keeps its own distinct signature pattern for scarves knitted from *qiviut*. Villagers also produce stoles, tunics, hats and smoke rings, circular scarves that fit around the head like a hood. About 250 women are employed as knitters.

In Southcentral Alaska musk oxen can be viewed from May to September at the Musk Ox Farm in Palmer (phone (907) 745-4151; www.muskoxfarm.org/). In the Interior, look for them at the university's Research Station on Yankovich Road in Fairbanks; (907) 474-7207.

NATIONAL FORESTS
(See also Land Use; National Parks; National Wilderness Areas; Timber) Alaska has two national forests, the Tongass and the Chugach. The Tongass occupies most of the panhandle, or southeastern portion of the state. The Chugach extends south and east of Anchorage along the Southcentral Alaska coast, encompassing most of the Prince William Sound area. These two national forests are managed by the USDA Forest Service for a variety of uses. They provide forest products for national and international markets, minerals, recreational opportunities,

During extremely cold weather, musk oxen stand still to conserve energy. From *Alaska's Mammals* by Dave Smith (text) and Tom Walker (photographs).

Rescued by an Angel

Panik the musk ox was in trouble. The fuzzy female calf, born in the early 1990s at the Musk Ox Farm in Palmer, was hardly 10 days old when she collapsed in the field where she was staying with her mother and was taken to a veterinary clinic for intravenous feeding. The calf was thin, listless and suffering from diarrhea.

By the time she was released from the clinic, the calf had become a social outcast to her herd, and was in danger of not thriving because of loneliness. A black poodle used as a playmate didn't help. Then the farm came up with the notion of borrowing a lamb.

Angel, a two-month-old white lamb, was brought over from a dairy farm in Point McKenzie. A friendship and a healthy musk ox began when the calf and lamb competed for the bottle. The pair nursed together, slept together, munched on weeds together and frolicked together.

"She may have survived without the lamb, but she wouldn't be as happy," veterinarian Ron Williams told the *Anchorage Daily News.*

—1993 *The Alaska Almanac*®

wilderness experiences and superb scenery and pristine vistas.

Nearly 250 public recreation cabins are maintained in the Tongass and Chugach National Forests. They accommodate visitors from all over the world and are a vacation bargain, including a boat on some freshwater lakes. Fees for the cabins are from $25 to $45 a night. All Tongass and Chugach National Forest cabins are reserved through the National Recreation Reservation System: (877) 444-6777 toll-free; (518) 885-3639 international; TDD (877) 833-6777; www.recreation.gov.

The forests are home to some of Alaska's most magnificent wildlife. It is here that the bald eagle and brown (grizzly) bears may be encountered in large numbers. Five species of Pacific salmon spawn in the rivers and streams of the forests and smaller mammals and waterfowl abound. The Forest Service is charged with the management of this rich habitat. The Alaska Department of Fish and Game manages the wildlife species that this habitat supports.

There are many recreational opportunities in the national forests of Alaska including backpacking, fishing, hunting, photography, boating, nature study and camping. For information concerning recreational opportunities, contact the USDA Forest Service office nearest the area you are visiting.

The Alaska National Interest Lands Conservation Act (ANILCA) designated approximately 5.5 million acres of wilderness as 14 units within the 17-million-acre Tongass National Forest. It also added three new areas to the forest: the Juneau Icefield, Kates Needle and parts of the Barbazon Range, over 1 million acres.

The Tongass Timber Reform Act (TTRA) of 1990 amended ANILCA and designated five additional wilderness areas and an addition to the existing Kootznoowoo Wilderness, as well as 12 backcountry semi-primitive roadless areas managed primarily for fish, wildlife and recreation resources. The lands bill also provided extensive additions to the Chugach National Forest.

The charts on the next page show the effect of the Alaska Lands Act on the Tongass and Chugach National Forests.

NATIONAL HISTORIC PLACES (SEE ALSO Archaeology)

A "place" on the National Register of Historic Places is a district, site, building, structure or object significant for its history, architecture, archaeology or culture. The National Register also includes National Historic Landmarks.

Wilderness Units in Tongass National Forest

Wilderness Areas Established Dec. 2, 1980, by ANILCA	Acres
Coronation Island Wilderness	.19,232
Endicott River Wilderness	.98,729
Kootznoowoo Wilderness* (Admiralty Island National Monument)**	.955,921
Maurelle Islands Wilderness	.4,937
Misty Fiords National Monument**	.2,142,243
Petersburg Creek–Duncan Salt Chuck Wilderness	.46,777
Russell Fiord Wilderness	.348,701
South Baranof Wilderness	.319,568
South Prince of Wales Wilderness	.90,996
Stikine–LeConte Wilderness	.448,926
Tebenkof Bay Wilderness	.66,839
Tracy Arm–Fords Terror Wilderness	.653,179
Warren Island Wilderness	.11,181
West Chichagof–Yakobi Wilderness	.264,747

Wilderness Areas Established Nov. 28, 1990, by TTRA	
Chuck River Wilderness	74,298
Karta Wilderness	39,889
Kuiu Wilderness	60,581
Pleasant–Lemesurier–Inian Islands Wilderness	23,096
South Etolin Wilderness	83,371
Total acreage	**5,753,211**

* Kootznoowoo Wilderness includes 18,486 acres (including 24 acres of nonnational forest land) in the Young Lake Addition established by TTRA.

** Designated monuments under ANILCA; first areas so designated in the national forest system. These wildernesses include only the public lands above mean high tide.

National Forest Lands in Alaska	Tongass	Chugach
Total acreage before ANILCA	15,555,388	4,392,646
Total acreage after ANILCA	16,954,713	5,940,040*
Wilderness acreage created	5,753,211	None created
Wilderness study	None created	2,019,999 acres

* This lands act provides for additional transfers of national forest land to Native corporations, the state and the U.S. Fish and Game Department of an estimated 296,000 acres on Afognak Island, and an estimated 242,000 acres to the Chugach Native Corporation.

The register is an official list of properties recognized by the federal government as worthy of preservation. Listing in the register includes a nomination process, notification of the property owner and reviews by the State Historic Preservation Office, the Alaska Historical Commission and the Keeper of the National Register. Limitations are not placed on a listed property. The federal government does not attach restrictive covenants to the property or seek to acquire it. Listing in the register means a property is accorded national recognition for its significance in U.S. history or prehistory.

Benefits of listing include tax credits on income-producing properties and qualification for federal matching funds for preservation, maintenance and restoration work when such funds are available. Listed properties are guaranteed a full review process for potential adverse effects by federally funded, licensed or otherwise

The Great Past of the Great Land

Alaska's archaeology holds the key to two mysteries of human experience: human adaptation to northern latitudes, and early human migrations from Asia to North and South America.

Whether passing through Alaska to more southerly lands, or settling in for centuries, people have always adapted to extremes: light and dark, water and ice, thick forest and windswept tundra, a glut of fish, game, birds, and berries, or none. Whereas animals adapt primarily physically to their environment, human adapt primarily through culture. Culture includes the size and structure of families and communities; beliefs and practices, such as spiritual and health rituals; the technology people use to feed and shelter themselves, and to play; intellectual and practical knowledge; and art and music.

—Ellen Bielawski, Ph.D., *In Search of Ancient Alaska*

assisted projects. Such a review usually takes place while the project is being planned. Alternatives are sought to avoid damaging or destroying the property.

Alaska has 390 sites and more than 1,500 sites, structures, buildings and objects listed in the National Register of Historic Places. For details, contact the Office of History and Archaeology, 550 W. Seventh Ave., Suite 1310, Anchorage, AK 99501-3565; www.dnr.state.ak.us/parks/oha_web. Among them:

Most visited site: Totem Bight State Park in Ketchikan.

Oldest standing Russian Orthodox Church: Ascension of Our Lord Chapel, Karluk.

Oldest standing building: Russian–American Co. Magazine (Erskine House), National Historic Landmark, Kodiak.

Oldest standing U.S. government buildings: U.S. Army Storehouses, No. 3 and No. 4 in Portland Canal and at Hyder.

The most recent additions to the list of historic places in Alaska are:

DIL-161 Site. This archaeological site has more than 40 identified features that have the potential to provide significant information about the early inhabitants and the development of large settled villages in western Alaska more than 2,000 years ago. Distinct floors were found in each of the eight features tested, and hearths were found in three of them. Nearly 6,100 artifacts were recovered during testing including fiber tempered and check stamped ceramics, chipped stone sideblades, chipped and ground adzes, chipped stone projectile points, drills and scrapers. The artifacts are similar to those that define the Norton tradition. DIL-161 Site is the largest and oldest site known, tested and dated in the region.

Hoben Park. Residents of Seward, interested in promoting their town as the "Gateway to Alaska," completed a park near the railroad depot and main dock in time for President Warren G. Harding's visit to Alaska in July 1923. Harding was the first U.S. president to visit Alaska. He came to drive in the golden spike signaling completion of the 170-mile government-built Alaska Railroad connecting the year-round port at Seward with the Interior hub city of Fairbanks. Seward residents expected the railroad to bring more visitors to their town. The residents wanted the park for the enjoyment of travelers arriving by train or by sea. A local businessman and former mayor, Hedley V. "Harry" Hoben, for whom the park is now named, had his office across the street and had his employees maintain the park until his death in 1948. Seward residents are working with the city government to rehabilitate Hoben Park to its historic appearance.

Hydaburg Totem Park. Established in 1939, the park preserves the totemic art of the Haida people of Southeast Alaska. The park is located in the center of Hydaburg, a community founded in 1911 when families from the villages of Howkan, Klinkwan and Sukkwan moved to the site to get a U.S. government school for their children. The park has three totems carved before 1939 and moved to the park, sixteen carved between 1939 and 1942 as a Civilian Conservation Corps (CCC) project and two carved in 1971 to replace ones that had decayed. The Hydaburg park is one of six totem-pole projects conducted by the CCC in cooperation with the U.S. Forest Service to provide jobs during the Depression, to preserve the cultural and artistic traditions of the Native people and to encourage tourism. Haida carvers, led by master carver John Wallace, did the work at Hydaburg. The taller totems stand in a circle around the perimeter of the park, smaller ones stand in a circle inside the larger one and a stone carving is at the center. The Hydaburg park joins CCC parks at Kasaan, Saxman, Ketchikan, Wrangell and Sitka documented and listed in the National Register.

NATIONAL PARKS, PRESERVES AND MONUMENTS
The National Park Service administers approximately 54 million acres of land in Alaska, consisting of 15 units of national parks, national preserves and national monuments. The Alaska National Interest Lands Conservation Act of 1980 (SEE Land Use)—also referred to as ANILCA—created 10 new National Park Service units in Alaska and changed the size and status of three existing Park Service units: Denali National Park and Preserve (formerly Mount McKinley National Park); Glacier Bay National Monument, now a national park and preserve; and Katmai National Monument, now a national park and preserve. (SEE map, pages 146–47) In 2006, Alaska's national parks, preserves and monuments attracted a record 2.47 million visitors.

National parks are traditionally managed to preserve scenic, wildlife and recreational values; mining, cutting of house logs, hunting and other resource exploitation are carefully regulated within park, monument and preserve boundaries, and motorized access is restricted to automobile traffic on authorized roads. However regulations for National Park Service units in Alaska recognize that these units contain lands traditionally occupied and used by Alaska Natives and rural residents for subsistence activities.

To accommodate these users, management of some parks, preserves and monuments in Alaska provides for subsistence hunting, fishing and gathering activities, and the use of such motorized vehicles as snowmobiles, motorboats and airplanes where these activities are customary. National preserves permit sport hunting.

Information is available at the Alaska Public Lands Information Centers: 605 W. Fourth Ave., Suite 105, Anchorage 99501, (907) 271-2737; 250 Cushman St., Suite 1A, Fairbanks 99701, (907) 456-0527; 50 Main St., Ketchikan 99901, (907) 228-6220; and P.O. Box 359, Tok 99780, (907) 883-5667. The Web site for the information centers is www.nps.gov/aplic. A list of National Park Service parks, preserves and monuments follows.

The USDA Forest Service manages another two national monuments: Admiralty Island National Monument, 937,000 acres; and Misty Fiords National

Only in Juneau could most of the city lose power when an overly ambitious bald eagle carrying a deer head crashed into transmission lines. There's an old joke: How many guys from Alaska does it take to screw in a lightbulb? None—we don't have electricity!

Monument, 2.1 million acres, both in Southeast Alaska and part of the National Wilderness Preservation System. (SEE ALSO National Wild and Scenic Rivers; National Wilderness Areas)

There are two NPS-affiliated areas in Alaska: the Aleutian World War II National Historic Area at Unalaska (www.nps.gov/aleu) and the Iñupiat Heritage Center in Barrow (www.nps.gov/inup). The former was designated in 1996 to educate and inspire people about the history and the role of the Aleut people and the Aleutian Islands in World War II. The federal government does not own or manage the park, which is overseen by the Ounalashka Corp., a Native village corporation. The National Park Service provides technical assistance. The Iñupiat Heritage Center is affiliated with the New Bedford Whaling National Historic Park in New Bedford, Mass. In the 19th century, more than 2,000 whaling voyages departed New Bedford for the western Arctic. The National Park Service has helped with exhibits and other technical assistance.

National Park Service units in Alaska are:

Aniakchak National Monument and Preserve, mailing address: P.O. Box 245, King Salmon 99613; www.nps.gov/ania. 466,000 acres. Features the Aniakchak dry caldera.

Bering Land Bridge National Preserve, National Park Service, P.O. Box 220, Nome 99762; www.nps.gov/bela. 2,697,000 acres. Lava fields, rare plants, archaeological sites, migratory waterfowl.

Cape Krusenstern National Monument, National Park Service, P.O. Box 1029, Kotzebue 99752; www.nps.gov/cakr. 649,000 acres. Archaeological sites.

Denali National Park and Preserve, National Park Service, P.O. Box 9, Denali Park 99755-0009; www.nps.gov/dena. 6,075,000 acres. Mount McKinley, abundant wildlife.

Gates of the Arctic National Park and Preserve, National Park Service, P.O. Box 30, Bettles 99726; www.nps.gov/gaar. 8,473,000 acres. Brooks Range, wild and scenic rivers, wildlife.

Glacier Bay National Park and Preserve, National Park Service, P.O. Box 140, Gustavus 99826-0140;

www.nps.gov/glba. 3,283,000 acres. Glaciers, marine wildlife.

Katmai National Park and Preserve, National Park Service, P.O. Box 7, King Salmon 99613; www.nps.gov/katm. 4,094,000 acres. Valley of Ten Thousand Smokes, brown bears.

Kenai Fjords National Park, National Park Service, P.O. Box 1727, Seward 99664; www.nps.gov/kefj. 670,000 acres. Fjords, Harding Icefield, Exit Glacier, waterfowl, sea otters.

Klondike Gold Rush National Historical Park, National Park Service, P.O. Box 517, Skagway 99840; www.nps.gov/klgo. 13,000 acres, including 15 restored turn-of-the-century structures; Chilkoot Trail.

Kobuk Valley National Park, National Park Service, P.O. Box 1029, Kotzebue 99752; www.nps.gov/kova. 1,751,000 acres. Archaeological sites, Great Kobuk Sand Dunes, river rafting.

Lake Clark National Park and Preserve, National Park Service, 240 W. Fifth Avenue, Suite 236, Anchorage 99501; www.nps.gov/lacl. 4,030,000 acres. Backcountry recreation, fishing, scenery.

Noatak National Preserve, National Park Service, P.O. Box 1029, Kotzebue 99752; www.nps.gov/noat. 6,570,000 acres. Abundant wildlife, river floating.

Sitka National Historical Park, National Park Service, 103 Monastery St., Sitka 99835; www.nps.gov/sitk. 113 acres. Russian Bishop's House, totems, trails.

Wrangell–St. Elias National Park and Preserve, National Park Service, P.O. Box 439, Copper Center 99573-0439; www.nps.gov/wrst. 13,176,000 acres. Rugged peaks, glaciers, expansive wilderness.

Yukon–Charley Rivers National Preserve, National Park Service, P.O. Box 167, Eagle 99738; www.nps.gov/yuch. 2,527,000 acres. Backcountry recreation, river floating.

NATIONAL PETROLEUM RESERVE—ALASKA (SEE ALSO Oil and Gas) In 1923, President Warren G. Harding signed an executive order creating Naval Petroleum Reserve Number 4 (NPR-4),

(Continued on page 148)

NATIONAL INTEREST LANDS

ARCTIC OCEAN

CHUKCHI SEA

ARCTIC CIRCLE

NATIONAL WILDLIFE REFUGE SYSTEM

1 Alaska Maritime NWR*
  Chukchi Sea Unit
  Bering Sea Unit
  Aleutian Islands Unit
  Alaska Peninsula Unit
  Gulf of Alaska Unit
2 Alaska Peninsula
3 Arctic
4 Becharof
5 Innoko
6 Izembek
7 Kanuti
8 Kenai
9 Kodiak
10 Koyukuk
11 Nowitna
12 Selawik
13 Tetlin
14 Togiak
15 Yukon Delta
16 Yukon Flats

St. Lawrence Island

Nome

BERING SEA

Nunivak Island

Iliamna Lake

Home

Aleutian Islands

Amatignak Is

Kodia

Kodiak Island

Unimak Island

Unalaska

PACIFIC OCEAN

Umnak Island

NATIONAL FOREST SYSTEM

34 Chugach National Forest
35 Tongass National Forest
36 Admiralty Island National Monument**
37 Misty Fiords National Monument**

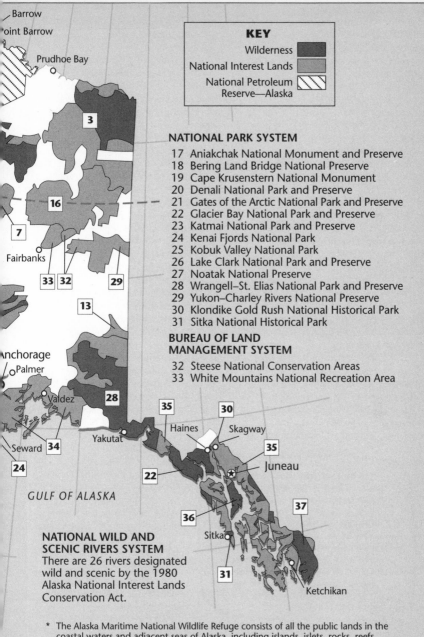

Barrow
Point Barrow
Prudhoe Bay

KEY
Wilderness
National Interest Lands
National Petroleum
Reserve—Alaska

3

16

7

Fairbanks

33 **32**   **29**

13

Anchorage
Palmer

Valdez   **28**

Seward **34**
24

Yakutat

GULF OF ALASKA

NATIONAL PARK SYSTEM
17 Aniakchak National Monument and Preserve
18 Bering Land Bridge National Preserve
19 Cape Krusenstern National Monument
20 Denali National Park and Preserve
21 Gates of the Arctic National Park and Preserve
22 Glacier Bay National Park and Preserve
23 Katmai National Park and Preserve
24 Kenai Fjords National Park
25 Kobuk Valley National Park
26 Lake Clark National Park and Preserve
27 Noatak National Preserve
28 Wrangell–St. Elias National Park and Preserve
29 Yukon–Charley Rivers National Preserve
30 Klondike Gold Rush National Historical Park
31 Sitka National Historical Park

BUREAU OF LAND MANAGEMENT SYSTEM
32 Steese National Conservation Areas
33 White Mountains National Recreation Area

35   **30**

Haines   Skagway

35

Juneau

22

37

36   Sitka

NATIONAL WILD AND SCENIC RIVERS SYSTEM
There are 26 rivers designated wild and scenic by the 1980 Alaska National Interest Lands Conservation Act.

31

Ketchikan

* The Alaska Maritime National Wildlife Refuge consists of all the public lands in the coastal waters and adjacent seas of Alaska, including islands, islets, rocks, reefs, capes and spires.
** Admiralty Island and Misty Fiords national monuments are part of the Tongass National Forest, which includes 17 other wilderness areas.

147

(Continued from page 145)

the last of four petroleum reserves to be placed under control of the U.S. Navy. The secretary of the navy was charged to "explore, protect, conserve, develop, use and operate the Naval Petroleum Reserves," including NPR-4, on Alaska's North Slope. (SEE map, pages 146–47)

The U.S. Geological Survey (USGS) had begun surface exploration in the area in 1901. Following creation of the 23-million-acre reserve, the Navy conducted exploration programs. From 1944 to 1953, extensive surveys were undertaken, 36 test wells were drilled and nine oil and gas fields were discovered. The largest oil field, near Umiat, contained an estimated 70 million to 120 million barrels of recoverable oil. Active exploration was suspended in 1953.

In 1974, the Arab oil embargo, coupled with the knowledge of large petroleum reserves at nearby Prudhoe Bay, brought about renewed interest in NPR-4, and Congress directed the Navy to resume its exploration program.

In 1976, all lands within NPR-4 were redesignated the National Petroleum Reserve Alaska (NPR-A) and jurisdiction was transferred to the secretary of the interior. In 1980, Congress authorized the secretary to oversee an expeditious program of competitive leasing of oil and gas tracts in the reserve, clearing the way for private development of the area's resources.

By mid-1983, three competitive bid lease sales involving 7.2 million acres of NPR-A had been held. A lease sale scheduled for 1984 was cancelled when no bids were received. Interest from the oil companies lessened, and leases were allowed to expire. Currently there are 1,185 active oil and gas leases, covering nearly 2.8 million acres.

The Interior Department, through USGS, continued exploration of NPR-A into the 1980s. Past naval explorations and those conducted by USGS resulted in the discovery of oil at Umiat and Cape Simpson, and several gas fields including Walakpa, Gubic and Point Barrow. The North Slope Borough is developing reserves in the Walakpa field to provide gas for heating and electrical generation for Barrow.

Data gathered indicates NPR-A may contain recoverable reserves of 1.85 billion barrels of crude oil and 3.74 trillion cubic feet of natural gas. Such optimistic data fueled bidding in a May 1999 lease sale. Alaska's two largest oil companies at that time, BP Exploration (Alaska) and Arco Alaska won interest in 87 percent of the leases. Anadarko Petroleum Co. was also a successful bidder in this lease sale. Bidding on the 5,700-acre blocks between Teshekpuk Lake and the Colville River totaled $105 million.

In 2000, Phillips Alaska Inc. bought Arco's interest in Alaska. NPR-A Sale 2002, held in June 2002, awarded bids on 60 tracts totaling nearly 580,000 acres. Successful bidders included Phillips Alaska, Inc., TotalFinaELF E&P USA, Inc., EnCana Oil & Gas (USA), Inc. and Paul L. Craig.

On Aug. 30, 2002, Phillips Alaska, Inc. changed its name to ConocoPhillips Alaska, Inc.

NPR-A leases are currently being explored. Since 2000, the Alaska Oil and Gas Conservation Commission has issued 24 permits to drill wells on NPR-A leases. Information from 17 of those wells has been released to the public record.

> A bird-watcher cruising the streets of Anchorage's Mountain View neighborhood with binoculars at sunrise was pulled over by two Anchorage Police cars in November. He explained that he was looking for a rare Eurasian Bullfinch that was reported on the Internet. The officers shook him down for ID, insurance, registration and checked the bird-watcher's record before explaining, "We don't get a lot of this in Mountain View."

Rafters prepare to launch on the Chulitna River in Denali State Park. Photo by Tricia Brown.

NATIONAL WILD AND
SCENIC RIVERS (SEE ALSO Rivers)

The Alaska National Interest Lands Conservation Act (ANILCA) of 1980 gave wild and scenic river classification to 13 streams within the National Park System, six in the National Wildlife Refuge System and two in Bureau of Land Management Conservation and Recreation areas. (SEE map, pages 146–47) An additional five rivers are located outside designated preservation units. Twelve more rivers were designated for further study and possible wild and scenic classification.

The criteria for wild and scenic river classification covers more than just float trip possibilities. Scenic features, wilderness characteristics and recreational opportunities that would be impaired by alteration, development or impoundment are also considered.

Rivers are classified into three categories under the Wild and Scenic Rivers Act. The wild classification is most restrictive of development or incompatible uses—it stresses the wilderness aspect of the rivers. The scenic classification permits some intrusions upon the natural landscape. The recreational classification is the least restrictive category. A specified amount of land back from the river's banks is also put in protected status to ensure access, use and the preservation of aesthetic values for the public.

For those desiring to float these rivers, special consideration must be given to put-in and take-out points because most of the designated wild and scenic rivers are not accessible by road. This means that voyagers and their crafts must be flown in and picked up by charter Bush planes. Because Federal Aviation Administration regulations prohibit the lashing of canoes and kayaks to pontoons of floatplanes when carrying passengers, inflatable rafts and folding canvas or rubber kayaks are often more convenient and less expensive to transport.

Further information on rivers and river running can be obtained from the Alaska Public Lands Information Centers: 605 W. Fourth Ave., Suite 105, Anchorage 99501, (907) 271-2737; 250 Cushman St., Suite 1A, Fairbanks 99701, (907) 456-0527; 50 Main St., Ketchikan 99901, (907) 228-6220; and P.O. Box 359, Tok 99780, (907) 883-5667; www.nps.gov/aplic.

Information is also available from the U.S. Fish and Wildlife Service, 1011 E. Tudor Road, Anchorage 99503, www.r7.fws.gov; and the Bureau of Land Management, 222 W. Seventh Ave., No. 13, Anchorage 99513, www.blm.gov. Information for rivers within park units or managed by the National Park Service is also available from the particular park headquarters. (SEE ALSO National Parks, Preserves and Monuments)

Rivers Within National Park Areas

Alagnak—Katmai National Preserve

Alatna—Gates of the Arctic National Park

Aniakchak—Aniakchak National Monument; Aniakchak National Preserve

Charley—Yukon–Charley Rivers National Preserve

Chilikadrotna—Lake Clark National Park and Preserve

John—Gates of the Arctic National Park and Preserve

Kobuk—Gates of the Arctic National Park and Preserve

Mulchatna—Lake Clark National Park and Preserve

Noatak—Gates of the Arctic National Park and Noatak National Preserve

North Fork Koyukuk—Gates of the Arctic National Park and Preserve

Salmon—Kobuk Valley National Park

Tinayguk—Gates of the Arctic National Park and Preserve

Tlikakila—Lake Clark National Park and Preserve

Rivers Within National Wildlife Refuges

Andreafsky—Yukon Delta NWR

Ivishak—Arctic NWR

Nowitna—Nowitna NWR

Selawik—Selawik NWR

Sheenjek—Arctic NWR

Wind—Arctic NWR

General information on rivers not listed in refuge brochures may be obtained from respective refuge offices by addressing queries to refuge managers. Addresses for refuges are given in the brochures.

Rivers Within Bureau of Land Management Units

Beaver Creek—The segment of the main stem from the confluence of Bear and Champion Creeks within White Mountains National Recreation Area to the Yukon Flats National Wildlife Refuge boundary.

Birch Creek—The segment of the main stem from the south side of Steese Highway downstream to the bridge at Milepost 147.

Rivers Outside of Designated Preservation Units

Alagnak—Those segments or portions of the main stem and Nonvianuk tributary lying outside and westward of Katmai National Park and Preserve.

Delta—The segment from and including all of the Tangle Lakes to a point one-half mile north of Black Rapids.

Fortymile—The main stem within Alaska, plus tributaries.

Gulkana—The main stem from the outlet of Paxson Lake to the confluence with Sourdough Creek; various segments of the west fork and middle fork.

Unalakleet—Approximately 80 miles of the main stem.

Rivers Designated for Study for Inclusion in Wild and Scenic Rivers System

Colville

Etivluk–Nigu Rivers

Kanektok

Kisaralik

Koyuk

Melozitna

Porcupine

Sheenjek (lower segment)

Situk

Squirrel

Utukok

Yukon (Rampart section)

NATIONAL WILDERNESS AREAS (SEE ALSO Cabins) Passage of the 1980 Alaska National Interest Lands Conservation Act (ANILCA) added millions of acres to the National Wilderness Preservation System. Agencies that oversee wilderness areas in Alaska include the National Park Service, U.S. Fish and Wildlife Service and USDA Forest Service. (SEE map, pages 146–47)

Passage of the Tongass Timber Reform Act in 1990 designated an additional 300,000 acres of the Tongass National Forest as wilderness.

Approximate wilderness allocations to different agencies in Alaska are: USDA Forest Service, 5.7 million acres; National Park Service, 32 million acres; U.S. Fish and Wildlife Service, 18.7 million acres.

Wilderness, according to the federal Wilderness Act of 1964, is land sufficient in size to enable the operation of natural systems without undue influence from human activities in surrounding areas and should be places in which people are visitors only. Alaska wilderness regulations follow the stipulations of the Wilderness Act as amended by the Alaska Lands Act.

Specifically designed to allow for Alaska conditions, the rules are considerably more lenient about transportation access, human-made structures and use of mechanized vehicles. The primary objective of a wilderness area continues to be the maintenance of the wilderness character of the land.

Some characteristics of Alaska wilderness areas:

Subsistence. Subsistence uses including hunting, fishing, trapping, berry gathering and use of timber for cabins and firewood may be allowed in some areas.

Cabins. Public recreation or safety cabins continue to be maintained and may be replaced.

Fish. Fish habitat enhancement programs, such as construction of fish weirs, fishways and spawning channels, may be allowed.

Guides. Special-use permits for guides and outfitters are allowed.

Access. Private, state and Native lands surrounded by wilderness areas are guaranteed access through wilderness areas.

Transport. Use of fixed-wing airplanes, motorboats and snowmachines for traditional activities and for access to villages and homesites is allowed to continue.

NATIONAL WILDLIFE REFUGES

Congress has designated 16 National Wildlife Refuges in Alaska, totaling nearly 82 million acres. (See map, pages 146–47) The refuges have 10 designated wilderness areas and 6 rivers designated National Wild and Scenic Rivers. At just under 20 million acres each, both the Arctic National Wildlife Refuge and the Yukon Delta National Wildlife Refuge are among the largest wildlife refuges in the world. Refuges are managed by the U.S. Fish and Wildlife Service's Region 7 at 1011 E. Tudor Road, Anchorage 99503.

National wildlife refuges in Alaska were established to conserve fish and wildlife populations and habitats in their natural diversity. Refuges are open to the public for many noncommercial recreational and subsistence uses including wildlife observation, photography, boating, camping and hiking. Hunting, fishing and trapping are allowed in accordance with state regulations and those set by the Federal Subsistence Board.

Visitors are encouraged to contact the refuge manager for information on special closures or other special conditions. Commercial guiding, air taxi operations and other commercial uses may be authorized by special permit. Subsistence activities are permitted, as is the use of snowmachines, motorboats and nonmotorized surface transportation methods for traditional activities. With adequate snow cover, recreational snowmachining is allowed in the Kenai Refuge. Transportation in off-road vehicles, including all-terrain vehicles, motorcycles and airboats, is not permitted.

Most refuges are in remote areas—only the Kenai and Tetlin Refuges are accessible from the highway system. Airplane access is allowed but helicopter access requires a permit and must be determined compatible with refuge purposes.

Refuge managers may be contacted at their field headquarters listed below or through www.r7.fws.gov.

Alaska Maritime National Wildlife Refuge, 95 Sterling Highway, Suite 1, Homer 99603 (4.5 million acres). Seabirds, sea lions, sea otters, harbor seals, walrus, whales.

Alaska Peninsula National Wildlife Refuge, P.O. Box 277, King Salmon 99613 (3.5 million acres). Brown bears,

caribou, moose, sea otters, bald eagles, peregrine falcons, wolves, wolverines, migrating whales.

Arctic National Wildlife Refuge, 101 12th Ave., Box 20, Room 236, Fairbanks 99701 (19.5 million acres). Caribou, polar bears, grizzly bears, wolves, Dall sheep, peregrine falcons, musk oxen, snowy owls.

Becharof National Wildlife Refuge, P.O. Box 298, King Salmon 99613 (1.2 million acres). Brown bears, bald eagles, caribou, moose, salmon.

Innoko National Wildlife Refuge, P.O. Box 69, McGrath 99627 (4.25 million acres). Migratory waterfowl, beaver, lynx, marten, moose.

Izembek National Wildlife Refuge, P.O. Box 127, Cold Bay 99571 (417,000 acres). Black brant (coastal geese), brown bears.

Kanuti National Wildlife Refuge, 101 12th Ave., Fairbanks 99701 (1.4 million acres). Waterfowl.

Kenai National Wildlife Refuge, P.O. Box 2139, Soldotna 99669-2139 (1.9 million acres). Moose, salmon, mountain goats, Dall sheep, bears, lynx, wolves.

Kodiak National Wildlife Refuge, 1390 Buskin River Road, Kodiak 99615 (1.9 million acres). Brown bears, black-tailed deer, bald eagles, river otters.

Koyukuk National Wildlife Refuge, P.O. Box 287, Galena 99741 (3.5 million acres). Wolves, bears, moose, waterfowl.

Nowitna National Wildlife Refuge, P.O. Box 287, Galena 99741 (1.5 million acres). Migratory waterfowl, moose, bears, furbearers.

Selawik National Wildlife Refuge, P.O. Box 270, Kotzebue 99752 (2.1 million acres). Caribou, migratory birds.

Tetlin National Wildlife Refuge, P.O. Box 779, Tok 99780 (700,053 acres). Migratory waterfowl, Dall sheep, moose, bears, ptarmigan.

Togiak National Wildlife Refuge, P.O. Box 270, Dillingham 99576 (4.1 million acres). Caribou, walrus, seabirds, moose.

Yukon Delta National Wildlife Refuge, P.O. Box 346, Bethel 99559 (19.1 million acres). Migratory birds, musk oxen and reindeer are found on Nunivak Island.

Yukon Flats National Wildlife Refuge, 101 12th Ave., Fairbanks 99701 (12 million acres). Waterfowl, moose, bears.

NATIVE ARTS AND CRAFTS

(See also Baleen; Baskets; Beadwork; Ivory; Masks; Native Peoples; Potlatch; Skin Sewing; Totem Poles)

Traditional arts and crafts of Alaska's Natives were produced for ceremonial and utilitarian purposes. These objects were not thought of as art in the Western sense but as pieces and designs to fulfill specific needs. Native art also reflected spiritual values and the environment each group inhabited.

Alaska Natives are known for their ingenious use and manipulation of natural materials to supply life's needs. Roots, bark, grasses, wood, fur, quills, skins, feathers and the sea's resources are still used to produce containers, clothing, hunting implements, ceremonial regalia and many other items.

Today, most Native utilitarian objects are modern adaptations using plastic, metal and glass. But many traditional Native designs and natural materials are still used to create ceremonial objects, and Alaska Native arts and crafts are widely

Aleut artist Peter Lind created this traditional-style bentwood visor.
Photo by Roy Corral.

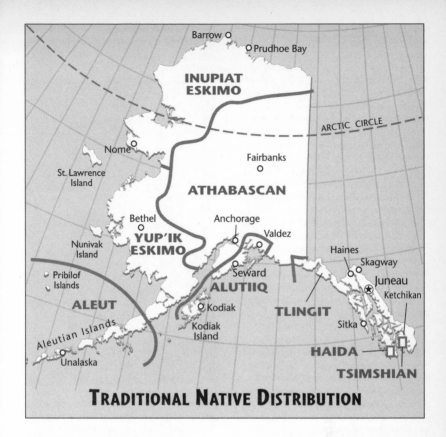

TRADITIONAL NATIVE DISTRIBUTION

sought by collectors, museums and tourists. This new market has proven beneficial to Native artists and to Native culture as it moves from a subsistence lifestyle to a cash economy.

The Iñupiat and Yup'ik people groups, like other Alaska Natives, are divided geographically and linguistically. Because their coastal environment offers few forest resources, the Eskimo peoples have learned to rely on the tundra and the sea. The Iñupiat of Northern Alaska are known for making objects out of sea mammal parts—especially walrus ivory, baleen and whale bone. Their ivory carving and scrimshaw work is world-renowned. More contemporary work in which stiff baleen is coiled into elegant baskets is gaining recognition.

The Yup'ik of Western Alaska also utilize sea mammals in their art. In addition, they rely heavily on the coastal rye grass for their intricate coiled baskets

and mat work. Yup'ik ceremonial masks—carved primarily of driftwood, assembled and painted—are distinctive in the global tribal mask-making tradition. Both the Iñupiat and Yup'ik groups produce warm, beautiful clothing using the furs and skins of land and sea mammals.

The Aleut (Unangan) people of the Pribilof and Aleutian Islands, and the Alutiiq of Kodiak Island on the Southcentral coast, also make attractive baskets from rye grass but they use a twining technique. The Aleut are known for their traditional capes made of sea mammal gut and painted bentwood hunting hats and visors.

The Athabascan Indians of Alaska's Interior live in a region abundant with forest and river resources. They make decorative beaded clothing and other items, often on tanned, smoked moose hide; birch bark is formed into lightweight canoes, baby cradles and containers. Athabascans are also known for their skill in sewing skins into clothing.

The Tlingit, Haida and Tsimshian people of southeastern Alaska are part of the Pacific Northwest Coast Indian culture, which extends down the coast of British Columbia and into Washington State. Each member of this culture is born into a family clan and as such receives his or her own totemic crest—an animal form representing the clan. These crests are reproduced in many art forms such as elaborate ceremonial regalia; carvings in wood, metal or stone; paintings or prints; and jewelry. The carvers of the Northwest Coast, best known for monumental totem poles, record legendary happenings and honor important people or events. Artwork adheres to a complex, formal design system and is highly stylized and dramatic. Fine Northwest Coast pieces such as carved and painted wooden hats, rattles, masks and bentwood boxes are sought worldwide by collectors and museums.

NATIVE PEOPLES Alaska's 106,000

Native people make up about 16 percent of the state's total population. Of those, the majority are Eskimo, Indian and Aleut (Unangan). Although many live in widely scattered villages along the coastline and great rivers of Alaska, about 24,000 Natives lived in Anchorage as of 2005. The Fairbanks North Star Borough had a Native population of more than 6,800.

At the time Europeans came in contact with the Natives of Alaska in 1741, Russians estimated the Native population at 100,000. The Eskimo, Indian and Aleut people lived within well-defined regions: There was little mixing of ethnic groups. All were hunting and gathering people who did not practice agriculture.

Indian. In southeastern Alaska, the herring, salmon, deer and other plentiful foods permitted the **Haida** (HIGH-duh) and **Tlingit** (KLINK-it) Indians to settle in permanent villages and develop a culture rich in art.

The **Athabascan** (ath-uh-BA-scun) people lived chiefly in the Interior. They were nomadic people whose principal sources of food were caribou, moose and fish. Hard times and famines were frequent

John Charlie, in decorated moosehide dance clothes, and his grandfather, Neil Charlie. From *Children of the Midnight Sun* by Tricia Brown (text) and Roy Corral (photographs).

for all Athabascans except the Tanaina and Ahtna groups who lived along the Gulf of Alaska and could rely on salmon.

Alaska's **Tsimshian** (sim-she-AN) Indians moved in 1887 from their former home in British Columbia to Annette Island in Southeast Alaska, under the Rev. William Duncan, an Anglican missionary. The Tsimshian today live in Metlakatla, on Annette Island, and are primarily fishermen.

Many of the Haida today live in Hydaburg on the south end of Prince of Wales Island in southeastern Alaska. Their ancestors lived in Canada, and it is believed they migrated to Alaska in the 1700s. The Haida excel at totem carving and are noted for skilled working of wood, bone, shell, stone and silver.

The Tlingit populated most of the Alaska panhandle. The Tlingit, who migrated west from what is now Canada before the first European contact, commercially dominated the interior Canadian Indians, trading eulachon oil, copper pieces and Chilkat blankets for various furs and beaded clothing. Like the Haida and Tsimshian, Tlingit are part of the totem culture; totems provide a record of major events in family or clan history.

The Eyak (EE-yack) people of the Copper River delta, while a distinctive Native group, were heavily influenced by their neighbors, the Athabascans and the Tlingit. They are the smallest of Alaska's Native groups, numbering only about 170 individuals. In 1995 the Eyak celebrated their culture by holding a potlatch, their first in 80 years.

Eskimo. The Eskimo peoples have traditionally lived in villages along the harsh Bering Sea and Arctic Ocean coastlines, as well as on King Island, St. Lawrence Island, Little Diomede Island and Nunivak Island. The inland Eskimos of southwestern Alaska settled along the lower reaches of Alaska's two largest rivers, the Yukon and Kuskokwim. Two major groups of Eskimos are the Yup'ik (YOU-pik), of southwestern Alaska, and the Iñupiat (in-YOU-pea-at) of northern Alaska. The Siberian Yupik primarily live on St. Lawrence Island.

Depending on village location, Yup'ik and Iñupiat Eskimos historically subsisted on traditional foods such as berries, salmon, waterfowl, ptarmigan, caribou, whales, walruses and seals. Winter dwellings were built partially underground, supported by driftwood and/or whale ribs and covered with sod.

Aleut (Unangan). (al-ee-OOT). The Aleut people have traditionally lived on the Alaska Peninsula and along the Aleutian Chain. When the Russians reached the Aleutians in the 1740s, practically every island was inhabited. Decimated by contact with whites, only a few Aleut settlements remain, including two established by Russians on the Pribilof Islands, St. Paul and St. George. The Aleuts lived in permanent villages, taking advantage of sea life and land mammals for food. Their original dwellings were large, communal structures housing as many as 40 families. After Russian occupation they lived in smaller houses, many adopting the Russian-style log cabin. Today many Aleuts are commercial fishermen.

Alutiiq (a-LOO-tik). The Alutiiq people lived on Kodiak Island and some coastal areas of the Kenai Peninsula and Prince

Indian Bread

1 envelope dry yeast	1 teaspoon salt
¼ cup very warm water	1 egg
1 cup milk	3 ½ cups flour
¼ cup sugar	1 cup raisins
¼ cup shortening	About 6 cups cooking oil for deep-frying

Sprinkle dry yeast into warm water—110° to 115°F—in a small bowl and let stand while mixing other ingredients. In a saucepan, over medium heat, mix milk, sugar, shortening and salt until dissolved and blended. Let mixture cool. Then add egg and yeast water and stir in flour and raisins gradually until it forms a soft dough. Place in a greased bowl and lightly grease the top of the dough. Cover and let rise until doubled in size—about 1½ hours.

Place on a floured surface and knead air bubbles from dough. Pinch off small pieces and stretch them to oval shapes, being careful not to stretch them too thin. Make a hole in the center of each and place them on a clean, floured surface. Allow them to rise again until doubled in size. Heat oil in frying pan at high heat until it is bubbling hot. Deep-fry the little breads, a few at a time, turning them until both sides are golden brown. Place them on napkins or other absorbent paper to drain grease.

—Vivian James, Angoon, *Cooking Alaskan*

William Sound. For more than two centuries, outsiders have mistakenly grouped them with the Aleut people or other Southcentral coastal groups, but the Alutiit (plural) began reclaiming their unique identity as recently as the mid-1980s. Beginning with the first Russian attack on Kodiak in 1784, this Native group was most altered by contact with Europeans.

Rapid advances in communications, transportation and other services to remote villages have altered Native life in Alaska. Economic changes, from a subsistence economy to a cash-driven economy, culminated in the passage of the Alaska Native Claims Settlement Act in 1971. It gave Alaska Natives $962.5 million and 44 million acres of land as compensation for the loss of lands historically occupied or used by their people.

Native Regional Corporations

Twelve in-state regional business corporations were formed under the 1971 Alaska Native Claims Settlement Act to manage money and land received from the government. (SEE map on page 157) A 13th corporation was organized for Natives residing outside Alaska.

Ahtna Inc. (Copper River Basin), 406 W. Fireweed Lane, Suite 201, Anchorage 99503; (907) 868-8250; www.ahtna-inc.com.

Aleut Corp. (Aleutian Islands), 4000 Old Seward Highway, Suite 300, Anchorage 99503; (907) 561-4300; www.aleutcorp.com.

Arctic Slope Regional Corp. (Arctic Alaska), P.O. Box 129, Barrow 99723; (907) 852-8633; or 3900 C St., Suite 801, Anchorage 99503-5963; (907) 339-6000; www.asrc.com.

Bering Straits Native Corp. (Seward Peninsula), P.O. Box 1008, Nome 99762; (907) 443-5252; www.beringstraits.com.

Bristol Bay Native Corp., 111 W. 16th Ave., Suite 400, Anchorage 99501; (907) 278-3602; www.bbnc.net.

Calista Corp. (Yukon–Kuskokwim Delta), 301 Calista Court, Suite A, Anchorage 99518-3028; (907) 279-5516; www.calistacorp.com.

Chugach Alaska Corp. (Prince William Sound), 560 E. 34th Ave., Anchorage 99503; (907) 563-8866; www.chugach-ak.com.

Cook Inlet Region Inc. (Cook Inlet region), 2525 C St., Suite 500, Anchorage 99503; (907) 274-8638; www.ciri.com.

Doyon Ltd. (Interior Alaska), 1 Doyon Place, Suite 300, Fairbanks 99701-2941; (907) 459-2000; www.doyon.com.

Koniag Inc. (Kodiak area), 4300 B St., Suite 407, Anchorage 99503; (907) 561-2668, or 104 Center Ave., Suite 205, Kodiak 99615; (907) 486-2530; www.koniag.com.

NANA Regional Corp. (Kobuk region), P.O. Box 49, Kotzebue 99752; (907) 442-3301; or 1001 E. Benson Blvd., Anchorage 99508; (907) 265-4100; www.nana.com.

Sealaska Corp. (Southeast), One Sealaska Plaza, Suite 400, Juneau 99801-1276; (907) 586-1512; www.sealaska.com.

The 13th Regional Corp. (outside Alaska), 1156 Industry Drive., Seattle, WA 98188; (206) 575-6229; www.the13thregion.com.

Statewide Nonprofits

Alaska Federation of Natives, 1577 C St., Suite 300, Anchorage 99501.

Alaska Inter-Tribal Council, 1569 S. Bragaw St., Suite 102, Anchorage 99508.

Alaska Native Health Board, 3700 Woodland Drive, Suite 300, Anchorage 99517.

Alaska Native Tribal Health Consortium, 4000 Ambassador Drive, Anchorage 99508.

First Alaskans Institute, 606 E St., Suite 200, Anchorage 99501.

Native American Rights Fund, 420 L St., Suite 505, Anchorage 99501.

Rural Alaska Community Action Program, (RurAL CAP), P.O. Box 200908, Anchorage 99520.

Association of Alaska Housing Authorities, 4300 Boniface Parkway, Anchorage 99504.

Regional Nonprofits

Aleutian Islands: **Aleutian/Pribilof Islands Association,** 201 E. Third Ave., Anchorage 99501.

Eastern Aleutian Tribes, 3380 C St., Suite 100, Anchorage 99503.

NATIVE REGIONAL CORPORATIONS

Barrow
Prudhoe Bay
NANA Regional Corp.
Arctic Slope Regional Corp.
Bering Straits Native Corp.
ARCTIC CIRCLE
Doyon Limited
Nome
Fairbanks
Cook Inlet Region Inc.
Calista Corp.
Ahtna Inc.
Bethel
Anchorage
Sealaska Corp.
Bristol Bay Native Corp.
Juneau
Aleut Corp.
Chugach Alaska Corp.
Kodiak
Aleutian Islands
Koniag Inc.
Unalaska
Thirteenth Corp.
Seattle

Arctic Slope Region: **Arctic Slope Native Association,** Ltd., P.O. Box 29, Barrow 99723.

Iñupiat Community of the Arctic Slope, P.O. Box 934, Barrow 99723.

Bering Straits Region: **Kawerak, Inc.,** P.O. Box 948, Nome 99762.

Norton Sound Health Corp., P.O. Box 966, Nome 99762.

Bristol Bay Region: **Bristol Bay Native Association,** P.O. Box 310, Dillingham 99576.

Bristol Bay Area Health Corp., P.O. Box 130, Dillingham 99576.

Copper River Native Region: **Copper River Native Association,** P.O. Box H, Copper Center 99573.

Chugach Region: **Chugachmiut, Inc.,** 1840 S. Bragaw, Suite 110, Anchorage 99508.

Cook Inlet Region: **Cook Inlet Tribal Council,** 3600 San Jeronimo Drive, Anchorage 99508.

Southcentral Foundation, 4501 Diplomacy Drive, Anchorage 99508.

Interior Alaska Region: **Fairbanks Native Association,** 201 First Ave., Suite 200, Fairbanks 99701.

Tanana Chiefs Conference, 122 First Ave., Suite 600, Fairbanks 99701.

Kodiak Region: **Kodiak Area Native Association,** 3449 E. Rezanof Drive, Kodiak 99615.

Northwest Alaska Region: **Maniilaq Association,** P.O. Box 256, Kotzebue 99752.

Southeast Alaska Region: **Central Council of the Tlingit and Haida**

Indian Tribes of Alaska, 320 W. Willoughby Ave., Suite 300, Juneau 99811.

Southeast Alaska Regional Health Consortium, 3245 Hospital Drive, Juneau 99801.

Ketchikan Indian Corp., 2960 Tongass Ave., Ketchikan 99901.

Yukon–Kuskokwim Region: **Association of Village Council Presidents,** P.O. Box 219, Bethel 99559.

Yukon–Kuskokwim Health Corp., P.O. Box 528, Bethel 99559.

Kuskokwim Native Association, P.O. Box 127, Aniak 99615.

13th Region: **13th Regional Heritage Foundation,** 1156 Industry Drive, Seattle, WA 98188.

Native Village Corporations

In addition to the 13 regional corporations managing money and land received as part of the Alaska Native Claims Settlement Act, eligible Native villages were required to form corporations and to choose lands made available by the settlement act. The 203 Native villages that formed village corporations eligible for land and money benefits are listed under their regional corporation.

Ahtna Inc. Cantwell, Chistochina, Chitina, Copper Center, Gakona, Gulkana, Mentasta Lake, Tazlina.

Aleut Corp. Akutan, Atka, Belkofski, False Pass, King Cove, Nelson Lagoon, Nikolski, St. George, St. Paul, Sanak, Sand Point, Unalaska, Unga.

Arctic Slope Regional Corp. Anaktuvuk Pass, Atmautluak, Atqasuk, Barrow, Kaktovik, Nuiqsut, Point Hope, Point Lay, Wainwright.

Bering Straits Native Corp. Brevig Mission, Council, Golovin, Inalik/Diomede, King Island, Koyuk, Mary's Igloo, Nome, St. Michael, Shaktoolik, Shishmaref, Solomon, Stebbins, Teller, Unalakleet, Wales, White Mountain.

Bristol Bay Native Corp. Aleknagik, Chignik, Chignik Lagoon, Chignik Lake, Clark's Point, Dillingham, Egegik, Ekuk, Ekwok, Igiugig, Iliamna, Ivanof Bay, Kokhanok, Koliganek, Levelock, Manokotak, Naknek, Newhalen, New Stuyahok, Nondalton, Pedro Bay, Perryville, Pilot Point, Portage Creek, Port Heiden, South Naknek, Togiak, Twin Hills, Ugashik.

Calista Corp. Akiachak, Akiak, Alakanuk, Andreafsky, Aniak, Bethel, Bill Moore's Slough, Chefornak, Chevak, Chuathbaluk, Chuloonawick, Crooked Creek, Eek, Emmonak, Georgetown, Goodnews Bay, Hamilton, Hooper Bay, Kalskag, Kasigluk, Kipnuk, Kongiganak, Kotlik, Kwethluk, Kwigillingok, Lime Village, Lower Kalskag, Marshall/Fortuna Ledge, Mekoryuk, Mountain Village, Napaimute, Napakiak, Napaskiak, Newtok, Nightmute, Nunapitchuk, Ohogamiut, Oscarville, Paimiut, Pilot Station, Pitka's Point, Platinum, Quinhagak, Red Devil, Russian Mission, St. Mary's, Scammon Bay, Sheldon's Point, Sleetmute, Stony River, Toksook Bay, Tuluksak, Tuntutuliak, Tununak, Upper Kalskag.

Chugach Alaska Corp. Chenega Bay, Eyak, Nanwalek, Port Graham, Tatitlek.

Cook Inlet Region Inc. Chickaloon, Eklutna, Knik, Ninilchik, Salamatof, Seldovia, Tyonek.

Doyon Ltd. Alatna, Allakaket, Anvik, Beaver, Birch Creek, Chalkyitsik, Circle, Dot Lake, Eagle, Evansville, Fort Yukon, Galena, Grayling, Healy Lake, Holy Cross, Hughes, Huslia, Kaltag, Koyukuk, Manley Hot Springs, McGrath, Minto, Nenana, Nikolai, Northway, Nulato, Rampart, Ruby, Shageluk, Stevens Village, Takotna, Tanacross, Tanana, Telida.

Koniag Inc. Afognak, Akhiok, Anton Larsen Bay, Ayakulik, Bells Flats, Kaguyak, Karluk, Litnik, Old Harbor, Ouzinkie, Port Lions, Port William (Kodiak), Uganik, Uyak, Woody Island.

NANA Regional Corp. Ambler, Buckland, Deering, Kiana, Kivalina, Kobuk, Kotzebue, Noatak, Noorvik, Selawik, Shungnak.

Sealaska Corp. Angoon, Craig, Hoonah, Hydaburg, Kake, Kasaan, Klawock, Klukwan, Saxman, Sitka, Yakutat.

Source: *Na'eda, Our Friends,* by Alexandra J. McClanahan and Hallie L. Bissett—a comprehensive directory of Alaska Native corporations and tribal organizations, published in 2002 by The CIRI Foundation.

NENANA ICE CLASSIC (See also

Breakup) The Ice Classic is a gigantic betting pool offering $303,272 (in 2007) in cash prizes to the lucky winner—or winners—who guess the time, to the nearest minute, of the ice breakup on the Tanana River at the town of Nenana. Official breakup time each spring is established when surging ice dislodges a four-legged "tripod" and breaks an attached line, which stops a clock set to Yukon standard time.

Tickets for the classic sell for $2.50 each, entitling the holder to one guess. Ice Classic officials estimate more than $7 million has been paid to lucky guessers through the years. The event was sanctioned as a state lottery by the first state legislature in one of its earliest actions in 1959.

Over the years the Ice Classic has benefited Nenana. Fifty percent of the gross proceeds goes to the winners. Nenana residents are paid salaries for ticket counting and compilation, and about 15 percent is earmarked for upkeep of the Nenana Civic Center and as donations to the local visitors' center, the library, special events at the high school and various other charities.

The Internal Revenue Service also gets a chunk of withholding taxes on the payroll and a bite of each winner's share. In 2007, 22 winners split the pot, giving them $13,785.10 each.

Breakup times for the Nenana Ice Classic from 1918 through 2007 are arranged in order of day and time of breakup. (See chart on following page)

Another pool, the Kuskokwim Ice Classic, has been a tradition in Bethel since 1924. Initially, it was said that the winner was paid 20 fish or 20 furs but stakes are considerably higher now and the winner receives 50 percent of the total ticket sales.

NEWSPAPERS AND PERIODICALS

(Rates are subject to change.)

AK This Month, P.O. Box 202941, Anchorage 99520. Monthly. Annual rate: $25.

Alaska Angler, 221 Bentley Drive, Fairbanks 99701. Bimonthly. Annual rate: $49.

Alaska Bar Rag, 550 W. Seventh Ave, Suite 1900, Anchorage 99501. Quarterly. Annual rate: $25.

Alaska Bride & Groom, P.O. Box 221344, Anchorage 99522. Biannually. Annual rate: $13.90.

Alaska Business Monthly, P.O. Box 241288, Anchorage 99524-1288. Monthly. Annual rate: $29.95.

Alaska Coast Magazine, P.O. Box 110297, Anchorage 99511-0297. Monthly. Annual rate: $24.

Alaska Contractor (The), 8537 Corbin Drive, Anchorage 99507. Quarterly. Free.

Alaska Designs, P.O. Box 100515, Anchorage 99510-0515. Monthly (except August). Annual rates: $36 for nonmembers; free for members.

Alaska Digest, P.O. Box 221129, Anchorage 99522. Annually. Free.

Alaska Directory of Attorneys, 203 W. 15th Ave., Suite 102, Anchorage 99501. Biannually. Annual rate: $70.

Alaska Guide Report, P.O. Box 3591 Seward, 99664. Quarterly. Annual rate: $19.95.

Alaska Hispanic Yellow Pages, P.O. Box 112955, Anchorage 99511-2955. Annually. Free.

Alaska Home Magazine, 5630 Silverado Way, Suite 8, Anchorage 99518. Quarterly. Annual rate: $12.

Alaska Horse Journal, 310 N. Harriette St., Wasilla 99654-7627. Monthly (except January). Annual rate: $17.50.

In 2007, 89 Alaskans who entered the Nenana Ice Classic bet that the ice would go out in Nenana on April 31st— a day that doesn't even exist! In the 2006 contest, 106 people made the same worthless bet. Alaskans are statistically 16% smarter than they were a year ago, but it's still nothing to brag about.

April		
20, 1940 — 3:27 P.M.	1, 1991 —12:04 A.M.	8, 1966 —12:11 P.M.
20, 1998 — 4:54 P.M.	1, 1932 —10:15 A.M.	8, 1930 — 7:03 P.M.
23, 1993 — 1:01 P.M.	1, 1956 —11:24 A.M.	8, 1933 — 7:30 P.M.
24, 2004 — 2:16 P.M.	1, 1989 — 8:14 P.M.	8, 1968 — 9:26 P.M.
24, 1990 — 5:19 P.M.	2, 1976— 10:51 A.M.	8, 1986 — 9:31 P.M.
26, 1995 — 1:22 P.M.	2, 2006 — 5:29 P.M.	8, 1971 —10:50 P.O.
26, 1926 — 4:03 P.M.	2, 1960 — 7:12 P.M.	8, 2001 — 1:00 P.M.
27, 2007 — 3.47 P.M.	3, 1941 — 1:50 A.M.	9, 1923 — 2:00 P.M.
28, 2005 —12:01 P.M.	3, 1919 — 2:33 P.M.	9, 1955 — 2:31 P.M.
28, 1969 —12:28 P.M.	3, 1947 — 5:53 P.M.	9, 1984 — 3:33 P.M.
28, 1943 — 7:22 P.M.	4, 1967 —11:55 A.M.	10, 1931 — 9:23 A.M.
29, 1939 — 1:26 P.M.	4, 1973 —11:59 A.M.	10, 1972 —11:56 A.M.
29, 1958 — 2:56 P.M.	4, 1944 — 2:08 P.M.	10, 1975 — 1:49 P.M.
29, 1953 — 3:54 P.M.	4, 1970 —10:37 P.M.	10, 1982 — 5:36 P.M.
29, 2003 — 6:22 P.M.	5, 1957 — 9:30 A.M.	11, 1921 — 6:42 A.M.
29, 1983 — 6:37 P.M.	5, 1961 —11:31 A.M.	11, 1918 — 9:33 A.M.
29, 1999 — 9:47 P.M.	5, 1996 —12:32 P.M.	11, 1920 —10:45 A.M.
29, 1994 —11:01 P.M.	5, 1987 — 3:11 P.M.	11, 1985 — 2:36 P.M.
30, 1997— 10:28 A.M.	5, 1929 — 3:41 P.M.	11, 1924 — 3:10 P.M.
30, 1936 —12:58 P.M.	5, 1946 — 4:40 P.M.	12, 1927 — 5:42 A.M.
30, 1980 — 1:16 P.M.	5, 1963 — 6:25 P.M.	12, 1922 — 1:20 P.M.
30, 1942 — 1:28 P.M.	6, 1977 —12:46 P.M.	12, 1952 — 5:04 P.M.
30, 1934 — 2:07 P.M.	6, 1974 — 3:44 P.M.	12, 1937 — 8:04 P.M.
30, 1978 — 3:18 P.M.	6, 1950 — 4:14 P.M.	12, 1962 —11:23 P.M.
30, 1951 — 5:54 P.M.	6, 1928 — 4:25 P.M.	13, 1948 —11:13 A.M.
30, 1979 — 6:16 P.M.	6, 1954 — 6:01 P.M.	14, 1992 — 6:26 A.M.
30, 1981 — 6:44 P.M.	6, 1938 — 8:14 P.M.	14, 1949 —12:39 P.M.
	7, 1925 — 6:32 P.M.	15, 1935 — 1:32 P.M.
	7, 1965 — 7:01 P.M.	16, 1945 — 9:41 A.M.
May	7, 2002 — 9:27 P.M.	20, 1964 —11:41 A.M.
1, 2000 —10:47 A.M.	8, 1959 —11:26 A.M.	

Alaska Hunter, 221 Bentley Drive, Fairbanks 99701. Bimonthly. Annual rate: $49.

Alaska Journal of Commerce, 301 Arctic Slope, Suite 350, Anchorage 99518. Weekly. Annual rate: $45.

Alaska Justice Forum, 3211 Providence Drive, Anchorage 99508. Quarterly. Free.

Alaska magazine, 301 Arctic Slope Ave., Suite 300, Anchorage 99518. Monthly (ten issues). Annual rates: $24; outside the U.S. $30.

Alaska Media Directory, 6828 Cape Lisburne Loop, Anchorage 99504-3958. Annually. Annual rate: $88.

AlaskaMen magazine, 205 E. Dimond Blvd., Suite 522, Anchorage 99515. Phone (907) 522-1401. Annually. U.S. rate: $22 plus $5 shipping and handling; outside U.S.: $22 plus $8 shipping and handling.

Alaska Miner (The), 3305 Arctic Blvd., Suite 105, Anchorage 99503. Monthly. Mailed to members of Alaska Miners Association.

Alaska Miners Association Handbook and Service Directory, 3305 Arctic Blvd., Suite 105, Anchorage 99503. Annually. Mailed to members of Alaska Miners Association.

Alaska Native Directory, P.O. Box 221129, Anchorage 99522. Updated regularly. Annual rate: $167.50.

Alaska Native Yellow Pages, P.O. Box 112955, Anchorage 99511-2955. Annually. Annual rates: (advance subscription) $35, free to Alaska Native community.

Alaska Pet News, P.O. Box 4083, Palmer 99645. Quarterly. Annual rate: $25.

Alaska Post, 723 Postal Service Loop, Fort Richardson 99505-5900. Weekly. Free.

Alaska Professional Hunter (The), HC 60, Box 299C, Copper Center 99573. Quarterly. Annual rate: $40.

Alaska Rider, P.O. Box 110297, Anchorage 99511. Monthly. Annual rate: $35.

Alaska Star, 16941 N. Eagle River Loop, Eagle River 99577. Weekly. Annual rates: $25 home delivery, $30 mail.

Alaska Wellness Magazine, 926 W. 20th Ave., Anchorage 99503. Bimonthly. Annual rate: $20.

Alaska Women Speak, P.O. Box 210045, Anchorage 99521. Quarterly. Annual rate: $16.

Alaskan Bowhunter, P.O. Box 220830, Anchorage 99522-0830. Quarterly. Free to members.

Alaskan Equipment Trader, 301 Arctic Slope, Suite 350, Anchorage 99518. Monthly. Annual rate: $6.

Alaskan Supersaver Classified (The), P.O. Box 140851 Anchorage 99514-0851. Weekly. Free.

Anchorage Daily News, P.O. Box 149001, Anchorage 99514-9001. Daily. Annual rate: Anchorage home delivery $159.

Anchorage Visitors Guide, 524 W. Fourth Ave., Anchorage 99501-2212; www.anchorage.net. Annually. Free.

Arctic Sounder, P.O. Box 290, Kotzebue 99752. Weekly. Annual rates: second-class mail $55; first class $100.

Army in Alaska Guidebook and Telephone Book, 8537 Corbin Drive, Anchorage 99507. Annually. Free to transferring new personnel to Alaska for the Army, Civil Service and retirees.

Bearfoot Travel Guides, 2440 East Tudor Road, Suite 122, Anchorage 99507. Annually. Free.

Boat Broker Outdoors (The), P.O. Box 32757, Juneau 99803. Monthly. Free to Southeast communities; $12 mailed.

Book of Good Deals (The), 1399 W. 34th Ave., Suite 204, Anchorage 99503. Bimonthly. Free.

NUGGETS

Rare, turn-of-the century Nome newspapers are being kept in the city morgue's freezer, until a method for drying them is determined, after they fell victim to leaky bathroom plumbing. The director of the Carrie McLain Museum arrived at work in early August 1997 to find boxes of newspapers saturated with water that had leaked through the ceiling. The water came from faulty plumbing for a urinal. The damaged issues were dated 1902 through 1924. They included the Nome News, Nome Daily Nugget **and** Nome Tri-Weekly Nugget. **The oldest issues suffered most from the dousing.**

—1998 *The Alaska Almanac*®

Bristol BayTimes, P.O. Box 1770, Dillingham 99576. Weekly. Annual rates: second-class mail $55; first class $100.

Capital City Weekly, P.O. Box 32757, Juneau 99803. Weekly. Annual rates: Home delivery, free; $52 mailed.

Catholic Anchor, 225 Cordova St., Anchorage 99501. Biweekly. Annual rate: $22.

Chamber (The), 8537 Corbin Drive, Anchorage 99507. Quarterly. Free.

Chickaloon News (The), P.O. Box 1105, Chickaloon 99674. Quarterly rate: $30.

The *Nome Nugget* reported on a combined memorial service and picnic. The picnic was held *after* the scattering of the ashes so remnants wouldn't wind up in the potato salad.

Chilkat Valley News, P.O. Box 630, Haines 99827. Weekly. Annual rates: $36 in Haines; $64 first class; $42 mailed in state; $48 outside Alaska.

Chugiak–Eagle River Business and Service Directory, P.O. Box 770353, Eagle River 99577. Biannually. Free.

Clarion Dispatch, P.O. Box 3009, Kenai 99611. Weekly. Free.

Copper River Record, P.O. Box 277, Glennallen 99588. Biweekly. Annual rates: $15 (locally), $20 everywhere else.

Cordova Times, P.O Box 200, Cordova 99574. Weekly. Annual rates: second-class mail $55; first class $100.

Cuisine Scene, 540 E. Fifth Ave, Anchorage 99501. Biannually. Free.

Current Drift, P.O. Box 110297, Anchorage 99511. Monthly. Annual rates: $35, mailed free to members.

Daily Sitka Sentinel, 112 Barracks St., Sitka 99835. Monday through Friday. Annual rate: $80.

Delta Discovery (The), P.O. Box 1028, Bethel 99559. Weekly. Annual rate: $60.

Delta Wind, P.O. Box 986, Delta Junction 99737. Biweekly. Rate: $1.25 per issue.

Denali Summer Times, P.O. Box 40, Healy 99743. Annually. Free.

Dutch Harbor Fisherman, P.O. Box 920472, Unalaska 99692. Weekly. Annual rates: second-class mail $55; first class $100.

Eielson AFB Guide Book and Telephone Book, 8537 Corbin Drive, Anchorage 99507. Annually. Free.

Elmendorf AFB Guide Book and Telephone Book, 8537 Corbin Dr., Anchorage 99507. Annually. Free.

Ester Republic (The), P.O. Box 24, Ester 99725. Monthly. Annual rate: $20.

Fairbanks Daily News-Miner, P.O. Box 70710, Fairbanks 99707. Daily. Annual rates: $357 Alaska; $450 outside Alaska.

Fairbanks Magazine (The), 921 Wood Way, Fairbanks 99709-4732. June through October. Rate: $2.25 per issue.

Fairweather Reporter, P.O. Box 176, Gustavus 99826. Monthly. Annual rate: $20.

First Alaskans Magazine, 301 Calista Court, Suite B, Anchorage 99518. Quarterly. Free.

Fish Alaska Magazine, P.O. Box 113403, Anchorage 99511. Monthly (ten issues). Annual rate: $30.

For Sale Magazine, P.O. Box 110297, Anchorage 99511-0297. Bimonthly. Annual rate: $26.

Free Map of Alaska, P.O. Box 200846, Anchorage 99520. Annually. Free.

Frontiersman, 5751 E. Mayflower Court, Wasilla 99654. Three times weekly. Annual rates: $62 home delivery; $87 Mat–Su; $95 Alaska; $120 outside Alaska.

Great Lander Bushmailer, Great Lander Fairbanks and Great Lander Mat-Su, 3110 Spenard Road, Anchorage 99503. Monthly. Free.

Homer Alaska Tribune, Inc., 601 E. Pioneer Ave., Suite 109, Homer 99603. Weekly. Annual rate: $39.

Homer News, 3482 Landings St., Homer 99603. Weekly. Annual rates: $38 Kenai Peninsula Borough; $48 Alaska; $59 outside Alaska; $106 first class.

Island News, P.O. Box 19430, Thorne Bay 99919. Weekly. Annual rate: $57.50.

Juneau Empire, 3100 Channel Drive, Juneau 99801-7814. Monday through Friday and Sunday. Annual rate: $135 (plus local tax).

Juneau Guide, 3100 Channel Drive, Juneau 99801-7814. Annually. Free.

Kaniqsirugut News, P.O. Box 966, Nome 99762. Bimonthly. Free.

Ketchikan Daily News, P.O. Box 7900, Ketchikan 99901. Monday through Saturday. Annual rates: $135 local; $191 mail.

Kodiak Daily Mirror, 1419 Selig St., Kodiak 99615. Monday through Friday. Annual rates: $105 Kodiak; $150 Alaska; $200 outside Alaska.

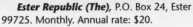

The *Cordova Times* claimed that a police recruit was asked, "What would you do if you had to arrest your mother?" He answered, "Call for a backup."

Local Paper (The), 516 Stedman, Ketchikan 99901. Weekly. Free.

Marine Yellow Pages, 3452 Lake Lynda Drive, Suite 363, Orlando, FL 32817. Annually. Free.

MILEPOST (The), 301 Arctic Slope Ave., Suite 300, Anchorage 99518. Annually. Rate: $26.95.

Mukluk News, P.O. Box 90, Tok 99780. Bimonthly. Annual rate: $20.

Mushing, P.O. Box 149, Ester 99725; Bimonthly. Annual rate: $24.

Nenana Messenger News, P.O. Box 396, Nenana 99760. Weekly. Annual rates: $39 first class; $24 online.

Nome Nugget, P.O. Box 610, Nome 99762. Weekly. Annual rates: $60; outside Alaska $65.

Northview, P.O. Box 200070, Anchorage 99520-0070. Monthly. Annual rate: $35.

Northern Light (The), 3211 Providence Drive, Anchorage 99508. Weekly. Free.

North Star Weekly, 3650 Braddock St., Suite 3, Fairbanks 99701. Weekly. Free.

On Board, 431 W. First Ave., Anchorage 99501. Annually. Free.

Peninsula Clarion, P.O. Box 3009, Kenai 99611. Sunday through Friday. Annual rate: $96.

Petersburg Pilot, P.O. Box 930, Petersburg 99833. Weekly. Annual rates: $44 Petersburg; $56 Alaska; $66 outside Alaska; $98 first class.

Petroleum News, P.O. Box 231651, Anchorage 99523-1651. Weekly. Annual rate: $78.

Press (The), P.O. Box 241841, Anchorage 99524-1841. Weekly. Free locally. Annual rates (mailed): $30 (in state), $70 (out of state).

Prince William Sound Visitor's Guide, 301 Calista Court, Suite B, Anchorage 99518. Annually. Free.

Senior Voice, 325 E. Third Ave., Suite 300, Anchorage 99501. Monthly. Annual rates: $15; outside Alaska $20.

Seward Phoenix Log, P.O. Box 89, Seward 99664. Weekly. Annual rates: second-class mail $55; first class $100.

Seward Visitor's Guide, P.O. Box 89, Seward 99664. Annually. Free.

Skagway News, P.O. Box 498, Skagway 99840-0498. Semimonthly. Annual rates: $35 second class; $45 first class.

Sourdough Sentinel, Third Wing, Public Affairs, 6920 12th St., Elmendorf Air Force Base 99506-2530. Weekly. Free.

Sun Star, P.O. Box 756640, Fairbanks 99775-6640. Weekly. Annual rate: $35.

Talkeetna Good Times, P.O. Box 967, Talkeetna 99676. Annually. Free.

Talkeetna Times, P.O. Box 967, Talkeetna 99676. Semimonthly. Annual rates: $48 U.S.; $58 outside U.S.

Tidbits of the Tundra, P.O. Box 111113, Anchorage 99511. Weekly. Free.

Transponder (The), P.O. Box 241185, Anchorage 99524, Bimonthly. Annual rate: $35.

True North, Journalism and Public Communications Department, Bldg. K, 3211 Providence Drive, Anchorage 99508. Annually. Free.

Tundra Drums, Box 868, Bethel 99559. Weekly. Annual rates: $55 second class; $100 first class.

Turnagain Times, P.O. Box 1044, Girdwood 99587. Semimonthly. Annual rates: $18 Alaska; $24 outside Alaska; Call for international rates.

Unalaska/Dutch Harbor Visitor's Guide, 301 Calista Court, Suite B, Anchorage 99518. Annually. Free.

Valdez Star, P.O. Box 2949, Valdez 99686. Weekly. Annual rates: $30; $55 second class.

Valley Sun, 5751 E. Mayflower Court, Wasilla 99654. Weekly. Free to Matanuska–Susitna Borough box holders.

Warriors, 8537 Corbin Drive, Anchorage 99507. Quarterly. Free.

Welcome to Anchorage/Welcome to Wasilla, 8537 Corbin Drive, Anchorage 99507. Annually. Free.

Wrangell Sentinel and Wrangell Guide, P.O. Box 798, Wrangell 99929. Weekly. Annual rates: $38; $53 Alaska; $63 outside Alaska; $85 first class.

Wrangell–St. Elias News, McCarthy, P.O. Box MXY, Glennallen 99588. Bimonthly. Annual rate: $11.

NOME Located on the shores of Norton Sound on the Seward Peninsula's south coast, Nome, with a population of just over

3,500, is the transportation and commercial center for northwestern Alaska.

Nome owes its name to a misinterpretation of the notation "? name" on a chart in 1850. The question mark was taken as a "C" standing for Cape, and the letter "a" in "name" was read as an "o." Originally the settlement was named Anvil City when gold was found in the Anvil Creek area in the summer of 1898.

The real gold stampede to Nome began in June 1899, when an estimated 30,000 miners rushed to Nome to stake claims and pitch their tents along the beaches of the Bering Sea Coast. That year, Nome was the largest city in the Alaska Territory. Miners quickly fled when their claims didn't pay, and by 1906 most of the gold and the prospectors were gone.

The mean average daily temperature in winter is –8°F and summer temperatures range from 40°F to 50°F. Mean annual snowfall, occurring from late September through early June, is 53 inches.

A 3,350-foot-long granite wall built by the U.S. Army Corps of Engineers protects Nome from the sea. It is 65 feet wide at the base, 16 feet wide at its top and 18 feet above mean low water.

Although not connected by road to the rest of the state, Nome boasts more than 300 miles of road in the area—the second-largest city road system in the state. There is no winter maintenance of the roads.

The city of Nome has several schools, including the Northwest College, and the distinction of having the state's oldest first-class school district. It also offers many churches; a library and museum containing more than 6,000 photographs of the gold rush, Eskimo history and the Bering Land Bridge culture; and a historical park with a nonworking gold dredge and mining equipment from the gold rush days. For a fee, visitors may still try their luck panning the sands of the Nome beaches.

Throughout the year Nome offers many festivals and celebrations including its most famous event—the finish of the Iditarod Trail Sled Dog Race. There's the Bering Sea Ice Classic Golf Tournament played on the frozen Bering Sea in March; a Polar Bear Swim on Memorial Day; a Midnight Sun Festival in June, featuring a raft race on the Nome River with many a strange craft taking part;

NUGGETS

Nome may be situated on treeless tundra, but that doesn't stop Nome's citizens from recycling their left-over Christmas trees by placing them in holes in the sea ice behind Fat Freddie's restaurant. The forest started as a gag in 1991, but has become an annual tradition. This year the "forest" was the largest ever, with more than 70 trees. The instant grove attracts "wildlife," such as pink wooden pigs, plywood walruses and plastic flamingos.

—1995 The Alaska Almanac®

a 12.5-mile run to the top of 1,977-foot Anvil Mountain on July 4; and a Labor Day Bathtub Race. Other events include snowmobile races, snowshoe, softball games and the largest state basketball tournament.

The city today is a jumping-off point for flights to Russia (only an hour-long flight away), surrounding Bush villages and tours of the Arctic. For details, consult www.nomealaska.org.

NO-SEE-UMS The words describe a small, biting, two-winged midge. In its usual swarms this tiny, gray-black, silver-winged gnat is a most persistent pest and annoys all creatures. The insect is difficult to see when it's flying alone. While no-see-ums don't transmit disease, their bites are irritating. Protective clothing, netting and a good repellent are recommended while in dense brush or near still-water ponds. Tents and recreational vehicles should be well screened.

OIL AND GAS (See also National Petroleum Reserve; Pipeline) Alaska's first exploratory oil well was drilled in 1898 on the Iniskin Peninsula, Cook Inlet, by Alaska Petroleum Co. Oil was encountered in this first hole at about 700 feet but a water zone beneath the oil strata cut off the oil flow. Total depth of the well was approximately 1,000 feet.

The first commercial oil discovery was made in 1902 at Katalla, near the mouth of the Bering River east of Cordova. This field produced until 1933.

As early as 1921, oil companies surveyed land north of the Brooks Range for possible drilling sites. In 1923, the federal government created Naval Petroleum Reserve Number 4 (now known as National Petroleum Reserve Alaska; SEE National Petroleum Reserve), a 23-million-acre area of Alaska's North Slope. Wartime needs speeded up exploration.

From 1944 to 1953, the U.S. Navy pioneered an exploration program establishing the feasibility of large-scale Arctic oil exploration, though the discoveries were subcommercial. The discovery of Prudhoe Bay and the Arab oil embargo prompted the Navy to mount a second exploratory program from 1974 to 1977. In 1977, responsibility for the program was transferred to the USGS. Overall, two subcommercial gas accumulations were found on the Barrow peninsula and were developed for local use. Between 1981 and 1984, the U.S. Department of the Interior leased oil and gas tracts in the reserve, but oil companies were focusing most of their attention elsewhere.

In the mid-1990s, oil companies began developing smaller fields close to the eastern edge of the reserve, spurring new interest in what lay within NPRA. BP and ConocoPhillips launched an aggressive exploration program in the reserve during 2001.

Today, all of Alaska's oil is produced from two regions, the North Slope and Cook Inlet.

North Slope. Discovered in 1968, Prudhoe Bay was the first commercial North Slope oil field to produce oil. Commercial production began in 1977, when Alyeska Pipeline Service Co. completed the pipeline between Prudhoe Bay and the port at Valdez. North Slope fields had produced a total of more than 14.6 billion barrels as of the end of 2005, 79 percent of it from Prudhoe Bay, 15 percent from Kuparuk and 6 percent from other fields.

Three North Slope satellite developments began production in the Prudhoe Bay area during 1993: Point McIntyre, by far the largest; North Prudhoe Bay State; and West Beach. The Niakuk pool began producing in 1994, Midnight Sun in 1998, Aurora and Polaris in 2000, Borealis in 2001 and Orion in 2002.

Kuparuk River Oil Pool production increased at Milne Point during late 1995. Other recent Kuparuk River Oil Pool developments are Tabasco, in April 1998; Tarn in July 1998; Meltwater, in 2001; and Palm, which started production in 2002. Within the Kuparuk River Unit, the first

Getting Alaska Oil to Market

How does a barrel of oil travel along the 800-mile trans-Alaska oil pipeline?

Oil from the Prudhoe fields is 145°F to 180°F when it is pumped to the surface of the North Slope. The oil is cooled to about 120°F before it enters the pipeline.

The pipeline is 48 inches in diameter; much of it is raised above the permafrost but at 21 spots it dives underground. Oil takes five to six days to travel the 800 miles from Prudhoe Bay to the terminal at the ice-free port of Valdez. Ten pump stations hustle the oil along. On the way, it crosses 834 rivers and streams, three major mountain ranges and an earthquake fault line. Caribou and other wildlife wander under raised parts of the pipeline. At Valdez, the crude is loaded onto oceangoing oil tankers.

As of 2006, Alyeska Pipeline Service Co. has shipped more than 15 billion barrels of Alaska North Slope crude since the pipeline start-up in 1977.

regular production from the West Sak Oil Pool since 1986 began in late 1997. To the north, at Milne Point, Schrader Bluff Oil Pool production began to increase in November 1999. During 2003, "heavy oil" production began from the shallower Ugnu undefined oil pool at Milne Point. These recent additions have somewhat offset the regional decline in oil production.

Recent exploration has resulted in several discoveries that will contribute significantly to North Slope production. The Colville River field, discovered in 1994, is the largest of these and began production in November 2000. Production at the Northstar began in 2001. Various satellite developments are being evaluated throughout the North Slope. New additions can only partially limit the decline at Prudhoe Bay and the other larger oil fields. On the North Slope, 14 exploration wells were permitted in 2005: seven by ConocoPhillips, three by FEX L.P., two by Kerr-McGee and one each by Pioneer Natural Resources Alaska and the U.S. Department of the Interior. Kerr-McGee also was permitted two wells and one sidetrack in the state waters of the Beaufort Sea north of Oliktok Point.

Cook Inlet. Companies first discovered Cook Inlet oil at Swanson River on the Kenai Peninsula in 1957 and began production in 1959. In 1962, the first offshore oil in Cook Inlet was discovered, making the inlet one of three successful areas in the United States for offshore oil production. Currently there are 16 production platforms in Cook Inlet, one of which produces only natural gas. The Forest Oil Corporation's Osprey Platform was set in 2000 and first production was reported in December 2001.

Regional production in Cook Inlet peaked in 1970 at 226,000 barrels daily (82 million barrels for the year) and subsequently declined to 17,054 barrels a day in 2006. By the end of 2006, Cook Inlet fields had produced 1.3 billion barrels of oil, 48 percent of this from McArthur River, 17 percent from Swanson River and 35 percent from the other fields. Two fields, West McArthur River and Sunfish (Tyonek Deep), were discovered in 1991. West McArthur River

NUGGETS

On May 11, 2007, both the Alaska House and Senate overwhelmingly passed separate, though similar, versions of the Alaska Gasline Inducement Act proposed by Gov. Sarah Palin. The AGIA is a multibillion dollar project designed to encourage producers and independent pipeline companies to compete for rights to build an Alaska natural gas pipeline. The bill establishes a bidding process and financial incentives that include tax breaks coupled with strict timetables and other regulations opposed by BP PLC, Exxon Mobil Corp. and ConocoPhillips. The state plans to issue a request for applications during the summer of 2007, and a license to the winning bid in the spring of 2008.

began production in 1993 and had produced 11 million barrels by the end of 2006. Cumulative production from Redoubt Shoal totaled 2,098,716 bbls at the end of 2006.

Gas production from the Cook Inlet continues at significant levels with 193 billion cubic feet produced during 2006. Forest Oil Corporation continues to develop the West Foreland gas reservoir and Redoubt Shoals Oil Field. Marathon Oil's Wolf Lake Field continued producing in 2006, as did Aurora Gas LLC's Nicolai Creek Field. Marathon began production from the Kasilof Tyonek Undefined Gas Pool in 2006 and produced 306,769 mcf. In the Cook Inlet Basin, four permits for exploration wells were approved during 2006. Of these, Aurora received three, and Storm Cat Energy Corporation received one permit.

There is no current coalbed methane exploration activity in Southcentral Alaska.

Projected Reserves and Production. The Division of Oil and Gas estimates Alaska's total proven and developed oil reserves to be 6.3 billion barrels. Natural gas reserves are estimated at 37.1 trillion cubic feet, but probable reserves are approximately 100 trillion feet. North Slope fields hold 98 percent of the proven oil and 95 percent of the state's proven gas reserves. The balance is in Cook Inlet.

Oil. Reserve estimates of oil for North Slope fields have increased through the years. In January 1986, Prudhoe Bay had produced 4.4 billion barrels and reserves were 5.8 billion barrels. By January 1998 the field had produced nearly 10.2 billion barrels and reserves were estimated at 3.2 billion barrels. Much of the increase in ultimate recovery was due to improved technology, such as increased horizontal drilling and enhanced oil recovery. Technology may further increase future reserve estimates, but the main variables in recovering oil will be the perceived oil prices and the cost of production.

North Slope oil production peaked in 1988 at 2 million barrels a day and subsequently declined to 0.78 million barrels a day in 2006. The Division of Oil and Gas estimates that combined production from operating fields and to-be-developed fields will decline to 416,000 barrels a day by 2027.

Cook Inlet fields will continue to produce well for years to come, although production is estimated to decline to about 5,000 barrels a day by 2027. Cumulative production for the five-year period from 2003 to 2007 will be an estimated 32 million barrels.

Since 1987, Alaska and Texas have alternated as the No. 1 state in oil production. The top five oil-producing states in 2005 were Texas, Alaska, California, Louisiana and Oklahoma, according to the U.S. Department of Energy, Energy Information Administration. Alaska currently provides about 17 percent of the nation's domestic production of oil.

The Petroleum Profits Tax (PPT) was signed into law in August 2006. This new production tax system replaces the prior economic limit factor-based system (or ELF) by taxing net revenues and offering credits for capital expenditures, exploration costs, prior year investments and individual,

company-based allowances. Under the PPT system, producers that invest in Alaska oil and gas activities would experience a lower tax burden.

Natural Gas. All Alaska gas is produced from the North Slope, mostly from the Prudhoe Bay area, and from Cook Inlet, the same two regions that produce the state's oil. The production regimes of the two regions are very different because their markets are very different.

On the North Slope, most of the extracted gas is injected back into the reservoirs. Cumulative natural gas lifted from North Slope fields is about 61.9 trillion cubic feet. Of this, approximately 56.2 trillion cubic feet has been reinjected for enhanced oil recovery, leaving about 5.7 trillion cubic feet in cumulative gas consumed for industrial and lease operations on the North Slope by the end of 2006.

Alaska Oil and Natural Gas Production

Year	Oil*	Natural Gas**
1992	654.2	449.126
1993	604.8	455.835
1994	594.9	469.038
1995	571.3	499.008
1996	544.0	490.591
1997	507.7	481.910
1998	462.6	477.043
1999	415.4	472.572
2000	388.2	474.396
2001	384.9	517.418
2002	388.2	473.406
2003	382.8	474.683
2004	360.2	480.643
2005	338.9	495.110
2006	291.3	454.270

* Millions of barrels

** Billions of cubic feet, includes gas sold and used for lease operations, North Slope and Cook Inlet, excludes gas reinjected.

Source: Alaska Department of Natural Resources, Division of Oil & Gas

Attempts to commercialize the natural gas have been ongoing for some time. In 1977, the Alaska Natural Gas Transportation System, a gas pipeline, was authorized by the federal government, but efforts to develop Alaska North Slope natural gas reserves were hampered by the high cost of bringing it to market.

In 2000, a surge in demand for natural gas in the Lower 48, higher gas prices, advances in technology and regulatory changes spurred oil companies operating on the North Slope to launch a $125-million-gas-line feasibility study. In 2002 the Alaska Legislature extended the Stranded Gas Development Act (SGDA) providing a negotiating framework to help advance North Slope Gas development.

In October 2004, the U.S. Congress passed energy legislation that includes important incentives and regulatory guidance to commercialize Alaska North Slope gas. In December 2004, the Federal Energy Regulatory Commission (FERC) held hearings in Alaska on the open season process pursuant to requirements in federal law and later enacted regulations.

Private energy companies and government agencies continue to express interest in Alaska North Slope gas as a bridge to declining North American gas supply in the coming decades. In June 2007, Gov. Sarah Palin signed the Alaska Gas Line Inducement Act into law. This legislation provides a framework of incentives to encourage development of Alaska's vast North Slope natural gas resources.

Cook Inlet fields lie near the Anchorage and Kenai local utility markets. Natural gas produced from Cook Inlet is also consumed in a LNG plant (for export to Japan) and a fertilizer plant near Kenai, Alaska. Regional production reached an all-time high of 223 billion cubic feet a year in 1996. It dipped to 197 billion cubic feet in 2006. Cook Inlet fields had produced a cumulative net 7.3 trillion cubic feet by the end of 2006.

Financial. Alaska receives its oil and gas revenues from oil and gas production tax, property tax, royalties and corporate income tax. Most of the revenue received from taxes and royalties goes into the General Fund, for general state spending. Following the passage of HB11 in 2003,

25 percent of the royalty revenue now goes into the principal of the Permanent Fund, and 0.5 percent of mineral bonuses and royalties go into the Public School Trust Fund. The state's share of all lease bonuses from the National Petroleum Reserve-Alaska (NPR-A) goes into the NPR-A Fund, a fund that implements a federal requirement that the state use its share of NPR-A oil revenue to satisfy the needs of local communities most affected by development in the NPR-A. Settlements of tax and royalty disputes between the state and oil and gas producers go into the Constitutional Budget Reserve Fund.

Royalties and production taxes constitute the largest part of both restricted and unrestricted revenue. In fiscal 2006, the state of Alaska received $4.3 billion in royalties and taxes (including previous revisions, settlements and contributions to the Permanent Fund) from its oil and gas resources; approximately 89 percent of its unrestricted revenue comes from petroleum taxes and royalties. Since 1965, the state has collected more than $59 billion in unrestricted oil and gas revenues.

OOSIK An *oosik* is the baculum, or penis bone, of the male walrus. The *oosik* is a symbol of strength and potency in some Alaska Native cultures. It is also a novelty item found in shops selling Native crafts. Oosiks generally measure from one to two feet long and are priced accordingly, with the longest costing upwards of $250.

PARKA This garment worn by Eskimos was one of their main pieces of clothing. Parka styles, materials used and ornamentation (such as pieced calfskin or beadwork trim) varied from village to village. The cut of parkas also changed from north to south.

The work parka was worn with the skin on the outside and the fur inside. Work parkas were meant to be serviceable, not beautiful. Often worn with pants made from skins, they provided excellent protection from the cold. These parkas usually used a secondhand worn ruff on the hood. Very poor persons did not have ruffs on their parkas at all, and if a person owned a parka without a ruff, he or she was given a ruff to use. When that person died, the ruff was cut off the parka and returned to the original owner.

A fancy parka, reserved for special occasions, used the skin of the male ground squirrel, which produces large gray pelts. These decorated parkas had intricate fancywork with wolverine tassels and trims and were topped with a wide wolf ruff, made in layers so the ruff stood out from the face. The fancy parka had furs inside and out. Wealth was judged by the quality of a wearer's best parka.

The Aleut rain parka was made from *oogruk* (bearded seal) intestine. Instead of a fur ruff around the face of the hood, the rain parka had a folded *oogruk* piece that served as a sinew drawstring casing.

Yup'ik and Iñupiat people used the skins of many different animals for parkas including seal, reindeer, caribou and ground squirrel. Wolf and wolverine were prized for ruffs. Also used to make parkas were skins from the wolf fish and bird skins—leaving the feathers on the outside—

Warm and beautiful, these "fancy parkas" showcase a skin-sewer's artistry.
Courtesy of the Murie Family Collection.
From *Arctic Dance* by Charles Craighead and Bonnie Kreps.

including those of murre, cormorants and diving fish ducks.

PERMAFROST
Permafrost is defined as ground that remains frozen for two or more years. In its continuous form, permafrost underlies the entire Arctic region to depths of 2,000 feet. In broad terms, continuous permafrost occurs north of the Brooks Range and in the alpine region of mountains, including those of the Lower 48.

Discontinuous permafrost occurs south of the Brooks Range and north of the Alaska Range. Much of the Interior and parts of Southcentral Alaska are underlain by discontinuous permafrost.

Permafrost affects many buildings and natural bodies. It influences construction in the Arctic because building on it may cause the ground to thaw and if the ground is ice-rich, structures will sink. Arctic and subarctic rivers typically carry 55 percent to 65 percent of the precipitation that falls onto their watersheds, roughly 30 percent to 40 percent more than rivers of more temperate climates. Consequently, northern streams are prone to flooding and carry high silt loads.

Permafrost is responsible for the thousands of shallow lakes dotting the arctic tundra because groundwater is held on the surface.

A tunnel excavated in permafrost during the 1960s near Fox, about 11 miles north of Fairbanks, is maintained cooperatively by the University of Alaska Fairbanks and the U.S. Army Cold Regions Research and Engineering Laboratory. One of the few such tunnels in the world, it offers unique research opportunities on a 40,000-year-old accumulation of sediments and ice.

PERMANENT FUND
In 1976 Alaska voters approved a constitutional amendment to establish a dedicated fund: the Alaska Permanent Fund. The amendment provides that "At least 25 percent of all mineral lease rentals, royalties, royalty sales proceeds, federal mineral revenue-sharing payments and bonuses received by the state be placed in a permanent fund, the principal of which may only be used for income-producing

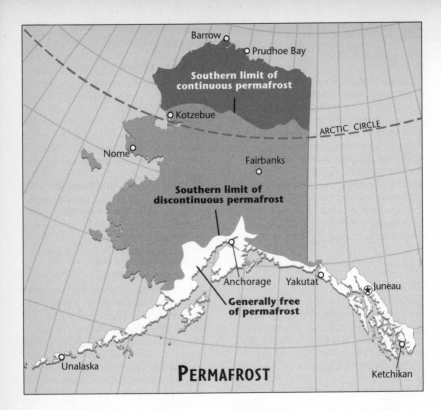

Barrow

Prudhoe Bay

**Southern limit of
continuous permafrost**

Kotzebue

ARCTIC CIRCLE

Nome

Fairbanks

**Southern limit of
discontinuous permafrost**

Anchorage   Yakutat

Juneau

**Generally free
of permafrost**

Unalaska

PERMAFROST

Ketchikan

investments." Fund-realized earnings come from interest on bonds, stock dividends and from real estate rent payments, in addition to any capital gains on the sales of these assets. The Legislature may spend the realized earnings. Unrealized earnings from appreciation/depreciation of the value of assets accrue to Fund principal.

In 1980 the Legislature established the Permanent Fund Dividend Program. Initially, eligible residents were to receive a $50 dividend for each year of residency since 1959. However, the U.S. Supreme Court declared the 1980 program unconstitutional on the grounds that it created different classes of residency. In 1982 a revised version was signed into law. Under that plan, an initial $1,000 dividend was paid to applicants who had lived in the state for at least six months prior to applying. Since then, dividends have been distributed each year to every qualifying applicant. The

annual dividend amount formula takes half of the approximate average of the Fund's realized income for the last five years and divides that among qualified applicants.

In the 30 years since the first deposit of $734,000, Alaska's Permanent Fund has received $9 billion in oil royalty deposits. Through a diversified portfolio of investments, these deposits have grown to a value of almost $33 billion on June 30, 2006, while paying out more than $14 billion in dividends since 1982. Investment revenues for 2006 were $3 billion, five times that year's oil royalty deposit of $601 million, proving that the Fund has been successful in saving and expanding a portion of Alaska's oil wealth. Each qualified Alaskan received a dividend of $1,107 in the fall of 2006.

The Alaska Permanent Fund has become a model that is studied the world over. To learn more about the Fund, visit www.apfc.org.

PIONEERS' HOMES

The first pioneers' home was established in Sitka in 1913 for "indigent prospectors and others who have spent their years in Alaska." Of the thousands of stampeders who came north between 1896 and 1900, 933 men and women submitted applications. However the home was not open to women until 1950; upon statehood in 1959, it was opened to Natives.

Currently six state-supported pioneers' homes offer assisted-living care for some 600 older Alaskans. The homes offer a range of service levels, providing assistance with activities of daily living, intermittent health care and recreation, with an emphasis on care of individuals with Alzheimer's disease and related disorders.

Applicants must be 65 years of age or older, must have lived continuously in Alaska for one year immediately preceding application, must have a need for the services provided in the homes and, if able, must pay rent established by the Department of Administration.

For additional information about pioneers' homes, contact the Director of the Division of Alaska Pioneer Homes, P.O. Box 110690, Juneau 99811-0690; (907) 465-4422; fax (907) 465-4108; www.hss.state.ak.us/dalp.

Anchorage Pioneers' Home, 923 W. 11th Ave., Anchorage 99501-4399; (907) 276-3414.

Fairbanks Pioneers' Home, 2221 Eagan Ave., Fairbanks 99701-5709; (907) 456-4372.

Juneau Pioneers' Home, 4675 Glacier Highway, Juneau 99801-9518; (907) 780-6422.

Ketchikan Pioneers' Home, 141 Bryant St., Ketchikan 99901-5575; (907) 225-4111.

Palmer Pioneers' Home, 250 E. Fireweed Ave., Palmer 99645-6699; (907) 745-4241.

Sitka Pioneers' Home, 120 Katlian St., Sitka 99835-7585; (907) 747-3213.

PIPELINE

Alyeska Pipeline Service Co., builder and operator of the Trans-Alaska Pipeline System, is a consortium of five oil companies:

BP Pipelines (Alaska), Inc., 46.93 percent
ConocoPhillips Transportation Alaska, Inc., 28.29 percent
ExxonMobil Pipeline Co., 20.34 percent
Koch Alaska Pipeline Co. LLC, 3.08 percent
Unocal Pipeline Co., 1.36 percent

Pipeline length: 800 miles; slightly less than half that length is buried, the remainder is on 78,000 aboveground supports, located 60 feet apart and built in a flexible zigzag pattern. There are more than 800 river and stream crossings. Normal burial of pipe was used in stable soils and rock; aboveground pipe—insulated and jacketed—was used in thaw-unstable permafrost areas. Thermal devices prevent thawing around vertical supports. The pipeline has 151 stop-flow valves.

Pipe: Specially manufactured coated pipe with zinc anodes installed to prevent corrosion. Size is 48 inches in diameter, with thickness from 0.462 to 0.562 inch.

Cost: $8 billion, which includes terminal at Valdez but excludes interest on money raised for construction.

Amount of oil pumped through pipeline: As of May 7, 2004, more than 14 billion barrels of oil had been pumped through the pipeline. The current flow represents approximately 17 percent of total U.S. oil production. At any one moment, there are about 9 million barrels of oil in the line.

NUGGETS

The U.S. Census Bureau director flew into remote Unalakleet in chilly January, donned a borrowed parka and rode into town on a dogsled for an afternoon of Native dancing and a potluck, hosted by the mostly Eskimo village of about 800. Officials hoped all the attention would improve Alaska's census return rate, worst in the nation in 1990.

—2000 *The Alaska Almanac*®

Operations: Control center at Valdez terminal and pump stations along the line monitor and control pipeline.

Terminal: 1,000-acre site at Port Valdez, northernmost ice-free harbor in the United States, with 18 tanks providing storage capacity of 9.2 million barrels of oil.

Valdez ship-loading capacity: 110,000 barrels an hour for each of three berths; 80,000 barrels per hour for one berth.

Length and cost of pipeline haul road built by Alyeska: 360 miles, from the Yukon River to Prudhoe Bay; $150 million.

Yukon River Bridge: Only bridge (2,295 feet long) to span the Yukon in Alaska. Built in 1974–75; officially named E. L. Patton Yukon River Bridge in 1982 by Alaska Legislature. Patton was president of Alyeska during pipeline construction.

Important dates: July 1968, Prudhoe Bay oil field discovery confirmed; **1970,** lawsuits filed to halt construction, Alyeska Pipeline Service Co. formed; **Nov. 16, 1973,** presidential approval of pipeline legislation; **April 29, 1974,** construction begins on North Slope Haul Road (now the Dalton Highway) and is completed 154 days later; **March 27, 1975,** first pipe installed at Tonsina River; **June 20, 1977,** first oil leaves Prudhoe Bay, reaches Valdez terminal **July 28; Aug. 1, 1977,** first tanker load of oil shipped aboard the SS *ARCO Juneau;* **June 13, 1979,** tanker number 1,000 (SS *ARCO Heritage)* sails; **July 15, 1983,** 3 billionth barrel of oil leaves pump station; **Sept. 15, 1986,** 5 billionth barrel of oil leaves pump station; **Feb. 16, 1988,** 6 billionth barrel arrives at the marine terminal; **May 2, 1988,** *Chevron Mississippi* is 8,000th tanker to load crude oil at marine terminal; **March 24, 1989,** *Exxon Valdez* tanker runs aground after departing the marine terminal and spills more than 11 million gallons of North Slope crude into Prince William Sound; **Dec. 28, 1992,** SS *ARCO California,* 12,000th tanker to load; **March 1994,** 10 billionth barrel is pumped from the North Slope into the pipeline; **April 1996,** 22,000-gallon spill from defective valve; **June 20, 1997,** 20th anniversary of the pipeline system; **Aug. 8, 1997,** Pump Station 6 placed in standby status, the fourth station to be idled due to

As seen from Richardson, the Trans–Alaska Pipeline on its route from Prudhoe Bay to Valdez. From *The World-Famous Alaska Highway* by Tricia Brown.

declining oil output; **Aug. 27, 2000,** the 13 billionth barrel of North Slope crude is delivered through the pipeline to Valdez; **Oct. 4, 2001,** pipeline was shut down for three days to repair damage caused by a bullet hole; **Nov. 3, 2002,** 7.9 magnitude earthquake hit along Denali Fault, approximately 50 miles from pipeline. Although slightly damaged, pipeline was reported by engineers to have performed as originally designed; **Nov. 26, 2002,** State of Alaska renews pipeline right-of-way for 30 years; **March 2006,** oil field worker discovers 201,000-gallon oil spill from corroded pipe, the largest spill in North Slope history; **August 2006,** BP Alaska temporarily shuts down half of Prudhoe following a small spill, also due to corrosion.

Joint Pipeline Office: The Joint Pipeline Office, established in 1990, is composed of nine state and federal regulatory and management agencies. Each agency has responsibilities either for issuing permits or for monitoring the operation and environmental safety of pipelines in Alaska.

State agencies include the Department of Natural Resources, Department of Environmental Conservation, Department of Fish and Game and the Office of the Governor.

PLACE-NAMES
Alaska has a rich international heritage of place-names. Names of British (Barrow), Spanish (Valdez), Russian (Kotzebue), French (La Perouse), American (Fairbanks) and Native Alaskan (Sitka) origin dot the map.

Some Alaska place-names are quite common. There are about 70 streams called Bear Creek in Alaska (not to mention Bear Bay, Bear Bluff, Bear Canyon, Bear Cove and Bear Draw) and about 50 called Moose Creek.

Many place-names have an unusual history. Moose Pass is said to derive its name from a 1903 incident when a mail carrier driving a dog team had difficulty gaining the right-of-way from a large moose.

POISONOUS PLANTS (See also Mushrooms)
Alaska has few poisonous plants, compared to the number of

Deadly Monkshood

They're so beautiful a flower, so innocent in appearance, that it seems unkind to bandy about the nefarious ways these flowers have been used. But monkshood in particular is so deadly poisonous that it is essential foragers be aware. . . . In medieval times, monkshood was called "thung" (a name for any deadly plant) and was used for warfare; the root was placed in water holes and wells to poison water supplies of pursuing armies. *The Herb Book* says that witches smeared the root on their broomsticks and bodies, took a dose of delirium-producing belladonna, and then went "flying." On a more mundane plane, the roots were mixed with toasted cheese to kill rats.

—Janice Schofield,
Discovering Wild Plants

species growing here. Nonetheless, some extremely poisonous plants thrive. Baneberry (*Actaea rubra),* water hemlock (*Cicuta douglasii* and *C. mackenzieana),* fly agaric mushroom (*Amanita muscaria),* monkshood (*Aconitum species)* and false hellebore (*Veratrum species)* are the most dangerous. Be sure you have properly identified plants before harvesting for food. Alaska has no poison ivy or poison oak, found in almost all other states, but Alaska's cow parsnip produces a photoreactive chemical that can cause blisters and burns.

POLITICAL PARTIES
A recognized political party in Alaska is an organized group that represents a political program and either nominates a candidate for governor who received at

least 3 percent of the total votes cast for governor in the preceding general election, or has registered enough voters to equal 3 percent of the votes cast for governor in the last election. Until it qualifies as a political party under this definition, an independent political group may field candidates for statewide and districtwide offices by filing nominating petitions.

Alaska's four political parties are:

Alaskan Independence Party, Chair: Lynette Clark, 2521 Old Steese Hwy., N., Fairbanks 99712; (907) 457-1884.

Alaska Democratic Party, Chair: Jake Metcalf; P.O. Box 231230, Anchorage, 99523-1230; (907) 258-3050.

Alaska Libertarian Party, Chair: Jason Dowell, PMB 373, 205 E. Dimond Blvd., Anchorage 99515; (907) 727-5298.

Alaska Republican Party, Chair: Randolph A. Ruedrich, 1001 Fireweed Lane, Anchorage 99503; (907) 276-4467.

POPULATIONS AND ZIP CODES

According to the Alaska Department of Labor and Workforce Development, many areas of Alaska gained population in the past decade. Between 1990 and 2000, Alaska's population increased by 14 percent, compared with a 13 percent increase in the U.S. population. The greatest overall growth occurred in Anchorage, which accounted for 42 percent of the state's population in 2000.

Populations for cities and communities (SEE pages 174–82) are Alaska Department of

(Continued on page 184)

Community	Year Incorporated	Population	Zip
Adak	2001	146	99546
Akhiok (AH-key-ok)	1972	44	99615
Akiachak (ACK-ee-a-chuck)	—	633	99551
Akiak (ACK-ee-ack)	1970	367	99552
Akutan (ACK-oo-tan)	1979	741	99553
Alakanuk (a-LACK-a-nuk)	1969	663	99554
Alatna	—	33	99720
Alcan Border	—	12	NA
Aleknagik (a-LECK-nuh-gik)	1973	241	99555
Aleneva	—	46	NA
Allakaket (alla-KAK-it)	1975	94	99720
Ambler	1971	277	99786
Anaktuvuk Pass (an-ak-TOO-vuk)	1957	299	99721
Anchor Point	—	1,803	99556
Anchorage, Municipality of	1920	282,813	
(includes Chugiak, Eagle River, Eklutna and Girdwood)			
Fort Richardson	—	—	99505
Elmendorf Air Force Base	—	—	99506
Mountain View	—	—	99508
Spenard Station	—	—	99509
Downtown Station	—	—	99510
Huffman Station	—	—	99511
Alyeska Pipeline Co.	—	—	99512
Federal Building	—	—	99513
Russian Jack Station	—	—	99514
Main Office (Airport)	—	—	99519
Eastchester Station	—	—	99520
Muldoon Station	—	—	99521
Sand Lake Station	—	—	99522
Lake Otis Station	—	—	99523

Community	Year Incorporated	Population	Zip
Midtown Station	—	—	99524
Anderson	1962	279	99744
Andreafsky	—	140	N/A
Angoon	1963	482	99820
Aniak (AN-ee-ack)	1972	512	99557
Anvik	1969	88	99558
Arctic Village	—	146	99722
Atka	1988	73	99547
Atmautluak (at-MAUT-loo-ack)	1976; dissolved 1996	304	99559
Atqasuk	1983	237	99791
Attu Coast Guard Station	—	20	99619
Barrow	1959	4,065	99723
Bear Creek	—	1,922	NA
Beaver	—	72	99724
Beluga	—	21	NA
Bethel	1957	5,812	99559
Bettles	1985	25	99726
Big Delta	—	728	99737
Big Lake	—	3,082	99652
Birch Creek	—	29	NA
Brevig Mission	1969	324	99785
Buckland	1966	418	99727
Buffalo Soapstone	—	755	NA
Butte	—	3,166	NA
Cantwell	—	204	99729
Central	—	89	99730
Chalkyitsik (chawl-KIT-sik)	—	65	99788
Chase	—	30	NA
Chefornak (cha-FOR-nack)	1974	460	99561
Chenega Bay	—	69	99574
Chevak	1967	908	99563
Chickaloon	—	282	99674
Chicken	—	29	99732
Chignik	1983	85	99564
Chignik Lagoon	—	70	99565
Chignik Lake	—	120	99548
Chiniak	—	44	99615
Chisana	—	9	NA
Chistochina	—	103	99586
Chitina	—	116	99566
Chuathbaluk	1975	95	99557
Circle	—	95	99733
Circle Hot Springs (see Central)	—	0	NA
Clam Gulch	—	165	99568
Clarks Point	1971	69	99569
Coffman Cove	1989	162	99918
Cohoe	—	1,260	99669
Cold Bay	1982	87	99571
Coldfoot	—	13	99701
College	—	11,825	99708
Cooper Landing	—	357	99572
Copper Center	—	402	99573

Community	Year Incorporated	Population	Zip
Copperville	—	191	NA
Cordova	1909	2,211	99574
Covenant Life	—	310	NA
Craig	1922	1,105	99921
Crooked Creek	—	122	99575
Crown Point	—	81	NA
Deering	1970	138	99736
Delta Junction	1960	1,039	99737
Deltana	—	1,896	NA
Diamond Ridge	—	690	NA
Dillingham	1963	2,397	99576
Diomede (DY-o-mede)	1970	110	99762
Dot Lake	—	32	99737
Dot Lake Village	—	22	NA
Douglas	1902	4,850	99824
Dry Creek	—	94	NA
Dutch Harbor (see Unalaska)	1942	NA	99692
Eagle	1901	100	99738
Eagle River/Chugiak	—	30,000	99577
Eagle Village	—	70	NA
Edna Bay	—	41	99950
Eek	1970	287	99578
Egegik (EEG-gah-gik)	1985	76	99579
Eielson Air Force Base	—	4,447	99702
Eklutna	—	368	99567
Ekwok (ECK-wok)	1974	111	99580
Elfin Cove	—	29	99825
Elim (EE-lum)	1970	294	99739
Emmonak (ee-MON-nuk)	1964	754	99581
Ester	—	1,938	99725
Evansville	—	18	NA
Excursion Inlet	—	8	NA
Eyak	—	130	NA
Fairbanks, City of	1903	30,522	
Main Office	—	—	99701
Eielson Air Force Base	—	4,447	99702
Fort Wainwright	—	—	99703
North Pole Station	—	—	99705
Main Office Boxes	—	—	99706
Downtown Station	—	—	99707
College Branch	—	—	99708
Steese Contract Station	—	—	99710
Badger Station	—	—	99711
Salcha	—	—	99714
Two Rivers Station	—	—	99716
False Pass	1990	54	99583
Farm Loop	—	1,255	NA
Ferry	—	31	NA
Fishhook	—	2,917	NA
Fort Greely	—	756	99731
Fort Yukon	1959	596	99740
Four Mile Road	—	39	99703

Community	Year Incorporated	Population	Zip
Fox	—	369	99712
Fox River	—	639	NA
Fritz Creek	—	1,723	99603
Funny River	—	729	99669
Gakona (ga-KOH-na)	—	234	99586
Galena (ga-LEE-na)	1971	636	99741
Gambell	1963	643	99742
Game Creek	—	21	NA
Gateway	—	3,830	NA
Georgetown	—	3	NA
Girdwood	—	236	99587
Glacier View	—	264	NA
Glennallen	—	525	99588
Golovin (GAWL-uh-vin)	1971	154	99762
Goodnews Bay	1970	242	99589
Grayling	1969	174	99590
Gulkana	—	177	99586
Gustavus (ga-STAY-vus)	—	441	99826
Haines	1910	1,492	99827
Halibut Cove	—	24	99603
Happy Valley	—	472	NA
Harding–Birch Lakes	—	45	NA
Healy	—	993	99743
Healy Lake	—	46	NA
Hobart	—	2	NA
Hollis	—	156	NA
Holy Cross	1968	204	99602
Homer	1964	5,454	99603
Hoonah	1946	829	99829
Hooper Bay	1966	1,157	99604
Hope	—	143	99605
Houston	1966	1,537	99694
Hughes	1973	68	99745
Huslia (HOOS-lee-a)	1969	259	99746
Hydaburg	1927	352	99922
Hyder	—	92	99923
Iguigig (ig-ee-AH-gig)	—	53	99613
Iliamna (ill-ee-YAM-nuh)	—	82	99606
Jakolof Bay (Red Mountain)	—	39	NA
Juneau, City and Borough of	1900	30,650	
Main Office	—	—	99801
Federal Boxes	—	—	99802
Mendenhall Station	—	—	99803
State Government Offices	—	—	99811
Auke Bay Station	—	—	99821
Douglas	—	—	99824
Kachemak	—	458	NA
Kake	1952	536	99830
Kaktovik	1971	288	99747
Kalifornsky	—	6,914	99669
Kaltag	1969	199	99748
Karluk	—	27	99608

Community	Year Incorporated	Population	Zip
Kasaan (Ka-SAN)	1976	59	99950
Kasigluk (ka-SEEG-luk)	1982; dissolved 1996	542	99609
Kasilof (ka-SEE-loff)	—	547	99610
Kenai (KEEN-eye)	1960	6,864	99611
Kenny Lake	—	414	99573
Ketchikan	1900	7,622	99901
Kiana (Ky-AN-a)	1964	401	99749
King Cove	1947	807	99612
King Salmon	—	409	99613
Kipnuk (KIP-nuck)	—	668	99614
Kivalina	1969	391	99750
Klawock (kla-WOCK)	1929	776	99925
Klukwan	—	112	99827
Knik–Fairview	—	11,238	NA
Knik River	—	652	NA
Kobuk	1973	135	99751
Kodiak	1940	5,937	99615
U.S. Coast Guard Station	—	1,941	99619
Kokhanok (KO-ghan-ock)	—	168	99606
Koliganek (ko-LIG-a-neck)	—	165	99576
Kongiganak (kon-GIG-a-nuck)	—	411	99559
Kotlik	1970	611	99620
Kotzebue (KOT-sa-bue)	1958	3,104	99752
Koyuk	1970	368	99753
Koyukuk (KOY-yuh-kuck)	1973	88	99754
Kupreanof (ku-pree-AN-off)	1975	32	99833
Kwethluk (KWEETH-luck)	1975	721	99621
Kwigillingok (kwi-GILL-in-gock)	—	378	99622
Lake Louise	—	89	NA
Lake Minchumina (min-CHOO-min-a)	—	20	99757
Lakes	—	7,901	NA
Larsen Bay	1974	90	99624
Lazy Mountain	—	1,347	NA
Levelock (LEH-vuh-lock)	—	61	99625
Lime Village	—	25	99627
Livengood	—	25	NA
Lowell Point	—	76	NA
Lower Kalskag	1969	269	99626
Lutak	—	44	NA
Manley Hot Springs	—	78	99756
Manokotak (man-a-KO-tack)	1970	423	99628
Marshall	1970	387	99585
McCarthy	—	60	99588
McGrath	1975	321	99627
McKinley Park	—	145	99755
Meadow Lakes	—	6,492	NA
Mekoryuk (ma-KOR-ee-yuk)	1969	217	99630
Mendeltna	—	62	NA
Mentasta Lake	—	114	99780
Metlakatla	1944	1,377	99926
Meyers Chuck	—	11	99903
Minto	—	186	99758

Community	Year Incorporated	Population	Zip
Moose Creek	—	578	NA
Moose Pass	—	204	99631
Mosquito Lake	—	158	NA
Mountain Village	1967	796	99632
Mud Bay	—	136	NA
Naknek (NACK-neck)	—	577	99633
Nanwalek	—	228	99603
Napakiak (nuh-PAH-key-ack)	1970	370	99634
Napaskiak (nuh-PASS-key-ack)	1971	464	99559
Naukati Bay	—	129	99950
Nelchina	—	51	NA
Nelson Lagoon	—	63	99571
Nenana (nee-NA-na)	1921	359	99760
New Allakaket	—	34	NA
New Stuyahok (STU-ya-hock)	1972	472	99636
Newhalen	1971	167	99606
Newtok	1976; dissolved 1997	323	99559
Nightmute	1974	237	99690
Nikiski	—	4,179	99635
Nikolaevsk	—	297	99556
Nikolai	1970	98	99691
Nikolski	—	31	99638
Ninilchik (Nin-ILL-chick)	—	784	99639
Noatak (NO-uh-tack)	—	470	99761
Nome	1901	3,540	99762
Nondalton	1971	193	99640
Noorvik	1964	636	99763
North Pole	1953	1,710	99705
Northway	—	79	99764
Northway Junction	—	61	NA
Northway Village	—	87	NA
Nuiqsut (noo-IK-sut)	1975	417	99789
Nulato	1963	290	99765
Nunam Iqua	1974	156	99666
Nunapitchuk (noo-nah-PIT-chuck)	1982	547	99641
Old Harbor	1966	192	99643
Oscarville	—	64	NA
Ouzinkie (oo-ZINK-ee)	1967	193	99644
Palmer	1951	5,574	99645
Paxson	—	28	99737
Pedro Bay	—	55	99647
Pelican	1943	106	99832
Perryville	—	120	99648
Petersburg	1910	3,129	99833
Petersville	—	20	NA
Pilot Point	1992	66	99649
Pilot Station	1969	574	99650
Pitka's Point	—	109	99658
Platinum	1975	38	99651
Pleasant Valley	—	683	NA
Point Baker	—	16	99927
Point Hope	1966	737	99766

Community	Year Incorporated	Population	Zip
Point Lay	—	235	99759
Point MacKenzie	—	232	NA
Pope–Vannoy Landing	—	6	NA
Port Alexander	1974	64	99836
Port Alsworth	—	112	99653
Port Clarence	—	23	NA
Port Graham	—	136	99603
Port Heiden	1972	79	99549
Port Lions	1966	211	99550
Port Protection	—	59	99927
Portage Creek	—	20	99576
Primrose	—	79	NA
Prudhoe Bay	—	2	99734
Quinhagak (QUIN-a-gak)	1975	648	99655
Rampart	—	21	99767
Red Devil	—	29	99656
Red Dog Mine	—	33	NA
Ridgeway	—	1,961	NA
Ruby	1973	183	99768
Russian Mission	1970	329	99657
St. George Island	1983	120	99591
St. Marys/Andreafsky	1967	551	99658
St. Michael	1969	446	99659
St. Paul Island	1971	460	99660
Salamatof	—	906	99611
Salcha	—	946	99714
Sand Point	1966	890	99661
Savoonga (suh-VOON-guh)	1969	712	99769
Saxman	1930	422	99901
Scammon Bay	1967	520	99662
Selawik (SELL-a-wick)	1977	841	99770
Seldovia	1945	287	99663
Seldovia Village	—	159	NA
Seward	1912	2,627	99664
Shageluk (SHAG-a-look)	1970	124	99665
Shaktoolik (shack-TOO-lick)	1969	214	99771
Shemya Station	—	27	NA
Shishmaref (SHISH-muh-reff)	1969	615	99772
Shungnak (SHOONG-nack)	1967	260	99773
Silver Springs	—	113	NA
Sitka	1963/1971	8,833	99835
Skagway	1900	854	99840
Skwentna	—	71	99667
Slana	—	94	99586
Sleetmute	—	91	99668
Soldotna	1967	3,807	99669
Solomon	—	2	NA
South Naknek	—	74	99670
Stebbins	1969	612	99671
Sterling	—	5,036	99672
Stevens Village	—	63	99774
Stony River	—	53	99557

Community	Year Incorporated	Population	Zip
Sunrise	—	22	NA
Susitna	—	24	NA
Sutton–Alpine	—	1,278	99674
Takotna (Tah-KOT-nuh)	—	53	99675
Talkeetna (Tal-KEET-na)	—	840	99676
Tanacross	—	146	99776
Tanaina	—	6,987	NA
Tanana (TAN-a-nah)	1961	261	99777
Tatitlek	—	117	99677
Tazlina	—	188	NA
Telida	—	3	NA
Teller	1963	258	99778
Tenakee Springs	1971	109	99841
Tetlin	—	149	99779
Thom's Place	—	7	NA
Thorne Bay	1982	482	99919
Togiak (TOE-gee-yack)	1969	783	99678
Tok (TOKE)	—	1,347	99780
Toksook Bay	1972	598	99637
Tolsona	—	24	NA
Tonsina	—	90	NA
Trapper Creek	—	415	99683
Tuluksak (tu-LOOK-sack)	1970; dissolved 1997	493	99679
Tuntutuliak (TUN-too-TOO-li-ack)	—	407	99680
Tununak	1975; dissolved 1997	333	99681
Twin Hills	—	77	99576
Two Rivers	—	627	99716
Tyonek (ty-O-neck)	—	199	99682
Ugashik	—	17	NA
Unalakleet (YOU-na-la-kleet)	1974	727	99684
Unalaska (UN-a-LAS-ka)	1942	3,947	99685
Upper Kalskag/Kalskag	1975	271	99607
Valdez (val-DEEZ)	1901	3,690	99686
Venetie (VEEN-a-tie)	—	187	99781
Wainwright	1962	517	99782
Wales	1964	139	99783
Wasilla (wah-SIL-luh)	1974	6,775	
Post Office	—	—	99687
Delivery	—	—	99654
Whale Pass	—	61	NA
White Mountain	1969	224	99784
Whittier	1969	117	99693
Willow	—	1,973	99688
Willow Creek	—	193	NA
Wiseman	—	22	99790
Womens Bay	—	703	NA
Wrangell	1903	1,911	99929
Y (developed area between Willow and Talkeetna)	—	1,085	NA
Yakutat (YAK-a-tat)	1948/1992	634	99689

* 2006 State Demographer estimates

(NA = Not Available)

Populations by Census Areas

Key	Census Area	1970	1980	1990	2000
	Alaska	302,583	401,851	550,043	626,932
1	North Slope Borough	3,451	4,199	5,979	7,385
2	Northwest Arctic Borough	4,048	4,831	6,113	7,208
3	Nome	5,749	6,537	8,288	9,196
4	Yukon–Koyukuk	7,045	6,471	6,681	6,551
5	Fairbanks North Star Borough	45,864	53,983	77,720	82,840
6	Southeast Fairbanks	4,308	5,676	5,913	6,174
7	Wade Hampton	3,917	4,665	5,791	7,028
8	Bethel	8,917	10,999	13,656	16,006
9	Dillingham	2,510	3,232	4,012	4,922
10	Bristol Bay Borough	1,147	1,094	1,410	1,258
11	Yakutat Borough	385	563	705	808
12	Matanuska–Susitna Borough	6,509	17,816	39,683	59,322
13	Anchorage Municipality	126,385	174,431	226,338	260,283
14	Kenai Peninsula Borough	16,586	25,282	40,802	49,691
15	Kodiak Island Borough	9,409	9,939	13,309	13,913
16	Valdez–Cordova	4,979	8,348	9,952	10,195
17	Skagway–Hoonah–Angoon	2,792	3,478	4,385	3,436
18	Haines Borough	1,401	1,680	2,117	2,392
19	Juneau Borough	13,556	19,528	26,751	30,711
20	Sitka Borough	6,073	7,803	8,588	8,835
21	Wrangell–Petersburg	4,920	6,167	7,042	6,684
22	Prince of Wales–Outer Ketchikan	3,782	3,822	6,278	6,146
23	Ketchikan Gateway Borough	10,041	11,316	13,828	14,070
24	Lake and Peninsula Borough	1,362	1,384	1,668	1,823
25	Denali Borough	NA	1,402	1,792	1,893
26	Aleutians East Borough	1,301	1,643	2,464	2,697
27	Aleutians West Census Area	6,533	6,125	9,478	5,465

Source: Alaska Department of Labor, Census 2000

Growth of Alaska's Major Cities

City	1900	1920	1940	1950	1970	1980	2000
Anchorage*	NA	1,856	4,229	11,254	48,081	174,431	260,283
Barrow	NA	NA	NA	NA	2,104	2,207	4,581
Cordova	NA	955	938	1,165	1,164	1,879	2,454
Fairbanks	NA	1,155	3,455	5,771	14,771	22,645	30,224
Juneau	1,864	3,058	5,729	5,956	6,050	19,528	30,711
Kenai	290	332	303	321	3,533	4,324	6,942
Ketchikan	459	2,458	4,695	5,305	6,994	7,198	7,922
Kodiak	341	374	864	1,710	3,798	4,756	6,334
Nome	12,488	852	1,559	1,876	2,357	2,301	3,505
Petersburg	NA	879	1,323	1,619	2,042	2,821	3,224
Seward	NA	652	949	2,114	1,587	1,843	2,830
Sitka	1,396	1,175	1,987	1,985	6,075	7,803	8,835
Valdez	315	466	529	554	1,005	3,079	4,036
Wrangell	868	821	1,162	1,263	2,029	2,184	2,308

*Includes Eklutna

Source: Alaska Department of Labor, Census 2000

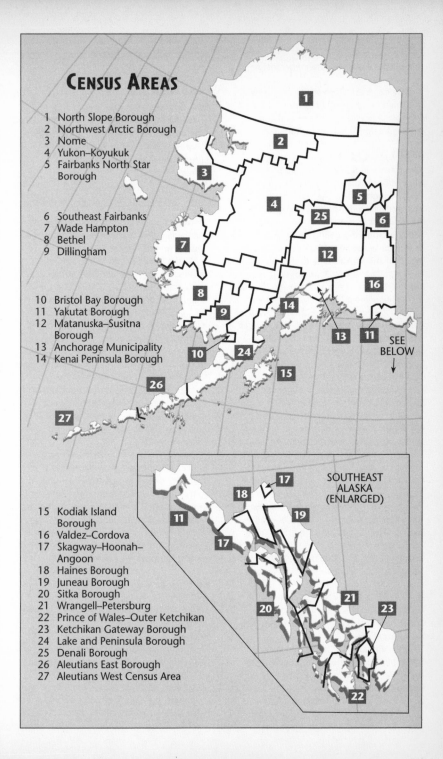

CENSUS AREAS

1 North Slope Borough
2 Northwest Arctic Borough
3 Nome
4 Yukon–Koyukuk
5 Fairbanks North Star
  Borough

6 Southeast Fairbanks
7 Wade Hampton
8 Bethel
9 Dillingham

10 Bristol Bay Borough
11 Yakutat Borough
12 Matanuska–Susitna
   Borough
13 Anchorage Municipality
14 Kenai Peninsula Borough

15 Kodiak Island
   Borough
16 Valdez–Cordova
17 Skagway–Hoonah–
   Angoon
18 Haines Borough
19 Juneau Borough
20 Sitka Borough
21 Wrangell–Petersburg
22 Prince of Wales–Outer Ketchikan
23 Ketchikan Gateway Borough
24 Lake and Peninsula Borough
25 Denali Borough
26 Aleutians East Borough
27 Aleutians West Census Area

SEE
BELOW

SOUTHEAST
ALASKA
(ENLARGED)

(Continued from page 174)

Labor 2006 estimates, based on the 2000 national census.

Entries lacking zip codes are communities without a U.S. post office. Population numbers also are available online at http://almis.labor.state.ak.us.

POTLATCH
This Native gathering, primarily an Indian custom, is held to commemorate major life events.

Traditional Native foods are served, songs and dances are performed, and gifts are distributed to attendees. A funeral potlatch might include the giving away of the deceased's possessions to relatives or to those who had shown kindness to the deceased.

Before the U.S. and Canadian governments outlawed the practice in the 1880s, potlatches were a focal point of Native society. The host family might give away all its possessions to demonstrate its wealth to the guests. Each guest in turn would feel obliged to hold an even more sumptuous potlatch. The outlawing of potlatches resulted in the disintegration of many aspects of Native culture. Potlatch restrictions were repealed in 1951.

QIVIUT
This material is the downy soft undercoat of the musk ox. *Qiviut* (KIV-ee-ute) is prized for its light weight and exceptional warmth. It is said to be eight times warmer than sheep's wool. It is knitted by hand into hats, scarves and other garments by members of the Oomingmak Musk Ox Producers' Cooperative. The cooperative is made up of approximately 250 Native women from Western Alaska villages. Each garment bears the distinctive traditional pattern of the village where it was made.

RADIO STATIONS
Alaska's numerous radio stations broadcast a variety of music, talk shows and religious and educational programs.

The Alaska Public Radio Network (APRN) is a consortium of 25 public radio stations around the state. APRN is based in Anchorage and produces daily and weekly programming for its member stations. Throughout Alaska, some stations often offer special programming for Native

NUGGETS

In late July 1995 the Alaska Public Radio Network shut down its Interior bureau headquartered in Fairbanks following hefty budget cuts.

—1996 *The Alaska Almanac*®

listeners, such as Native American music, news and entertainment, as well as a Native Word of the Day.

Alaska Public Broadcasting, Inc. is a partnership between the Alaska Public Radio Network and the Alaska One public television cooperative. It is operated as a service bureau to provide staff support services to the Alaska Public Broadcasting Commission (APBC), the Alaska Rural Communications Service Council (ARCS) and to the Alaska Satellite Interconnection Project Management Group (SIP).

Many radio stations in Alaska also broadcast personal messages, long a popular and necessary form of communication in Alaska—especially in the Bush.

To accommodate these messages— and radio's unique role in providing vital weather information to fishermen and hunters—the United States and Canada agreed to grant some Alaska radio stations international communication status. The "clear channel" status provides protection against interference from foreign broadcasters. Personal messages are heard on:

Barrow. *Tundra Drum,* KBRW 680 kHz; KBRW-FM 91.9 MHz; P.O. Box 109, Barrow 99723; listen in at www.kbrw.org.

Bethel. *Mukluk Messages,* KYKD-FM 100.1 MHz; Voice for Christ Ministries, I AM Radio Network, P.O. Box 00474, Nenana 99760; message line (907) 832-5426; www.vfcm.org/kykd.htm.

Tundra Drums, KYUK 640 kHz; P.O. Box 468, Bethel 99559; (907) 543-3131; www.kyuk.org.

Dillingham. *Bristol Bay Messenger,* KDLG 670 kHz; Dillingham City School District, P.O. Box 670, Dillingham 99576; (907) 842-1670; www.prx.org/station/kdlg.

Fairbanks. *Pipeline of the North,* KIAK-FM 102.5 MHz; Clear Channel Worldwide, 546 Ninth Ave., Fairbanks 99701; (907) 457-1025; www.kiak.com.

Galena. *Yukon Wireless,* KIYU 910 kHz; Community Radio of Alaska, P.O. Box 165, Galena 99741; (907) 656-1488; www.kiyu.com.

Glennallen. *Caribou Clatters,* KCAM 790 kHz; P.O. Box 249, Glennallen 99588; phone (907) 822-5226; fax (907) 822-3761; e-mail caribouclatters@yahoo.com; www.kcam.org.

Haines/Skagway. *Listener Personals,* KHNS-FM 102.3 MHz; P.O. Box 1109, Haines 99827; (907) 766-2020 in Haines; (907) 983-2853 in Skagway; e-mail khns@khns.org; www.khns.org.

Homer. *Bushlines,* KBBI 890 kHz; Kachemak Bay Broadcasting, 3913 Kachemak Way, Homer 99603; (907) 235-7721, ext. 229; www.kbbi.org.

Kenai/Soldotna. *Tundra Tom Tom,* KSRM 920 kHz; 40960 Kalifornsky Beach Road, Kenai 99611; (907) 283-5811; www.ksrm.com.

Ketchikan. *Muskeg Messenger,* KRBD-FM 105.3 MHz; 123 Stedman St., Ketchikan 99901; (907) 225-9655; www.krbd.org.
  Public Service Announcements, KTKN 930 kHz; Alaska Broadcast Communications, Inc., 526 Stedman St., Ketchikan 99901; e-mail ktknkgtw@gci.net; www.ktkn.com.

Kodiak. *Highliner Crabbers,* KVOK 560 kHz; Kodiak Island Broadcasting Co., Inc., P.O. Box 708, 99615; (907) 486-5159; e-mail kvok@ak.net; www.kvok.com.

Kotzebue. *Messages,* KOTZ 720 kHz; P.O. Box 78, 99752; (907) 442-3434; fax (907) 442-2292; e-mail kotz@otz.net; www.kotz.org.

McGrath. *Messages,* KSKO 870 kHz; Kuskokwim Public Broadcasting Corp., P.O. Box 70, 99627; (907) 524-3001; fax (907) 524-3436; www.kskoradio.org.

Nome. *Ptarmigan Telegraph,* KICY 850 kHz; KICY-FM 100.3 MHz; Arctic Broadcasting Association, P.O. Box 820, Nome 99762-0820; (907) 443-2213; www.kicy.org.
  Village Hot Lines, KNOM 780 kHz; KNOM-FM 96.1 MHz; P.O. Box 988, Nome 99762; (907) 443-5221; e-mail hotline@knom.org; www.knom.org.

North Pole. *Trapline Chatter,* KJNP 1170 kHz; KJNP-FM 100.3 MHz; P.O. Box 56359, North Pole 99705; 99705; (907) 488-2216; e-mail kjnp@mosquitonet.com; www.mosquitonet.com/~kjnp/fm.html.

Petersburg. *Muskeg Messages,* KFSK-FM 100.9 MHz; Narrows Broadcasting Corp., P.O. Box 149, Petersburg 99833; (907) 772-3808; www.kfsk.org.
  Channel Chatters, KRSA 580 kHz; P.O. Box 650, Petersburg 99833; (907) 772-3891; fax (907) 772-4538; e-mail krsa@krsa.net; www.krsa.net.

> Alaska is still the state with the highest percentage of men, and the smallest percentage of women, although this is not always a good thing for the women. The authors of a guide to Alaska men, *Catch and Release,* quoted an Oregon woman who said to a new Alaska male acquaintance, "You and Fairbanks have a lot in common. You're both cold, remote and trashy."

Sitka. *Muskeg Messages,* KCAW 90.1 MHz or KCAW-FM 104.7 MHz; 2 Lincoln St., Suite B, Sitka 99835-7538; (907) 747-5877; http://kcaw.org.

Valdez. *Billboard,* KCHU 770 kHz; KCHU-FM 88.1 MHz; P.O. Box 467, Valdez 99686; (907) 835-5080; www.alaska.net/~kchu.

Wrangell. *Radiograms,* KSTK-FM 101.7 MHz; P.O. Box 1141, Wrangell 99929; (907) 874-2345; http://kstk.org.

RAILROADS (SEE ALSO Skagway)

The Alaska Railroad is the northernmost railroad in North America and was for many years the only one that was owned by the federal government. Ownership has been transferred to the state. The Alaska Railroad rolls on 470 miles of mainline track from the ports of Seward and Whittier to Anchorage, Cook Inlet and Fairbanks in the Interior.

The Alaska Railroad began in 1912 when Congress appointed a commission to study transportation problems in Alaska. In March 1914, President Woodrow Wilson authorized railroad lines in the Territory of Alaska to connect open harbors on the southern coast of Alaska with the Interior. The Alaska Engineering Commission surveyed railroad routes in 1914 and, in April 1915, the president announced the selection of a route from Seward north 412 miles to the Tanana River (where Nenana

The White Pass & Yukon Route railway still operates its historic steam engine.
Photo by Tricia Brown.

is now located), with branch lines to Matanuska coalfields. The main line was later extended to Fairbanks. Construction of the railroad began in 1915 from a wilderness construction camp on Cook Inlet. Almost overnight, a tent city of 2,000 sprang up and Anchorage was born.

On July 15, 1923, President Warren G. Harding drove in the golden spike at Nenana, signifying completion of the railroad.

The Alaska Railroad offers year-round passenger and freight service. The railroad features flag-stop service along the Anchorage-to-Fairbanks corridor, as well as summer express trains to Denali National Park and Preserve and beyond to Fairbanks. Passenger service is daily between mid-May and mid-September, and in winter weekly service is available between Anchorage and Fairbanks. One-day excursions between Anchorage, Seward and Whittier are provided daily, mid-May to early September. In 2006, more than a half-million passengers rode the Alaska Railroad. For more information contact the Alaska Railroad, 327 W. Ship Creek Ave., Anchorage 99501; (800) 544-0552; www.alaskarailroad.com.

The privately owned White Pass & Yukon Route provided a narrow-gauge link between Skagway, Alaska, and Whitehorse, Yukon Territory. When it was built—1898 to 1900—it was the farthest north any railroad had operated in North America. The railway maintains one of

> Four days before the start of the 2005 Iditarod race, four-time champion Martin Buser cut off half of his middle finger with a table saw. At the start of the race, announcer "Super Dave" Stroh praised Buser's courage and character. Stroh told the crowd that Buser was such a nice guy, "he hardly uses his middle finger at all."

the steepest railroad grades in North America, climbing to 2,885 feet at White Pass in only 20 miles.

The White Pass & Yukon Route provided both passenger and freight service until 1982, when it suspended service until 1988. Currently, the route provides daily passenger service only. Contact the White Pass & Yukon Route, P.O. Box 435, Skagway 99840; (800) 343-7373; fax (907) 983-2734; www.whitepassrailroad.com.

REGIONS OF ALASKA The

state of Alaska is organized by geography and climate into six general regions.
(See map, pages 6–7)

Southeast. Southeast, Alaska's panhandle, stretches approximately 500 miles from Icy Bay, northwest of Yakutat, south to Dixon Entrance at the U.S.–Canada border beyond the southern tip of Prince of Wales Island. Massive ice fields, glacier-scoured peaks and steep valleys, more than a thousand named islands and numerous unnamed islets and reefs characterize this world where few flat expanses break the steepness. Spruce, hemlock and cedar cover many mountainsides and are harvested as timber.

Average temperatures range from 50°F to 60°F in July and from 20°F to 40°F in January. Average annual precipitation varies from 80 inches to more than 200 inches. The area receives from 30 inches to 200 inches of snow in the lowlands and more than 400 inches in the high mountains.

The region's economy revolves around fishing and fish processing, timber and tourism. Mining has increased with development of a world-class molybdenum mine near Ketchikan.

Airplanes and boats are the principal means of transportation. Only three communities in Southeast are connected to the road system: Haines, via the Haines Highway to the Alaska Highway at Haines Junction; Skagway, via Klondike Highway 2 to the Alaska Highway; and Hyder, to the continental road system via the Cassiar Highway in British Columbia. Juneau, on the Southeast mainland, is the state capital; Sitka, on Baranof Island, was the capital of Russian America.

Southcentral/Gulf Coast. The Southcentral/Gulf Coast region curves 650 miles north and west of Southeast Alaska and includes Kodiak Island. About two-thirds of the state's residents live in the arc between the Gulf of Alaska on the south and the Alaska Range on the north, the region commonly called Southcentral. On the region's eastern boundary, only the Copper River valley breaches the mountainous barrier of the Chugach and St. Elias Mountains. On the west rise lofty peaks of the Aleutian Range. Within this mountainous perimeter course the Susitna and Matanuska Rivers.

The irregular plain of the Copper River lowland has a colder climate than the other major valley areas. The January average for Kenny Lake is –2°F. The January average for the Talkeetna airport is 10°F. July temperatures average 50°F to 60°F in the region.

Regional precipitation ranges from a scant 17 inches annually in drier areas to more than 76 inches a year at Thompson Pass in the coastal mountains.

Vegetation varies from the spruce-hemlock forests of Prince William Sound to mixed spruce and birch forests in the Susitna Valley to tundra in the highlands of the Copper River–Nelchina Basin.

Alaska agriculture historically has been most thoroughly developed in the Matanuska Valley. The state's dairy industry is centered there and at a project at Point MacKenzie, across Knik

Arm from Anchorage. Vegetables thrive in the area, which is well-known for its giant cabbages.

Hub of the state's commerce, transportation and communications is Anchorage, on a narrow plain at the foot of the Chugach Mountains, and bounded by Knik Arm and Turnagain Arm, offshoots of Cook Inlet. The population of Alaska's largest city is closely tied to shifts in the state's economy.

Alaska's major banks, oil companies and the Alaska Railroad have headquarters in Anchorage. The city's port handles most of the shipping in and out of the state. Valdez, to the east of Anchorage on Prince William Sound, is the southern terminal of the trans-Alaska oil pipeline, which transports oil from Prudhoe Bay on the North Slope.

Interior. Great rivers have forged a broad lowland, known as the Interior, in the central part of the state between the Alaska Range on the south and the Brooks Range on the north. The Yukon River carves a swath across the entire state. In the Interior, the Tanana, Porcupine, Koyukuk and several other rivers join with the Yukon to create summer and winter highways. South of the Yukon, the Kuskokwim River rises in the hills of the western Interior before beginning its meandering course across the Bering Sea coast region.

Winter temperatures in the Interior commonly drop to –50°F or colder. Ice fog sometimes hovers over Fairbanks and other low-lying communities when the temperature falls below zero. Controlled by the extremes of a continental climate, summers usually are warmer than in any other region; high temperatures can climb to 90°F. The climate is semiarid, with about 12 inches of precipitation recorded annually.

Immense forests of birch and aspen bring vibrant green and gold to the Interior's landscape. Spruce covers many of the slopes and cottonwoods thrive near river lowlands. But in northern and western reaches of the Interior, the North American taiga gives way to tundra. In highlands above tree line and in marshy lowlands, grasses and shrubs replace trees.

Gold lured the first large influx of non-Natives to Alaska's Interior. From 1903 to 1910, the largest community in the region was the booming gold-mining camp of Fairbanks. Now the city on the banks of the Chena River is a transportation and supply center for eastern and northern Alaska. The main campus of the University of Alaska overlooks the city.

About 100 miles east of Fairbanks, farmers at the Delta project work to build a foundation for agriculture based on barley. At Healy, southwest of Fairbanks, the state's only operating coal mine produces coal used to generate electricity for the Interior. The rest of the Interior relies primarily on a subsistence economy, sometimes combined with a cash economy where fishing or seasonal government jobs are available.

Northern/Arctic. Beyond the Brooks Range, more than 80,000 square miles of tundra interlaced with meandering rivers and countless ponds spread out along the North Slope. In far northwestern Alaska, the Arctic curves south to take in Kotzebue and other villages of the Kobuk and Noatak River drainages.

Short, cool summers and temperatures between only 30°F and 40°F allow the permanently frozen soil to thaw just a few inches. Winter temperatures range well below zero but the Arctic Ocean moderates temperatures in coastal areas. Severe winds sweep along the coast and through mountain passes. Cold and wind often drop the windchill-factor temperature far below the actual temperature. Most areas receive less than 10 inches of precipitation a year but the terrain is wet in summer because of little evaporation and frozen ground.

Traditionally the home of Iñupiat Eskimos, the Arctic was inhabited by few non-Natives until oil was discovered at Prudhoe Bay in the 1960s. Today the region's economy is focused on Prudhoe Bay and neighboring Kuparuk oil fields. Petroleum-related jobs support most of the region's residents. Subsistence hunting and fishing fill any economic holes left by the oil industry.

The largest Iñupiat Eskimo community in the world, Barrow is the center of commerce and government activity for the region. Airplanes, the major means of transportation, fan out from there to the region's far-flung villages.

The Dalton Highway, formerly called the North Slope Haul Road, connects the Arctic with the Interior. The 416-mile road is open to the public all the way to Deadhorse. Permits are no longer required to drive the highway.
(See Dalton Highway)

Western/Bering Sea Coast. Western Alaska extends along the Bering Sea coast from the Arctic Circle south to where the Alaska Peninsula joins the mainland near Naknek on Bristol Bay. Home of Iñupiat and Yup'ik Eskimos, the region centers around the immense Yukon–Kuskokwim River Delta, the Seward Peninsula to the north and Bristol Bay to the south.

Summer temperatures range from about 30°F to about 60°F. Winter readings generally range from just above zero to near 30°F. Wind chill lowers temperatures considerably.

Total annual precipitation is about 20 inches; northern regions are drier.

Much of the region is covered with tundra, although a band of forest covers the hills on the eastern end of the Seward Peninsula and Norton Sound.

NUGGETS

Trespassers will be dismantled? Flooding of the Koyukuk River in the fall of 1994 uprooted and carried off many Allakaket homes. About eight of the houses just switched neighborhoods, coming to rest on State land adjacent to the local airfield. The State notified homeowners that their houses were trespassing and might interfere with local air traffic. Officials and homeowners worked together to move the houses, but two of them had to be dismantled, sources say.

—1995 *The Alaska Almanac*®

In the south near Bristol Bay the tundra once again gives way to forests. In between, the marshy flatland of the great Yukon–Kuskokwim Delta spreads out for more than 200 miles.

Gold first attracted non-Natives to the hills and creeks of the Seward Peninsula.

To the south, only a few anthropologists and wildlife biologists entered the world of the Yup'ik Eskimos of the delta. At the extreme south, the world's largest sockeye salmon run drew fishermen to the riches of Bristol Bay.

The villages of Western Alaska are linked by air and water, dogsled and snow-machine. Commerce on the delta radiates from Bethel, largest community in Western Alaska. To the north, Nome dominates commerce on the Seward Peninsula, while several fishing communities rely on the riches of Bristol Bay.

Southwestern/Alaska Peninsula and Aleutians. Southwestern Alaska includes the Alaska Peninsula and Aleutian Islands. From Naknek Lake, the peninsula curves southwest about 500 miles to the first of the Aleutian Islands; the Aleutians continue south and west more than 1,000 miles. Primarily a mountainous region with about 50 volcanic peaks, only on the Bering Sea side of the peninsula does the terrain flatten out.

More than 200 islands, roughly 5,500 square miles in area, form the narrow arc of the Aleutians, which separate the Pacific Ocean from the Bering Sea. Nearly the entire chain is in the Alaska Maritime National Wildlife Refuge. Unimak Island, closest to the Alaska Peninsula mainland, is 1,000 miles from Attu, the most distant island. Five major island groups make up the Aleutians, all of which are treeless except for a few scattered stands that have been transplanted.

The Aleutian climate is cool. Summer temperatures range to about 50°F and winter readings reach 20°F or colder. Winds are almost constant and fog is common. Precipitation ranges from 21 inches to more than 80 inches annually. The peninsula's climate is somewhat warmer than the islands' in summer and cooler in winter.

189

Aleuts (Unangan), original inhabitants of the chain, still live at Atka, Atka Island; Nikolski, Umnak Island; Unalaska, Unalaska Island; Akutan, Akutan Island; and False Pass, Unimak Island.

The quest for furs first drew Russians to the islands and peninsula in the 1700s. The traders conquered the Aleuts and forced them to hunt marine mammals. After the United States purchased Alaska in 1867, fur traders switched their efforts to fox farming. Many foxes were turned loose on the islands, where they flourished and destroyed native wildlife.

With the collapse of the fur market in the 1920s and 1930s, the islands were left to themselves. This relative isolation was broken during World War II when Japanese military forces bombed Dutch Harbor and landed on Attu and Kiska Islands. The United States military retook the islands, and after the war the government resettled Aleuts living in the western Aleutians to villages in the eastern Aleutians, closer to the mainland.

Today fishing provides the main economic base for the islands and the peninsula. Many Aleuts go to Bristol Bay or Unalaska to fish commercially in summer.

RELIGION
Nearly every religion practiced in American society is found in Alaska. Anchorage alone has nearly 200 churches and temples. Following is a list of addresses for some of the major ones:

Alaska Baptist Convention, 1750 O'Malley Road, Anchorage 99507.

All Saints Episcopal Church, Eighth Avenue and F Street, P.O. Box 100686, Anchorage 99510-0686.

Amazing Grace Lutheran Church, 10830 Elmore Road, Anchorage 99516.

Anchorage Friends Church (Native), 2824 E. 18th Ave., Anchorage 99508.

Anchorage Moravian Church, 4105 Turnagain Blvd., Suite 217, Anchorage 99517.

Assembly of God District Council, 1048 W. International Airport Road, Suite 101, Anchorage 99518.

Baha'i Faith, 13501 Brayton Drive, Anchorage 99516.

ChangePoint, 6689 Seafood Drive, Anchorage, 99518.

Sunset on the Yukon River at the village of Rampart. From *Two in a Red Canoe* by Matt Hage and Megan Baldino.

The Russian Orthodox church at Kenai is among the oldest buildings in the state. Photo by Tricia Brown.

Chapel by the Sea, 14730 Turnagain Bluff Way, Anchorage 99515-4153.

Christian Church of Anchorage, 10800 Lake Otis Parkway, Anchorage 99516.

Christian Science Church, 1347 L St., Anchorage 99501.

Church of Jesus Christ of Latter Day Saints, 13161 Brayton Drive, Anchorage 99516.

Congregation Beth Sholom, 7525 Northern Lights Blvd., Anchorage 99504.

First Presbyterian Church, 616 W. 10th Ave., Anchorage 99501.

First United Methodist Church, 725 W. Ninth Ave., Anchorage 99501.

Greater Friendly Temple Church of God in Christ, 6310 DeBarr Road, Anchorage 99508.

Holy Family Cathedral, 800 W. Fifth Ave., Anchorage 99501.

Islamic Center of Alaska, 5630 Silverado Way, Anchorage 99518.

Jehovah's Witnesses, 2301 Strawberry Road, Anchorage 99507.

Lubavitch Jewish Center of Alaska, Congregation Shomrei Ohr, 1210 E. 26th Ave., Anchorage 99508.

St. Innocent Russian Orthodox Cathedral, 401 Turpin St., Anchorage 99504.

Salvation Army, 143 E. Ninth Ave., Anchorage 99501.

Trinity Christian Reformed Church, 3000 E. 16th Ave., Anchorage 99508.

Unity Church of Anchorage, 1300 E. 68th Ave., Suite 109, Anchorage 99518.

REPTILES
For all practical purposes, reptiles are not found in Alaska outside of captivity. The northern limits of North American reptilian species may be the latitude at which their embryos fail to develop during the summer. Three sightings of a species of garter snake, *Thamnophis sirtalis,* have been reported on the banks of the Taku River and Stikine River.

RIVERS
(SEE ALSO National Wild and Scenic Rivers; Yukon River) There are more than 3,000 rivers in Alaska.

The 10 longest are:

Yukon River—1,400 miles in Alaska; the remainder is in Canada.

Porcupine River—555 miles; a major tributary of the Yukon River.

During the 2006 Christmas season, PETA wrote to an Anchorage Methodist church demanding that they stop using real animals in their live nativity scene. The church had never used live animals in the first place, and PETA seemed unconcerned about the baby Jesus lying in a manger in frigid temperatures. They only cared about not freezing their sheep, their cows, and their asses.

Koyukuk—554 miles
Kuskokwim—540 miles
Tanana—531 miles
Innoko—463 miles
Colville—428 miles
Noatak—396 miles
Kobuk—396 miles
Birch Creek—314 miles

The major navigable Alaska inland waterways are:

Chilkat. Navigable by shallow-draft vessels to village of Klukwan, 25 miles above mouth.

Kobuk. Controlling channel depth is about 5 feet through Hotham Inlet, 3 feet to Ambler and 2 feet to Kobuk Village, about 210 river miles.

Koyukuk. Navigable to Allakaket by vessels drawing up to 3 feet during normally high river flow and to Bettles during occasional higher flows.

Kuskokwim. Navigable (June 1 to Sept. 30) by 18-foot-draft oceangoing vessels from mouth upriver 65 miles to Bethel. Shallow-draft (4-foot) vessels can ascend river to mile 465. McGrath is at mile 400.

Kvichak. The river is navigable for vessels of 10-foot draft to Alaganak River, 22 miles above the mouth of Kvichak River. Remainder of this river (28 miles) navigable by craft drawing 2 feet to 4 feet, depending on the stage of the river. Drains into Lake Iliamna, which is navigable an additional 70 miles.

Naknek. Navigable for vessels of 12-foot draft for 12 miles with adequate tide. Vessels with 3-foot draft can continue an additional 7.5 miles.

Noatak. Navigable (late May to mid-June) for shallow-draft barges to a point about 18 miles below Noatak village. Shallow-draft vessels can continue on to Noatak.

Nushagak. Navigable (June 1 to Aug. 31) by small vessels of 2½-foot draft to Nunachuak, about 100 miles above the mouth. Shallow-draft, oceangoing vessels can navigate to mouth of Wood River at mile 84.

Porcupine. Navigable to Old Crow, Yukon Territory, by vessels drawing 3 feet, during spring runoff and fall rain floods.

Stikine. Navigable (May 1 to Oct. 15) from mouth 165 miles to Telegraph Creek, British Columbia, by shallow-draft, flat-bottom riverboats.

Susitna. Navigable by stern-wheelers and shallow-draft, flat-bottom riverboats to confluence of Talkeetna River, 75 miles upstream, but boats cannot cross bars at mouth of river. Not navigable by oceangoing vessels.

Tanana. Navigable by shallow-draft (4-foot), flat-bottom vessels and barges from the mouth to Nenana and by smaller river craft to the Chena River 201 miles above the mouth. Craft of 4-foot draft can navigate to Chena River on high water to University Avenue Bridge in Fairbanks.

Yukon. Navigable (June 1 to Sept. 30) by shallow-draft, flat-bottom riverboats from the mouth to near the head of Lake Bennett. It cannot be entered or navigated by oceangoing vessels. Controlling depths are 7 feet to Stevens Village and 3 feet to 5 feet from there to Fort Yukon.

ROADHOUSES

An important part of Alaska history, roadhouses were modest quarters that offered bed and board to travelers along early-day Alaska trails. Because most travel was done in winter, many roadhouses provided accommodations for sled-dog teams.

By 1920, there were roadhouses along every major transportation route in Alaska. Most roadhouses have vanished, though a few of the historic roadhouses survive, including Gakona Lodge on the Glenn Highway, Paxson Lodge at the junction of the Richardson and Denali Highways and Talkeetna Roadhouse.

The Cape Nome Roadhouse was a major stopover for dog teams and also served as a temporary orphanage. Several roadhouses are included in the National Register of Historic Places. Some historic roadhouses are now museums or occupied by businesses.

ROCKS AND GEMS

(SEE ALSO Gold; Jade; Minerals and Mining) Gemstones are not easy to find in Alaska. Rockhounds must hunt for them and often walk quite a distance. The easiest specimens to collect are float-rocks scattered by glaciation. These rocks are found on ocean beaches and railroad beds, and in creeks and rivers all over Alaska. In most rock-hunting areas, every instance of high water, wind, heavy rain and a melting patch of snow and ice uncovers a new layer, so you can hunt repeatedly in the same area and make new finds.

The easiest gemstones to search out are in the crypto-crystalline group of quartz minerals. These gems have crystals not visible to the naked eye. They are the jaspers, agates, cherts and flints.

Thunder eggs, geodes and agatized wood (all in the chalcedony classification) occur in Alaska. Thunder eggs have a jasper rind enclosing an agate core. Harder-to-find geodes usually have an agate rind with a hollow core filled with crystals. Agatized and petrified woods come in various colors and often show the plant's growth rings. Sometimes even the bark or limb structure is visible on agatized and petrified woods.

Crystalline varieties of quartz can also be found: amethyst (purple), citrine (yellow), rose quartz (pink), rock crystal (clear) and smoky quartz (brown).

Other gems to search for in Alaska are onyx, feldspar, porphyry, jade, serpentine, soapstone, garnet, rhodonite, sapphire, marble, staurolite, malachite and covelite (blue copper).

RUSSIAN ALASKA (See also

Baranov, Alexander; Bering, Vitus; History; Seward, William H.; Veniaminov, Ioann) Russian presence in Alaska began with the 1741 voyages of Vitus Bering and Alexei Chirikov. Their exploration of the Aleutian Islands and the Alaska mainland spurred dozens of voyages by Russian fur entrepreneurs, or *promyshlenniki*.

By the mid-1800s, Russians had explored most of the coast of southern and southwestern Alaska and some of the Interior. Their interest in Alaska lay primarily in exploiting the rich fur resources of the region, especially sea otters and fur seals.

In 1799, the Russian post known today as Old Sitka was established. That same year, a trade charter was granted to the Russian–American Co., a monopoly authorized by the czar in 1790 to control activities in Alaska.

During the entire Russian period, from 1741 to 1867, there were rarely more than about 500 Russians in Alaska at any one time. Nevertheless, the Aleuts, Eskimos and Indians whom the Russians encountered felt the devastating effects of foreign contact. Native populations declined drastically from introduced diseases. The population of the Aleut people, the first to succumb to Russian occupation, was reduced to less than 20 percent of the precontact level through warfare, disease and starvation. The Tlingit, Haida and Chugach people may have been reduced by 50 percent.

The Russians also brought to the new land their customs, religion and language, which, through subjugation and the efforts of Orthodox missionaries, brought great changes in traditional technologies, social patterns and religious beliefs.

In 1867, facing increasing competition and frustrated in its efforts to expand, the Russians sold Alaska to the United States for $7.2 million.

One of the foremost legacies of the Russian period is the Russian Orthodox Church, still a vital aspect of Native culture in Southwestern, Southcentral and Southeast Alaska. Visitors to Kenai, Kodiak, Sitka and smaller Native communities will see the familiar onion-shaped domes of the Russian Orthodox churches.

RUSSIAN CHRISTMAS Russian

Christmas is the Russian Orthodox obser-vance of the birth of Christ. It begins on Jan. 7—Twelfth Night, 12 days after Dec. 25.

A Mat-Su Valley inmate caused damage to the Point McKenzie prison by attacking a door with an ax! How did a prisoner get an ax in the first place? We can only assume that Wal-Mart is now selling some really really big cake pans.

Boalotchkee (Russian Buns)

1 pound butter
5 eggs
2 cups sour cream
¾ teaspoon baking soda

2 pounds flour
1 pound sugar
Nuts
Beaten egg yolk

Combine butter and eggs. Mix sour cream and soda; combine with butter-egg mixture.
Sift flour on board and mix with sugar. Make a hole in the middle and add the egg mixture.
Knead the dough with hands, constantly sprinkling the board with flour. Shape into round
buns, place in lightly oiled shallow pan, brush with beaten egg yolk and sprinkle with any
kind of chopped nuts. Bake at 350°F until done, about 18 to 25 minutes.

—Ann Lewis, St. Herman's Sisterhood Club, Kodiak, *Cooking Alaskan*

The holiday, called *Selavi*, is celebrated for seven days, with church services including songs in Slavonic, fireworks and special foods. Part of the tradition involves carrying a star from house to house, caroling and sharing food and small gifts.

Russian Christmas is observed in cities and towns with Orthodox parishes, such as Akutan, Anchorage, Dillingham, Eklutna, Juneau, Kenai, Kodiak, Lower Kalskag, Naknek, New Stuyahok, Newhalen, Ninilchik, Nushagak, Pedro Bay, St. Paul, St. George, Seldovia and Sitka.

SALMON STRIPS

These strips are salmon that has been dried or smoked for a long time until it's very chewy. The food is a staple in winter for rural Alaskans and their dogs. Other terms for this food are salmon jerky, strips, salmon candy or dry fish.

SCHOOL DISTRICTS
(SEE Education)

SEWARD

Located on Resurrection Bay, on the east coast of the Kenai Peninsula, Seward lies 127 miles south of Anchorage by road or 35 minutes by plane. Population is just over 2,600.

The city is named for U.S. Secretary of State William H. Seward, who was instrumental in negotiating the purchase of Alaska from Russia. The city of Seward was founded in 1902 by surveyors for the Alaska Railroad as the ocean terminus of the railroad.

Resurrection Bay is a year-round ice-free harbor, and Seward is an important cargo, fishing and cruise ship port. The economy of the town is based on tourism, a coal terminal, fisheries and government offices. Visitors enjoy wildlife and glacier tours, sportfishing expeditions, kayaking, photography safaris, nature cruises, RV facilities, hotels, dozens of bed-and-breakfast establishments, art galleries, coffeehouses, dogsled tours and hiking.

The Alaska SeaLife Center was unveiled in 1998. Other attractions in the area include Exit Glacier (accessible by trail), Kenai Fjords National Park and Chugach National Forest. From puffins to oyster-catchers to bald eagles, more than 100 species of birds abound. Substantial numbers of marine mammals inhabit or migrate through Seward's coastal waters, including sea otters, Steller sea lions, dolphins and Pacific gray whales.

For information about Kenai Fjords National Park, call (907) 224-7500; www.nps.gov/kefj. For information about Seward, contact the Chamber of Commerce at (907) 224-8051; www.seward.com.

SEWARD, WILLIAM H. (SEE ALSO
Russian Alaska) William H. Seward, the man who negotiated the purchase of Alaska from Russia, was born in New York in 1801. He was admitted to the bar in 1822 and eventually became governor

of New York for two terms (declining a third). Seward returned to his law practice until 1849, when he was elected to the United States Senate and served for two terms. In 1860, Seward was a candidate for the presidential nomination, but failing to receive it, he then supported Lincoln. He was appointed secretary of state in 1861, and held that position until 1869.

Due to the rapidly declining fur trade and the economizing and streamlining of the St. Petersburg regime in Russia, operations such as the Russian-American Co. were deemed expendable. The Grand Duke Constantine urged the sale of Alaska to the United States in 1857, but the American Civil War in 1861 forestalled talks.

On Good Friday, April 24, 1865, four conspirators, among them John Wilkes Booth, plotted triple assassinations set for 10:15 P.M. The targets were President Abraham Lincoln, Vice President Andrew Johnson, and Secretary of State William Henry Seward. While Booth mortally wounded President Lincoln at Ford's Theatre, his coconspirator, Lewis Powell, attacked Seward in his home. Still weak and bedridden from a carriage accident, Seward was stabbed and slashed in the face, and his adult son Frederick suffered a fractured skull, before Powell was subdued. So great were their injuries that neither man was expected to recover, but in time both regained their health.

At the conclusion of the war, the czar's representative began immediate negotiations with Secretary of State Seward, who was eager to buy, and a selling price of $7.2 million was agreed upon—about 2 cents an acre. The treaty was signed on March 30, 1867, and ratified by the Senate on June 20. Formal handover did not occur until Oct. 18.

Newspaper editorials denounced the acquisition of the apparently worthless real estate, ridiculed the agreement as "Seward's Folly" and caricatured Alaska as "Walrussia" and "Seward's Icebox."

After leaving office in 1869, Seward traveled around the world; he visited Alaska in 1869. He died in 1872.

SHIPPING

Vehicles. Persons shipping vehicles between Washington and Anchorage are advised to shop around for the carrier that offers the services and rates most suited to the shipper's needs. Not all carriers offer year-round service, and freight charges vary greatly depending upon the carrier and the weight and height of the vehicle. Rates quoted here are only approximate. Sample fares per unit: northbound, Washington to Anchorage, under 66 inches in height, $1,355; over 66 inches and under 78 inches, $1,730. Southbound, Anchorage to Washington, any unit under 84 inches, $931. Fuel surcharges and terminal handling charges may be applied.

Not all carriers accept rented moving trucks and trailers, and a few of those that do accept them require authorization from the rental company to carry its equipment to Alaska. Check with the carrier and your rental company before booking service.

Make your reservation at least two weeks in advance, and prepare to have the vehicle at the carrier's loading facility two days prior to sailing. Carriers differ on what items they allow to travel inside

An employee of the Alaska Sealife Center in Seward reported to us that when biologists had difficulty supplying live king crabs for exhibit in the $55 million facility, the Center finally called the mail-order live seafood department of Anchorage's New Sagaya grocery. The crabs are thriving and the visitors are happy as clams.

the vehicle, from nothing at all to goods packaged and addressed separately. Coast Guard regulations forbid the transport of vehicles holding more than one-quarter tank of gas, and none of the carriers listed allows owners to accompany their vehicles in transit. Remember to have fresh antifreeze installed in your car or truck prior to sailing.

At a lesser rate, you can ship your vehicle aboard a state ferry to southeastern ports. However you must accompany your vehicle or arrange for someone to drive it on and off the ferry at departure and arrival ports.

Carriers that will ship cars, truck campers, house trailers and motorhomes from Anchorage to Seattle/Tacoma include:

The Alaska Railroad, 327 W. Ship Creek Avenue, Anchorage 99501; (800) 321-6518; www.akrr.com.

Alaska Vehicle Transport, 467 W. Chipperfield Drive., Anchorage 99503; (800) 354-6007, (907) 561-2899; www.alaskavehicletransport.com.

Horizon Lines of Alaska, LLC, 1717 Tidewater Road, Anchorage 99501; (907) 274-2671; www.horizon-lines.com.

Totem Ocean Trailer Express, Inc., 2511 Tidewater Road, Anchorage 99501; (800) 234-8683; (907) 276-7252; www.totemocean.com.

In the Seattle/Tacoma area, contact:

A.A.D.A. Systems, P.O. Box 2323, Auburn, WA 98071; (800) 929-2773, (253) 826-8876; www.aada.net.

The Alaska Railroad, 5615 W. Marginal Way S.W., Seattle, WA 98106; (800) 843-2772; www.akrr.com.

Horizon Lines of Alaska, LLC, 1675 Lincoln Ave., Bldg. 300, Tacoma, WA 98421; (253) 882-1600; www.horizon-lines.com.

Totem Ocean Trailer Express, Inc., 500 Alexander Ave., Tacoma, WA 98421; (206) 628-4343 or (800) 426-0074 (outside Washington, Alaska and Hawaii); www.totemocean.com.

Vehicle shipment between southeastern Alaska ports and Seattle is provided by:

Alaska Marine Lines, 5615 W. Marginal Way S.W., Seattle, WA 98106;

Loose Shoes

A shipment of Nike athletic shoes bound for Tacoma, Washington, from Los Angeles spilled from the container ship during a storm in northern California and, as of mid-December 2002, was bobbing toward the Gulf of Alaska and the Aleutian coasts. Curtis Ebbesmeyer, a Washington state oceanographer, estimated that the 17,000 pairs of shoes were moving at a speed of up to 18 miles a day, and urged Alaskans to be on the lookout in a few months. One beachcomber from Washington's Olympic Peninsula told Ebbesmeyer that two shoes had washed up on a nearby beach in late January. To his dismay, they were sizes 10½ and 8½. Both were left shoes.

---

(206) 764-8346 or (800) 326-8346; www.lynden.com; (serves Ketchikan, Thorne Bay, Craig, Klawok, Wrangell, Petersburg, Sitka, Juneau, Haines, Skagway, Yakutat and Hawk Inlet).

Northland Services, 6700 W. Marginal Way S.W., Seattle, WA 98106; (800) 426-3113; www.northlandservicesinc.com; (serves Ketchikan, Craig, Thorne Bay, Metlakatla, Wrangell, Petersburg, Juneau, Sitka and Haines).

For shipping to Bush areas:

Northern Air Cargo, 3900 Old International Airport Road, Anchorage 99502; (907) 243-3331; (800) 727-2141; www.nacargo.com.

Household Goods and Personal Effects. Many moving van lines have service to and from Alaska through their agency connections in most Alaska and Lower 48 cities. To initiate service, contact the van line agents nearest your starting point.

Northbound goods are shipped to Seattle and transferred through a port agent to a waterborne vessel for transportation to Alaska. Few shipments go overland to Alaska. Southbound shipments are processed in a like manner through Alaska ports to Seattle, then on to the destination.

Haul-it-yourself companies provide service to Alaska. It is possible to ship a rented truck or trailer into southeastern Alaska aboard the carriers that accept privately owned vehicles. A few of the carriers sailing between Seattle and Anchorage also carry rented equipment. However, shop around for this service because it has not been common practice in the past—rates can be very high if the carrier does not yet have a specific tariff established for this type of shipment. You will not be allowed to accompany the rented equipment.

SITKA

SITKA The town of Sitka (population 8,833), one of the most scenic of Southeast Alaska's cities, is located on the west side of Baranof Island in the shadow of Mount Edgecumbe, about 95 miles southwest of Juneau.

Tlingit Indians originally occupied the townsite until Alexander Baranov, chief manager of the Russian–American Co., built a trading post and fort in 1799 just north of their settlement. The Indians burned down the fort, and in 1804 Baranov defeated the alliance of local Tlingits, driving them from their settlement and naming the site New Archangel Bay. By 1810, New Archangel was thriving as the capital of Russian Alaska. New Archangel was later renamed Sitka, meaning "by the sea" in the Tlingit language.

Today, tourism and commercial fishing are the mainstays of the town's economy. The climate of Sitka is mild and wet, with an annual precipitation of 95 inches and an average daily temperature of 33°F in January and 55°F in July.

Among the many sights in Sitka are Castle Hill, where Russia turned Alaska over to the United States in 1867; the Sitka Pioneers' Home (the first of six pioneers' homes built in Alaska); and Sitka National Historical Park, which reflects both the community's Tlingit heritage and its Russian past with two units: the Fort Site and the Russian Bishop's House. A replica of the old Russian Blockhouse, the original Russian Bishop's House (built in 1842) and the Indian Fort Site are preserved as part of the Sitka National Historical Park.

Visitors can see Sitka's historical roots in St. Michael's Cathedral, which contains priceless icons saved from a fire that destroyed the old cathedral in 1966. The existing structure was rebuilt from the original plans. The Sheldon Jackson Museum boasts one of the finest collections of Native arts and crafts in Alaska.

Located within walking distance from downtown Sitka is the Alaska Raptor Center, offering self-guided or guided interpretive tours. The facility treats injured birds of prey so they can return to the wild.

Annual events include the Sitka Summer Music Festival, featuring world-renowned chamber music, and the Island Institute Writers' Conference in June. Alaska Day Celebration in October celebrates the transfer of Alaska from the Russians. Whale Fest, an annual celebration of Sitka's marine life, takes place the first weekend in November.

For more information, contact the Sitka Convention and Visitors Bureau, P.O. Box 1226, Sitka 99835; (907) 747-5940; www.sitka.org.

SITKA SLIPPERS

SITKA SLIPPERS Also known as Alaska tennis shoes, Wrangell sneakers or Petersburg sneakers, Sitka slippers are heavy-duty rubber boots worn by residents of rainy southeastern Alaska.

An Anchorage builder once sent an entire harbor to Wainwright through the U.S. mail thanks to special bush delivery rates. The cost of stamps on 6,000 concrete blocs and 4,600 bags of cement was only a fraction of any other shipping method.

SKAGWAY (See also Chilkoot Trail)

Skagway, population 854, is found at the north end of Taiya Inlet on Lynn Canal in Southeast Alaska, about 90 air miles north of Juneau. The climate at Skagway averages 57°F in summer, 23°F in winter and the city has an annual precipitation of about 30 inches. Skagway serves as a gateway to the Alaska Highway in Southeast Alaska.

Skagway began as a gold rush town, springing up overnight as fortune seekers made their way from Skagway, up the White Pass and Chilkoot Trails, to the Yukon goldfields.

In July 1897, Skagway was little more than a tent town. Within months the town swelled to more than 20,000, with dance halls and gambling houses, saloons and residences. Frontier Skagway was once described as "hell on earth." Two years later the Klondike gold rush was over, and by 1903 Skagway's population had dwindled to 500.

Today, tourism is Skagway's main economic activity. The town serves the Alaska State Ferry and many cruise ships. Nearly 865,000 visitors came to Skagway during the summer of 2006. A favorite tourist attraction, the White Pass & Yukon Route railway, has added a new steam engine, No. 40, from Colorado. (See also Railroads)

Visitors may walk Skagway's historical district, featuring false-fronted buildings and boardwalks of the Klondike Gold Rush National Historical Park. Other attractions include the Trail of '98 Museum and The Days of 1898 Show with Soapy Smith, a play that relates the history of the town in the days of one of its most notorious con men.

Prepared hikers can climb the 33-mile Chilkoot Trail, the historic route of the gold seekers over 3,739-foot Chilkoot Pass to Lake Bennett. Relics are still visible along the trail.

For more information on Skagway, consult the Skagway Convention and Visitors Bureau, P.O. Box 1029, Skagway 99840; (907) 983-2854; fax (907) 983-3854; www.skagway.com.

SKIING

Both cross-country and downhill skiing are popular forms of outdoor recreation in Alaska from November through May. There are developed ski facilities in several Alaska communities, backcountry powder skiing is available by

The historic Slide Cemetery, near Skagway, holds the remains of avalanche victims on the Trail of '98. Photo by Tricia Brown.

charter helicopter or ski-equipped aircraft, and cross-country skiing opportunities are virtually limitless. It is also possible to ski during the summer months by chartering a plane to reach glacier skiing spots.

Several cross-country ski races are held each year. The largest, the Alaska Nordic Ski Cup Series, determines contestants for the Arctic Winter Games and Junior Olympic competitions. The series of five races is held in Anchorage, Homer, Salcha and Fairbanks. The World Masters Cross Country Ski Championships were held in Anchorage in February 1992, and Valdez is now home to the World Extreme Ski Championships in April.

In the 1992 Winter Olympics, Hilary Lindh of Juneau turned all eyes to Alaska when she won the silver medal for the downhill. Lindh's was the first individual-merit Olympic medal ever won by an Alaskan.

"Moe-mania" struck when Alaskan Tommy Moe captured the gold medal in the downhill and silver in the supergiant slalom at the 1994 Olympics in Lillehammer, Norway.

Anchorage. There are two major downhill ski areas in the Anchorage area: Alyeska Resort and Alpenglow at Arctic Valley.

Alyeska Resort, 40 miles southeast of Anchorage, is the state's largest ski resort, offering nine chairlifts with runs up to 2 miles long. Nearly half of the mountain is equipped for night skiing, and one chairlift is reserved for racer training. The resort also offers snowshoeing and cross-country skiing. Alyeska is open year-round, offering skiing from November through April and sightseeing in the summer. Hours of operation are 10:30 A.M. to 5:30 P.M. in winter, with Friday and Saturday night skiing until 9:30 P.M.; summer hours are 10:30 A.M. to 9:30 P.M. daily.

The Alyeska Prince Hotel, an eight-story, 307-room inn opened in 1994, includes six restaurants, an indoor pool, exercise and health facilities and meeting rooms. The resort features a high-speed tramway capable of carrying 60 passengers at a time to two restaurants high on the slopes.

Alpenglow, a few miles from Anchorage, is owned and operated by the Anchorage Ski Club, a nonprofit corporation. Arctic Valley is open on winter weekends and holidays. Facilities include two double chairlifts, a T-bar/Poma lift combination and three rope tows on beginner slopes.

Several smaller alpine slopes maintained by the municipality of Anchorage include Far North Bicentennial Park; Russian Jack Springs Park, with rope tows; and Hilltop, south of town, featuring the closest chairlift to the Anchorage area.

There are several popular cross-country ski trails in the Anchorage area in city parks. These include Russian Jack Springs, with nearly 5 miles of trails, all lighted; Kincaid Park, site of the first World Cup and U.S. National races in Alaska and the United States in March 1983, with 24 miles of trails, 6 miles lighted, and a warm-up chalet; Far North Bicentennial Park, with 3 miles of trails, about 2 miles lighted; Hillside Park, with 10.8 miles of trails, 1.5 miles lighted; Tony Knowles Coastal Trail, with 9 miles of trails, none lighted; and Chester Creek Greenbelt, with 6.2 miles of trails, none lighted.

Cross-country skiers also can find trails in Chugach State Park; in Hatcher Pass north of Anchorage and in the Turnagain Pass area; in Chugach National Forest, about 57 miles south of Anchorage; and at Sheep Mountain Lodge along the Glenn Highway. Call the Nordic Skiing Association, (907) 276-7609; www.anchoragenordicski.com.

Cordova. The Sheridan Ski Club operates the Mount Eyak Ski Hill about seven blocks from downtown Cordova. The season starts in mid-November and extends until mid-May, depending on snow.

Fairbanks. Cleary Summit and Skiland, about 20 miles from town on the Steese Highway, both privately owned and operated, have rope tows, with a chairlift at Cleary Summit; Birch Hill, located on Fort Wainwright, is mainly for military use; the University of Alaska has a small slope and rope tow; and Chena Hot Springs Resort at Mile 57 on the Chena Hot Springs Road has a small alpine ski area that uses a tractor to transport skiers to the top of the hill.

Popular cross-country ski trails in the Fairbanks area include Birch Hill recreation area, about 3 miles north of town on the Steese Expressway to a well-marked turnoff, then 2 miles in; the University of Alaska Fairbanks, with 26 miles of trails that lead to Ester Dome; Creamers Field trail near downtown; Salcha cross-country ski area, about 40 miles south of town on the Richardson Highway, with a trail system also used for ski races; Two Rivers trail area, near the elementary school at Mile 10 on the Chena Hot Springs Road; and Chena Hot Springs Resort, offering cross-country ski trails for both novice and more experienced skiers.

Kenai Peninsula. Most communities on the lower Kenai have trails or areas for skiing, including Anchor Point, Seldovia and Ninilchik. The best concentration of trails and slopes for Nordic, backcountry and downhill skiing is in the Homer area. Among them are Baycrest–Diamond Ridge, Homestead Trail, Ohlson Mountain and McNeil Canyon. Skiing on glaciers (accessible by helicopter) is possible in the Kenai Mountains across Kachemak Bay from Homer. Skijoring (cross-country with a dog towing you) is increasingly popular in Homer.

Palmer. Hatcher Pass, site of the Independence Mine State Park, north of Palmer, is an excellent cross-country ski area

A pair of backcountry skiers heads into Turnagain Pass in the Chugach National Forest. Photo by Roy Corral.

traditionally used for dyeing garments and footgear. Most sewers prefer sinew (animal tendon) as thread, although in some areas sinew cannot be obtained and waxed thread or dental floss is substituted. Skins commonly used for making parkas and mukluks include seal, reindeer, caribou and ground squirrel. Wolf and wolverine are prized for ruffs.

Parka styles, materials and ornamentation (such as pieced calfskin or beadwork trim) vary from village to village, and among Athabascan, Yup'ik, Iñupiat and Siberian Yupik sewers. The cut of parkas changes from north to south.

In most regions, mukluk styles and material vary with changes in season and weather conditions. Mukluks advertise the skill of their makers and the villages where they were made.

The manufacture of moccasins and children's toys, primarily clothed dolls and intricately sewn balls, still reflects the traditional ingenuity of skin sewers.

SKOOKUM *Skookum* means strong
or serviceable. The word originated with the Chehalis Indians of western Washington and was incorporated into the Chinook jargon, a trade language dating from the early 1800s.

A *skookum chuck* is a narrow passage between a saltwater lagoon and the open sea. In many areas of Alaska, because of extreme tides, *skookum chucks* may resemble fast-flowing river rapids during changes of the tide.

SOAPSTONE This soft, easily
worked stone is often carved into art objects by Alaskans. Most of the stone is imported. Alaska soapstone is mined in the Matanuska Valley by blasting, a process that leaves the stone susceptible to fracture when carved.

SOLDOTNA Located 150 highway
miles south of Anchorage, Soldotna is a hub city on the Kenai Peninsula. The Kenai River runs through Soldotna, and the town's fate and fortune are closely tied to the river, which is famous for its trophy-size king salmon. It's here that anglers meet up with guides and stock up on food and supplies for a day of fishing.

with several maintained trails. The lodge has a coffee shop and warm-up area. The ski area is open from October through May.

Southeast. Eaglecrest Ski Area on Douglas Island, 12 miles from Juneau, has a 4,800-foot-long chairlift, a Platter Pull lift, a 3,000-foot-long chairlift and a day lodge. Cross-country ski trails are also available. Eaglecrest is open from November to May. A few smaller alpine ski areas are located at Cordova, Valdez, Ketchikan and Homer. All have rope tows.

SKIN SEWING (SEE ALSO Beadwork;
Mukluks; Parka) The craft of sewing tanned hides and furs was highly developed among Alaska Natives. Although commercially made garments are now often worn by Eskimo villagers, women who are exceptional skin sewers still not only ensure the safety of family members who must face the harsh outdoors, but are regarded as a source of pride for the entire community.

Sewers place great importance on the use of specific materials, some of which are only available seasonally. Winter-bleached sealskin can only be tanned during certain seasons. Blood, alder bark and red ochre are

The city was named for nearby Soldotna Creek. Soldotna's first homesteaders were World War II veterans who were given a preference in selecting property in 1947. Today the city has more than 3,800 residents, many of whom make their living from commercial fishing, tourism and the oil and gas industry.

Soldotna is home of the Peninsula Winter Games each January, and the Progress Days Festival in July, which commemorates the completion of a gas pipeline in 1960.

The visitor center for the Kenai National Wildlife Refuge can be found in Soldotna. The sprawling refuge surrounds the town and offers fishing, canoeing and prime wildlife viewing. Information on the town is available from the Soldotna Chamber of Commerce and Visitor Information Center, 44790 Sterling Highway, Soldotna 99669; (907) 262-9814; www.soldotnachamber.com.

SOURDOUGH Carried by many early-day pioneers, this versatile, yeasty starter was used to make bread, doughnuts and hotcakes. Sourdough cookery remains popular in Alaska today. Because the sourdough supply is replenished after each use, it can remain active and fresh indefinitely.

A popular claim of sourdough cooks is that their batches trace back to pioneers at the turn of the century.

The name "sourdough" also came to be applied to any Alaska or Yukon old-timer.

SPEED LIMITS The basic speed law in Alaska states the speed limit is "no speed more than is prudent and reasonable." The maximum speeds are 15 miles per hour in an alley, 20 miles per hour in a business district or school zone, 25 miles per hour in a residential area and 55 miles per hour on most roadways. The speed limit on portions of the Parks, Seward and Glenn Highways is 65 miles per hour.

Locally, municipalities and the state may, and often do, reduce or alter maximums.

SPRUCE BARK BEETLE Spruce bark beetles are cold-blooded insect pests that feed on the trees' phloem, a thin layer of nutrient tissue just under the bark. Adults are blackish brown cylinders, about ¼ inch long, bearing reddish or black wing covers. The range of *Dendroctonus rufipennis* (Kirby) extends from Alaska through British Columbia to the Pacific Northwest, into areas of Montana, Idaho and Utah, and across the northern Great Lakes states and Canada's Maritime Provinces. The beetle has a one- to three-year life cycle and will infest all spruce species.

After the mosquito, the spruce bark beetle is the most notorious insect of the north. Over the past decade the boreal forests of Alaska have endured a widespread spruce beetle outbreak. Up to 3 million acres of spruce forest show the unsightly results of beetle activity, and billions of board feet of potential lumber have been lost in Alaska during the current beetle epidemic.

Within the Municipality of Anchorage, for example, more than 80,000 acres of spruce forest have seen up to 90 percent spruce mortality blamed on beetles. Since 1990, cumulative spruce beetle damage has been documented on Kenai Peninsula from aerial surveys. The damage covers more than 1.4 million acres belonging to multiple owners.

Because warmer, drier springs encourage beetles while simultaneously placing trees under moisture stress, the meteorological effects of El Niño and a general warming trend since the early 1990s are considered contributing factors. In turn, beetle-killed trees create a fire hazard as well as a windstorm hazard.

To promote their annual fund-raising concert, the Fraternal Order of Alaska State Troopers took out newspaper ads. The opening act on the bill was Brewer and Shipley, and the troopers' ad proudly proclaimed that their greatest hit was "One Toke Over The Line!"

STATE FORESTS Created in 1983,
the 1.78-million-acre Tanana Valley State Forest is located almost entirely within the Tanana River basin and includes 200 miles of the Tanana River.

Principal tree species are paper birch, quaking aspen, balsam poplar, black spruce, white spruce and tamarack. There are many rivers, streams and lakes with significant fish, wildlife, recreation and water values. Nearly all of the land is open for mineral development. Rivers and trails throughout the river basin provide additional access. The Eagle Trail State Recreation Site is the only developed facility and has 35 campsites. Contact the Regional Forester, Northern Region, 3700 Airport Way, Fairbanks 99709; (907) 451-2705.

The Haines State Forest was created in 1982 and contains 286,208 acres, including the watersheds of the major Chilkat River tributaries. Topography ranges from sea level to more than 7,000 feet. Forest growth is diverse, but is dominated by western hemlock, Sitka spruce, black cottonwood and willow.

About 15 percent of the forest is dedicated to timber harvest with an annual allowable harvest of 5.88 million board feet. All large commercial sales have been replanted since the 1970s.

The Haines State Forest also offers recreation such as hiking, hunting, fishing, skiing and camping. Contact the Division of Forestry's Haines Area Office, P.O. Box 263, Haines 99827; (907) 766-2120.

STATE PARK SYSTEM (See map
pages 204–205) The Alaska State Park system began in July 1959 with the transfer of federally managed campgrounds and recreation sites from the Bureau of Land Management to the new state. Since October 1970, the Division of Parks and Outdoor Recreation has managed the sites.

The Alaska State Park system consists of a wide variety of individual units divided into seven park management areas. Included are recreation sites, recreation areas, historical parks, historic sites, state trails, state parks (Afognak Island, Chilkat, Chugach, Denali, Kachemak Bay, Point Bridget, Shuyak Island and Wood–Tikchik), marine parks, a wilderness park, special management area and a preserve.

The Kenai River Special Management Area is renowned for its salmon fishing.

The 49,000-acre Alaska Chilkat Bald Eagle Preserve has the world's largest concentration of bald eagles. Wood–Tikchik State Park is Alaska's most remote state park and, with 1.6 million acres of wilderness, is the largest contiguous state park in the United States. All told, Alaska's State Park system embraces more than 3 million acres and hosts 3 million visitors a year.

Alaska State parks offers 56 cabins for rent from Fairbanks to Ketchikan. Fees range from $25 to $75 per night. Campsites are available on a first-come, first-served basis usually for $10 to $15 nightly. Daily use of improved boat launches is $10 to $15, depending on location. Use of sanitary

Basic Recipe for Sourdough Hotcakes

2 cups sourdough starter
2 tablespoons sugar
4 tablespoons oil
1 egg

½ teaspoon salt
1 scant teaspoon soda;
    full teaspoon if starter
    is real sour

Into the sourdough, dump sugar, salt, egg and oil. Mix well. Add soda the last thing, when ready for batter to hit the griddle. Dilute soda in 1 tablespoon of warm water. Fold gently into sourdough. *Do not beat*. Notice deep, hollow tone as sourdough fills with bubbles and doubles bulk. Bake on hot griddle to seal brown. Serve on hot plates.

—Ruth Allman, *Alaska Sourdough*

dump stations is $5. These are located at Big Delta State Historical Park, Byers Lake Campground, Chena River State Recreation Site, Eagle River Campground (Chugach State Park), Harding Lake State Recreation Area and Ninilchik State Recreation Area. There is free use of the dump station at Buskin River State Recreation Site. A daily parking fee of $1 to $6 is charged at selected park units.

A yearly camping pass is no longer available for residents; a yearly boat launch pass is $75; a yearly parking pass is $40. An Alaska resident may purchase a combination day use/boat launch pass for $100. A second pass of any kind may be purchased for a discount to the same resident family living at the same address. Second-pass prices are: boat launch, $40; daily parking, $20.

In addition to camping and picnicking, many units offer hiking trails, boating and fishing, as well as winter activities. Most developed campgrounds have picnic tables, firepits, water and latrines. General information on the state park system is available from Alaska State Park Information, 550 W. Seventh Ave., Suite 1260, Anchorage 99501-3561, or at www.alaskastateparks.org.

State park units are managed by seven area offices:

Chugach Area, HC 52, P.O. Box 8999, Indian 99540; (907) 345-5014.

Kenai Office, P.O. Box 1247, Soldotna 99669; (907) 262-5581.

Kodiak Area Office, 1400 Abercrombie Drive, Kodiak 99615; (907) 486-6339.

Mat–Su/Copper Basin Area Office, HC 32, Box 6706, Wasilla 99654; (907) 745-3975.

Northern Area, 3700 Airport Way, Fairbanks 99709; (907) 451-2695.

Southeast Area Office, 400 Willoughby Ave., Suite 400, Juneau 99801; (907) 465-4563.

Wood–Tikchik Office, 550 W. 7th Ave., Suite 1380, Anchorage 99501; (907) 269-8698.

Director's Office, 550 W. 7th Ave., Suite 1380, Anchorage 99501; (907) 269-8700.

STATE SYMBOLS

Flag—Alaska's state flag was designed in 1926 by Benny Benson, a seventh-grade Aleut boy who entered his design in a territorial flag contest. The Alaska Legislature adopted his design as the official flag of the Territory of Alaska on May 2, 1927. The flag consists of eight gold stars—the Big Dipper and the North Star—on a field of blue. In Benny Benson's words, "The blue field is for the Alaska sky and the forget-me-not, an Alaska flower. The North Star is for the future state of Alaska, the most northerly of the Union. The Great Bear—symbolizing strength."

(Continued on page 206)

203

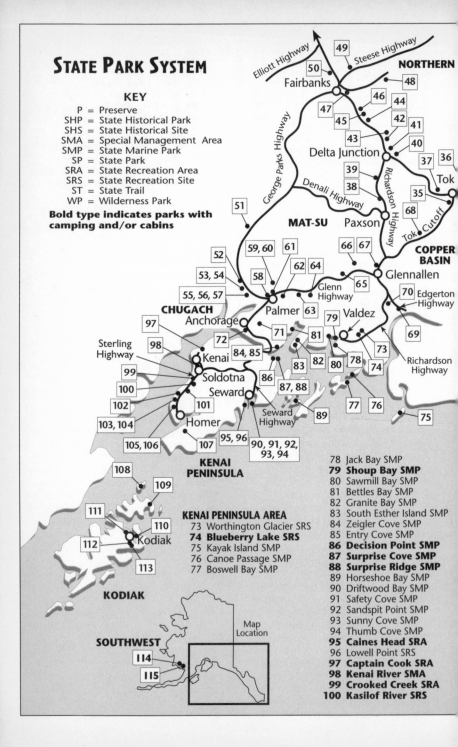

STATE PARK SYSTEM

KEY

P = Preserve
SHP = State Historical Park
SHS = State Historical Site
SMA = Special Management Area
SMP = State Marine Park
SP = State Park
SRA = State Recreation Area
SRS = State Recreation Site
ST = State Trail
WP = Wilderness Park

Bold type indicates parks with camping and/or cabins

NORTHERN

Elliott Highway
Steese Highway
Fairbanks
George Parks Highway
Delta Junction
Denali Highway
Richardson Highway
Paxson
Tok
Tok Cutoff
COPPER BASIN
Glennallen
Edgerton Highway
MAT-SU
CHUGACH
Anchorage
Glenn Highway
Palmer
Valdez
Richardson Highway
Sterling Highway
Kenai
Soldotna
Seward
Homer
Seward Highway
KENAI PENINSULA
KODIAK
Kodiak
SOUTHWEST
Map Location

KENAI PENINSULA AREA

73 Worthington Glacier SRS
74 Blueberry Lake SRS
75 Kayak Island SMP
76 Canoe Passage SMP
77 Boswell Bay SMP

78 Jack Bay SMP
79 Shoup Bay SMP
80 Sawmill Bay SMP
81 Bettles Bay SMP
82 Granite Bay SMP
83 South Esther Island SMP
84 Zeigler Cove SMP
85 Entry Cove SMP
86 Decision Point SMP
87 Surprise Cove SMP
88 Surprise Ridge SMP
89 Horseshoe Bay SMP
90 Driftwood Bay SMP
91 Safety Cove SMP
92 Sandspit Point SMP
93 Sunny Cove SMP
94 Thumb Cove SMP
95 Caines Head SRA
96 Lowell Point SRS
97 Captain Cook SRA
98 Kenai River SMA
99 Crooked Creek SRA
100 Kasilof River SRS

SOUTHEAST AREA
1 Dall Bay SMP
2 Black Sands Beach SMP
3 Totem Bight SHP
4 Refuge Cove SRS
5 Settlers Cove SRS
6 Grindall Island SMP
7 Thom's Place SMP
8 Joe Mace Island SMP
9 Petroglyph Beach SHS
10 Beecher Pass SMP
11 Security Bay SMP
12 Magoun Islands SMP
13 Baranof Castle SHS
14 Halibut Point SRS
15 Old Sitka SHP

16 Big Bear/Baby Bear SMP
17 Taku Harbor SMP
18 Oliver Inlet SMP
19 Funter Bay SMP
20 Shelter Island SMP
21 Juneau Trail Sys. ST
22 Johnson Creek SRS
23 Wickersham SHS
24 Gruening SHP
25 Eagle Beach SRA
26 Point Bridget SP
27 St. James Bay SMP
28 Sullivan Island SMP
29 Chilkat Islands SMP
30 Chilkat SP
31 Portage Cove SRS
32 Chilkoot Lake SRS
33 Mosquito Lake SRS
34 Chilkat Bald Eagle P

NORTHERN AREA
35 Eagle Trail SRS
36 Tok River SRS
37 Moon Lake SRS
38 Fielding Lake SRS
39 Donnelly Creek SRS

40 Clearwater SRS
41 Delta SRS
42 Big Delta SHP
43 Quartz Lake SRA
44 Birch Lake SRS
45 Harding Lake SRA
46 Salcha River SRS
47 Chena River SRS
48 Chena River SRA
49 Upper Chatanika River SRS
50 Lower Chatanika River SRA

MAT-SU/COPPER BASIN AREA
51 Denali SP
52 Willow Creek SRA
53 Nancy Lake SRA
54 Nancy Lake SRS
55 Rocky Lake SRS
56 Big Lake North SRS
57 Big Lake South SRS
58 Finger Lake SRS
59 Independence Mine SHP
60 Summit Lake SRS
61 Kepler-Bradley Lakes SRA
62 King Mountain SRS
63 Long Lake SRS
64 Matanuska Glacier SRS
65 Little Nelchina SRS
66 Lake Louise SRA
67 Dry Creek SRS
68 Porcupine Creek SRS
69 Liberty Falls SRS
70 Squirrel Creek SRS

CHUGACH AREA
71 Chugach SP
72 Potter Section House SHS

101 Johnson Lake SRA
102 Clam Gulch SRA
103 Ninilchik SRA
104 Deep Creek SRA
105 Stariski SRS
106 Anchor River SRA
107 Kachemak Bay SP&WP

KODIAK AREA
108 Shuyak Island SP
109 Afognak Island SP
110 Woody Island SRS
111 Fort Abercrombie SHP
112 Buskin River SRS
113 Pasagshak SRS

SOUTHWEST AREA
114 Wood–Tikchik SP
115 Aleknagik SRS

(Continued from page 203)

Alaska was proclaimed the 49th state of the Union on Jan. 3, 1959. The drafters of the constitution for Alaska stipulated that the flag of the territory would be the official flag of the state of Alaska. When the flag was first flown over the capital city on July 4, 1959, Benny Benson led the parade that preceded the ceremony, carrying the flag of eight stars on a field of blue, which he had designed 33 years before.

Seal—The first governor of Alaska designed a seal for the then-District of Alaska in 1884. In 1910, Gov. Walter E. Clark redesigned the original seal, which became a symbol for the new Territory of Alaska in 1912. The constitution of Alaska adopted the territorial seal as the seal for the state of Alaska in 1959.

Represented in the state seal are icebergs, northern lights, mining, agriculture, fisheries, fur seal rookeries and a railroad.

Song—*Alaska's Flag*
Eight stars of gold on a field of blue—
Alaska's flag.
May it mean to you the blue of the sea,
the evening sky,
The mountain lakes, and the flow'rs
nearby;
The gold of the early sourdough's dreams,
The precious gold of the hills and streams;
The brilliant stars in the northern sky,
The "Bear"—the "Dipper"—and, shining
high,
The great North Star with its steady light,
Over land and sea a beacon bright.
Alaska's flag—to Alaskans dear,
The simple flag of a last frontier.
(© University of Alaska)

The lyrics were written by Marie Drake as a poem that first appeared on the cover of the October 1935 *School Bulletin,* a territorial Department of Education publication that she edited while assistant commissioner of education.

The music was written by Elinor Dusenbury, whose husband, Col. Ralph Wayne Dusenbury, was commander of Chilkoot Barracks at Haines from 1933 to 1936. Elinor Dusenbury wrote the music several years after leaving Alaska because, she later said, "I got so homesick for Alaska I couldn't stand it."

The Territorial Legislature adopted "Alaska's Flag" as the official song in 1955.

Other State Symbols

Bird—Willow ptarmigan, *Lagopus lagopus,* a small arctic grouse that lives among willows and on open tundra and muskeg. Its plumage changes from brown in summer to white in winter; feathers develop in winter to cover the entire lower leg and foot. Common from Southwestern Alaska into the Arctic. Adopted in 1955.

Fish—King salmon, *Oncorhynchus tshawytscha,* an important part of the Native subsistence fisheries and a significant species to the state's commercial salmon fishery. This anadromous fish ranges from beyond the southern extremes of Alaska to as far north as Point Hope. Adopted in 1962.

Flower—Forget-me-not, *Myosotis alpestris.* Adopted in 1949.

Fossil—Woolly mammoth. Adopted in 1986.

Gem—Jade. Adopted in 1968.
(See Jade)

Insect—Four-spot skimmer dragonfly, *Libellula quadrimaculata.* Adopted in 1995.

Land Mammal—Moose, *Alces alces.* Adopted in 1998.

Marine Mammal—Bowhead whale, *Balaena mysticetus.* Adopted in 1983.
(See Whales; Whaling)

Mineral—Gold. Adopted in 1968.
(See Gold)

Motto—North to the Future. Adopted in 1967.

Sport—Dog mushing. Adopted in 1972. (See Dog Mushing)

Tree—Sitka spruce, *Picea sitchensis,* the largest and one of the most valuable trees in Alaska. Sitka spruce grows to 160 feet in height and 3 feet to 5 feet in diameter. Its long, dark green needles surround twigs that bear cones. It is found throughout Southeast and the Kenai Peninsula, along the Gulf Coast and along the west coast of Cook Inlet. Adopted in 1962. (See Timber)

Salmon fillets are hung to dry at a family fish camp near the village of Fort Yukon. From *Two in a Red Canoe* by Matt Hage and Megan Baldino.

SUBSISTENCE (SEE ALSO Whaling)

Alaska is unique among states in that it has established the subsistence use of fish and game as the highest-priority consumptive use. Alaska's legislature passed subsistence priority laws in 1978, 1986 and 1992. In addition, Congress passed a priority subsistence law in 1980 for federal lands in Alaska. Studies by the Alaska Department of Fish and Game have shown that many rural communities in Alaska depend upon subsistence hunting and fishing for a large portion of their diets and raw materials. Subsistence is defined by federal law as "the customary and traditional uses by rural Alaska residents of wild, renewable resources for direct personal or family consumption as food, shelter, fuel, clothing, tools or transportation; for the making and selling of handicraft articles out of nonedible by-products of fish and wildlife resources taken for personal or family consumption; and for the customary trade, barter or sharing for personal or family consumption."

Residents of rural areas annually harvest about 44 million pounds of wild foods; urban residents harvest about 10 million pounds. The wild food harvest is primarily fish (60 percent by weight), followed by land mammals (20 percent)

and marine mammals (14 percent); birds, shellfish and plants each account for 2 percent of the annual harvest. On average, rural Alaskans eat about a pound of wild food per person daily.

All state residents may hunt and fish for subsistence on all lands and waters in subsistence use areas, unless federal regulations limit opportunity to only federally qualified rural residents on federal lands and waters.

State subsistence fishing regulations are available from the Alaska Department of Fish and Game, P.O. Box 115526, Juneau 99811-5526; (907) 465-4147; www.subsistence.adfg.state.ak.us. State subsistence hunting regulations are included with the annually published state hunting regulations, also available from the Alaska Department of Fish and Game. Federal subsistence hunting and fishing regulations are available as a pamphlet from U.S. Fish and Wildlife Service, Office of Subsistence Management, 3601 C St., Suite 1030, Anchorage 99503; (800) 478-1456; (907) 786-3888; http://alaska.fws.gov/asm/index.cfm.

SUNDOGS

Sundogs are "mock suns" (parhelia) usually seen as bright, rainbow-hued spots on opposite sides of the winter sun. This optical phenomenon is created by the refraction of sunlight through tiny ice crystals suspended in the air. The ice crystals are commonly called "diamond dust."

TAIGA (See also Tundra) Taiga (TIE-guh) is
a moist coniferous forest that begins where the tundra ends. Taken from a Russian word that means "land of little sticks," this name is applied to the spindly white spruce and black spruce forests found in much of Southcentral and Interior Alaska.

TALKEETNA A small town in the
shadow of a very big mountain, Talkeetna is where climbers gather before making their assaults on Mount McKinley.

Located 120 miles north of Anchorage, Talkeetna sits at the confluence of the Susitna, Chulitna and Talkeetna Rivers. It was established as a trading post for gold miners in 1896 and boomed during construction of the Alaska Railroad in the early 1900s.

Today many of its 840 residents make their living by providing services to the more than 1,000 climbers who pass through the town each spring and from the fast-growing tourism industry. Local

The one-street town of Talkeetna is a favorite destination for Anchorage day-trippers. Photo by Tricia Brown.

air taxis fly climbers and tourists into the Alaska Range, landing on glaciers amid the towering peaks. Guides cater to those who come for hunting, fishing and rafting.

Talkeetna's downtown is a mix of rough-hewn log cabins and historic buildings and is listed on the National Register of Historic Places. The town has a friendly, comfortable feel to it and residents have come up with some unusual forms of entertainment. In December, the Talkeetna Bachelor Society invites single women to prove their skills in frontier living and meet local men at the Bachelor Auction and Wilderness Woman Contest. In July the Talkeetna Historical Society holds its Moose Dropping Festival. No, it doesn't involve dropping moose. Rather, it offers games and contests that center around the use of dried moose droppings.

TELECOMMUNICATIONS
History.

Alaska's first telecommunications project, begun in the 1860s, was designed to serve New York, San Francisco and the capitals of Europe, not particularly the residents of Nome or Fairbanks. It was part of Western Union's ambitious plan to link California to Russian America (Alaska) with an intercontinental cable that would continue under the Bering Strait to Siberia and on to Europe. Men and material were brought together on both sides of the Bering Sea, but with the first successful Atlantic cable crossing in 1867, the trans-Siberian intercontinental line was abandoned.

The first operational telegraph link in Alaska was laid in September 1900, when 25 miles of line were stretched from military headquarters in Nome to an outpost at Port Safety. It was part of a $450,000 plan by the Army Signal Corps to connect scattered military posts in the territory with the United States. By the end of 1903, landlines linked Western Alaska, Prince William Sound and Interior and Southeast Alaska, where underwater cable was used.

Plagued by ice floes that repeatedly tore loose the underwater cables laid across Norton Sound, the military developed wireless telegraphy to span the icy water in

1903. It was the world's first application of radio-telegraph technology and marked the completion of a fragile network connecting all military stations in Alaska with the United States. Sitka, Juneau, Haines and Valdez were connected by a line to Whitehorse, Yukon. Nome, Fort St. Michael, Fort Gibbon (Tanana) and Fort Egbert (Eagle) were linked with Dawson, Yukon. A line from Dawson to Whitehorse continued to Vancouver, British Columbia, and Seattle.

In 1905, the 1,500 miles of landlines, 2,000 miles of submarine cables and the 107-mile wireless link became the Washington–Alaska Military Cable and Telegraph System (WAMCATS). This, in turn, became the Alaska Communications System in 1935, reflecting a shift to greater civilian use and a system relying more heavily on wireless stations than landlines. The Alaska Communications System operated under the Department of Defense until RCA Corp., through its division RCA Alascom, took control in 1971.

Alaska Communications Systems Group, Inc.

Former telecommunications executives of Alascom and Pacific Telecom founded ACS in 1998. Headquartered in Anchorage, ACS is a facilities-based integrated telecommunications provider. The largest local exchange carrier (LEC) in Alaska, ACS is the only Alaskan provider that owns its entire infrastructure for local and long distance telephone, Internet and wireless services. ACS is one of two statewide service providers in the Alaska wireless market and the only one with a CDMA network offering high-speed mobile data via 3G EV-DO technology. In addition, through a partnership with DISH Network, ACS offers satellite television.

With a nearly 640-mile fiber-optic network, the ACS family of companies provides communications services to three-fourths of the state's population, serving residents in 74 communities, including the population centers of Anchorage, Fairbanks, Juneau, Kenai/Soldotna, Kodiak and Sitka. It is a publicly traded company (NASDAQ: ALSK).

Additional information on ACS is available at www.alsk.com.

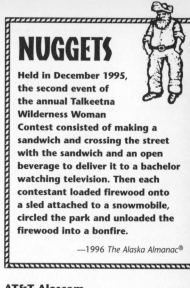

NUGGETS

Held in December 1995, the second event of the annual Talkeetna Wilderness Woman Contest consisted of making a sandwich and crossing the street with the sandwich and an open beverage to deliver it to a bachelor watching television. Then each contestant loaded firewood onto a sled attached to a snowmobile, circled the park and unloaded the firewood into a bonfire.

—1996 *The Alaska Almanac*®

AT&T Alascom.

What is now AT&T Alascom began as the Washington–Alaska Military Cable and Telegraph System (WAMCATS), a "talking wire" strung overland in 1900 across vast wilderness. Headquartered today in Anchorage, AT&T Alascom has some 300 employees and is a wholly owned subsidiary of AT&T. Both the Federal Communications Commission (FCC) and the Regulatory Commission of Alaska (RCA) certify AT&T Alascom.

On October 27, 1982, Alascom launched its own telecommunications satellite, *Aurora I,* from Cape Canaveral, Fla. It was the first telecommunications satellite dedicated to a single state, the first completely solid-state satellite to be placed in orbit and the first long-distance service to Alaska's smallest rural communities.

On May 29, 1991, Alascom launched its second satellite, *Aurora II,* from Cape Canaveral. Replacing the original *Aurora,* this satellite uses similar design, updated with modern technology, to increase life span. *Aurora III,* the company's third Alaska-dedicated satellite, was successfully launched from Kourou, French Guiana, on December 19, 2000.

AT&T Alascom has installed more than 350 microwave and satellite earth stations in Alaska. The company's integrated business and residential options include long distance, local, data, video and Internet services.

In 2005 AT&T joined forces with SBC Communications making AT&T Alascom part of the largest telecommunications company in the United States and one of the largest companies in the world.

For more information about the company go to www.AttAlascom.com.

General Communication Inc.

GCI (NASDAQ: GNCMA) is an Alaska-based company providing voice, video and data communication services to residential, commercial and government customers. It is listed on Standard & Poor's Small Cap Index, employs approximately 1,300 Alaskans and has revenues of $450 million.

Bob Walp and Ron Duncan founded GCI in 1979 in an Anchorage Bootlegger's Cove apartment. These entrepreneurs wanted to bring competition to long-distance calling with a breakthrough technology called "digital." At the time, phone calls averaged $1 per minute and service was anything but reliable. Consumers voted with their feet and within a few years GCI captured approximately 50 percent of the market.

GCI continued to grow in the Alaska market, and today provides local and long-distance calling, cable TV, broadband Internet, wireless, distance education and telehealth services throughout the state. These services are provided over company-owned, physically diverse and redundant fiber optic, satellite and metropolitan area network facilities

We asked a bookstore owner what Alaskans are most likely to read. She replied, "You mean other than *Playboy*?"

within Alaska and to the Lower 48. More information about the company can be found at www.gci.com.

TELEVISION STATIONS

Television in Anchorage and Fairbanks was available years before satellites were sent into orbit. The first satellite broadcast to the state was Neil Armstrong's walk on the moon in July 1969. Television reached the Bush in the late 1970s with the construction of telephone earth stations that could receive television programming via satellite transmissions. The state funds Alaska Rural Communication Service (ARCS), which broadcasts general and educational programming to more than 200 rural communities. For more information about ARCS, contact the Department of Administration, Information Services, 5900 E. Tudor Road, Anchorage 99507; (907) 269-5744.

Regular network programming (ABC, CBS, NBC and PBS) on a time-delayed basis is provided through the RATNet system. Most of the stations listed here carry a mixture of network programming, with local broadcasters specifying programming. Some stations carry locally produced programming. Cable television is available in areas throughout Alaska.

The following list shows the commercial and public television stations in Alaska:

Anchorage. KAKM Channel 7 (public television); 3877 University Drive, 99508.

KCFT (UHF 35/Cable 19); P.O. Box 210830, 99521-0830.

KDMD (UHF 33/GCI Cable 6); 1310 E. 66th Ave., 99518.

KIMO Channel 13; 2700 E. Tudor Road, 99507.

KTBY Channel 4; 440 E. Benson Blvd., 99503.

KTUU Channel 2; 701 E. Tudor Road, Suite 220, 99503.

KTVA Channel 11; 1007 W. 32nd Ave., 99503.

KYES Channel 5; 3700 Woodland Drive, Suite 800, 99517.

Bethel. KYUK Channel 15 (public television); P.O. Box 468, 99559.

NUGGETS

KUAC-TV in Fairbanks is watched by more people per capita than any other public television station in the country.

—*1989 The Alaska Almanac®*

Fairbanks. KATN Channel 2; 516 Second Ave., Suite 400, 99701.

KDMD-LPTV Channel 32; 1310 E. 66th Ave., Anchorage 99518.

KFXF Channel 7; 3650 Braddock St., Suite 2, 99701.

KTVF Channel 11; 3528 International Way, 99701.

KUAC Channel 9 (public television); University of Alaska, P.O. Box 755620, 99775-5620.

KXD Channel 13; 3650 Braddock St., Suite 2, 99701.

Juneau. KATH Channel 5/Cable 15; 1107 W. Eighth St., Suite 1, 99801.

KJUD Channel 8; 175 S. Franklin St., 99801.

KTNL-LPTV UHF 24/Cable 14; 3161 Channel Drive, 99801.

KTOO Channel 3/10 (public television); 360 Egan Drive, 99801.

Ketchikan. KUBD Channel 4/Cable 4; 516 Stedman St., 99901.

Kodiak. KMXT-LPTV Channel 9 (public television); 620 Egan Way, 99615.

K11UQ Channel 11, 1623 Mill Bay Road, 99615.

North Pole. KJNP Channel 4; P.O. Box 56359, 99705-1359.

Sitka. KSCT Channel 5; 520 Lake St., 99835.

KTNL Channel 13/Cable 6; 520 Lake St., 99835.

Unalaska. K08IW-LPTV Channel 8; P.O. Box 181, 99685

TIDES (See also Bore Tide) In southeastern Alaska, Prince William Sound, Cook Inlet and Bristol Bay, salt water undergoes extreme daily fluctuations, creating powerful tidal currents. Some bays may go totally dry at low tide.

A long-held belief that Cook Inlet's tide swings were the second-greatest in North America was shattered in 2003 when the *Anchorage Daily News* reported that measurement sites throughout Canada's Bay of Fundy and elsewhere sustained greater tidal fluctuations than those of Cook Inlet. Even so, with a maximum diurnal range of 38.9 feet during spring tides, upper Cook Inlet near Anchorage remains one of the greatest tidal ranges in North America. According to the National Ocean Service, the greatest single tidal swing measured near Anchorage totaled 39.4 feet and occurred on the night of Jan. 29–30, 1979. And the greatest tidal range in North America was measured at Minas Basin in Nova Scotia's Bay of Fundy, with spring tides over 50 feet.

Following are diurnal ranges for some coastal communities: Bethel, 4 feet; Cold Bay, 7.1 feet; Cordova, 12.4 feet; Haines, 16.8 feet; Herschel Island, 0.7 feet; Ketchikan, 15.4 feet; Kodiak, 8.5 feet; Naknek River entrance, 22.6 feet; Nikiski, 20.7 feet; Nome, 1.6 feet; Nushagak, 19.6 feet; Point Barrow, 0.4 feet; Port Heiden, 12.3 feet; Port Moller, 10.8 feet; Sand Point, 7.3 feet; Sitka, 9.9 feet; Valdez, 12 feet; Whittier, 12.3 feet; Wrangell, 15.7 feet; Yakutat, 10.1 feet.

TIMBER (See also Spruce Bark Beetle) According to the U.S. Forest Service, 127 million acres of Alaska's 365 million acres of land surface are forested, 12 million acres of which are classified as timberland. Commercial forestland is forestland capable of producing in excess of 20 cubic feet of industrial wood per acre per year.

Alaska has two distinct forest eco-systems: the Interior forest and the coastal rain forest. The vast Interior forest covers 114 million acres, extending from the south slope of the Brooks Range to the Kenai Peninsula, and from Canada to Norton Sound. More than 7 million acres of white spruce, paper birch, quaking aspen, black cottonwood and balsam poplar stands are considered timberland, comparing favorably in size and growth with forests of the Great Lakes states of Minnesota, Wisconsin and Michigan. There are an additional 2.8 million acres capable of producing as timberland but which are unavailable for harvest because they are in parks or wilderness.

The state forest in the Tanana Valley contains half of the Tanana basin's productive timberland, about 1.1 million acres. A state-prepared prospectus to encourage investment proposals can be seen at www.alaskaforestproducts.com. The state is currently gathering more timber inventory data to aid potential timber industry investors.

The coastal rain forests extend from Cook Inlet to the Alaska–Canada border south of Ketchikan, and they continue to provide the bulk of commercial timber volume in Alaska. Of the 13.9 million acres of forested land, 5 million acres are classified as timberland. Under the management plan for the Tongass National Forest in southeastern Alaska, only 576,000 acres were available for harvest. An additional 2.6 million acres of timber stands are capable of producing more than 20 cubic feet per acre per year, but are in parks and wilderness.

Western hemlock and Sitka spruce provide most of the timber harvest for domestic and export lumber and pulp markets. Western red cedar and Alaska cedar make up most of the balance, along with mountain hemlock, lodgepole pine and other species.

Lands from which substantial volumes of timber are harvested are divided into two distinct categories: privately owned by Native corporations and villages under the 1971 Native Claims Settlement Act, and publicly owned and managed federal, state and borough lands. Timber harvests from publicly owned lands are carried through short-term open sales and Small Business Administration set-aside sales.

The forest products of Alaska are also divided somewhat along the same lines as land ownership. By federal law, timber harvested from federal lands cannot be exported without processing. While processors dependent on federal lands produce primarily rough-sawn lumber, pulpwood, veneer, railroad ties and chips, the Native corporations primarily produce round logs, which find more buyers along the Pacific Rim, especially in Japan and Korea. The Alaska forest manufacturing industry does some custom cutting for the Japanese market, but most of the products from the mills are sold in the Pacific Northwest.

There are about 20 mills in Southeast Alaska with a combined capacity of about 370 million board feet per year. Three of the larger mills are located in Wrangell, Klawock and Ketchikan. In addition, a group of investors is seeking a timber supply to allow the opening of an existing veneer plant in Ketchikan.

The timber supply from federal land, which comprises about 94 percent of the land in Southeast Alaska, has dropped from over 400 million board feet in 1990 to about 50 million board feet for the last few years. Meanwhile, the markets for forest products in the Pacific Northwest are at sustained high levels. Both the Forest Service and the State of Alaska have committed to restoring a timber supply adequate to support a viable, sustainable manufacturing industry. In 2006, about 75 million board feet of timber were harvested from private lands in Southeast Alaska, and

NUGGETS

Larry Hadselford, the camp cook at the El Cap Gold Mine near Ketchikan, got more than he bargained for when he walked to the camp outhouse. He was just about to sit down when he heard a noise. Turning around he looked straight into a bear's eyes, its head sticking up through the seat hole. Four men shoved the outhouse over, freeing the animal, which promptly ran away.

—1988 *The Alaska Almanac®*

another 30 million board feet from State and Mental Health Trust timberlands. In addition, about 35 million board feet of timber were harvested from private timberlands on Afognak Island. For more timber information: www.akforest.org; www.dnr.state.ak.us/forestry; www.fs.fed.us/r10.

TIME ZONES

More than 90 percent of Alaska residents are on Alaska time, one hour behind the West Coast (Pacific time). The far reaches of the Aleutian Islands and St. Lawrence Island observe Hawaii–Aleutian time, two hours behind Pacific time.

Until 1983, Alaska had four time zones: Pacific time (in southeastern Alaska); Yukon time (in Yakutat); Alaska time (from just east of Cold Bay and west of Yakutat northward, including Nome); and Bering time (including Nome, far Western Alaska and the Aleutians). Consolidating these time zones aided business and improved communications.

TOTEM POLES (SEE ALSO Native Arts and Crafts; Potlatch)

In the prehistory of southeastern Alaska and the Pacific Northwest coast, the Native way of life was based on the rich natural resources of the land, respect for living things and a unique and complex social structure. Totemic art reflects this rich culture.

Carved from the huge cedar trees of the northern coast, totem poles are a traditional art form among the Natives of the Pacific Northwest and southeastern Alaska. Although the best-known type of totem pole is tall and freestanding, totemic art also is applied to house frontal poles, house posts and mortuary poles. Totem poles are bold statements that make public records of the lives and history of the people who had them carved; they represent pride in clans and ancestors.

Animals of the region are most often represented on the poles. Commonly depicted are eagles, ravens, frogs, bears, beavers, wolves and whales. Also represented are figures from Native mythology: monsters with animal features, humanlike spirits and legendary ancestors.

A Tlingit Octopus Totem pole at the Totem Bight State Park in Ketchikan. From *Alaska's Totem Poles* by Pat Kramer.

Occasionally included are objects, devices, masks and charms and, more rarely, art illustrating plants and celestial phenomena.

The poles were traditionally painted with natural mineral and vegetable pigments. Salmon eggs were chewed with cedar bark to form the binder for the ground pigment. Traditional colors are black, white and red-brown; green, blue-green, blue and yellow are also used, depending on tribal convention.

This year, Alaska will host nearly 1.5 million tourists and visitors. Last year, one of them asked the concierge at the Millennium Hotel, "What time does the 3 o'clock shuttle leave?"

The range of colors broadened when modern paints became available. Totem art grew rapidly in the late 18th century, with the introduction of steel European tools acquired from explorers and through the fur trade. Large totem poles were a thriving cultural feature by the 1830s and signified social standing. For example, wealthy Tlingit often commissioned the Tsimshian to carve totems for them.

Totem-pole carving almost died out between the 1880s and 1950s during the enforcement of a law forbidding the potlatch, the core of Northwest Coast Indian culture. The potlatch ceremony is held to observe events such as marriages; guests are invited from near and far, dancing and feasting take place, property is given away and often poles are raised to commemorate the event. Since the anti-potlatching law was repealed in 1951, a revival of Native culture and the arts has taken place, and many tribes are actively carving and raising poles again. (See Potlatch)

Totem poles were left to stand as long as nature would permit, usually about 50 to 60 years. Once a pole became so rotten that it fell, it was left to decay naturally or used for firewood. Some totem poles still standing in parks today are 40 to 50 years old. Heavy precipitation and acid muskeg soils hasten decomposition even though cedar is resistant to decay.

Collections of fine totem poles may be seen either outdoors or in museums in several Alaska communities including Ketchikan, Wrangell, Hydaburg and Sitka. Carvers practice their art at cultural centers in those towns as well as in Haines and Saxman.

TOURISM Although Alaska has been attracting tourists for more than 100 years, residents sometimes are surprised that the visitor industry has quietly become one of the state's top basic-sector employers. A 2004 study conducted for the Alaska Department of Commerce, Community and Economic Development estimates that the travel and tourism industry accounts for about 39,420 direct and indirect jobs and $1.15 billion in labor income. At least 13 of Alaska's top 100 employers are tied to the visitor industry. Tourism is a renewable resource that brings dollars to all regions of Alaska. The total spending by and on behalf of travelers is $1.6 billion. The direct impact of sales and services to travelers for recreation, lodging, transportation, food and beverages, souvenirs, clothing and other expenses is $856 million.

The state of Alaska has long recognized the value of the visitor industry. For the fiscal year 2006, the Alaska State Legislature appropriated up to $5 million toward an estimated $10 million tourist marketing campaign to promote Alaska

---

A Fallen 'Giant'

For more than 20 years, a single white spruce stood five miles from town in the treeless tundra of the Baldwin Peninsula. Rumored to have been planted by homesick Air Force personnel from a nearby base, the tree was surrounded by a white picket fence and a sign designating the tree the "Kotzebue National Forest."

In June 1993, the tree was pushed over after it had been partially cut by vandals, leaving only a stump.

A radio broadcast about the felling caught the attention of Matt Tyrala of Anchorage, executive director of Alaska TREES (Tree Recycling and Ecology Education Systems). Tyrala arranged to have a 10-year-old, 6-foot replacement white spruce shipped free from Nenana by Alaska Airlines—a gift worth $2,000 for pining Kotzebue residents. The previous "forest" had been just 3 feet tall.

—1994 *The Alaska Almanac*®

as a visitor destination. The Alaska Travel Industry Association will contribute up to $5 million to the campaign.

Alaska welcomed more than 1.6 million summer visitors between May 1 and Sept. 30, 2006. This represents a slight decrease from the total number of summer visitors to Alaska in 2005. With Alaska's population estimated at 663,661 as of June 30, 2006, the presence of more than 1.6 million visitors translates into more than two visitors for every resident of the state. The present growth in tourism is primarily due to the continued increases in cruise ship visitors.

The majority of summer visitors were cruise ships passengers (59 percent), while most others arrived by international and domestic air (36 percent). The remaining 5 percent of Alaska's summer visitors arrived by highway or ferry.

Alaska's scenic beauty, trophy fish, abundant wildlife and unique history remain its biggest attractions. The adventure travel market is growing in Alaska; an increasing number of visitors participate in river rafting, kayaking, backcountry trekking and other wilderness experiences.

Further information is available from the Alaska Travel Industry Association at www.travelalaska.com or www.alaskatia.org, and from the Alaska Office of Economic Development, www.commerce.state.ak.us/oed.

TREES AND SHRUBS (See also

Spruce Bark Beetle) According to the U.S. Department of Agriculture, the number of native tree species in Alaska is less than in any other state. Species of trees and shrubs in Alaska fall under the following families: yew, pine, cypress, willow, bayberry, birch, mistletoe, gooseberry, rose, maple, elaeagnus, ginseng, dogwood, crowberry, pyrola, heath, dispensia, honeysuckle and composite.

Commercial timber species include white spruce, Sitka spruce, western hemlock, mountain hemlock, western red cedar, Alaska cedar, balsam poplar, black cottonwood, quaking aspen and paper birch.

Rare tree species include the Pacific yew, Pacific silver fir, subalpine fir, silver willow and Hooker willow.

North of the Brooks Range, the tundra-covered land slopes gently toward the Arctic Ocean. Photo by Tricia Brown.

TUNDRA Characteristic of arctic and subarctic regions, tundra is a treeless plain that consists of moisture-retaining soils and permanently frozen subsoil. Tundra climates, marked by frequent winds and low temperatures, are harsh on plants. Soils freeze around root systems and winds wear away portions exposed above rocks and snow. The three distinct types of Alaska tundra—wet, moist and alpine—support low-growing vegetation that includes a variety of delicate flowers, mosses and lichens.

According to *Alaska Science Nuggets,* every acre of arctic tundra contains more than 2 tons of live fungi that survive by feeding on dead organic matter. Since the recession of North Slope ice age glaciers 12,000 years ago, a vegetative residue has accumulated a layer of peat 3 to 6 feet thick overlying the tundra.

ULU A traditional Eskimo woman's knife designed for scraping and chopping, this fan-shaped tool was originally made of stone with a bone handle. The term derives from the Yup'ik word *uluaq* and the Siberian Yupik word *ulaaq.*

Today, an *ulu* is often shaped from an old saw blade, and a wood handle is attached. Commercially made *ulus* are sold in the tourist trade. Signs at Alaska's major airports remind travelers to check their *ulus* in their baggage.

UMIAK (See also Baidarka)

The Eskimo *umiak* is a traditional skin-covered boat whose design has changed little over the centuries. Although *umiaks* are mostly powered by outboard motors today, paddles are still used when stalking game and when ice might damage a propeller. Because *umiaks* must often be pulled long distances over pack ice, the boats are lightweight and easily repaired. The frames are wood, often driftwood found on beaches, and the covering can be sewn if punctured. The bottom is flat and the keel is bone, which prevents the skin from wearing out as it is pulled over the ice.

Female walrus skins are the preferred covering because they are the proper thickness when split (bull hides are too thick and often scarred) and because it takes only two skins to cover a boat. Sometimes female walrus skins are unavailable, so skins of the bearded seal, or *oogruk,* may be used. It may take six or seven skins to cover an umiak.

Umiak is the Iñupiat word for skin boat and is commonly used by the coastal Eskimos throughout Alaska. St. Lawrence Islanders speak the Siberian Yupik language, and their word for skin boat is *angyaq.*

UNALASKA/DUTCH HARBOR (See also Military; World War II)

Located on Unalaska Island, the second-largest island in the Aleutian chain and 800 miles southwest of Anchorage, Ounalashka, or Unalaska, was the Russian–American Co.'s headquarters for the sea otter fur trade in the 1700s. At the turn of the 20th century, Unalaska was a major stop for ships heading to and from the Nome goldfields.

The international port of Dutch Harbor is located across a bridge from Unalaska on Amaknak Island. The U.S. Army and Navy began building installations there in 1939; in June 1942, Japanese bombers attacked the area, and most of the local Aleut people were evacuated. A memorial to those killed in the Aleutians in World War II is in Memorial Park near the cemetery.

Unalaska/Dutch Harbor is a significant port and gateway to the Bering Sea region. The climate is referred to as the "Cradle of the Storms." Here the warm Japan Current meets the colder air and water currents of the Bering Sea, creating an annual rainfall of 60.5 inches and colossal winds. Rare plants and birds and the historic Cathedral of the Holy Ascension of Christ draw visitors to the island. The Unalaska/Dutch Harbor area remains ice-free year-round and large canneries form the basis of the local economy, making it one of the most productive seafood processing ports in the United States.

UNIVERSITIES AND COLLEGES

Higher education in Alaska may be achieved through the University of Alaska system and private institutions. The university system includes three regional multicampus universities, one community college and a network of services for rural Alaska. The three regional institutions are the University of Alaska Anchorage (UAA), the University of Alaska Fairbanks (UAF) and the University of Alaska Southeast (UAS). University of Alaska institutions enrolled more than 34,000 students in 2006.

Campuses of the University of Alaska Southeast are located in Juneau, Sitka and Ketchikan. The University of Alaska Anchorage campus in that city is supplemented by a network of extended schools that includes Kenai Peninsula College, Kodiak College, Matanuska–Susitna College and Prince William Sound Community College, as well as the Chugiak–Eagle River

This winter's Food Bank of Alaska newsletter reported that the "Point McKenzie Correctional Farm, a facility for lower level offenders, has a meat-processing facility and trains *inmates* how to be *butchers.*"

No Stroll in the Woods

After a long time of tramping upward through moss-floored spruce forest and then copses of dwarf birch, we at last came to the timberline, the bare heath dotted with purple anemones and yellow dwarf daisies and mountain avens, and this should have been pure pleasure. But there is a test involved in all of this climbing. After miles of muskeg, your leg muscles are heavy and complaining. . . . as we neared the top, I said: "If I just sat down here, would you find me on your way back?"

"No," Olaus said emphatically, "I don't want to come back this way; I want to go down over there to the left, on that other slope. You're doing fine—just fine—you can make it!"

So I did.

—Margaret E. Murie, *Two in the Far North*

Campus, a branch campus in Kachemak Bay and several military centers.

University of Alaska Anchorage units include the Center for Alcohol and Addiction Studies; Center for Economic Development; Center for Economic Education; Center for Human Development, University Affiliated Program; Environment and Natural Resources Institute, which includes the Alaska Natural Heritage Program, Alaska State Climate Center and the Arctic Environment and Natural Resources Institute; Institute for Circumpolar Health Studies; Institute of Social and Economic Research; and the Justice Center.

University of Alaska Fairbanks includes the main campus in Fairbanks; Bristol Bay Campus in Dillingham; Chukchi Campus in Kotzebue; Interior Campus with offices in Fairbanks and centers in Fort Yukon, McGrath, Tok and Unalaska; Kuskokwim Campus in Bethel; Northwest Campus in Nome; and Tanana Valley Campus in downtown Fairbanks.

University of Alaska Fairbanks research facilities include the Alaska Cooperative Fishery and Wildlife Research Unit; Alaska Native Language Center; Alaska Synthetic Aperture Radar Facility; Arctic Region Supercomputing Center; Center for Cross-Cultural Studies; Center for Global Change and Arctic Systems Research; Consortium for Research in Rural Alaska; Environmental Technology Laboratory; Fishery Industrial Technology Center; Forest Products Technology Center; Forest Soils Laboratory; Geophysical Institute; Georgeson Botanical Garden; Institute of Arctic Biology; Institute of Marine Science; Institute of Northern Engineering; Juneau Center for Fisheries and Ocean Sciences; Large Animal Research Station; Mineral Industry Resource Laboratory; Petroleum Development Laboratory; Poker Flat Research Range; Polar Ice Coring Office; Seismology Laboratory; Transportation Research Center; University of Alaska Museum; Water Research Center; and West Coast National Undersea Research Center.

The Alaska Cooperative Extension and the Alaska Sea Grant College Program interpret and report some of the university's research results to the residents of Alaska.

For more information:
University of Alaska Anchorage, 3211 Providence Drive, Anchorage 99508, www.uaa.alaska.edu; **Kenai Peninsula College,** 34820 College Drive, Soldotna 99669, www.kpc.alaska.edu; **Kodiak College,** 117 Benny Benson Drive, Kodiak 99615, www.koc.alaska.edu; Matanuska–Susitna College, P.O. Box 2889, Palmer 99645, www.matsu.alaska.edu; **Prince William Sound Community College,** P.O. Box 97, Valdez 99686, www.uaa.alaska.edu/pwscc.

University of Alaska Fairbanks, P.O. Box 757500, Fairbanks 99775, www.uaf.edu; Bristol Bay Campus, P.O. Box 1070, Dillingham 99576, www.uaf.edu/bbc; Chukchi Campus, P.O. Box 297, Kotzebue 99752-0297, www.chukchi.alaska.edu; College of Rural Alaska, P.O. Box 756500, Fairbanks 99775-6500, www.uaf.edu/rural; Interior Aleutians Campus, P.O. Box 756720, Fairbanks 99775-6720, www.uaf.edu/iac; Kuskokwim Campus, P.O. Box 368, Bethel 99559, www.bethel.uaf.edu; Northwest Campus, Pouch 400, Nome 99762, www.nwc.uaf.edu; Tanana Valley Campus, 604 Barnette Street, Fairbanks 99775, www.tvc.uaf.edu.

University of Alaska Southeast, Juneau Campus, 11120 Glacier Highway, Juneau 99801, www.uas.alaska.edu; **Ketchikan Campus,** 2600 Seventh Ave., Ketchikan 99901, www.ketch.alaska.edu; **Sitka Campus,** 1332 Seward Ave., Sitka 99835, www.uas.alaska.edu/sitka.

For information on private institutions of higher learning:

Alaska Bible College, P.O. Box 289, Glennallen 99588; www.akbible.edu.

Alaska Pacific University, 4101 University Drive, Anchorage 99508; www.alaskapacific.edu.

Sheldon Jackson College, 801 Lincoln St., Sitka 99835; www.sheldonjackson.edu.

Many other schools and institutes in Alaska offer religious, vocational and technical study. For a listing of these and other schools, write for the Directory of Postsecondary Educational Institutions in Alaska, Alaska Commission on Postsecondary Education, 3030 Vintage Blvd., Juneau 99801-7100.

> The University of Alaska Anchorage campus has 16 acres of roof, 17 acres of lawn, 26 acres of interior floor space, 46 acres of pavement, and uses 80 acres of toilet paper each year.

VENIAMINOV, IOANN

Father Ioann (Ivan Popov) Veniaminov (1797–1879) often has been called "Paul Bunyan in a cassock." A figure of commanding height and proportions, a linguistic genius who could build furniture and clocks with his own hands, Veniaminov was a central figure in early efforts to convert Alaska's Native population to the Russian way of life through Orthodoxy.

Veniaminov was a Russian Orthodox priest who served as a missionary in the Aleutians and in Southeast Alaska. In each place, he learned the local language and devised a written alphabet for the local Native group, allowing him to translate some books of the Bible. In the Aleutians he traveled thousands of miles by kayak to visit his enormous parish. He rose to become Bishop of Russian America, with his headquarters at Sitka, and eventually was appointed Metropolitan of Moscow. His writings on Aleut language and ethnology are still standard references. A volcano on the Aleutian Peninsula is named after him. Revered as Saint Innocent, Veniaminov is one of the four Orthodox saints of Alaska.

VOLCANOES (SEE map, pages 126–27)

Volcanoes on the Aleutian Islands, on the Alaska Peninsula and in the Wrangell Mountains are part of the "Ring of Fire" that surrounds the Pacific Ocean basin. More than 80 potentially active volcanoes dot Alaska, about half of which have had at least one blast since 1760, the date of the earliest written record of eruptions.

Pavlof Volcano, in the Aleutian Range, is one of the most active of Alaska volcanoes, having had more than 40 reported eruptions since 1790. A spectacular eruption of Pavlof in April 1986 sent ash 10 miles high, causing black snow to fall on Cold Bay; it remained active through August 1988, producing lava and mud flows. The March 27, 1986, eruption of Augustine Volcano (4,025 feet) in lower Cook Inlet sent ash 8 miles high and disrupted air traffic in Southcentral Alaska for several days.

Southcentral's Mount Redoubt erupted Dec. 14, 1989, its first eruption since 1968.

Mount Augustine's 1986 eruption halted air traffic. Photo by B. Young, USGS, courtesy Alaska Volcano Observatory. From *Alaska's Natural Wonders* by Robert H. Armstrong and Marge Hermans.

The biggest blasts sent ash throughout most of Southcentral Alaska and disrupted air traffic. This eruption continued until April 1990. Mount Spurr erupted in June, August and September 1992. Anchorage received the brunt of ash fallout from the August eruption, which halted air traffic out of the city for several days. Flights were briefly interrupted again during the September eruption.

In January 2006, the Augustine Volcano, located on an uninhabited island in Southcentral Alaska, began to erupt for the first time in 20 years. The series of eruptions prompted ash fall advisories and occasional interruptions in airline schedules.

The most violent Alaska eruption in historical times occurred over a 60-hour period in June 1912 from Novarupta Volcano. The eruption darkened the sky over much of the Northern Hemisphere for several days, deposited almost a foot of ash on Kodiak, 100 miles away, and filled the Valley of Ten Thousand Smokes (within Katmai National Park) with more than 2.5 cubic miles of ash during its brief but extremely explosive duration. The eruption caused the collapse of adjacent Mount Katmai volcano to form a crater

2.5 miles across and 3,400 feet deep. This crater now contains a deep blue lake.

About 80 percent of active volcanoes in the U.S., and 8 percent of the world's known above-water historically active volcanoes are in Alaska. Hardly a year goes by without one or two eruptions from a volcano in this state.

1645 B.C.—Aniakchak Caldera forms on the Alaska Peninsula, ejecting over 16 cubic miles of debris and creating a crater six miles across.

About 1600 B.C.—Hayes Volcano destroys itself in seven eruptions within 100 years, each eruption producing as much ash as the 1980 eruption of Mount St. Helens.

1796 A.D.—Bogoslof erupts

1812—Augustine Volcano

1883—Fire Island appears, another result of Bogoslof eruptions; Augustine Volcano

1908—Augustine Volcano

1909—Bogoslof

1912—Novarupta/Katmai

1931—Bogoslof; Aniakchak Caldera, one of the largest historical eruptions in Alaska

1935—Augustine Volcano

1953—Mount Spurr

1953–74—Trident

1963–64—Augustine Volcano

1976—Augustine Volcano

1977—Ukinrek Maars

1980—Makushin

1986—Augustine Volcano

1986–88—Pavlof

1989–90—Mount Redoubt

1990—Kiska

1992—Mount Spurr

1999—Shishaldin

2005–06—Augustine Volcano

WAVES (See also Bore Tide; Earthquakes; Tides) Alaska's recorded seismic history is very short yet extremely active. Alaska responds to movement in the Aleutian–Alaska megathrust zone, where the edge of the Pacific plate descends under the North American plate. These vertical movements of the earth's crust result in vertical motion of the seafloor, which can produce great seismic waves known as tsunamis. In fact, these crustal movements in the Alaska

Peninsula, Aleutians and Gulf of Alaska can produce Pacific-wide tsunamis.

In southeastern Alaska, the Fairweather Fault lies inland. Though this fault has not triggered tectonic tsunamis as in other Alaska areas, it can unleash nearby underwater landslides, which may cause tsunamis.

According to the Alaska Tsunami Warning Center in Palmer, Alaska has had seven tsunamis that caused fatalities in recorded history. These were of local origin and occurred between 1788 and 1964. Tsunamis originating in Alaska Pacific waters have caused all of the fatalities reported on the West Coast and in Alaska, and most of those in Hawaii. The most recent damaging tsunami was in 1964 following the March 27 Good Friday earthquake. That wave destroyed three Alaska villages before reaching Washington, Oregon and California, and continued to cause damage as far away as Hawaii, Chile and Japan.

The word *tsunami* is taken from the Japanese words *tsu,* meaning "harbor," and *nami,* meaning "great wave." Often called tidal waves, tsunamis are not caused by tides. Generated by earthquakes occurring on or below the seafloor, tsunamis can race across the Pacific Ocean at speeds of up to 600 miles per hour. Tsunamis rarely cross the Atlantic. Traveling across the open ocean, the waves are only a few feet high and can be up to 100 miles from crest to crest. They cannot be seen from an airplane or felt in a ship at sea. Once they approach shore, however, shallower water causes the waves to grow taller by increasingly restricting their forward motion. Thus, a 2-foot wave traveling 500 miles per hour in deep water becomes a 100-foot killer at 30 miles per hour as it nears the shore. The wave action of a tsunami can repeat every 15 to 30 minutes, and the danger for a given area is generally not considered over until the area has been free from damaging waves for two hours.

Another type of wave action that occurs in Alaska is a seiche. A seiche is a long, rhythmic wave in a closed or partially closed body of water. Caused by earthquakes, winds, tidal currents or pressure, the motion of a seiche resembles the back and forth movement of a tipped bowl of water. The water moves only up and down, and can remain active from a few minutes to several hours. The highest recorded wave in Alaska, 1,740 feet, was the result of a seiche that took place in Lituya Bay on July 9, 1958. This unusually high wave was caused by an earthquake-induced landslide that stripped trees from the opposite side of the bay.

More information about earthquakes and tsunamis is available from the West Coast and Alaska Tsunami Warning Center at http://wcatwc.arh.noaa.gov.

WEATHER (See Climate)

WHALES (See also Baleen; Whaling) Fifteen
species of both toothed and baleen whales
are found in Alaska waters.

Toothed whales include sperm,
beluga, orca (or killer whale), pilot, beaked
(three species), dolphins (two species) and
porpoises (two species). Another toothed
whale, the narwhal, a full-time resident
of the Arctic, is almost never seen in
Alaska waters. St. Lawrence Islanders call
narwhals *bousucktugutalik*, or "beluga with
tusk," due to a tusk that grows from the
left side of the upper jaw on bulls only.
Spiraling in a left-hand direction, the tusk
can reach lengths up to 8 feet on an adult.

Baleen whales that inhabit Alaska
waters include gray, bowhead, blue,
northern right, fin (or finback), humpback, minke (or little piked) and sei.
Baleen refers to the hundreds of strips of
flexible fingernail-like material that hang
from the gum of the upper jaw. The strips
are fringed and act as strainers that
capture krill—tiny shrimplike organisms—
as well as other prey upon which whales
feed. Once the baleen fills with prey,
whales force water back out through the
sides of their mouth, swallowing the food
left behind. Baleen whale females are
usually larger than males.

Gray whales. According to the Alaska
Department of Fish and Game, gray
whales have the distinction of being the
most primitive of the living *mysticete*
("moustached") or baleen whales. They
can regularly be observed in large numbers
from Alaska shores, and are found in the
North Pacific Ocean and adjacent waters
of the Arctic Ocean. There are two
geographically isolated stocks: the Korean
or western Pacific stock, and the California

or eastern Pacific stock. The California
stock migrates between Baja California and
the Bering and Chukchi Seas, a round-trip
of 10,000 miles, the longest migration of
any marine mammal.

Grays are mottled gray in color
and covered with scars, abrasions and
clusters of parasitic barnacles that are
most abundant on their heads and
backs, the parts exposed to air when
the animals breathe.

The estimated daily consumption of an
adult gray whale is about 2,600 pounds.
In the approximately five months spent
in Alaska waters, one whale eats about
396,000 pounds of food, primarily
amphipod crustaceans. Gray whales feed
on the bottom by sucking tube-dwelling
amphipods out of the sandy sediment and
leaving large oval feeding imprints behind.
Scientists can study these imprints and
gain knowledge about feeding habits.
Muddy feeding trails are often seen when
gray whales surface after feeding dives.

Gray whales were called "devil fish"
by early whalers because they were so
aggressive and protective of their young
when hunted.

Adult grays are about 36 to 50 feet long
and weigh from 16 to 45 tons. Females are
larger than males at any given age. They
have been known to live up to 70 years,
but the average life span is about 50 years.

Beluga whales. The beluga, or
white whale, belongs to the *odontocetes*
("toothed") group, which includes sperm
and killer whales, dolphins and porpoises. Its
closest relative is the narwhal. Belugas range
widely in arctic and subarctic waters, and
two populations occur in Alaska. The Cook
Inlet population can be found in Turnagain
Arm and in the Shelikof Straits region,
although some belugas have been seen east
to Yakutat Bay and west to Kodiak Island.
Belugas of the western Arctic population
range throughout the Bering, Chukchi and
Beaufort Seas. These whales winter in the ice
of the Bering Sea, moving in summer over
1,500 miles to concentration areas along the
coast from Bristol Bay to the Mackenzie River
delta in northwestern Canada.

In Alaska, large groupings occur in the
Bristol Bay area, Norton Sound, Kotzebue
Sound and Kasegaluk Lagoon. In Bristol

Bay, belugas sometimes swim more than 100 miles a day.

Belugas are very vocal animals, producing a variety of grunts, clicks, chirps and whistles, which are used for navigating, finding prey and communicating. Because of their talkative nature, they are known as "sea canaries." Belugas are also masters of echolocation, using their sophisticated sonar to detect fish and navigate in shallow waters or among gill nets without getting stranded. In some areas, they may dive more than 2,000 feet to feed on the bottom. At birth, belugas are dark blue-gray fading to white by the age of 5 or 6. Adult males are 11 to 16 feet long and weigh 1,000 to 2,000 pounds; adult females may reach 12 feet in length. Belugas can live up to 40 years. Numbers of beluga in Cook Inlet have greatly reduced in the last decades and in 1997, the National Marine Fisheries Services listed it as a "Species of Concern."

Orcas. Also known as killer whales or blackfish, orcas are the largest member of the dolphin family. They range from the Beaufort Sea to Antarctica. In Alaska, two different stocks are designated resident and transient. A third stock offshore is being researched. It is thought that orcas migrate, riding currents south in the winter. The most unusual feature of the orca is the high dorsal fin, which has no muscle but may serve the whale as a keel would a boat. The fin on older males can grow to 6 feet in height.

Orcas are considered very intelligent and to possess all mammalian senses except smell. They take catnaps on the surface of the water and hunt in pods using complex, cooperative patterns of attack. Prey includes sea lions, salmon, seals, porpoises, halibut, shark, squid, belugas and other whales. Male killer whales average 23 feet in length; females are smaller. Average life span is 30 to 40 years.

WHALING (See Also Whales) Decimated
by commercial whaling in the late 1880s, the bowhead population today is growing. It is estimated that 199 whales are added to the stock yearly; the 1999 population numbered 8,000 to 9,000.

Bowhead whales have been protected from commercial whaling for decades by a number of agreements, including the Convention for the Regulation of Whaling (1931), the International Convention for the Regulation of Whaling (1947), and by the Marine Mammal Protection Act (1972) and the Endangered Species Act (1973).

Blue, humpback, sei, fin, Northern right, bowhead and sperm whales are on the federal endangered species list. Gray whales are also protected.

Commercial whaling for grays has been banned by the International Convention for the Regulation of Whaling since 1947. These conventions and regulations do allow for subsistence harvest by Natives. Since 1978, the International Whaling Commission (IWC) has regulated the Native taking of both bowheads and grays. The IWC reclassified the eastern stock of gray whales from a protected species to a sustained management stock with an annual catch limit of about 179 whales. The entire catch limit of grays and bowheads is reserved for Natives or by member governments on behalf of Natives. However, gray whales are not hunted in Alaska.

At a convention in 1994, the IWC revised the bowhead catch limit for Alaska, so that bowheads landed from 1995 to 1998 would not exceed 204. Hunters were forbidden to strike, land or kill calves or any bowhead accompanied by a calf.

Other species of large baleen whales, such as minke and fin whales, are occasionally taken by Alaska Eskimos for food. It is not necessary to report minke harvests. The only toothed whale taken by Eskimos is the beluga, and its harvest is monitored by the Alaska Beluga Whale Committee. Approximately 200 to 300 belugas are landed annually.

WILDLAND FIRES

Fire season starts in April or May, when winter's dead vegetation is vulnerable to any spark. Human activity is the leading cause of wildland fires; however, lightning strikes are responsible for most of the wildland acreage that has burned. In June, thunderstorms bring as many as 3,000 lightning strikes a day to the Alaska Interior. By mid-July in a normal year, rainfall in Interior Alaska increases.

When wildland fires threaten inhabited areas, the Bureau of Land Management (BLM) Alaska Fire Service (in the northern half of the state) and the State of Alaska Division of Forestry (in the southern half of the state) provide initial fire protection to private lands, as well as land managed by BLM, National Park Service, U.S. Fish and Wildlife Service, Native corporations and the state. Wildland fire protection in Southeast Alaska is provided by the USDA Forest Service. Through the use of the Alaska Interagency Fire Management Plan, Alaska is the only state with a fire plan that covers the entire state and all ownerships.

All land management agencies in Alaska have placed their lands in one of four protection categories—critical, full, modified and limited. These protection levels set priorities for firefighting.

With its 570,374 square miles of land, Alaska is more than twice the size of Texas. Most of this vast area has no roads, and transportation for firefighters is usually by airplane or helicopter. Fire camps are remote. Mosquito repellent is a necessity, but headlamps are often not required when the midnight sun shines all night. Aircraft bring in all supplies, even drinking water. Radios are the main means of communication with headquarters. Black spruce burns very quickly. Firefighters use chain saws to cut the trees and Pulaskis to cut through the underlying vegetation. It is nearly impossible to transport heavy equipment to fires in remote areas. Bulldozers are not used because they damage the delicate permafrost layer, leading to dramatic erosion.

Firefighters don't depend on lookout towers in the wilderness to spot wildland fires. Today, computers detect the ionization from a lightning strike anywhere

NUGGETS

When sourdoughs brag about walking to school at –70°F, there's evidence the windchill wasn't all that bad. A new formula from the National Weather Service and its Canadian counterpart for windchill now measures those same conditions at –44°F.

—2002 *The Alaska Almanac*®

in the state, determine the latitude and longitude of the strike and display it on a computer screen. Detection specialists then fly to the areas of greatest risk.

When a fire is reported, dispatchers use maps, computers and other resources to determine which agency manages the land and whether the fire should be aggressively attacked. Remote automatic weather stations report weather conditions all over Alaska, enabling weather forecasters to predict thunderstorms in any part of the state. Smoke jumpers and airplanes with fire-retardant chemicals are positioned close to the predicted thunderstorm activity.

The largest single fire ever reported in Alaska burned 800,000 acres 60 miles north of Tanana in 1969. Unusually dry weather in 1990 made it one of the most severe fire seasons on record in Alaska. Lightning was the primary cause of more than 900 fires, with an average of 2,000 strikes a day between June 26 and July 5.

In 1996, conditions that were drier than normal made it difficult to control a wildland fire that began near Big Lake, 60 miles northwest of Anchorage. Fire spread for more than a week, burning 37,500 acres and destroying 454 structures. Smoke blanketed Anchorage and the Matanuska–Susitna Valley. Fire crews from the Lower 48 were brought in to help fight the blaze, which threatened populated areas. Alaska wildland fires have destroyed more acreage in the past, but none have claimed more property.

The 2004 wildfire season broke all previous records: 701 fires burned a total of nearly 6.6 million acres. In 2005, 4.6 million acres burned making it the third-largest season. The 2006 fire season was more modest with only 266,000 acres burned. However, the Lower 48 had their record-breaking season in 2006—burning over 9 million acres. Alaska sent 55 village crews to assist with their fires.

Alaska Wildland Fires*

Calendar Year	No. of Fires	Acres Burned
1997	716	2,026,899
1998	413	176,000
1999	486	1,005,428
2000	369	756,296
2001	349	216,230
2002	545	2,210,868
2003	476	602,718
2004	701	6,590,140
2005	624	4,663,880
2006	307	266,268

* Combined AFS (federal) and state coverage

WILDFLOWERS Wildflowers in

Alaska usually are small, delicate and seldom showy. More than 1,500 plant species occur in the state including trees, shrubs, ferns, grasses and sedges, as well as flowering plants.

Alpine regions are particularly rich in flora and some of these species are rare. Anywhere there is tundra there is apt to be a bountiful population of flowers. The Steese Highway (Eagle Summit), Richardson Highway (Thompson Pass), Denali Highway (Maclaren Summit), Denali National Park and Preserve (Polychrome Pass), Seward Highway (Turnagain Pass), Glenn Highway just north of Anchorage (Eklutna Flats) and a locale near Wasilla (Hatcher Pass) are wonderful wildflower-viewing spots. All are readily accessible by car.

Forget-me-not, Alaska's state flower.

Less easily accessible floral Edens are some of the Aleutian Islands, Point Hope, Anvil Mountain and the Nome–Teller Road (both near Nome), Pribilof Islands and other remote areas.

Alaska's official flower, the forget-me-not *(Myosotis alpestris),* is a diminutive beauty found throughout much of the state in alpine meadows and along streams. Growing to 18 inches tall, forget-me-nots are recognized by their bright blue petals surrounding a yellow eye. A northern "cousin," the arctic forget-me-not *(Eritrichium aretioides),* grows in sandy soil on the tundra, or in the mountains, and reaches only 4 inches in height.

WINDCHILL FACTOR

(See also Hypothermia) The windchill factor can lower the effective temperature by many degrees. While Alaska's regions of lowest temperatures also generally have little wind, activities such as riding a snowmobile or even walking can produce the same effect on exposed skin.

The windchill factor, when severe, can lead to frostnip (the body's early-warning signal of potential damage from cold—a "nipping" feeling in the extremities), frostbite (formation of small ice crystals in the body tissues) or hypothermia (dangerous lowering of the body's core temperature). Other factors that combine with windchill and bring on these potentially damaging or fatal effects are exposure to wetness, exhaustion and lack of adequate clothing.

The National Weather Service now employs a new windchill temperature index, which provides an accurate calculation of frostbite danger. Web site for National Weather Service, Alaska Region: www.arh.noaa.gov.

Calculating Windchill

Temperature (Fahrenheit)	Wind Speed (mph)			
	10	20	30	45
30	21	17	15	12
20	9	4	1	−2
10	−4	−9	−12	−16
0	−16	−22	−26	−29
−10	−28	−34	−39	−44
−20	−41	−48	−53	−58
−30	−53	−61	−67	−72
−40	−66	−74	−80	−86
−45	−72	−81	−87	−93

WINDS (See also Climate; Windchill Factor)

Some of Alaska's windiest weather has been recorded on the western islands of the Aleutian chain. Causes are the same as elsewhere—planet rotation and the tendency of the atmosphere to equalize the difference between high and low pressure fronts. A few winds occur often and significantly enough to be given names: chinook, taku and williwaw.

Chinook. Old-timers describe chinook winds as unseasonably warm winds that can cause a thaw in the middle of winter. What they also cause are power failures and property damage, especially in the Anchorage bowl where in recent years hundreds of homes have sprung up on the sides of the Chugach Mountains, where chinook winds howl. One such wind occurred on April Fool's Day in 1980, causing $25 million in property damage. Parts of Anchorage were without power for 60 hours.

Until recently, it was not possible to predict chinook winds in Anchorage. Today, however, meteorologists can tell if the winds are gathering, when they will arrive and their relative strength. It was learned that such a warm wind could only originate in Prince William Sound and that its speed had to be at least 55 miles per hour or faster just to cross the 3,500-foot Chugach Mountains. Other factors include a storm near Bethel and relatively stable air over Anchorage. Meteorologists accurately predict chinook winds 55 percent of the time.

Taku. Taku winds are the sudden, fierce gales that sweep down from the ice cap behind Juneau and Douglas. Takus are shivering cold winds capable of reaching 100 miles per hour. They have been known to send a piece of two-by-four lumber flying through the wall of a frame house.

Williwaw. Williwaws are sudden gusts of wind that can reach more than 110 miles per hour after wind builds up on one side of a mountain and suddenly spills over into what may appear to be a relatively protected area. Williwaws are a bane of Alaska mariners.

The term was originally applied to a strong wind in the Strait of Magellan.

WORLD ESKIMO–INDIAN OLYMPICS

Several hundred Native athletes from Alaska and the circumpolar nations compete each year in the World Eskimo–Indian Olympics, in Fairbanks. Held during four days in July, the games draw participants from all of Alaska's Native populations (Iñupiat, Yup'ik, Aleut, Athabascan, Tlingit, Haida and Tsimshian). The Inuit peoples of Canada, Greenland and Russia also are invited to participate, as well as Native Americans from the Lower 48 states.

Feats may seem exotic—even painful—but they have roots in a hunting, fishing and gathering culture that rewards endurance, observation and cooperation. Spectators thrill to the knuckle hop and the ear-weight competition. Other traditional Native sports and competitions include the greased pole walk, fish cutting, stick pull, Indian and Eskimo dancing, men's and women's blanket toss and the spectacular two-foot and one-foot high kicks. Some of the more boisterous games include a lively game of tug-of-war and the muktuk-eating contest.

Each year the judges choose a Native queen to reign over the Olympics. Over the next year she makes appearances

The March 3, 2003, Anchorage windstorm posted a record gust of 109 mph. I saved the dump fee receipt for the twigs, leaves, branches, and needles on my yard. Fifth-grade arithmetic shows there were 3.5 billion pounds of junk deposited on the municipality—which would weigh the same as a line of moose from Anchorage to the Panama Canal!

throughout the state and represents the Olympics at the National Congress of American Indians.

For schedules and advance tickets, contact the World Eskimo–Indian Olympics, P.O. Box 72433, Fairbanks 99707; (907) 452-6646; www.weio.org.

2006 World Eskimo–Indian Olympic Games, First-Place Winners

Race of the Torch: *Men,* Casey Ferguson; *Women,* Crystal Tobuk

One-Hand Reach: *Men,* Jesse Frankson; *Women,* Tracy Bacon

Alaskan High Kick: *Men,* Jesse Frankson; *Women,* Danielle Malchoff

Indian Stick Pull: *Men,* David Thomas; *Women,* Emily Frantz

Eskimo Stick Pull: *Men,* Matthew Evans; *Women,* Kimberly Delk

Ear Pull: *Men,* Keith Bacon; *Women,* Asta Keller

Toe Kick: *Men,* Aki Anderson; *Women,* Carol Pickett

Kneel Jump: *Men,* Jesse Frankson; *Women,* Amber Vaska

Scissor Broad Jump: *Men,* Chris Warrior; *Women,* Donna Frantz

One-Foot High Kick: *Men,* Jesse Frankson; *Women,* Erica Meckel

Two-Foot High Kick: *Men,* Karl Frankson; *Women,* Danielle Malchoff

Greased Pole Walk: *Men,* Billy Bodfish; *Women,* Jasmin Simeon

Arm Pull: *Men,* Brian Randazzo; *Women,* Rhonda Baker-Joseph

Ear Weight: *Men,* Chad Nusinginya; *Women,* Sheila Randazzo

Blanket Toss: *Men,* Larry Lucas; *Women,* Domonique Kippi

Drop the Bomb: *Men,* Lee McCotter; *Women,* Crystal Tobuk

4-Man Carry: Chris Warrior

Knuckle Hop: *Men,* Tony Avalos; *Women,* Crystal Tobuk

Fish-Cutting Contest: Willa Eckinwieller

Muktuk Eating: Charlie Brower

Miss WEIO: Ashley Stickman (Kotzebue)

Miss Congeniality: (3-way tie) Nichole Gregory (Galena), Keeley Kaveolook (North Pole), Shannon Sanchez (Barrow)

The one-foot kick is among the ancient Native games featured at the World Eskimo–Indian Olympics. Photo by Roy Corral.

Most Traditional: Ashley Stickman (Kotzebue)

Most Photogenic: Shannon Sanchez (Barrow)

Most Talented: Andrea Painter (Nome)

Dance Team: *Indian,* FNA/JOM; *Eskimo,* Barrow

Seal Skinning: Charlie Brower

WORLD WAR II (See also Military; Unalaska/Dutch Harbor)

World War II propelled development of modern Alaska. In 1940 Congress authorized the construction of Fort Richardson outside of Anchorage.

After the bombing of Pearl Harbor, Alaska's strategic importance as a staging area for supplying forces in the North Pacific was apparent. The construction of the Alaska Canada Military Highway (the Alcan) began in March 1942, providing an overland route from the Lower 48 into Alaska.

The Japanese bombed a small military base at Dutch Harbor on June 3, 1942, in

Yukon Quest Winners and Times

Year	Musher	Days	Hrs.	Min.	Prize
1996	John Schandelmeier, Paxson	12	16	47	20,000
1997	Rick Mackey, Nenana	12	05	55	20,000
1998	Bruce Lee, Denali Park	11	11	27	30,000
1999	Ramy Brooks	11	07	59	30,000
2000	Aliy Zirkle, Two River	10*	22	01	30,000
2001	Tim Osmar	11	15	10	30,000
2002	Hans Gatt	11	04	22	30,000
2003	Hans Gatt	10**	16	28	30,000
2004	Hans Gatt	10	17	54	30,000
2005	Lance Mackey	11	00	32	30,000
2006	Lance Mackey	10***	07	47	30,000
2007	Lance Mackey	10	02	37	40,000

* Due to poor trail conditions, the 2000 race ended at Takhini Hot Springs, near Whitehorse.

** Due to poor trail conditions, the 2003 race was restarted at Carmackson Feb. 11, 2003. Times are taken from the restart.

*** Due to poor trail conditions, the 2006 race ended in Dawson City.

an attack that was designed to divert American forces north while engaging the American fleet in the central Pacific at Midway. The diversion failed and the battle at Midway became a turning point in the Pacific war.

On June 7, 1942, some 1,200 Japanese troops landed on the Aleutian islands of Attu and Kiska, where they built an air base, bunkers and antiaircraft emplacements aimed at preventing the United States from using the Aleutians to launch an attack on Japan. Although the Japanese presence on the islands posed no real threat to the United States, foreign occupation was unthinkable. But the ensuing fight to drive the Japanese from the Aleutians was as much a battle against the bad weather as it was against enemy forces. More American aircraft were lost to the violent 120-mph winds, the dense fog and constant storms than to Japanese fire.

On May 11, 1943, after nearly a year of Japanese occupation, 11,000 American troops landed on Attu and engaged in a bloody battle with 2,600 Japanese troops. At the end of the month, 550 Americans were dead and 1,148 were wounded. Of the Japanese, only 28 prisoners were taken; American soldiers buried 2,351 Japanese troops killed in combat. Hundreds of others were presumed to have died and been buried in the hills or were thought to have committed suicide.

The battle for Kiska was different. On July 28, 1943, the 5,000-man Japanese garrison evacuated the island in dense fog. For three weeks, U.S. forces continued to bomb and shell the island, unaware that the island had been abandoned. In August, 35,000 Allied soldiers arrived on the island, but found only a few stray Japanese dogs.

NUGGETS

Birdface, the parrot of Skagway, was the prime suspect in a fire investigation on board his owner's fishing boat. Birdface has a habit of moving things around, and apparently deposited some old rags on the stove. Bystanders extinguished the flames before serious damage occurred, and though Birdface was unharmed, his seafaring days are over.

—1992 *The Alaska Almanac*®

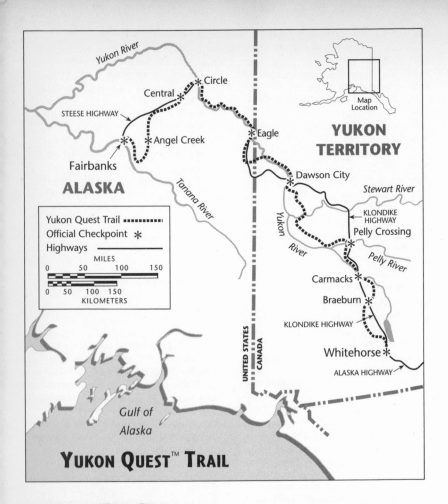

YUKON QUEST™ TRAIL

YUKON QUEST INTERNATIONAL SLED DOG RACE

(SEE ALSO Dog Mushing; Iditarod Trail Sled Dog Race) The Yukon Quest International Sled Dog Race was begun by Roger Williams and LeRoy Shank in 1983 to foster a long-distance sled dog race between Fairbanks, Alaska, and Whitehorse, Yukon Territory. The first race took place in February 1984, when 26 teams competed, and had a purse of $50,000.

Named for the old-time winter "Highway of the North," the Yukon River, the 1,000-mile trek usually takes between 11 and 14 days to complete, depending on weather and trail. The Quest is held in February and is one of the toughest of

sled-dog races. During their journey between the two cities, teams retrace the footsteps of Native Alaskans, gold rush miners, trappers, explorers and missionaries (SEE map, page 228). Mushers cross four major summits and diverse, challenging terrain. They travel 250 miles on the frozen Yukon River and cross the longest unguarded international border in the world.

The direction of the race alternates each year. Between the start and finish lines are a series of official checkpoints.

The longest distance between checkpoints is 290 miles, between Dawson City and Carmacks. The only checkpoint at which a musher may receive help is at

Dawson City, where a 36-hour layover is mandatory. Rules allow for a minimum of 8 dogs and a maximum of 14 dogs at the start. Five dogs are the minimum allowed at the finish, and only four dogs can be dropped during the course of the race. Each musher may use only one sled throughout the race, and mandatory equipment includes a sleeping bag, hand ax, snowshoes, promotional material and eight booties per dog. Information on the Yukon Quest is posted at www.yukonquest.com.

2007 Yukon Quest Results

Musher	Days	Hrs.	Min.
1. Lance Mackey	10	02	37
2. Hans Gatt	10	09	19
3. Gerry Willomitzer	10	12	09
4. William Kleedehn	10	12	12
5. Aaron Burmeister	11	01	10
6. Michelle Philips	11	01	47
7. Sebastian Schnuelle	11	02	40
8. Mike Jayne	11	03	15
9. Hugh Neff	11	09	26
10. Dave Dalton	11	14	02
11. John Schandelmeier	11	14	53
12. William Hanes	12	00	51
13. Russ Bybee	12	04	46
14. Kelly Griffin	12	08	01
15. Brent Sass	12	08	06
16. Richie Beattie	13	00	43
17. Benedikt Beisch	13	06	02
18. Regina Wycoff	13	07	27
19. Tom Benson	13	14	01
20. Kyla Boivin	14	07	50
21. Bob McAlpin	14	22	35

Dog mushing is Alaska's great sport. From *Fairbanks: Alaska's Heart of Gold* by Tricia Brown (text) and Roy Corral (photos).

YUKON RIVER (SEE ALSO Rivers) The

Yukon River is the longest river in Alaska, flowing in a 2,000-mile arc (1,400 miles in Alaska) from its British Columbia headwaters across the Interior's forested hills, narrow mountain valleys and vast tundra flats to the Bering Sea. The fifth-largest river in North America, the third-largest in the United States, the Yukon River watershed drains 330,000 square miles—a third of Alaska.

Archaeological evidence indicates that humans may have lived along the river more than 20,000 years ago. Historically, two Native groups occupied the Yukon valley: the Yup'ik Eskimos and the Athabascans. Most Native villages were established on the north bank of the river, apparently the preferred side of the river, to fish for the millions of migrating king, coho and chum salmon that returned to the river system to spawn. These fish return to the Yukon today and fish traps and summer fish camps can still be seen along the river. With the arrival of European trappers, the Yukon became a well-used supply route for the Interior. Travel was by steamboat or canoe during the summer and by dogsled from October to May, when the river was frozen. In Alaska, the Yukon has never been dammed and is crossed by only one bridge, the Yukon River Bridge. It is on the Dalton Highway near Stevens Village, just south of the Arctic Circle.

The Yukon River attracts canoeists, kayakers and others for float trips. Many commercial guides offer excursions, and the popular jumping-off point is at Eagle. A summer float trip downriver through Yukon–Charley Rivers National Preserve to Circle is 154 river miles and averages 5 to 10 days. Also available are float trips from Dawson City, Yukon, to Circle that make a stop halfway at Eagle. You can rent canoes in Eagle or choose a trip with a local commercial guide with gear supplied. For information on proper clothing, weather conditions and best time to make a float, contact the National Park Service, Box 167, Eagle 99378; (907) 547-2233.

ZIP CODES
(SEE Populations and Zip Codes)

Yearly Highlights, 2006-2007

Following are brief accounts of Alaska news from mid-2006 to mid-2007. Primary sources are the *Anchorage Daily News, Juneau Empire, Fairbanks Daily News-Miner, Mat-Su Valley Frontiersman* and the Associated Press.

Pipeline Woes. In March 2006, an oil field worker discovered a 201,000-gallon oil spill from a corroded pipe at Prudhoe Bay, the largest spill in North Slope history. BP Alaska temporarily shut down half of Prudhoe, the largest oil field in the U.S., after another corroded pipe led to a small leak (up to 210 gallons) the following August. An internal report at the time indicated widespread corrosion problems.

Mazdas, Anyone? The *Cougar Ace,* a ship traveling under the flag of Singapore, listed 60 degrees onto its port side on July 23, 2006, while transferring its ballast in the Pacific Ocean south of the Aleutian Islands. Maritime rules require the release of water ballast to prevent the introduction of foreign aquatic life into U.S. waters. The U.S. Coast Guard and the Alaska Air National Guard rescued the entire 23-member crew by helicopter, although one naval architect was killed when he slipped while aboard the then-sideways ship and hit his head.

The ship's cargo included 4,700 new Mazda cars from Japan headed for ports in British Columbia, Washington and California. Mazda spokesman Jay Amestoy stated that all Mazda vehicles on board the ship, regardless of damage, would be sold as used cars with full new-car warranties.

Beware of the Grizzlies. The 4,200 folks in Barrow are accustomed to the occasional 1,000-pound polar bear meandering through their town when the bear's sea-ice habitat is near the shore. But in August 2006, the smaller and perhaps more aggressive tundra grizzly showed up. Two sightings of this less familiar and therefore more dangerous bear occurred in the research area, prompting temporary evacuation of scientists.

"Grizzlies will investigate humans, even if they're not hungry," stated Harry Brower Jr., a wildlife manager for the North Slope Borough. "We don't see that with polar bears." The grizzlies are exploring new areas in the Arctic, according to Geoff Carroll, wildlife manager for the Alaska Department of Fish & Game. Sightings have increased in the North Slope region, and local residents don't want them around.

October Deluge. Southcentral Alaska suffered from an unseasonably warm and wet autumn as record rainfall, mudslides and snowmelt hammered the communities of Valdez, Cordova and Seward, as well as the Matanuska-Susitna Valley.

Bridges and roads were washed out in Valdez, making life difficult for local residents and travelers. The City of Cordova recorded 22 inches of rain in two days, and the mayor declared a local disaster for the second time in two months due to flooding. The airport was awash with 3 feet of water, septic and fuel tanks flooded and wells were contaminated.

The Mat-Su Valley experienced more than $1 million worth of damage when rivers like the Little Susitna surged over their banks following more than two weeks of heavy rain. Fourteen bridges were washed out and 49 area roads damaged.

It's Governor Palin. Alaska voters chose change over experience in the November 2006 gubernatorial election. Republican candidate Sarah Palin rode a popular wave of anti-establishment momentum from her small-town roots in Wasilla over the incumbent Republican governor (and former U.S. Senator) Frank Murkowski and past Democrat (and former two-term governor) Tony Knowles. Palin is Alaska's first female governor and at 42, its youngest.

Farewell to the Shishmaref Cannonball. Alaska lost another Iditarod hero in December 2006, when legendary dog musher Herbie Nayokpuk, 77, died in Anchorage. Known as the "Shishmaref Cannonball," Nayokpuk lived most of his life on a remote island at the edge of the Bering Strait north of Nome, yet was known throughout the world. His nickname was a blending of his home village of Shishmaref with his head-on style both in dog mushing and in life. He ran the Iditarod 11 times, finishing second in 1980.

Alaska's First Astronaut. Bill Oefelein learned to fly while growing up in Anchorage. In December 2006, Alaskans were thrilled to see Oefelein become the state's first astronaut. Serving as pilot of the space shuttle *Discovery,* Oefelein was also in charge of using the shuttle's robotic arm to check out the condition of the spacecraft's outer skin prior to its docking with the space station. Later in the mission, Oefelein also took time for a question-and-answer session with students at the Challenger Learning Center in Kenai.

World Cup Skier. Kikkan Randall, a graduate of Anchorage's East High School and two-time Olympic medalist in cross-country skiing, became the first American woman to share the podium at a World Cup event when she finished third in a 1.2-kilometer freestyle sprint event in Rybinsk, Russia, in January. Randall told the Associated Press that her off-season training on Eagle Glacier near Anchorage helped her handle the course, which was hard and fast from the previous day's rain.

Mackey Makes History. A euphoric Lance Mackey made Alaska dog-mushing history by winning both the 1,000-mile Yukon Quest International Sled Dog Race (in February) and the 1,100-mile Iditarod Trail Sled Dog Race (in March) in the same year (2007). Lance wore the lucky No. 13 bib on his chest, the same number worn by both his father, Dick Mackey, and his half-brother, Rick Mackey, in their previous Iditarod victories.

Free Land. In an effort to draw additional residents to their small Interior community of 563 residents, in March 2007, the city council of Anderson offered 26 free, 1.3-acre wooded lots on a first-come, first-served basis to anyone willing to plunk down a refundable $500 deposit. As a class

project, local high school students created a Web site inviting those "tired of the hustle and bustle of the Lower 48, crime, poor schools and high cost of living" to trade it all in for the wonders of Alaska.

Thousands of interested people called (around the clock) from all 50 states as well as from Canada, Taiwan, India and South America. The first 26 people in line on the appointed day paid their $500, selected their lot and pledged to build a house measuring at least 1,000 square feet within the next two years.

Political Scandal. In May 2007, three current and former Alaska State Legislators were indicted on public corruption charges. The indictments charged Rep. Vic Kohring, a current member of the Alaska State House of Representatives; attorney and former Rep. Bruce Weyhrauch, who served from 2002 to January 2007; and former Rep. Pete Kott, who was a member of the House from 1992 to 2007 and served as Speaker of the House in 2003 and 2004. All three defendants were arrested in Juneau, and charged with ". . . selling their offices in Alaska's State House to an influential energy company in exchange for cash payments, loans, jobs for relatives and the promise of future employment," according to Assistant Attorney General Alice S. Fisher.

Moving Maggie. Following many years of impassioned public debate, in June 2007 the board members of the Alaska Zoo in Anchorage decided to relocate the state's only elephant, Maggie, to the Lower 48. The board is insistent, however, that certain conditions must be met prior to Maggie's move, including independent veterinary approval of the move, appropriate site selection and transportation details.

Various animal rights groups are frustrated at what they see as the zoo's procrastination in moving Maggie to a milder climate, preferably a sanctuary where she can live among other elephants. Others are equally vocal about losing Alaska's only elephant, and they worry about Maggie's stress as she's crated up and shipped far away from the only home—and climate— she's ever known.

Suggested Reading

Other Alaska books from Alaska Northwest Books®, WestWinds Press® and Graphic Arts Books, Portland, Oregon. For additional titles, see our Web site: www.gacpc.com.

Alaska Native Culture

Alaska Native Ways: What the Elders Have Taught Us. Roy Corral photography with text by Natives of Alaska; intro by Will Mayo. GAB, 2002.

Children of the Midnight Sun: Young Native Voices of Alaska. Tricia Brown and Roy Corral. AKNWB, 1998.

The Winter Walk: A Century-Old Survival Story from the Arctic. Loretta Outwater Cox, AKNWB, 2003.

Alaskan Adventures

A Place Beyond: Finding Home in Arctic Alaska. Nick Jans. AKNWB, 1996.

Alaska's Heroes: A Call to Courage. Nancy Warren Ferrell. AKNWB, 2002.

Alone across the Arctic: One Woman's Epic Journey by Dog Team. Pam Flowers with Ann Dixon. AKNWB, 2001.

The Kids from Nowhere: The Story Behind the Arctic Education Miracle. George Guthridge. AKNWB, 2006.

The Last New Land: Stories of Alaska, Past and Present. Wayne Mergler, ed. AKNWB, 1996.

Running with Champions: A Midlife Journey on the Iditarod Trail. Lisa Frederic. AKNWB, 2006.

Walking My Dog, Jane. Ned Rozell. AKNWB, 2005.

History/Biography

Alaska's History. Harry Ritter. AKNWB, 1993.

Arctic Dance: The Mardy Murie Story. Charles Craighead and Bonnie Kreps. GAB, 2002.

Bradford Washburn: An Extraordinary Life. Bradford Washburn and Lew Freedman. AKNWB, 2005.

Gold Rush Dogs. Claire Rudolf Murphy and Jane G. Haigh. AKNWB, 2001.

Gold Rush Women. Claire Rudolf Murphy and Jane G. Haigh. AKNWB, 1997.

On Patrol: True Adventures of an Alaska Game Warden. Ray Tremblay. AKNWB, 2004.

One Man's Wilderness. Sam Keith with Richard Proenneke. AKNWB, 1999.

Two in the Far North. Margaret E. Murie. AKNWB, 1978; rev. 1997.

Children

Goodbye, My Island. Jean Rogers and Rie Muñoz. AKNWB, 2001.

The Itchy Little Musk Ox. Tricia Brown and Debra Dubac. AKNWB, 2007.

Sharkabet: A Sea of Sharks from A to Z. Ray Troll, WWP, 2002.

Ten Rowdy Ravens. Evon Zerbetz and Susan Ewing. AKNWB, 2005.

Cookbooks

The Alaska Heritage Seafood Cookbook. Ann Chandonnet. AKNWB, 1999.

Alaska Sourdough. Ruth Allman. AKNWB, 1999.

Baked Alaska: Recipes for Sweet Comforts from the North Country. Sarah Eppenbach. AKNWB, 1997.

Humor

Mr. Whitekeys' Alaska Bizarre. Mr. Whitekeys. AKNWB, 1995.

Not Really an Alaskan Mountain Man. Doug Fine. AKNWB, 2004.

Natural History

Alaska's Fish. Robert H. Armstrong. AKNWB, 1996.

Alaska's Natural Wonders. Robert H. Armstrong and Marge Hermans. AKNWB, 2000.

Alaska's Seashore Creatures. Conrad Field and Carmen Field. AKNWB, 1999.

Midnight Wilderness: Journeys in Alaska's Arctic National Wildlife Refuge. Debbie Miller. AKNWB, 2000.

Travel/Photography

Alaska: Portrait of a State. Various photographers. GAB, 2006.

Alaska's Bush Planes. Jeff Schultz and Ned Rozell. AKNWB, 2003.

Alaska's Inside Passage. Kim Heacox. GAB, 1997.

Alaska's Kenai Peninsula: A Traveler's Guide. Andromeda Romano-Lax, Greg Daniels and Bill Sherwonit. AKNWB, 2001.

Alaska's Prince William Sound: A Traveler's Guide. Marybeth Holleman. AKNWB, 2000.

Chilkoot Pass: A Hiker's Historical Guide to the Klondike Gold Rush National Historical Park. Archie Satterfield. AKNWB, 1973; rev. 2004.

Denali: The Complete Guide. Bill Sherwonit. AKNWB, 2002.

Fairbanks: Alaska's Heart of Gold: A Traveler's Guide. Tricia Brown and Roy Corral. AKNWB, 2000.

Portrait of the Alaska Railroad. Kaylene Johnson and Roy Corral. AKNWB, 2003.

To the Top of Denali: Climbing Adventures on North America's Highest Peak. Bill Sherwonit. AKNWB, 1990; rev. 2000.

Two in a Red Canoe: Our Journey Down the Yukon. Megan Baldino and Matt Hage. AKNWB, 2005.

The World-Famous Alaska Highway. Tricia Brown. AKNWB, 2005.

Index

backpacking: See camping; hiking

baidarka, **20**

bald eagle, 29; foundation, 134

baleen, **21**, 23, 152–54, 121–22

baneberries, 27

barabara, **21**, 104–5

Baranov, Alexander, **21**, 197

barley, 10

Barnette, E. T., 69

Barren Ground caribou, 101, 115

Barrow, **22**; Chamber of Commerce, 44; health care, 97; Iñupiat Heritage Center, 132; Northern/Arctic region, *6–7,* 188–89; northernmost, 5; radio stations, 184; visitors information, 51

baseball, **22**

baskets, **23**, 152–54

bats, 117

beach ivory, 110

beadwork, **24**, 152–54; See also parka

bears, **24–26**, *119;* encounters and mishaps, *14, 24, 25, 212,* 230; hiking, 90; hunting, 101; mammals, 114–15; McNeil River State Game Sanctuary, 119–20; Pack Creek Bear Viewing Area, 42

Beatie, Chuck, *21*

beaver, 116

beluga whales, *108,* 221–22

Bering, Vitus, **26**, 193

Bering Land Bridge, 27, 145, *146–47;* See also archaeology

Bering Sea Coast region, 189

berries, 27

Bethel: Chamber of Commerce, 44; health care, 97; radio stations, 184; television stations, 210; Western/ Bering Sea Coast region, *6–7,* 189; Yupiit Piciryarait Cultural Center and Museum, 132

bidarka, bidarkee: See *baidarka*

Bielawski, Ellen, *143*

billiken, **27–28**

Birdface, the parrot, *227*

birds, bird-watching, **28–30**, *29,* 30, *148,* 206; See also *individual birds*

bison, 115

black bears, 25, 114

black icebergs, 102

black-tailed deer, 115

blanket toss, **30–31**

blankets, traditional, 45–46

bluethroat, 29

Boalotchkee (recipe), *194*

boating, *21,* **31–32**, *72; baidarka,* 20; cruises, 57; ferries, 70–72; information, 105; Inside Passage, 108; kayaking, 20, 32, 105; *umiak,* 216

bogs, 140

bookstores, *210;* See also libraries and archives

bore tide, 5, **32**, 211

boroughs, 83–84, *183*

boundaries, 10–11, 77–78

Brady Sr., Carl F., *10*

bread (recipe), *155*

breakup, **32**, 159, *203*

Brower, Charles D., 23

Brown, Tricia, *138*

brown bears, 25, 101, 114

brown lemmings, 117

bunny boots, **33**

buns (recipe), *194*

Bureau of Land Management, 40, 43, *146–47*

burning permits, 42

bus lines and shuttles, **33–34**

Buser, Martin, *186*

bush, **33**

bushy-tailed woodrats, 117

business information, 106

Butcher, Susan, *60*

butterflies, *42*

cabbage, **34**, *51;* See also agriculture

cabin fever, **34**

cabin sites, 95–96, 114

cabins, **34–35, 40–41**, 141, 151, 202–3; See also camping

cache, **41**

Calendar of Annual Events— 2008, **36–40**

Camp Point, 78

camping, **41–43**; information, 105; national forests, 140–41; national parks, 144–45; national wildlife refuges, 151–52; state parks, 202–3; See also cabins

candlefish: See hooligan

canoeing, 32; See also kayaks, kayaking

Cape Wrangell, 78

caribou, 101, 115

census data, 106, *171,* 182, *183*

chambers of commerce, **44–45**

Charlie, Neil and John, *154*

charter service, bus, 34

cheechako, **45**

Chilkat blanket, **45–46**

Chilkoot Trail, 46; See also gold

chinook wind, 225

Chirikov, Aleksei, 26, 193

chitons, **46**

Christmas nativity protest, *191*

Christmas tree forest, *164*

Chugach National Forest, 35, 41–42, 140–42, 141, *146–47*

cities: See communities, listed

clams, 73

"clear channel" status, 184

climatic data, **46–50**; breakup, 32, 159–60; daylight hours, 58; regions of Alaska, 187–90; statewide, 5; winds, windchill, 224–25

coal, **50**, 67, 124–25

cod, 74, 75

collared lemming, 117

collared pika, 117

colleges and universities, **216–18**

commercial fishing, 63, 65, **72–74**

communities, listed, 174–81; See also *individual listings*

Congressional delegation, 87

conk, **50**

Constitution of Alaska, **50–51**

construction industry, 65

Continental Divide, 51; See also mountains

Convention and Visitors Bureaus, 51–52

Cook, Captain James, **52**

Cook, Frederick, *130*

Cook Inlet, 52, 166

coppers, **52–53**; *See also* native arts and crafts

Cordova, *16;* Chamber of Commerce, 44; health care, 96, 98; Iceworm Festival, 103; museums, 132; skiing, 199; Southcentral/Gulf Coast region, *6–7,* **187–88**

cormorant, 30